The Bhagavad Gita and Inner Transformation

The Bhagavad Gita and Inner Transformation

NAINA LEPES

MOTILAL BANARSIDASS PUBLISHERS
PRIVATE LIMITED • DELHI

First (revised) Indian Edition: Delhi, 2008
*First printed in 1994 from USA by **Ist Book Library***

ISBN: 978-81-208-3186-5

MOTILAL BANARSIDASS
41 U.A. Bungalow Road, Jawahar Nagar, Delhi 110 007
8 Mahalaxmi Chamber, 22 Bhulabhai Desai Road, Mumbai 400 026
203 Royapettah High Road, Mylapore, Chennai 600 004
236, 9th Main III Block, Jayanagar, Bangalore 560 011
Sanas Plaza, 1302 Baji Rao Road, Pune 411 002
8 Camac Street, Kolkata 700 017
Ashok Rajpath, Patna 800 004
Chowk, Varanasi 221 001

Printed in India
BY JAINENDRA PRAKASH JAIN AT SHRI JAINENDRA PRESS,
A-45 NARAINA, PHASE-I, NEW DELHI 110 028
AND PUBLISHED BY NARENDRA PRAKASH JAIN FOR
MOTILAL BANARSIDASS PUBLISHERS PRIVATE LIMITED,
BUNGALOW ROAD, DELHI 110 007

To Sri Sathya Sai Baba
and
Swami Chinmayananda
(May 8, 1916 to August 3, 1993)

for your teachings
and your presence
and your unfathomable love

Contents

PREFACE

Without any conscious intention on my part, the *Gita* has become a secret driving force behind the unfoldment of my life. In the days of doubt, this wonderful book appeared and supported my spiritual search. Then for many years, I carried the tiny Juan Mascaro edition around with me, and read a bit here and there. Before long, I began turning to her wisdom in times of need. And she has remained a faithful guide ever since.

In 1988, while living in India at the ashram of Sri Sathya Sai Baba, I came to experience the miracle of divine energy—its inordinate power and indomitable capacity for quickening inner purification, healing, and love. Cradled by the presence of this higher energy, all the mundane annoyances, physical inconveniences and emotional turmoil became almost inconsequential. For the worlds of mind, matter, and emotions were being linked to the higher, the inner witness (*sakshi*), and purified. In this way, past conditioning and confusion could be seen, suffered, and left behind. Throughout this time of the coming together of the opposites, I continued reading the *Gita,* one verse early in the morning. And subsequent events would often illumine the meaning.

Then one day, after having been contented with eighteen years of independent study, I was suddenly overcome by a strong desire to study the *Gita* with a *Vedanta* scholar, who was also a God realized soul. I communicated this wish to Sai Baba in an inner way. The next day, an acquaintance approached and handed me a tiny piece of paper with a name, address and phone number written on it. She said, "Swami Chinmayananda will be in Bangalore at this address. Call and find out when you can receive his *darshan.* Sai Baba will also be going to Bangalore." Needless to say, I was stunned! Although I had heard the name Swami Chinmayananda before, I knew nothing about him.

Before calling, I attended his *Gita* teaching in a large tent at 6AM—and was uplifted by his spiritual dynamism, intelligence and humor. He was so articulate that I found myself struggling hard to remain centered, not to get lost in the words, but to maintain a connection with my inner consciousness. In the presence of this dynamic realized soul, simply listening to his teachings invited the mind to transcend itself and purify. Laughter, wisdom and holiness intermingled. And the knowledge streamed forth to be lived.

Upon returning to the U.S., I began reading commentaries of other *Gita* lovers and great souls. Soon I felt the urge to try to express in words something of the essence and meaning of each chapter in a flowing way, that would help strengthen my inner connection and integrate the spiritual, the psychological and the somewhat scholarly.

This writing has been very much influenced by Swami Chinmayananda's *The Holy Geeta* and by his videotaped lectures. Another important source has been *The Bhagavad Gita for Daily Living (3 volumes)* by Eknath Easwaran. Commentaries by Swami Chidbhavananda, Yogananda, and Ramanuja (translator, Swami Addidevananda), also contributed greatly to this book. And ultimately, the direct experience of the *lilas* and presence of Sri Sathya Sai Baba offered a real glimpse into the universality of Krishna's teachings, in a most individual way.

My wish is that this book will contribute to self-reflection, finer feeling, and deepen the journey of one's inner process. When this occurs, seeing, healing, and wholeness follow naturally without doing much of anything. As a companion to the *Gita*, the book would be more powerful if read slowly, so as to allow time for intuition and awareness to connect us with where we are. One approach might be to read a discourse of the *Gita*, the concordant chapter of this book, and afterwards return to the same *Gita* discourse again. Then notice whatever questions and personal thoughts emerge from each chapter. May the wisdom of loving consciousness ever guide us on our journey!

Acknowledgements

with deep gratitude to:

Chinu Cakrabarty for introducing me to the Gita
Kent Chu for being my first student
Ravi Kapoor for the Krishna picture
Barbara Yellin for her editing suggestions
all the well-wishers who offered their support and feedback

to Central Park in Manhattan
for serving as the perfect place
to write this book

and to Mr. N. P. Jain of
Motilal Banarsidass for publishing
this first Indian Edition

Further acknowledgements appear on page 451.

ABBREVIATIONS

BGDL — *The Bhagavad Gita for Daily Living*, Eknath Easwaran
DBG — *Discourses on the Bhagavad Gita,* Sri Sathya Sai Baba
TBG — *The Bhagavad Gita*, Swami Chidbhavananda
THG — *The Holy Geeta*, Swami Chinmayananda
SS — *Sanathana Sarathi*

CCMT — Central Chinmaya Mission Trust
PN — Prasanthi Nilayam
SSSBPT — Sri Sathya Sai Books and Publications Trust, Prasanthi Niliayam

SwA — Swami Adidevananda
SwC — Swami Chinmayananda
EE — Eknath Easwaran
JM — Juan Mascaro
SwV — Swami Vidyaprakashananda

The eighteen chapters of this book coincide with the eighteen chapters of the *Gita*. When a parenthesis containing a number appears in a sentence, for example (9), the number refers to the *Gita* verse in the concordant chapter.

INTRODUCTION

The *Bhagavad Gita* can be experienced as a powerful catalyst for transformation. *Bhagavad gita* means song of the spirit, song of the Lord. This extraordinary poem was sung by Krishna to Arjuna on the battlefield of Kurukshetra while multitudes of men stood by waiting to fight the largest battle in history.

In this eternal moment of intense dramatic necessity, we are shown how to live *in* the world and not be *of* the world; how to utilize living itself as a means of spiritual growth, no matter what the external circumstance; how to experience all our joys and sorrows and shortcomings as a means of spiritual upliftment. The *Gita* helps us integrate our separate personality into harmony with the whole. It teaches an alchemy of *transforming* our raw material as well as *transcending* it. Spirit and matter are equal partners. The individual and the divine are part of one whole.

This knowledge is revealed through a dialogue between Krishna and Arjuna. Krishna is the loving teacher; Arjuna is the questioning disciple. Krishna is a king; a married man with many duties. And he's also an *avatar*—one who descends to earth with the express purpose of uplifting humanity. Krishna is the inner Self—eternal, omniscient, present within each of us. Arjuna is the insecure individuality making its way in the world subject to confusion and doubt. An aim of the *Gita* is to help us forge a link with this inner Self as we dance through life, so we can come to know who we really are. Then genuine self confidence emerges.

Gradually throughout each chapter, Krishna teaches Arjuna the nature of Truth or Reality. This helps him come closer and closer to his inner Self until at the very end, Arjuna's memory of his true nature returns.

The knowledge of our true identity cannot occur without a battle. This battle takes place on the field of *dharma*. *Dharma* means justice, righteousness, the inner essence of a thing—that which sustains. Although the location of the war is called Kurukshetra, it is really placeless and timeless. This is a battle each of us will be compelled to fight, if we yearn for liberation.

Liberation from suffering, liberation from ignorance cannot occur without yearning for freedom. Like Arjuna we must know we do not know. And to gain freedom, we must learn to participate in the battle of life with right knowledge.

What makes the *Gita* a practical psychology of transformation is that it offers us the tools to connect with our deepest intangible essence. Only when the connection becomes ongoing does suffering cease. In order to be able to forge this inner link, much baggage must be discarded along the way. All the external conditioning which is not a reflection of our essence must gradually go. Our anger, fear, greed, jealousy, confusion, worry, attachment, selfishness, pride, expectations and desire to control must be given the means to melt down as the beginning process of the work. This occurs not only through technique, but also through ever heightening yearning, spiritual practice and consequent insight that proceeds from deep within each person. First we must recognize the tools and then learn how to use them.

The process consists of many small steps along the way of practice and understanding. As each fresh insight brings new joy and a different obstacle, a flow is established between inner knowing and outer happening. Events are no longer seen as separate and segmented but part of a giant continuity of great nature of which we are all a part. We are each students at the university of *prakriti* learning lessons from nature tailored to our individual level and inner needs. And eventually we might come to see that what constitutes liberation is the qualitative depth and breadth of our experiential vision.

There is no theory to be internalized and applied in this psychology. Ancient practices spontaneously induce what each person needs as the individual and the universal coincide. The work proceeds through intellectual knowledge of the playing field(*jnana yoga*), emotional devotion to the ideal(*bhakti yoga*) and right action that includes both feeling and knowledge(*karma yoga*). With ongoing purification we approach wisdom.

Each of the eighteen chapters presents a *yoga* or graduated means of linking the separate individuality with the selfless Self. *Yoga* derives from the Sanskrit "*yuj*," which means to join. The various philosophies and methods of joining the mind to eternal Truth find expression within each chapter. When the different aspects of oneself become connected to the One center, the goal of *yoga* is near.

Then all our seemingly individual thoughts and actions become linked to the higher Intelligence. If each individual who experiences an inner calling could work in accordance with his or her capacity to forge this connection, there would be peace and contentment within the individual, the family, the society and the world.

Gita Synopsis

I
emotions churn
confusion covers life
the sun always shines

II
permeating all
I have existed always
I never perish

My nature is bliss
pervading deep inside
My nature is Love

III
to know Me
act on in the world outside
as is your nature

offer the results to Me
let go of fear, doubt and craving
remember Me and revel
in the game of life

IV
the sacrifice of creation
brings worlds into being
we too can participate

everything we do or say
each austerity we practice
purification, contemplation, meditation

even our desire
our food, our very breath
a connection with the divine

become fit to be a cell
in the body of the Totality!

V

to truly know
I am not the doer
while continuing to do
wisdom accrues

in joyous equanimity
wherever and whatever
renunciation abides

VI

while moving
train the mind in silence
until wholeness

without movement
train the mind in stillness
until unity

"when he sees me in all
and he sees all in me
then I never leave him and
he never leaves me."

VII

invisible is
the true foundation of life
One Reality

nature pulsates
exuding loving consciousness
taste it

VIII

there are many worlds
of the living and the dead
pierce them all through love

at the last moment
when the great transition comes
be only in Me

IX

all are in Me
the Source of all that lives
worship Me with love

X

unborn I manifest
the essence of everyone
everything I am

XI

with the divine eye
see My presence continuous
beyond the realm of time

worlds of dazzling splendor
black holes and jaws of death
I maintain them all
ever peaceful

XII

I love them all
who worship Me with devotion
or dispassion

love only Me
in all creatures and happenings
with faith in My eternity

XIII
to know the field
and the knower of the field
is to know Me

beyond beginningless nature
beyond pleasure and pain
beyond matter and feeling consciousness
Know Me

XIV
three ropes of matter
ever bind us to the world
cut them

with the scissors of consciousness
know and feel and see
in utter detachment

XV
the tree of life
with root beyond the firmament
eternal essence seed

enmeshed in the tree we die
discover the root
and live

XVI
divine wealth
leads us to our Self
the path of light

the way of ignorance
haphazard and entrenched
perpetual darkness

become fit
to transcend
endless cycles!

XVII
whatever we do
do it with faith
whatever we say
say it with faith
whatever we give
give it with faith

a golden thread
sews all our actions
to the infinite

XVIII
surrender all selfishness
to Me
in wholesomeness

imperfect though your work may be
offer everything to Me
with remembrance love

and you will be stainless
and you will be in Me
***always**...*

ॐ

One

YOGA OF ARJUNA'S SORROW

Arjuna Vishada Yoga

	Gita verses
Description of the warriors of the two armies	1–11
The conches sound	12–19
Arjuna surveys the armies	20–27
The depression of Arjuna	28–47

emotions churn
confusion covers life
the sun always shines

As we begin our personal journey into the *Bhagavad Gita*, a question arises. For what purpose was the *Gita* offered by Krishna to Arjuna? And why is the *Gita* available to us today?

The purpose of the *Gita* is not to entertain although it is a very interesting text. It is not to gather intellectual knowledge although it is filled with wisdom. It is not to solve our problems of daily living, though if we come to follow the teachings, our perception of difficulty will transform itself into the actuality of opportunity. Although the *Gita* can be experienced as a guide to whatever we need and wherever we happen to be inside, its primary purpose is to guide us toward liberation. Its primary purpose is liberation.

Liberation from what? Liberation from the suffering caused by confusion and a clouded view of Reality. Liberation from the ignorance of our Real nature; from the ingrained conditioning that prevents our seeing. Liberation from the automatic emotions and actions, which hamper our capacity to love. Sri Nisargadatta Maharaj says, "Liberation is never *of* the person. It is always *from* the person."

The teachings help us peel away the shell step by step in accordance with our individual tendencies and inner nature. When a squirrel wishes to eat a nut first he must hold it; hold it firmly and look at it. He knows that the nut is his food. In order to reach the kernel, he must decide where to dig in his nails; find the right spot and the right angle so the shell can be crushed. First he turns the nut and explores. Then he holds on tightly and starts chipping away bit by bit, digging his sharp incisive teeth into the covering that prevents him from consuming the food. Only after this diligent, preliminary effort is he able to eat the nut—chew it, swallow it, and digest it.

Likewise, it is also necessary for us to look at ourselves, to observe our behavior under different conditions and circumstances like the squirrel turning the nut. And to ask ourselves, "who am I, who am I really"? If we are earnest in our observation and questioning, soon we will come to discover there is in fact a shell that covers our true nature.

Many of us seem content to live only in the shell and have little faith in the existence of the kernel. And some nuts are hard to crack while others remain hidden in the underbrush, unused and uneaten till they rot. As we begin to question and observe ourselves, we will see that so much of our energy, thoughts and actions are directed toward the maintenance and protection of the shell with little regard for the nourishing food of the kernel. It is through this process of seeing ourselves, experiencing ourselves both as shell and as kernel that the initiation into our evolution truly begins. Through ingesting the teachings of the *Gita*, we are being offered a way of viewing and working with ourselves that can initiate us into the world community of evolving human beings. This can eventually enable us to be of service to ourselves as well as to others. The quality of our individual lives and the life of the planet depend upon whether you and I accept the conscious choice to make the effort to evolve.

Evolution and Liberation

What then is evolution? Is it different from personal growth? The distinction can be viewed like this. The term personal growth refers to gaining skills, knowledge, freer emotional expression or expansiveness; for example, getting out of personal ruts, seeing new things about ourselves, being able to be more assertive, less rigid, or more related. Personal growth then, refers to refining the quality of our mental and emotional expression as we meet the world in the process of becoming. Usually, this entails the growth of the ego body self, which for most of us is the only aspect of the self we have access to. This is akin to the shell, the covering that contacts the external world. That which is tangible, which can be seen, felt, tasted or thought about is what we have been trained to develop in ourselves. That which is not accessible to the five senses, emotions and thoughts we have had little experience with. An enormous part of us lies buried for lack of education. Therefore, there is little understanding regarding the possibility of existence beyond the material and tangible.

It is only natural to have faith in what we've experienced and to doubt what we have not experienced. Personal growth, which relates to the development of the ego body self would then appear to be more accessible than evolution.

However, evolution remains a powerful urge deep within each of us. For some it is a conscious urge, for others, the deep desire remains unconscious. Evolution is our inherent capacity to reach another level of ourselves, a deeper level that exists within every human being but remains unknown and untapped. It is the innate inheritance of a human being to become his or her hidden higher nature—to shed one's self-centered thoughts and actions like the snake sheds its skin; to let go of all our fears, including the fear of death. When we can embrace our natural tendency to love without a trace of selfishness or attachment, we contribute beneficence to everyone and everything.

How then can this inherent human capacity to evolve into our higher nature connect with a catalyst that will awaken it from its dormant state?

The ability to evolve for a human being is not simply an automatic, imprinted biological function, as it is for an animal. For a human being is endowed with a brain that carries within it enormous potential—provided our consciousness is motivated to acknowledge and wish for the unfolding of this potential. For us there is a choice, unlike for the animal. So we ordinary mortals are in a position of feeling dimly the existence of something within; something mysterious, something beautiful, something noble, something expansive. We don't know what it is and we don't know how to tap it, how to allow this dimly perceived beauty to materialize and live through us amidst the hustle and bustle of everyday life.

Apart from an animal brain and a human brain, a higher endowment is present within us but remains unconnected to our consciousness. Most of us spend our lives living on the level of animals—breeding, acquiring, preserving, concerned primarily with self preservation, our relationships, our jobs, our power, our territory. Our conditioning has taught us to live under the illusion that exclusive concern with the shell will bring happiness. As we develop more human qualities such as kindness, compassion and the desire to contribute to the welfare of others, our minds become calmer. When the ego slowly relinquishes its spot as the center, there is less anxiety and deeper contentment. With a more peaceful mind, connections with our higher nature can begin to form. Then the urge for evolution, which is a part of our higher nature, unlimited by ego will begin to appear. A vast network of interconnections between the outer world and ourselves become more pronounced. Events become teachings. Life becomes a game—playful, light and highly serious all at once. We begin to see how external circumstance can both become our teacher and send us our teacher.

Says the ancient wisdom, "When the student is ready the teacher will appear." The university-of-life offers no formal degree except the degree of evolution that we encounter on the way—the capacity to transform ourselves from an animal person to a human person to a godly person. Our unshakable happiness and well being is dependent solely on this degree.

What then are the prerequisites for meeting a teaching in such a way that we will be open to receiving it? The main requirement is a deep feeling of urgency. Maybe there is a crisis in our lives that shakes us to the core—physical illness, psychological depression, unbearable conflict, loss of loved ones, money or position. Or maybe the urgency comes from a deep desire to know Truth, to find meaning, a new way of being, a real purpose for living. Or like the Buddha, to discover an end to suffering. For those of us who begin from the starting point of intellectual curiosity, a steady search brings the possibility of deepening one's initial conscious motivation so that the deeper, buried wish for this higher capacity present in all of us can eventually emerge.

From whatever route we approach a teaching, the path will intensify as we attempt first to reflect, understand and then to practice and experience for ourselves the universal content of the teaching within our own individual context. It is important that each person approach the teaching from where he or she is, without comparisons or trying to fit into a mold. We must each come to see where we are, accept where we are. This doesn't happen over night. It takes time.

In this way, the *process* of living our individual lives in the world affords the opportunity of becoming more balanced in body, emotions and intellect. Each individual, with our mixture of instincts, conditioned tendencies, faults and noble aspirations is the vehicle through which the higher nature gradually manifests, as our various parts become harmonized.

The Value of Conflict

For Arjuna, the sense of urgency comes from an emotional crisis. The greatest warrior of his age becomes paralyzed on the battlefield before the most monumental battle of his long career. He had been looking forward to this conclusive fight for many years. But something mysterious has changed it all. He goes with Krishna to survey the armies.

hear the sacred conch shells roar
in thundering cacophony
their forceful cries vibrate
instilling terror deep
within the hearts of men

the call to battle is
an invitation to enlightenment

This awe-inspiring clamor to all true warriors can serve as an initiation to liberation. Arjuna sees it all—each individual warrior, his relatives and kinsmen, his friends and teachers. Whirling clearly before his mind's eye, he sees the future consequences of the killing, the destruction of society. The fact that he would be the murderer of his relations penetrates his emotions with such powerful force that he becomes filled with fear, confusion, despondency and guilt. These emotions completely overwhelm him, take over all his reason and training. Never before has he felt such fear in battle. Never before has he been so overwhelmed by confusion. The only thing he's sure of is that the kingdom is not worth all the killing. Even if the enemy is evil, the consequences that ensue from the chaos of war do not feel right. He no longer wants to rule.

As Arjuna reaches rock bottom, it becomes impossible for him to continue living his life in the same way. Something entirely new is needed, something of a completely different quality, something utterly unknown. What elusive possibility can ever help him solve his dilemma? Now he is no longer a great warrior prince on the battlefield of life but rather an ordinary person like you and me, completely under the sway of his emotions.

In this condition, he totally questions and discards what he thought he always knew. His nature is sincere and devoted. Under every circumstance, he steadily tries to do what is ethical and live out his *dharma*. Face to face with the unknown, his overwhelming confusion forces him to take a quantum leap in inner development. Now he knows he does not know. He is absolutely paralyzed. He must honor his feelings and use them as a stepping stone into the unknown. Conventional authority figures cannot offer him any hope of relief. But he is blessed to have chosen Krishna as his charioteer, without even knowing what that means.

Essence of the Gita

The *Gita* is a story of human nature—of good and evil, of the beneficent tendencies and destructive tendencies present in every one of us. It subtly demonstrates how we each can participate in the battle against our negative tendencies and past conditioning, so we can acquire rulership of our true kingdom. In a sense, the entire *Gita* can be considered a teaching on how to live in the world fully engaged in our daily lives with the higher consciousness as our driver, symbolized here by Krishna.

One meaning of Krishna in Sanskrit is to draw near, to attract. The presence of Krishna is meant to attract us to our higher nature and steal us away from our preoccupation with the mundane to which we give so much undue importance. When we blindly follow our material desires, thinking they will bring us happiness, we end up never being satisfied. We always want more. For the nature of matter is to change, to dissolve, to love its glitter. But if we follow our higher nature, which is the substratum of all our desires and the support of the entire universe that our mind has created, we will eventually become that higher nature. If we follow our higher consciousness we will eventually evolve into That. Then the whole world is appreciated in fullness. And our desires shed their limiting power to bind.

We might ask, does the mind create the world or does the creator create the world? Who is the creator? When we are happy does the world not seem joyful? When we are sad does the world not seem depressing? Thus, the content of the mind gets *projected* onto the world to attract to us the experiences we need in order to work through the impurities in our mind and emotions. Who for example is the creator of our dreams? Experiences and thoughts get deposited in the mind and present to us a mirror of our inner emotional state. Just as our thoughts and emotions create our dreams, we alone give birth to our entire individual lives—all supported by the lap of the creator. In this way, we are each disciple Arjuna; we are each Self Krishna. When the tiny person is ready, the cosmic person(*Purusha*) reveals the secret wisdom.

So the crisis in the life of Arjuna contains some greater purpose than getting over his conflict neurosis. His midlife crisis is to help Arjuna make the quantum leap from living a life primarily supported by social structure, education, family, ritual, career and external duty to a life supported by the conscious inner striving, will and action that will lead him to the knowledge of his higher inner capacity, his higher Reality. *It is conscience based conflict that presents the possibility for liberation.*

In his depression, Arjuna stands at the crossroads between the known and the unknown, a life dictated by the duality of concrete egoistic desires(*preyas*) or the unity of the highest good(*sreyas*). Faith in the material world, acquired knowledge, relationships, wealth, authority figures and good deeds cannot solve his confusion. The only thing that can guide him out of the hell of his despondency is his openness to receiving Knowledge.

Living in Dharma

The first word in the Sanskrit *Gita* is "*dharma*." This stems from the root which means to support, to bear(*dhr*). Just as human beings support the earth, so the earth supports us. "*Dharma* protects those who protect *dharma*," states the Indian proverb.

On the external level, *dharma* can be translated as duty or a prescribed code of conduct. This is relative and varies from society to society. On a subtler level it can mean performing action that is in accordance with one's inner talents and intelligence—doing what feels harmonious. At a subtler level, *dharma* refers to just action: that behavior which is objectively true and virtuous in all times and places. And on the subtlest level, *dharma* means living in accordance with the law of our inner being, the Self and following This and This alone no matter what. To live in *dharma* is joyful!

Arjuna's confusion stems from the fact that his conscious mind knows nothing about the deepest level of *dharma*. And his attachment to the surface level as duty and family relationship clouds his sense of societal *dharma*—that he is a powerful warrior trained to protect the society from evil.

There is no inherent conflict between inner nature and outer duty. This notion is illusion. When we live in accordance with our deepest *dharma*, the other levels inevitably fall into place. Throughout the *Gita*, Krishna gradually leads Arjuna to the shattering of his illusion and confusion. The precedence of inner striving is lovingly revealed as the backdrop for the play of the universe, the cosmic dance, and the game of life—the point where the individual and the universe coalesce. The crisis of Arjuna is to help him evolve. The person *grows* within society and *evolves* within himself, both in partnership with the "external" and irrespective of what is "external." It is a quantum leap of being functioning from the space of conscious Self awareness. And through the gradual process of evolution, we too can be led towards liberation. The *yogis* say, the way is to melt the ego(*ahankara*) into the soul(*jivatman*) and the soul into the universal Spirit(*Brahman*). This is what the *Gita* will be teaching us.

Thus, the first discourse reveals how despair, conflict and suffering can lead us to a teaching that will initiate us into the way of *yoga*.

(See Appendix One for a discussion of background story and characters.)

Two

Yoga of Eternal Wisdom

Sankhya Yoga

	Gita verses
Arjuna expresses confusion and surrenders to Krishma	1–10
Eternal Truth of *Atma*; thou art That	11–30
The need to fight according to the warrior's *dharma*	31–38
Desireless action*(nishkama karma)*	39–53
The person of steady wisdom*(sthita prajna)*	54–72

permeating all
I have existed always
I never perish

My nature is bliss
pervading deep inside
My nature is Love

As the chapter opens, Arjuna is on the battlefield in a state of paralysis caused by a terrible emotional conflict. On the one hand is his rightful kingdom; on the other hand he would have to kill his teachers and family members in order to get it. And in the first discourse, he tells us he doesn't want the kingdom, he doesn't want to kill his relations and he has no wish to destroy the prevailing sense of order in the family, social structure, rituals and culture. For war kills not only people, it disrupts the entire way of life. He foresees the further future disintegration of morality and the values which held the society together. And he sees himself as the agent of all this destruction. In the face of conscience, Arjuna cannot blindly follow his role as warrior. Individuality and *dharma* must deepen—beyond group and social value to individual Self value, which includes all. He wants to follow his rightful duty but he doesn't know what that is.

The kinds of questions Arjuna asks are: "Is it better to drop out, or is it better to kill evil in the full knowledge you'll be destroying those you love and hundreds of thousands of people and the entire society in the process? As all worldly matter is mixed with elements of good and evil, in such a situation how could any action be commendable"? Since he cannot bear the thought of killing his own family, he comes to the conclusion that it is better to give up and withdraw. Arjuna says, "I will not fight"(9).

Krishna lets him talk. And Arjuna comes to express deeper layers of emotional pain until finally, he reaches a point where he experiences his helplessness fully. He is able to shed the persona of the great warrior prince and become a little child again crying in the lap of the father with total honesty, without a trace of pretense or pride. Alone, he is unable to extricate himself from this horrible dilemma. He is fully aware of his helplessness. Amidst the confusion rests a spark of alertness. It is in this spirit of renunciation and surrender that Arjuna takes refuge in Krishna. He places himself completely under the care of Krishna.

Here we might pause for a moment and ask, what do I take refuge in? What does it mean to take refuge in an ideal, a person, a way of living or one's inner consciousness?

When we encounter a crisis in our lives, the most important thing is to take refuge in what will truly help us as opposed to what will merely patch up the status quo. Only by embracing that which is qualitatively different from what we already know can a rebirth into a new way of living occur. We must be able to say, "I don't know." Otherwise, we just end up repeating the same mistakes again and again based on ignorance, insensitivity and lack of understanding.

From his conflict and consequent surrender, we see the purity of Arjuna's motivation. He wants to follow his inner conscience but his emotions act like clouds covering his clarity. The voice of conscience is the voice of our higher nature. But confusion veils discrimination regarding what is important and how to act on it.

With full knowledge of Arjuna's pure desire to do what is right for himself and the kingdom, Krishna begins to impart the teaching that will enable Arjuna to know his *dharma* and fight the battle of *Dharmakshetra* to the best of his ability(11). And if he so chooses, he can continue to practice the teachings throughout the entire battle of life, that he might one day be liberated from any further need for battle.

To be born as a human being offers us the opportunity to participate in the battle of life with consciousness that can lead to evolution and liberation.

The Real and the Unreal

Krishna begins with the highest teaching on the nature of Reality called nondualism(*advaita*). Reality is only One. All names and forms, all time and place and the vastness of space are part of this One. You and I are in fact this One. He tells us that life is continuous, eternal, unchanging; that you and I have always existed and will ever continue to exist. For it is only the bodies that come and go, come and go. It is only the packaging that is thrown away like old clothes that get worn out(22). "Within" the body lives something that ever remains. When a jar is broken, the space inside the jar still exists, no longer limited by the encasement and shape of the form. What we call death belongs only to the realm of the body. But Reality belongs to the realm that never dies. Why then mourn for a body?

The body is composed of the five elements, which are destructible. Reality is beyond that which can be destroyed, beyond the changing, beyond time and space. The *real* Self of every human being is indestructible.

The meaning of *advaita* is "not two"; not division into different categories of atoms, elements, shapes, bodies, names and personalities. In nondualism, all "separateness," from the smallest grouping of micro-atom to the largest galaxy or even space itself is an artifact dependent on our organs of perception. When we take in the world with the senses, mind and intellect we perceive the sense objects, emotions and thoughts. When we experience Reality through the inner eye we perceive the One, eternal, nondual. The aim is to perceive the world *through* the senses, mind and intellect in the knowledge this is all dynamic and changeable. This is not permanent Truth. *The aim is to discover the changeless within the realm of change.*

Krishna teaches the *Gita* to help Arjuna proceed from the level of conflict and division to a space of stillness and unity. For liberation can occur only when the seemingly separate individuality experiences itself as part of the unchanging totality, the One. We too can separate out our God Self from its merging imprisonment in the universe of names and forms, that we can come to perceive this formless Self: *Brahman* as it is—changeless, One without a second, within all levels of seeming causation and beyond.

Krishna tells Arjuna that he is experiencing himself as a potential murderer identified with his role as killer because of his attachment to his family, friends and teachers. The Self cannot kill or be killed. Arjuna is not a murderer. He is not the doer. He is meant to play out his role in life to the best of his ability. To participate in the battle rightly means to play out his role as a warrior fighting for a just cause to protect the people. In order to accomplish this, he cannot be identified with his cousins and teachers who are fighting for an unjust, egoistic cause. And he cannot mistake himself for his name and form and body. Whereas Duryodhana and the Kauravas are generally fighting out of selfishness, hatred, greed and desire for power, Arjuna and the Pandavas are fighting primarily for *dharma*: for justice, righteousness and the well being of all. Why in this truth find sorrow?

It is our identification with the body which is the root of all our confusion and pain. As long as we cling to the belief that we are the body ego mind form, with its relationships, possessions, thoughts and feelings, this prevents us from living in ultimate oneness. Identification with the body veils our true identity. When we take in Knowledge and begin to experience it, gradually this attachment to our name and form begins to dissolve. Now Krishna is helping Arjuna to separate out what is Real from what is unreal by explaining the nature of life and Reality.

> *Sankhya Yoga* teaches the wisdom to distinguish between the *Atma* and *anatma*, between the true Self and the false self, between the sentient and the insentient, between the eternal and the changing. (Sri Sathya Sai Baba, *Discourses on the Bhagavad Gita*, p.99)

> Dhritarashtra and the Kauravas represent those people who consider things which do not belong to them as their own. They represent the possessive nature. Even though he is not the body, he considers the body as his very Self. He is not the senses but he derives pride in thinking that he is the senses. Any person who considers a kingdom, which does not belong to him as his own is a Dhritharashtra. If you could observe all the people of Dhritharashtra's lineage, that is, those having this possessive attitude, you would find that they all identify themselves with the body and the senses. (ibid., p.101)

Thus, to participate in the battle of *Dharmakshetra* means to participate in our lives in a manner that will sever our attachment to everything that is not Real. This in turn allows us to experience the link to that which is Real. "The unreal never is; the Real never is not. This truth indeed has been seen by those who can see the true."(2:16)

There's a story told in India about the enormous power of a person who is not identified with the body and knows Reality:

> When Alexander the Great entered India, a scout was sent through the forest to pave the way for the King. He discovered an old man lying near a tree and told him, "Get up, get up. Alexander the Great is coming." The man didn't move. Then the soldier threatened to cut off his head if he didn't move. The man just laughed. By now Alexander was witnessing the scene. The old man just laughed contentedly as the soldier placed the sword at his neck. There was no trace of fear.
>
> The emperor saw the great effulgence on his face and he spoke to him, "My soldier has threatened to cut off your head and yet you seem very happy. If you were an ordinary person you would immediately surrender before him and ask for pardon. But you are only smiling. What is the meaning of this?"
>
> The *yogi* replied, "I am eternal truth awareness bliss. I am ever free. Your weapons can never harm me. Fire cannot burn me. Water cannot wet me. Wind cannot blow me away. I was never born and I will never die. I am the immortal *Atma*. That is my reality. Here this soldier is threatening to kill me by cutting the head off this body. That is totally ludicrous. Hearing that provoked me to laughter."
>
> The moment the emperor heard these words he was very surprised. He thought, "It is quite natural for people to get frightened when they are about to face death but rarely will anyone laugh and be so happy when they are about to die. In India there are people who have attained such a state of excellence in spiritual life that they are not even afraid of death. How can I plunder such a nation? No I won't do that." So Alexander turned his army away and went no further into India." (ibid., p.120)

First Krishna teaches from the perspective of the highest Reality which is unchanging and eternal(11-25). This unceasing Reality is called the supreme *Purusha* or *Paramatma*. Then he explains from the viewpoint of materialist philosophy(26), that the body as matter(*prakriti*) is always in a state of flux, ever changing; a temporary home for the soul on its journey to the eternal. Birth, death, birth, death revolve in ever-continuous cycle. The waves break into the shore, disappear and reappear again and again. For the waves are composed of the ocean, which is the substratum for the waves. But unlike the ocean, the inner Self is invisible. This one ongoing continuousness, the senses and mind can neither grasp nor see.

> Invisible before birth are all beings and after death invisible again. They are seen between two unseens. Why in this truth find sorrow? (2:28)

Here the philosophy of reincarnation is introduced: each human soul exists beyond the body and makes use of the body as a vehicle through which to evolve. Each birth offers us a different set of circumstances to experience living and purify our minds and emotions that we might work through our confusion and proceed toward wisdom. Each life offers something new, something needed; a different vantage point in time and space to discriminate what is Real from what is unreal. This brings us closer to clarity—the clear, formlessness eternal, timeless, unchanging unity—the One beyond all word or description.

When there is no more impurity, our inherent wholeness is no longer covered. We reclaim our true identity as an unsegmented segment of the totality. Then there is no more need to reincarnate, unless we consciously choose to descend to help humanity.

But this is all very difficult for the average intelligent person to comprehend—especially for a doubting skeptic like Arjuna, who possesses a rational intellect. He is a military man living in a society that follows rules and regulations. And without concrete evidence of the eternal, how can the ordinary reasoning skeptic know what in the world Krishna is talking about? It seems impossible.

So then Krishna teaches Arjuna from a conventional common sense point of view(31). It is your *dharma*. What will others say about you. It would be shameful for such a great warrior as yourself to have people say you ran away out of fear. You and I know it's not true but that's what everyone would say.

Thus we have the highest idealist philosophy, the materialist's viewpoint and simple folksy advice mixed together as one. By not remaining exclusively in the esoteric intellectual realm, Krishna reminds us it is this very mixture of which the stuff of life is made—the eternal, the material and the conventionally ordinary. Or with reference to philosophy, the three planes of existence can be called nondualism(*advaita*), qualified nondualism(*vasisthadvaita*) and dualism(*dvaita*). And we need to be able to relate to all three perspectives. For the three levels are in fact one Reality. Reality permeates all ways of viewing things, all aspects of life. The eternal is all pervasive whether we can experience it or not.

Being existence lives forever
there is no such thing as death
for this omnipresent source
of the universe

Truth can never change
its essence cannot alter
ever invisible it remains
supporting the divine movement
of the cosmos
that comes and goes and
returns to its source in its season

we are all part of
this divine movement and
we are each
its eternal unchanging existence
in reality there is no such thing as death

for the body is but a covering
over the essence of humankind
and the Spirit is our true home

water cannot wet it, fire cannot burn it
for the Spirit is indestructible

myriad of warriors come and go
while the Self remains
clusters of universes enter and exit
while the true nature remains

I have existed always
thunders the divine in me

five elements are the raw materials
divine building blocks of body and mind
that live in Spirit and change in form
in accordance with time and circumstance
but they are never destroyed

again and again we have entered
this drama of death and birth
under the sway of maya
blindly suffering our ignorance
again and again until
the precious moment when we embody
this exquisite awakening forever and ever

in the knowledge of universal continuity O disciple
live out your duty to yourself and humanity
do not forsake this precious battle of life
do not flee from opportunity

Three Laws of Vedanta

From a metaphysical perspective, *Vedanta* expounds three laws of causation, which lead us beyond the cause and effect relationship. The first principle is:

1. There cannot be an effect without a cause.

   Shankara's *Brahma Sutra Bhasya* delineates two kinds of causes—the material cause and the efficient cause. The material cause consists of the stuff from which something is made. Clay is the substance for ceramic pots, gold is the substance for jewellry. And the efficient cause is the creator, the one who makes the clay pot or the necklace. On this level of causation, the nondual one God is considered the creator of the universe of diverse names and forms. Here God transcends the universe. He is above it and separate from it. He is the master and we are the servants. This is the philosophy of dualism(*dvaita*). The second law of causation is:

2. The effect is nothing but the cause in different form.

 This implies the time-space dimension is not as segmented as the mind generally perceives it. If the cause for a present event was five years ago, that cause is part of the now effect and both cause and effect can be experienced as one present event. And all the different powers or gods can be viewed as a specific manifestation of the one illumining God energy.

 When applied to all creation, this law means that the effect, which is the universe, is nothing but God, consciousness, the Creator in a different form. At this level, God lives within the universe immanent in every name and form, from the frog and the freak to the sinner and the saint. God as enlivening energy pervades every atom of creation while qualitative differences between behaviors, forms and energies are still acknowledged. Here God walks among us and the relationship is intimate as Friend to friend, Lover to lover, while still maintaining mastery and Lordship. This is the philosophy of qualified nondualism(*visisthadvaita*). The third law of causation is:

3. When the cause is removed from the effect nothing remains.

 When the enlivening principle leaves the body, the five elements disintegrate and nothing remains of that particular form. Likewise, when God seemingly withdraws His presence from the universe, the form of the universe as we know it ceases. The Absolute still remains but the world apparently vanishes or changes in form. And when our conscious mind is merged in God consciousness, only Truth, Eternity, Reality exists. There is no external universe, no division into names, forms and energies. There are no words. All is One and One alone. All is God and only God. There are no distinctions. This is the philosophy of nondualism(*advaita*).

We develop into nondualism gradually through each of the three stages of worshipping God—first up in heaven, then through the energies in oneself and in the universe and later through merging with this One subtlest omnipresent energy. Then it is said the subject-object dichotomy wholly ceases. And there is nothing more to be experienced for everything is known. This is the experience of the fully realized soul. Our aim is to come to know this all-inclusive equality unity.

(For further elucidation on the three laws of *Vedanta* see "The Logic of Spirituality," Swami Chinmayananda, videos 1 & 2 of *The Holy Bhagavad Gita.*)

Knowledge and Practice

Krishna concludes his discourse on discriminating the nature of Reality in a utilitarian direction: how to put the highest philosophy into practice. For all knowledge is almost worthless unless it becomes a practical part of one's life. Intellectual knowledge leads only to imbalance unless it finds fulfillment in action, in some form of expression. To know something without practicing it can only create disharmony and conflict.

Picture an old fashioned scale with weights and balances. As the mind gets filled with information it cannot use, the scale sinks down with a heavy weight until it cannot move. It gets stuck. The human being, who does not translate his information into action gets weighted down with heaviness like the immovable scale. As our knowledge is practiced, insight appears. The burden in the brain gets lifted and the two halves of the scale equalize. For we need both taking in and giving out, thinking and doing. One without the other is foolishness.

First information must be reflected upon so that it can become knowledge. Then knowledge must be practiced so it can become feeling understanding. Since Krishna is trying to impart a sense for the nature of Reality, this balance is essential if we are ever to comprehend what he is talking about. The practice aspect of the philosophy is called *yoga*. Without diligent application, understanding is not probable. Without alert practice, liberation is not possible.

The question then arises, is it possible to practice something we might like to take on faith from Krishna but don't have enough experience to really believe? For example, the fact that each of us is eternal, that we never die would naturally lead to the conclusion that there is nothing to grieve for when a loved one dies. From the viewpoint of a realized soul this statement is absolutely true. But from the human perspective of love mixed with attachment and joy mixed with sorrow, trying to follow Krishna's injunction of "do not grieve" can lead only to suppression. When one does not yet perceive the real eternal continuity of life, it is natural for feelings of loss to dominate the psyche. As long as we live under the sway of *maya*, our emotions must be lived out on the human level in such a manner that they can become purified. This entails fully experiencing our joys and sorrows with some awareness of the ever lurking eternal presence supporting the drama of life and death.

Accepting *where* we are and working with ourselves *as* we are can lead to transformation whereas deluding ourselves into trying to fit into an ideal too far removed from the body, emotions and intellect can only encourage further imbalance. When we are identified with the body it is natural to mourn. When our bodily attachment is severed through experiential Knowledge it is natural not to mourn. And the spiritual student must tread the razor's edge between the two in his search to experience Reality, while the practice continues.

Yoga of the Higher Intelligence

As Krishna begins his discourse on the *yoga* of the higher Intelligence (*buddhiyoga*), a lost perspective on action is reintroduced (40-53). Since *Vedic* times, sacrifice (*yajna*) was considered a formal part of group worship called ritual action (*karma kanda*). This ceremony was believed to help the individual and the cosmos through purification of the elements; and it continues to this day. Now Vyasa is reintroducing the forgotten, ancient idea that *everyday action can also become worship.* Individual action acquires new importance in the cosmic scheme of things. As the intellect becomes purified and comes to reflect the light of knowledge, our very actions become infused with holiness. Everything we do, feel and think can be sacred action. Sacrifice(*yajna*) is not just ritual ceremony. It is the process of living.

> No step is lost on this path and no dangers are found. And even a little progress is freedom from fear. (2:40)

From the outset, we are assured that in *buddhi yoga* effort is never wasted. This universal law of cause and effect is very comforting and encouraging. Each chapter of the *Gita* will expand our vision regarding the meaning of effort. The general effort entails listening or ingesting, reflecting on the content, which becomes knowledge and then trying to live the knowledge, which leads to understanding. Even the smallest effort is meaningful. *Yoga* is both the path and the goal.

"*Yoga*" derives from the Sanskrit "*yuj*" which means to yoke, unite or join. Just as the oxen is yoked to the cart so that the driver can control the reins, the body, emotions and intellect are to be yoked to the higher nature. When this connection is present, one feels in harmony and behaves in balance with the essence of oneself. When this connection is lacking one lives in confusion, alienation and consequent suffering.

Usually the body wants one thing, the emotions something else and the intellect aspires to something of a far different order. Let's each think of examples in our own lives—from food to sex to relationships, material things and higher ideals. *External orientation inevitably breeds conflict*. This conflict between the varying desires of the body, emotions and intellect leads the mind to agitation and disappointment. As one practices the art of remembering the higher nature, which is one's Self, devotion enters the heart. The different parts of the person gradually become unified, linked together to one's higher nature. The oxcart now has a driver. And it is the reins of attention, which help create the link between the ox and the will of the driver.

But the average person finds it difficult to believe in and relate to his higher nature(42-45). He wants more tangible things, simply because there is no connection with his soul. So he lives under the illusion that things bring happiness. He prays for wealth, performs sacrifices for external things.[1] Just as the man of *Vedic* times worked to perform rituals to bend nature to his will, so today's person labors to acquire possessions. All work is sacrifice of something—time, energy, youth. But the status and possessions acquired from the work of ritual or the results of a nine to five job cannot in themselves dispel fear or bring security and happiness. For as these are based primarily on material desires, they are subject to change. *All things subject to change cannot bring lasting happiness.* Krishna therefore advises us to look beyond the world of nature, the material world of change, for our happiness—to realize that all happiness rests in discovering That support for the world of change; the unnamable cosmic ocean of the Self in one and all.

Three Qualities of Matter

The stuff of matter is present in our minds, thoughts and emotions as well as in all concrete living things be they called mineral, vegetable, animal or human. And all matter consists of the three *gunas*(45).

Guna means rope in Sanskrit. Each of us is tied by the rope of our subjective experience of life taken in by the senses and the mind. Our internal and external experience is based on the distribution of *gunas* within us. We perceive in accordance with our *gunas*.

There is *tamas*—inactivity, heaviness, inertia, sleepiness or passive receptivity, which is connected with the principle of dissolution. Its color is black. There is *rajas*—activity, passion, movement, dynamism, which is connected with the principle of creation. Its color is red. There is *sattva*—inner stillness, purity, righteousness, justice, wisdom, harmony, which is connected with the principle of preservation. Its color is white.

The *gunas* have been likened to the psychological moods of matter. They determine what experiences we have and how we understand these experiences. It is through our observation and understanding of the gunas working within that we can live out both personal growth and evolution.

The *cakras* of the subtle body help us to evolve. At first, the coiled serpent *kundalini* rests sleeping at the base of the spine in the root *cakra* called *muladhara*. As long as this powerful energy remains dormant, a person is primarily externally oriented, object oriented, selfishly oriented, governed by desire and attachment. The duality between subject and object persists. As the potential energy for evolution awakens through the process of listening to teachings, reflection, self-inquiry and spiritual practice, a change in our inner orientation begins to occur. The energy that had gone into sex, survival and individuality transforms into something new—a kind of rebirth.[2]

The *cakras* can be viewed as receiving centers for different forms of cosmic energy that help to cleanse our personality of its past conditioning. As the emotions become more purified and beneficent, egotism gradually departs. With no veils or dust covering the *cakras*, they begin to open and bloom and receive the light of divine energy. When the heart *cakra* opens, we enter the realm of genuine love, a love that is not based on egocentricity or attachment but on compassion for all.

Though the *cakras* are neither physical nor psychological, the gradual awakening of energy creates a balance between body and mind that transcends both. Whereas the *gunas* are constituents of matter, *kundalini* is divine subtle energy, which utterly transforms our inner state. The relationship between the two becomes a more evident process of interaction as we begin to evolve. By observing our functioning, we come to see how the body, the mind and our behavior are interrelated. This seeing evokes a genuine yearning that serves as fuel for our spiritual effort and inner transformation.

We begin as a *tamasic* person—lazy, sleepy, wanting to be fed and given love, not wanting to make efforts for ourselves. Then egocentric desire awakens. We grow into *rajas* and become motivated to work and acquire things for ourselves and our families. Before long, our suffering, caused by emotional selfishness, physical stress, confusion or feelings of alienation leads us to search for another way of being. We want to be useful, do something meaningful, understand life and be of service to others. *Sattva* begins to develop. In the realm of pure *sattva*, a person can rest or work, think or act, but whatever he does is for the good of the Self, the good of the whole. His motivation stems from purity of intention and not from personal gain.

Alongside Arjuna's dynamic, active nature is a pure motivation, a *sattvic* nature. Therefore, the quality of his mind, his actions and his life is very different from Duryodhana, who is primarily under the sway of his automatic *tamasic* instincts and egoistic *rajasic* greed.

To be *sattvic* is to work well for the *process* of what is being done in the moment and not for the sake of the reward one will receive—be it money, praise or intellectual satisfaction. Being present-oriented and process-oriented as opposed to primarily goal-oriented leads to peacefulness. This attitude saves one from the anxiety of thinking oneself a success if one wins and a failure if one loses(47). *For there is no such thing as win and lose, success and failure.* These are merely human judgements, which exist in the fantasy of the ego. They are devoid of the wisdom of universal law, the ever present totality, with its just interconnections of shifts and balances. What is truly worthwhile is to perform actions with remembrance of one's higher nature. Do not try to control the outcome. Leave the results to the lawfulness of the universe.

When we stop trying to control, when we no longer work primarily for a paycheck or strictly for the sake of winning, the ego begins to acknowledge something other than itself. This is the beginning of peacefulness, the dawn of wisdom. Thus, to be beyond the three *gunas* is to live in the world with the support of the wealth of Self Knowledge.

> Be in Truth eternal, beyond earthly opposites. Beyond gains and possessions, possess thine own soul. (2:45)

The process of coming to know one's real Self is *yoga*. "*Yoga* is wisdom in work," says Krishna; "*yoga* is dexterity in action"(50). The ability to be impartial, neither craving for success nor shunning failure brings evenness of mind. For failure from the perspective of the narrow ego is rightness from the perspective of the Self. The ability to do, to act in one's duty without regard for the result is wisdom(49). This attitude takes an enormous burden off a person and confers freedom from worry, doubt and anxiety. *The link with practicing wisdom renders action a yoga.*

The mind is to be linked only to the highest. Even scriptures can be an impediment if they are approached too long through the intermediary of the mind(52). One day, even scriptures are to be abandoned for the sake of wholly practicing contemplation within oneself or merging in one's own higher nature. Then there will come a time when we stop thinking about it and will *be* It. Everything that is not Oneself is to be surrendered. Only then can the process of *yoga* become the goal.

The Person of Steady Wisdom

Now Arjuna is truly becoming interested. He wants to understand what it is actually like to be the kind of person who lives in the knowledge of Reality. How does that person function? What are his ways?

This portion of the *Gita*(from *sloka* 55 onwards) describes the person of steady wisdom(*sthita prajna*). It holds before us a mirror of what a human being can become; shows how the positive force inherent as a seed in everyone can be experienced and lived. It describes those qualities that can be developed in each of us, which will lead to wisdom and happiness. And it tells how we can begin to nurture these qualities.

The first attribute, which is the guideline for all others is surrender—to surrender desire. "When a man surrenders all desires that come to the heart and by the grace of God finds the joy of God, then his soul has indeed found peace." What here is the meaning of surrender? Desire is natural for a human being. Why then should we give up desire?

There is desire of the body, desire of the emotions, desire of the intellect. Let's stop for a moment and try to be alert to the specific ways these three categories of desire operate in our individual lives... There are many desires. But when one want is satisfied another seems to pop up in its place. Our material and emotional desires never seem to be satisfied. And if we expect things and relationships or anything external to make us permanently happy we will end up disappointed. Then how are we to find joy and live in ongoing contentment?

There's a story of a powerful demon named Mahishasura who had conquered many worlds. The Goddess army was sent to combat him. One of his fiercest fighters named Raktabija was a terrible challenge to the warrior goddesses. Whenever a drop of his blood fell, two new demons were born. Our desires are like that. Cut off one desire and two more take its place. Soon thousands of demons emerged from his blood. Finally Kali came to the rescue and *drank the blood.* When our many desires become incorporated into the Goddess, into the mother of the universe, they return to their source. They become unified and lose their power to bind.

Thus, desire is conquered not by suppressing desire but by seeing that all desire for something external can be experienced at a deeper level, as That which supports the desire. This is the subtle realm of the Goddess. Behind every physical, emotional and material desire lurks the desire to be happy, the desire for completion, fullness, bliss and union. Bliss lives within each of us. But somehow we exchange our deepest desire for lesser ones. We exchange unity for multiplicity and then wonder why we are not satisfied. Krishna tells us that by contacting only one great desire, the desire for Truth, all our lesser desires will lose their power over us and we will come to know the joy of grace.

That one great wish beyond desire is in fact without attribute. The sages have called it *satchitananda*—being, awareness, bliss—three aspects of the aspectless. This bliss is constantly being showered on the universe but we are too dense to tune into its source. When we can wish for the source of bliss with all our being, we too will become our inherent bliss. The sage is he who surrenders all his desires to the source of bliss.

> That person attains peace who lives devoid of longing, free from the pull of desires, moving about without the sense of I-ness and my-ness. (2:71)

Desires bring agitation. The more desires we have that remain unfulfilled, the more agitated we become. The fewer desires we feel, the more peaceful we become. So the key to our happiness revolves around our recognition of the nature of desire.

We can begin by observing our desires. Are they noble, selfish or hurtful desires? Are they necessary for our well being? On what do they depend? By keeping our eyes open we can see that all material desires depend upon our identification with the ego—the illusory notion that my true identity rests in this name, form, body, thoughts and emotions. When I identify myself with this body, name and feelings, this is *maya*.[3]

Before the capacity to surrender can develop, we must have some observed experience of the effects of our desires; how they rule our lives, agitate our minds, trick us into thinking they will make us happy, while actually they keep us wedded to functioning on the narrow level of the ego. In order to detach from our desires we must be able to separate ourselves from the body ego mind self, to sever the major source of our identity from the ego. The sages say, we think we are a body with a soul but in actuality we are a soul with a body.

The transmutation of desire leads to rebirth into a life of sacredness. This is the central core around which all transformation of personality proceeds. When the ideas of the teaching begin to sink below the surface of awareness, we will be confronted with *the desire to discover Reality*. As this desire deepens, we become less scattered, more onepointed. Our varied desires gradually become reduced, one by one, as they melt into that one desire.

But until that time of inner readiness, we can view our varied desires with respect, as the expression of the life force within that is calling us to live out our destiny. The wish fulfilling cow named Kamadhenu, who lives inside each and every one of us, cannot be stolen by any other person. For our own desires are the most powerful determinants of our lives. When we yearn for something and work hard for it we often receive it. And the quality of our desires determines what we shall become. We become what our driving desire is, says the *Brhadaranyaka Upanishad.*

When we deeply wish to live our lives in the lap of Reality *the wish will be granted.* The means for confronting our inner obstacles will make themselves known.

Agitation is caused by the fact that we do not control the mind, the senses, the intellect and our desire. The mind is led outward by the senses and emotions. Under all circumstances, no matter how seemingly difficult, the man of steady wisdom remains unruffled by events and thoughts. His mind remains harmonized, yoked to the higher nature inside. Like a tortoise who draws his limbs into the protection of his shell, the sage draws in his senses, emotions and desires into the protection of the highest inner Self, in which he has taken refuge(58). Though he may experience desires he is not caught by them. As he knows the purpose of the drama of life, he is able to recognize all that changes and set his steady vision on that which is beyond change and brings lasting happiness. According to an Indian proverb, "Mountains may move but nothing can cause even a ripple in the mind of the perfect."

Hankering after pleasure induces its opposite—pain. When we want only one side of the coin, the other side is sure to respond without solicitation. This is universal law. Every coin has two sides—pleasure pain, honor shame, attachment alienation, loss gain. Each side continues alternating like a seesaw until we claim the center. When we are able to stand firmly between the opposites, at the spot that encompasses both, the seesaw immediately becomes still. The waves instantly lose their power to toss us about.

However, until we are able to let go of pain, it is important that we allow ourselves to experience our suffering with a sense of conscience; neither with guilt nor harsh superego but with remorse of conscience. For all our suffering results from our lack of perfection, our incompleteness, our as yet unknown intuition of our true identity. To suffer our lacks rightly with consciousness, without judgement will purify and lead to peacefulness.

The first step and the last rests in learning to *control the senses and develop will.* Through controlling the senses we become free from the prison of like and dislike. We approach nonfavoritism, equality. Will is an aspect of the power of the higher within us. With devoted remembrance, this power develops. Our lesser desires become transformed into *prema*, love of the highest. Krishna tells us that as our love increases, we become an embodiment of love itself. And we too can become persons of steady wisdom—liberated, immortal, free from death. Sri Sathya Sai Baba says:

> You are not the body, a bundle of flesh, blood and bones. Neither are you the unmanifested desires nor the manifested mind. You are also not the infatuating delusion that thwarts your liberation. But you are the eternal *Paramatma*, if only you recognize your innate power. The body, the senses, the mind and the intellect are only the vestures put on by many. Only when we understand the nature and significance of the adjuncts can we make proper use of them." (*Indian Culture and Spirituality*, p.11)

Thus, the second discourse reveals how we can each be reborn into a life of wisdom through the ongoing awareness of discriminating the Real from the unreal.

Three

Yoga of Action

Karma Yoga

	Gita verses
Action and the benefit of acting with detachment	1–8
The nature of sacrifice	9–16
Wheel of *dharma* as universal law for the well being of all	17–24
Wise and ignorant action, qualities of the *karma yogi*	25–35
Let go of desire and anger; be a warrior, conquer the mind	36–48

to know Me
act on in the world outside
as is your nature

offer the results to Me
let go of fear, doubt and craving
remember Me and revel
in the game of life

In the second chapter, the focus is on being, on the eternal, the changeless; that being inside oneself and everything alive which permeates all and everything. In the third chapter the emphasis is on becoming, on right action, on living in the world. Being is our birthright, a gift we have all been granted from birth. But few of us are in touch with our sense of existence, our eternal continuity, our inner essence present always without doing anything; without the props of role, position, money or relationships.

Becoming relates to evolution, to remaining in touch with our own inner nature as we dance through life. It is not blind action but action in accordance with ethics; what is right for us as individuals and as individuals living within a totality. In order for genuine evolution to occur, our actions must be connected to the pulse of life within us, within others and within the environment.

The inner yearning to evolve can serve as the link between being and becoming. This link can motivate us to awaken from sleep to consciousness, from dullness to alertness, from coarseness to a finer intelligence. It is said in the *Puranas* that God's motivation for creating the universe was his yearning to have company, to give love and relate to Himself in others. In the same way, our inner yearning for love and perfection is lived out through the ongoing creation of our individual universe. And this occurs through action.

The second discourse has been compared to the student stage of life(*brahmacharya*), where we gain the knowledge to distinguish the changing from the eternal, the Real from the unreal so that our lives can be based on the foundation of Truth and not on illusion. The third discourse has been likened to the householder stage of life(*grhasta*), where we practice applying what we have learned for the well being of ourselves, our families and the society. This requires action based on the clarity of Truth. [4]

Each action that we perform can be viewed as the most important thing in life. Why? Because our actions determine whether our lives will be happy or unhappy. It is our actions, the way we treat other people, which lead to how we will be treated; whether we feel loved or alienated, whether we have close friends or enemies, whether we live in a peaceful atmosphere or a hostile one. It is our actions that help us develop our talents and abilities or allow our innate gifts and inner qualities to wither away. It is our actions, which determine whether we find fulfillment in living or whether we die disappointed, running round the same old mechanical treadmill.

For we ourselves create an inner atmosphere that travels with us from birth to death. Each time we do something new, be it meaningful or trite, be it good or evil, we are setting the stage for a future event to rebound back to us in the form of good or evil. What we reap we sow. This is the law of cause and effect. This is the law of the universe. And this is called the law of *karma*. *Karma* means action.

Karma is not fate created by the stars. *Karma* is our present and future destiny created by our own past and present actions. If we could but comprehend the monumental significance of each of our actions, each of our words, we would be filled with awe-inspiring fear. We would know how important each moment is. We would value life and how we live it. We would think before we act. We would not allow one tiny movement or word to slip out automatically, without our conscious intention.

There is an ancient Indian proverb that says, "You sow an action, you reap a tendency; you sow a tendency, you reap a habit; you sow a habit, you reap your character; you sow your character, you reap your destiny."

What then do actions consist of? What do they stem from? And do we have a choice regarding how we will act?

At a simple individual level we can consider that an action results from a thought, a thought springs from a desire, either conscious or unconscious, and desires determine what we think about. Our thoughts lead to our words. So our desires and thoughts will determine our words and deeds. When our desires are filled with affection and good will, our thoughts, words, and actions will naturally create a positive environment. We will emanate positive vibrations. When our thoughts are filled with hatred, jealousy, competitiveness or ill will, this will be reflected in our words, our actions, and in the negative effect on the surrounding atmosphere. We will emanate negative vibrations. A conflicted and hostile atmosphere is filled with stress, agitation and unhappiness. An atmosphere where good will prevails can induce peacefulness and harmony in spite of any disagreement.

What I'm saying might appear obvious on the surface. *But it is so subtle we don't get it!* For if we truly understood the full ramifications of the connection between our desires, words, thoughts and actions, we would all be working diligently toward sainthood, toward our inherent perfection, toward infusing our desires, words and actions with pure intentions.

But few of us are aspiring saints. Krishna expounds the law of cause and effect in the third chapter to give us the opportunity to connect with our inner latent motivation that is totally positive, wholly perfect and often undiscovered. He truly wants us to understand the importance of having been granted a human body, a human life, the capacity for reason and the freedom to choose. We are given the choice to develop automatically, instinctively along the same lines as an animal or to evolve actively with consciousness in accordance with the brain that has been offered to a human being.

Our present desires, thoughts, words and actions have been greatly influenced by our conditioning; the way we've been brought up. What's happened to us molds our way of thinking and being. All our impressions, whatever we've taken in through the senses, emotions and thoughts, all our past experiences get deposited in the mind bank to form what are called *vasanas* or *samskaras*. Our *vasanas* are the inner predispositions, impressions or tendencies to act in a certain way. If a person lives among violence he will very likely acquire some violent *vasanas*. He will have the innate tendency to react aggressively to situations and repeat what he has been taught. If a person has been brought up in a peaceful, loving atmosphere, she will develop the tendency to respond in a patient, loving manner to people and situations, as her *vasanas* tend to be peaceful. These tendencies are said to be the accumulated impressions of many lifetimes and are based primarily on our past desires and actions. They greatly curtail our freedom of choice. But when we learn to perform action as a *yoga*, the raw material of our lives serves to melt our *vasanas*. And we gain detachment.

The sages have compared a human being to a cow tied to a post with a rope round her neck. Every living being is tied by this rope, the rope of our individual *samskaras*. But some ropes are longer than others; some are thicker, some are thinner. The longest rope is *sattvic*, the medium rope is *rajasic*, the shortest rope is *tamasic*. Yet they are all ropes. So where does this leave us in terms of freedom of choice?

If we are ignorant of our inner tendencies, we behave automatically without reflection. Then we are helpless slaves to our *samskaras*. If we can begin to observe our slavery, how the mind tricks us into thinking we're free, then the desire for genuine freedom will emerge. When we know that we are not free, the possibility for freedom becomes more real. The rope can begin to lengthen.

So Krishna is kindly telling us that the inalienable rights of life, liberty and the pursuit of happiness granted by the constitution are a drop in the bucket compared to internal freedom—freedom from the compulsion to act in accordance with our preprogrammed past tendencies, impressions and thought-channels. And since he is a kind teacher with a genuine interest in our well being, he offers us a way of living in the world that will eventually lead to the dissolution of our internal bondage, the end of our conditioning. This is the subject of *karma yoga*—how to link action to inner duty, to the Self, to the totality, to the changeless.

The Value of Action

The chapter begins with a question from Arjuna. He is confused. In the second chapter, he heard Krishna say that inaction is greater than action; that knowledge, wisdom stillness is the highest. If this is so why should he actively fight?

Every doubt, every question can lead us on to greater knowledge. To be able to formulate a right question, we must first reflect. When the question touches on a seeming paradox or contradiction, then an opportunity presents itself for expansion in our thinking, which can lead to integration. In the second chapter, Krishna was expounding the highest Truth, the actionless nature of the eternal. Why then does Krishna urge Arjuna to fight? Why does he urge us to act?

For Arjuna to discover and realize this actionless eternal, much action is required. But this is not compulsive action, not unthinking action. What is required is action within an acknowledged order. The movement of becoming is to be experienced as part of the totality. This is action with awareness, without any preconception. This kind of action is called work:

> There is a difference between work and mere activity. All nature works. Work is nature, nature is work. On the other hand, activity is based on desire and fear, on longing to possess and enjoy, on fear of pain and annihilation. Work is by the whole for the whole, activity is by oneself for oneself. (Sri Nisargadatta Maharaj)

Every creature is born to work, to do in accordance with his intelligence and talents as part of a whole. Lack of movement is impossible for a living being, as pulsation is an intrinsic part of life(9). From the smallest squirming amoeba to the largest rotating planet, everything is always in motion. Each breath is movement. If one's life is to be meaningful, each of us must live out his action, her capacities in accordance with *dharma*; with what we were meant to do and be in this life(8). There is one's own *dharma* on the level of the body ego and one's *dharma* on the deeper universal level. And the two are intertwined. Krishna greatly emphasizes the importance of discovering one's own *dharma* and performing it.

> Do thy duty even if it be humble rather than another's even if it be great. To die in one's duty is life: to live in another's is death. (3:35)

And one person's *dharma* is no better than another's. All are part of one whole. Maharaj says: "Do what you believe in and believe in what you do. All else is a waste of energy and time."

So the action essential for living is not blind action. It is action based on what is right for the individual. And action that is right for the individual will benefit the society. A contented individual who acts with positive motivation can bring harmony to everyone he comes in contact with, as well as to the society as a whole. A discontented person who has not yet found his *dharma* tends to contribute disharmony to others and to society. Most of us are somewhere in between with mixtures of motivation and action that consist of altruism and egotism, positive and negative, knowing and not knowing. But the true *dharma* of a human being is to see our seeming failings without harshness and strive toward the perfection that lives buried within; to live the art of peeling away the veils between ourselves and Reality. This can be accomplished only through acting on in the world in such a way that our *samskaras* become purified.

Thus the external dharma, the roles we are meant to play in the world are the means for contacting our internal dharma, which is to discover our purpose for living, to live in Truth, to experience Reality.

Desireless Action(*Nishkama Karma*) and the Ego

To act for the sake of *dharma*, duty or righteousness rather than egocentric desire is a first step toward lengthening the rope and decreasing the effect of our *vasanas*. The fewer *vasanas* we have the greater is our freedom of choice.

> Every selfless act, or sacred action is described in the *Vedas*. These come from the eternal. Therefore, the eternal is ever present in sacrifice, in every selfless act. Thus was the Wheel of Law set in motion. That man lives indeed in vain who in a sinful life of pleasures helps not in its revolution. (3:11-12)

By participating consciously in turning the wheel of *dharma*, our *vasanas* are eliminated. We willingly contribute to the good of the whole. This dedication and consecration affects the entire world.

> Egocentric actions leave their impressions behind which ultimately persecute the little ego with their reactions. All egocentric actions which are always motivated by selfish desires leave their ugly footprints upon the shores of the mind(*vasanas*) while actions

which are not ego motivated leave no trail, as birds leave no footprints as they move along in the sky. (Swami Chinmayananda)

If we act on in the world without ego and egocentric desire, we will not accumulate any new *vasanas*. And we will diminish the quantity of our existing tendencies. As extraneous conditioning and unnecessary desires dissolve, the ego(*ahankara*) melts into soul essence(*jivatman*). This leads us toward freedom.

At this juncture, let's differentiate between eastern and western concepts of the term ego. One word for ego in Sanskrit is *ahankara*, which means, "I doing;" I do this, I feel this, I think this. So ego believes the body mind form is the doer. Confusion arises between eastern and western psychology when we use such terms as "give up the ego," or "strengthen the ego." In India especially, when one says the ego should be given up what is usually being referred to is *egoism*, the identification of our Self with the body ego mind form or "I doing." In western psychology the term strengthening the ego has a very different connotation.

Ego strength usually refers to being able to function with a minimal amount of distortion from the defense mechanisms we've unknowingly adopted to keep our emotions and difficult situations away from consciousness. When a person can live in a way that's not too defensive, distorted, rigid, hysterical or authoritarian he's said to have ego strength. Interestingly enough, the positive connotation of ego strength can more readily occur only when we give up egoism. For identification with the results of "I doing" leads to anxiety, less focused concentration and poor results. The initial high of self-importance can never be sustained. And most attempts to maintain this false state induce a fall.

Krishna then teaches that it is possible to repair the past; it is possible to prepare a peaceful future; it is possible to live a blissful present. And purification through action, the method of *karma yoga*, which helps us dis-identify from the body mind form is the most important starting point. Through performing action as a *yoga*, the ego loosens its grip on the person, that our true essence can shine through.

This is why at the beginning of the chapter, Krishna responds to Arjuna's question by saying action is greater than inaction. *All other yogas need the foundation of action in order to be effective.* It is essential for each of us to participate in life in the world, to make use of the world as a means of transforming our negative tendencies. For without this transformation, the mind would be too agitated to embody the quality of concentration required for ongoing devotion, contemplation or meditation. By withdrawing from the battlefield before a substantial portion of our conditioning has been eliminated, we would be wasting a precious opportunity to purge the mind of its negative emotions.

> If you are not a man of action, what do you know of a task to be fulfilled? In the seed of thought, action, prayer and meditation coexist in the sensation of being... Do you not know that Creation itself issued from an action? To live is also an action. To live could be the action of recognizing the Man in the temple of the heart and serving Him perfectly. (*Lizelle Reymond*)

Preparing for Meditation

Karma yoga and worship as action are an organic preparation for contemplation, as they serve to purify the emotions and steady the wavering mind. Within the eastern traditions, it would be considered foolhardy for a person to attempt meditation before practicing selfless service(*seva*) and worship. Emotional expression is to be deepened and expanded through active idealism. Our ideals need to be *practiced*; our restlessness and agitation need to dissolve. Quasi-spiritual disciplines that promote mass meditation before a sufficient degree of personal emotional purification has occurred are commercially oriented and superficial. Meditation and money do not mix.

Psychotherapy or active work with the emotions can also serve as a prerequisite to prepare the mind for meditation.[5] For a mind excessively agitated by emotional turmoil is not yet ready for stillness. Therapy can help a person work through *karma*. The mental and emotional defilements, which get deposited in the *cakras* can gradually dissolve through releasing and transforming the energy of "negative emotions" such as rage, fear, envy, hatred or pride. But this is only a beginning. The seeds of past *karmas* can resprout at any time. Meditation is needed to burn out these seeds unto infinity.

Action as Unification

All the techniques offered in the *Gita* are meant to purify our inner equipment as well as connect us to understanding. Understanding can be viewed as a harmonious combination of knowledge, experience and feeling. Without the prerequisite of understanding, evolution is not possible. A technique or method which is devoid of reason or intellectual comprehension can be a helpful preliminary but in order to engage in actual practice, reflection and insightful feeling is also necessary. For techniques of perfection are different from taking pills or from instant results. Here the total person is being called upon to deepen his experience so that he can become motivated, ready and prepared to practice with his entire being. *As more of our self enters into our practice and more of our practice links us to our self, the process of becoming brings us closer to being.*

Thus, we are being called upon to understand the nature and importance of action for ourselves personally as well as for the society, the earth and the universe. In terms of time, space and personality, the ramifications of cause and effect are much broader, far deeper than our minds can imagine. Meteorologists tell us that what happens in the Pacific causes the Mississippi River to overflow. The Chinese cutting down forests in Tibet causes flooding in India. Underground nuclear testing influences the movement of the earth's plates throughout the globe. The same principle of interrelationship applies to our thoughts. For whatever we do or think has a ripple effect on everyone and everything. We are all interconnected through our thoughts, words and deeds. As part of the total composition of the five elements in the world, our thoughts effect what happens in the world. And our thoughts are very powerful.

Krishna teaches that underlying all selfless action is sacrifice(15). Every day, every night, through all the three states of consciousness—the waking state, the dream state, and the deep sleep state—we are always sacrificing or being sacrificed. With each breath, the allotted portion of our life is being depleted. We sacrifice our time, our energy and our youth toward a wide variety of purposes and pastimes either beneficial or harmful. Knowingly or unknowingly we are ever participating in the three forms of sacrifice—creation, preservation and destruction. Since sacrifice is the underlying principle in the world of change, there is a way of allowing our inevitable sacrifice to be with conscious intention rather than automatic inevitability. Automatic inevitability is the preprogrammed way of the animal. Conscious intention is the freer way of the human being. Intentional awareness, conscious integrated awareness(*prajna*) turns automatic sacrifice into consecrated action. And action with awareness is like 'no action' for it creates no new *vasanas*. Says Krishna:

> The world is in the bonds of action, unless the action is consecration. Let thy actions then be pure, free from the bonds of desire. (3:9) JM
>
> O Arjuna, works other than those performed for the sake of sacrifice bind this world. So perform work for the sake of sacrifice without attachment. SwV
>
> The world is imprisoned in selfish action, Kaunteya. Act selflessly, without any thought of personal profit. EE

We are being called upon to understand our place in the total scheme of things; that we each have a role to play which does not belong to us. Therefore, to work for results or for the purpose of fulfilling our desires leads only to the accumulation of further *vasanas*, more conditioning, more attachment. When we believe I am the doer, this brings us further from freedom. If we can act in the remembrance of who we are; that we are not working solely for the sake of the body ego but for that which supports the body ego, we are working toward freedom. For those who yearn to know Reality, the sole motivationless motivation for all our actions is the Self(18).

The teachers have advised that before we begin anything, we mentally dedicate the action to the higher consciousness or personal God through some form of remembrance. This ongoing sacrifice of the rulership of the ego when practiced consistently can lead to harmony, joy, and the fulfillment of our deeper desires. What is the deeper desire? We must each ask this question for ourselves. Call it universal love, a love which does not bind us to the material world;

call it the desire for freedom, a freedom which encompasses experiencing oneself as part of the whole; call it bliss, a joy which does not change with every passing cloud. Call it the deep inner yearning to be our own Self.

There is a seeming paradox involved in the idea of freedom of choice. When I can link my action to the Higher through some form of dedication or remembrance, I am aware that my action is not *my* action. It does not belong to me. There is a choice. The choice consists of acting in connection with the Totality or separated from it. Sri Sathya Sai Baba says:

> All the accomplishments and acquisitions in this world are transient and impermanent. Lured by them, men get inflated and ultimately court ruin. Hence, giving up the notions of one's own doership, man must regard God alone as the doer. He is the giver, He is the recipient and He is also the object that is given.

To the degree the higher acts through us, we become united with our true nature, which has been called "God." In review, the four levels of *dharma* mentioned in the first chapter are:

1. action in accordance with family relationships, prescribed codes of conduct and obligatory duty. These are relative.
2. action in accordance with one's inner gifts and intelligence; societal *dharma* or work. These are subjective.
3. action in accordance with virtue that transcends time and place. These are objective.
4. action synonymous with the Self, Divine Will, Truth or the light of higher Intelligence. This *Atma dharma* supports all action.

Each of these levels of *dharma* can be dedicated to the Higher and thereby performed without completely falling under the sway of our egocentric desire for results. "I want" can be tempered by the link of remembrance to "the Spirit in man and in all"(42). In this way, actions shed their tendency toward ambivalence and conflict. Through living our dharma, integration proceeds.

Karma Yoga in Practice

To help these ideas become more immediate let's visualize them. Picture a huge pot. Imagine what kind of stew you would like to make. Gather together the ingredients. Dedicate the act with some form of remembrance. Be sure the pot is clean. Wash the food, cut it, prepare it with love. Work calmly with quiet concentration. Enjoy what you are doing.

Start adding the ingredients. Let them cook. Stir. Put in some fresh spices. Stir. Add your loving awareness to the food. Observe. Watch. See yourself watching. Taste. See what's needed. Stir, cover. Regulate the temperature. Initially high so all the flavors boil and intermingle. Then simmer gently. Be watchful. Do not overcook. Remain ever awake.

The taste of the stew will depend on the ingredients, forethought, cleanliness and care that goes into the cooking, as well as on the vibrations of the cook. Likewise, the quality of our life is dependent on the purity of each of our thoughts, words and actions. Every ingredient we add to the stew of life contributes to the flavor. If our existence is tasteless or lacking in vitality, we probably have not yet discovered our own rightful ingredients. Maybe we are relying too much on our past conditioning and not enough on our inner essence. By learning the difference between what is truly nurturing and what leads to bondage, we begin to seek companions and environments that will uplift our heart, rather than simply entertain. The company we keep and the environments we frequent are essential influences on the state of our mind. As we strive to live out our higher ideals, the ingredients become more pure, more palatable. As we become motivated to develop the positive attributes of patience, forgiveness and contentment, the sweetness of the soul can be imbibed in the stew. The flavor of our emotions and thoughts determines the savor of our life.

The stew is not made by "God." It is supported by God, the Lord of our individual universe, which is created by us. And our individual *karma* is not some irrevocable destiny, but rather is changeably molded by the quality of our mind. *As we learn to alter the preoccupations of the mind, we can change our destiny.*

Now let's think for a moment about the kinds of influences we're subjected to every day. We are influenced by our habits, the effect of the media, movies, newspapers, violence, mechanicalness, computer speediness, habitual ways of relating to family and friends, what we talk about, what we work for, our goals, and so forth.

How can we begin to participate in shaping our destiny with humility, without trying to control, without focusing on results but on the process? How can we try to live our higher ideals? How can we participate in transforming our negative *karma* into positive *karma* and positive *karma* into no more *karma*? How can this partnership with the higher be formed? Remember, ordinary automatic action curtails our freedom by binding us to the result, whereas conscious action, linking the mind to the highest Self leads to liberation.

Spiritual Work(*Sadhana*)

For readers who are not familiar with spiritual practice, following are six steps, six forms of practice, *karma* or sacrifice, which offer the opportunity for linking the individuality with the Self and turning ordinary action into a *yoga*, into *Karma yoga*. These are: 1) remembrance or dedication; 2) conservation of energy or self-discipline(*tapas*); 3) selfless service(*seva*), giving and receiving; 4) nonviolence or nonhurtfulness of oneself and others(*ahimsa*); 5) inner reflection, *mantra* or prayer; 6) meditation(see chapter 6).

REMEMBRANCE is the inner awareness acknowledgment of one's true identity... I am He, I am He(*soham, soham*), I am. It is the feeling, intuitive awareness of being more than the ego, more than the emotions, more than the intellect; a more expansive experience of I. To live in closer communion with this real I is remembrance. Remembrance deepens with spiritual practice. It comes and goes throughout the range of our actions until it becomes permanent.

The temple of Apollo at Delphi in ancient Greece bore the inscription, "Know thyself." St. Augustine wrote, "Oh God always one and the same, if I know myself I shall know Thee." When Moses was on Mount Sinai, God revealed himself as, "I am that I am."

The great Indian saint Ramana Maharshi emphasized self-inquiry(*vichara*) as a precursor to remembrance. To ask ourselves, "Who am I? Who am I really"? And stay with the question intuitively as well as analytically. If someone asks who you are what would you say? You are not your profession; you are not your role in the family or in the world of work. Who then are you? Every response seems to echo, "not that, not that." Then who am **I**? As we continue questioning, we come to see that everything we call ourselves is only a part, only a role. All parts that can be thought of or verbalized are **not** I. Then who am I?

Remembrance begins as a kind of mind training; a way of helping the mind loosen its attachment to our sense of identity with the ego. Techniques of remembrance vary. But most modern day teachers in India recommend repeating a *mantra* or a name of God to help tune the mind to its larger reality. Some sages have said that the technique used is not as important as the motivation and earnestness behind the practice:

> Whatever you do for the sake of truth will take you to truth. Only be earnest and honest. The shape it takes hardly matters. (Maharaj)

TAPAS is translated as austerity or inner heat. It is actually a means of developing will, self-control and conserving energy. We tend to waste a lot of energy through unnecessary talking, unnecessary movements, unnecessary eating and needless worry. By noticing and confronting just one superfluous habit, we can begin to gain control over the body and mind so that the energy which now expresses itself at the gross level as egocentric agitation can be transformed into a softer, finer quality, radiating the energy of being.

Tapas can be practiced on the level of the physical body with reference to food, physical comforts, habits, talking, or sex. We can gradually and incrementally place a limit on our self-pampering. It can be practiced on the emotional level with reference to likes and dislikes, our dependencies on others, on things, our capacity to curb our temper and the automatic expression of our emotional negativity. We can say no to the expression of our negative emotions and just watch the behavior and feelings without being compelled to act them out externally. It can be practiced on the intellectual level with reference to reducing our desires and our over reliance on the rational intellect as a false means of security and control. In this way, we can consciously strive to diminish the tight grip of our *vasanas* on the inner essence of our individuality.

> *Tapas* means all self-denial and practices of self-control which the ego undertakes in order to integrate and revive its own capacities to seek its real identity with the eternal. (Swami Chinmayananda)

The sages, saints and heroes of India acquired great power from performing *tapas*. Even the egocentric *asura*s(the present day materialists with misguided values) or the demonic ones called *rakshasas*(the utterly evil ones) acquired powerful boons from the gods(the forces of nature) by performing austerities. *Tapas* can be done either for material or spiritual advancement. Most of us who work hard toward any specific goal are unconsciously performing *tapas* for material gain or outer recognition. We remain unaware however that this form of striving can be easily lost, as it is subject to the perishable world of change. *Only striving performed for evolutionary upliftment, spiritual improvement or the well being of others can have a more lasting effect.* This is because a link is being created with a higher energy, a higher consciousness that is more permanent, more pervasive and finer than matter.

All visible matter is created to perish. Thus, if we consciously link our energy to that which is subtler than gross matter, the dynamism from our effort will multiply, fueled by a force greater than our own ego.

SELFLESS SERVICE(*seva*) means performing actions not for oneself but for the higher in oneself and in others; acting not only for the sake of the body ego and its selfish desires but for the sake of *Atma* through duty, *dharma*, personal transformation and the greater good. This is action without desire for results and acceptance of whatever comes. To act without a sense of personal desire, without the possessive attachment of *I* and *my* leads to evenness and equanimity in success or failure, gain and loss, joy and sorrow. Yet, at the same time, selfless service is neither for the other nor for doing good deeds but for the sake of the Self. This quality of giving and being annihilates anxiety, opens the heart, and brings lasting contentment. The foundation of selfless service is love(*prema*).

The sun shines constantly without asking for a reward. The sun shines equally on all without reference to good or evil, like or dislike. The sun has been cited as the perfect example of selfless service. In the same way, the great souls(*mahatmas*) shower their love equally on all.

From the vantage point of a realized soul on true selfless service, the poet Kabir says, "Neither I repeat the rosary nor I serve God, nor I pronounce the names of God. The Supreme is serving me. I realize it and get full rest."

Until we realize this inner space of merging with divine consciousness, it behooves us to act on in the world with a spirit of dedication, thereby training the mind and ego to become aware that it is participating in serving the higher universal Being through dedicated action. In this way, the ego can become linked to the Self.

> Offer to me all thy works. Rest thy mind on the Supreme. Be free from vain hopes and selfish thoughts. With inner peace engage in battle. (3:30)

The battle consists of depotentiating and melting the binding effects of our past thoughts and actions.

AHIMSA has been translated as non-injury, non-violence, not harming oneself or others. To be harmless is indeed a very high state, for as long as we remain ignorant of Reality, of Truth, our incorrect views can hurt us and induce us to unknowingly harm others. A rigid egocentric stance cannot help but hurt others. Considering what we've already said about the power of our thoughts and actions, we realize how difficult the principle of nonviolence is to practice. As long as we act out negative thoughts, words and actions that do not take the totality into account, we will be harming ourselves by incurring further negative *vasanas*, and we will be hurting others as well. But as we begin to observe ourselves and suffer our predicament, we become motivated to change. Our tears purify. *To suffer our negative karma with conscious remembrance offers the opportunity to let go of further suffering.* When viewed in this way, our suffering is a gift. Once we begin in small ways to try to practice *ahimsa*, for example, to refrain from expressing a negative emotion, the effects can be extremely powerful and immediate. Through non-violence, Mahatma Gandhi toppled the British Empire in India. But he knew that in order to be used as an instrument for any external change, be it political or personal, he must first try to practice what he preaches.

There is a story told about a mother who came from far away to bring her son to speak to the great saint, Ramakrishna. When the mother asked him to speak to the boy, he told her to return in a week. When the week was up, Ramakrishna told him very firmly not to eat sweets, that sweets were not good for him. The mother asked why she had to remain there for a week, why couldn't he have said this a week ago? He replied, "I myself had to give up sweets before I could tell anyone else to do that or else it wouldn't work."

Likewise, in order to be able to effectively teach children or others positive values such as nonaggression, peacefulness and contentment, one must at least be making the effort to purge oneself of greed, hatred, competitiveness, violence and egoism.

> Nothing profits the world as much as abandoning profits. A man who no longer thinks in terms of loss and gain is the truly non-violent man for he is beyond all conflict. It is not doing good that comes first but ceasing to hurt, not adding to suffering. (Maharaj)

By practicing the first three principles, remembrance, conservation of energy and selfless service, purification will result. And *ahimsa* will begin to permeate our way of thinking and being.

PRAYER is the conscious wish to make a connection with the higher, a way of participation in invoking That energy to descend on oneself and the world in the form of grace. Many of us do not know how to pray or invoke the mind toward the higher. Some of us pray only by rote or when we feel needy and in trouble. Others are afraid to ask for help. Unifying the mind with a deeply felt wish can have a lasting effect on our future actions and destiny. For the agnostic who has little faith in the presence of God, wishing deeply for something of value can nourish one's soul.

Mantra is a device used to help the mind cross over to the higher. It usually takes the form of an inner repetition of a name of God, a seed syllable(*bijaksharam*) or a scriptural passage that has deep, hidden meaning which gradually reveals itself. The Sanskrit language is constructed based on the ancient mathematical knowledge of sound and its effects. *Certain sounds and gestures actually have the capacity to change the psyche of the person.* By repeating the *mantra,* one learns to tame the mind through exposing it to positive influence. The mind has been compared to a wild horse. The *mantra* has been likened to the food given to tame the horse. Through connecting with the *mantra*, the mind gradually becomes peaceful and filled with love.

All forms of prayer, reflection, contemplation and *mantra* can lead to purifying and integrating the small personality into the all-inclusive Self. This is a place where practice, process and goal converge, where work becomes stillness, where diversity is seen as unity, and where passion becomes *com*passion.

At the same time, practice does not *cause* the goal. Maharaj says, "There can be no causal connection between practice and wisdom. But the obstacles to wisdom are deeply affected by practice."

The sages say it can take many lifetimes of steady practice to be liberated. But no positive motivation is ever lost. Meanwhile, practice includes an acknowledgment and watchfulness of our animal tendencies.

> Even a wise man acts under the impulse of his nature; all beings follow nature. Of what use is restraint? Hate and lust for things of nature have their roots in man's lower nature. Let him not fall under their power. They are two enemies on his path. (3:33-4)

Detaching From Desire

When desire is directed solely toward our "lower nature," toward the material world of instincts, objects, emotions and thoughts, then we are stuck(37-40).

> The senses are called the important obstacles to knowledge because when the senses keep operating on their objects, the knowledge of the Self cannot arise. Even if the mind and intellect are quieted from their activity, still when desire, identified with will originating from *rajas* is operating, it by itself obstructs the

> knowledge of Self by inducing the senses to operate in their fields. Thus, understanding desire to be the foe antagonistic to *jnana yoga*(self-knowledge) and establishing the mind by means of the intellect in *karma yoga*, destroy this foe in the shape of desire, which is difficult to overcome. (Ramanuja, *Sri Ramanuja Gita Bhasya*, Swami Adidevananda, translator, p.154)

We begin by learning to control the senses, by training the senses not to roam out after every sense object—to see without seeing, to taste without tasting. When we are not a slave to the senses, it becomes easier to disidentify from the mind. But we cannot stop our desires for they are an expression of the life within us. It is not right to try to suppress our desires for this is an affront against nature. Whether the desire is for food, sex, possessions, recognition or knowledge, this is all a lawful expression, based on the age-old subtle impressions of the *vasanas*. But the same desires when seen as the creation of the One enliviner, can become linked with the higher. In this way, desire is not suppressed but rather is acknowledged and gradually transformed. Through this process, the desires of the lower nature become linked to the higher nature. And soon, the quality of our desires also becomes transformed.

> The waters of life are thundering over the rocks of objects—desirable or hateful. Remove the rocks by insight and detachment and the same waters will flow deep and silent and swift, in greater volume and with greater power. (Maharaj)

Insight can result from working with the emotions, thoughts and instincts through awareness, dreamwork or creative work. Detachment, on the other hand entails connecting the attention to the higher and letting go of everything else. This can bring direct intuitions from the higher Intelligence(*buddhi*). The first process entails descent into matter; the second works by attempting to detach from matter. The first includes the world; the second renders the specific contents of the world irrelevant. At different times, both processes are required for purging the *vasanas*.

Through the process of working on in the world fully engaged in discovering and deepening our *dharma*, Krishna helps us see how to transform our mundane actions and our daily lives into a *yoga*.

> Can you escape from *karma* oh man? Whatever your scholarship, whatever your daily worship, whatever penance you may perform, can you avoid the results of *karma*? Whether you fill your vessel in a small pond or the vast ocean, it will be filled only up to its capacity. (Sri Sathya Sai Baba, *Digest 2*, p.175)

Karma yoga teaches us how to reach an inner space where we will one day be free of cause and effect. The present moment is existence in *now*, free from the baggage of the past and anxiety for the future. Through training the mind, the heart and the hand in the way of *karma yoga*, we can prepare ourselves to discover the eternal presence. Thus, the third discourse reveals how action can become *yoga*.

Four

YOGA OF RENOUNCING ACTION IN KNOWLEDGE

Jnana Karma Sannyasa Yoga

	Gita verses
The imperishable *yoga* and the descent of the *avatar*	1–9
The power of *karma* and desireless action	10–18
The pure conduct of the Self realized soul*(jnani)*	19–23
Different kinds of sacrifice*(yajna)*	24–32
Effectiveness of the knowledge sacrifice*(jnana yajna)*	33–42

the sacrifice of creation
brings worlds into being
we too can participate

everything we do or say
each austerity we practice
purification, contemplation, meditation

even our desire
our food, our very breath
a connection with the divine

become fit to be a cell
in the body of the Totality!

In the third discourse, we observed how our desires translate into thoughts and thoughts into actions; that our values and actions are the ultimate determinants of our lives. We learned the difference between activity and right action; work in accordance with *dharma*, our deep inner prompting and outer duty. Work performed without the craving for results leaves no imprint, no baggage to bind and compel us toward identification with activity and further bondage. As long as we are identified with matter, the interplay of the *gunas*, we live under the law of cause and effect, endlessly spinning repetitive webs. These in turn create further events that must be lived through until our true Self is separated out from the matter envelopments of actions, emotions, thoughts and images that keep us imprisoned. As we become more focused on the nobler values and ideals, we begin to discriminate the Real from the unreal. The mind and intellect begin to serve the Real. And our desire for the unreal loosens its grip.

The eternal, transcendent, aspectless unity that was presented in the second chapter must somehow be experienced as existing in the world. *There must be a link between being and becoming, a bridge between that which is seemingly above and that which is seemingly below.* This bridge is the dynamic process of *karma yoga*, when practiced with the support of knowledge and devotion.

It is action, conscious action, action as service, as worship, as self-discipline, as sacrifice, as contemplation, which purifies the heart. These different forms of consecrated action lead to the melting of *maya*. This dissolution severs identification with the crust of mind and ego. With the dissolution of the ego, which is but a conditioned superimposition on the essence of the person, our true unmanifest individuality can be lived.

Our natural essenceless essence can be called the *Atman*. It shines through the individuality(*jiva*) to the degree the conditioned ego has let go of its identification with the body. This happens gradually. Thus, the fourth chapter can be viewed as presenting the ancient *yoga* that provides a link between action and Self Knowledge. *Clarifying the content and techniques of consecrated action serves as the bridge that takes us from action to wisdom.* It reveals that action need not be separate from wisdom if both are experienced through the conscious, dynamic process of living in the world. And the true basis for all *karma yoga* is love(*prema*).

That *Atma* which has been described as silence and stillness can enter the world as a creative dynamism(18). Through encompassing both stillness and movement, we see that the Self, which has neither attribute nor activity is not only present through action, but consecrated action itself serves as the link to the Self, which embodies no action.

In the fourth chapter we learn there is no split between action and knowledge. Through dedicated work, the stillness *Atma* filters through as a dynamic force that makes itself felt in the life of a person in the world. It is through ongoing contact with this dynamic stillness that we evolve. We participate in the divine descent as well as the divine ascent. With each experience of this contact, in whatever form, the ego slowly relinquishes its place to the essence. We are thus being offered intellectual understanding as well as the practical means for forging this link in our daily lives.

The sages say the way of knowledge(*jnana yoga*) is more difficult to follow because it requires certain inner and outer conditions. If subject to interruption or turbulence, much time can be wasted. But *karma yoga* can be practiced under any condition; wherever we find ourselves. And it also includes the knowledge that leads to Self Knowledge. The *karma yogi* is ever in touch with a link to the Self.

Ultimately, the *yoga* of action(*karma yoga*), the *yoga* of knowledge(*jnana yoga*) and the *yoga* of devotion(*bhakti yoga*) all lead to wisdom. Wisdom in Vedanta is more than an understanding of life and human nature that an older person can acquire from a life well lived. Wisdom is omniscience, omnipotence, omnipresence, knowing Reality, Truth, Oneself, the universe, the cosmos—an ongoing awareness beyond the mind, beyond experience in time and space, total knowledge, total love, total presence that exists within each of us as the eternal foundation of the world, beyond the duality of knower and known. We are thereby being shown how to live a life of action based on an awareness of the foundation of knowledge; how knowledge and action meet to initiate balance, induce integration and lead the seeker toward a firmer footing on the way to wisdom. Needless to say, the process is gradual!

Descent of the Avatar

In order to reach this wisdom which is ever within us, there must be contact with the teacher, the teaching and an alignment of mind between the teacher and the taught. Krishna begins through establishing the authenticity of the teaching by tracing it back to its original source, the causeless first cause. The teaching is both ancient and eternal, as the teacher is both ancient and eternal. Arjuna is definitely not being offered this knowledge merely to help him win the war.

Here for the first time, Krishna announces to his friend and brother-in-law that he is God. He is the *avatar* who descends to earth in human form from age to age to uplift humanity when mankind has forgotten the teaching. Be he called Krishna, Buddha, Jesus or Mohammed, the person whose mind is totally saturated with God consciousness can take on any name and form to present the eternal ancient teachings in a way that can be understood by the people of that era. All the fully realized souls in the history of humanity are in fact God. As Jesus said, "I and my Father are one." The Father is also one with all *avatars*. According to *Vendantic* experience, there is no discrepancy between one incarnation of God and another—all are permeated with God consciousness.

In the Hindu tradition, many *gurus* are considered *avatars* by their devotees. Yet very few are universally acknowledged as full *avatars,* who have perfected themselves in total identification with God.[6] Likewise in the Buddhist tradition, there are sixteen different levels of *boddhisattvas*; beings who descend to earth and take on human form out of compassion for suffering humanity. Krishna is traditionally considered one of the ten full *avatars*.

> When righteousness is weak and faints and unrighteousness exults in pride, then my Spirit arises on earth. For the salvation of those who are good, for the destruction of evil in men, for the fulfillment of the kingdom of righteousness, I come to this world from age to age. He who knows my birth as God and who knows my sacrifice, when he leaves his mortal body goes no more from death to death for he in truth comes to me. (4:7-9)

Krishna teaches that each of us carries within, the potential of living as full *avatar*, that our Real nature is Truth. The *avatar* is one who lives this Truth. But due to the veiling power of *maya*, this inner essence ever present in each of us remains unconnected to our consciousness. What always is, pure Truth becomes covered by the ignorance of our true nature, covered by desire, sullied by agitation, enveloped by the cloud of time as *vasanas* accumulate.

Reincarnation

Each lifetime offers a perfect set of circumstances for us to live through and purify our desires as a *karma yogi*, that we might cut through surface falsity and connect to the root of Knowledge. Then the sages say, the inner tendencies which created the particular birth will one day be exhausted.

It is nature's gift to us that we do not remember our past lives. Imagine all the unfinished business and attachment we have accumulated over the milleniums. In our present state of mind, the burden would be too heavy to carry.

But on the path of spiritual work, people do come to remember their past lives spontaneously. In the Buddhist tradition, children are chosen at a very young age by time tested methods as the reincarnations of various high lamas. And among lay people with no spiritual training, it has been found that children who have died a violent death often remember their past lives and former death(Stevenson, M.D.). It is not important however, whether we believe we have lived before or not. What is important is that we live this particular incarnation in as meaningful a way as possible.

Knowing Reality

This would mean ultimately to experience the rebirth of one's limited consciousness into the expansive awareness of cosmic consciousness.

> He who knows my birth as God and who knows my sacrifice, when he leaves his mortal body goes no more from death to death for he in truth comes to me. (4:9)

Once we have entered the higher state of consciousness, the sages say there is no longer the danger of returning to the delusion that I am the body, mind and ego, limited by time and space. *We can each participate in the sacrifice of this delusion.*

According to the *Gita*, to know God does not mean to know that Krishna is God or that Christ is God because this is just a mental idea that substitutes an embodied person for a universal experience. Taken literally, this dualistic level of understanding can lead to the conflict of "my God is true and your God is false." Rather, it is the totality of experience, the totality of awareness as symbolized by Krishna consciousness, Christ consciousness, Buddha consciousness, which is considered "God." When we know the birth of this level of consciousness within ourselves, the confusion of believing the small body ego I to be the real I, will vanish and the mind will merge with eternal Reality. This is Krishna's promise to us.

What exactly is required for an ordinary person like you and me to work on the path that will lead us to universal wisdom? In one *sloka* Krishna reveals a practical method toward liberation.

> Freed from attachment, fear and anger, absorbed in Me, taking refuge in Me, purified by the fire of knowledge, many have attained My Being. (4:10)

The first component in the process refers to allowing the emotions to become balanced. It is through *karma yoga* that we become progressively free from attachment, fear and anger. This is accomplished through living in the world with the inner attitude of the witness, observing oneself and one's reactions, giving one's best effort with ease without trying to control, allowing events to unfold without being identified. Through observing our attachments we become detached, through watching ourselves experiencing our fears we become fearless, through seeing the anger play out in us, we separate ourselves from it. We observe it all playing itself out like a CD, which stops when the piece is completed. Through this process, the energy of the witness reclaims or takes back unto itself the energy that had been dissipated into objects, other people and events. Thereby, our true identity comes to participate in living and our expenditure of energy is economized.

A carousel that keeps turning round the same circle again and again does so through the power of electricity. When the switch is turned off it stops. Attachment is like a switch. When it is turned off through watchfulness, all the other so-called negative emotions lose their power. Attachment is the switch that keeps the carousel of anger and fear, lust and greed ever turning through the perpetual mechanism of *maya*. As long as we believe the material world to be real, we remain on the carousel. As we begin to practice *karma yoga*, a link is established with the process that can liberate us from the ignorance of our true nature.

Freedom from attachment, fear and anger doesn't mean becoming a statue or a schizoid person and not experiencing these emotions. No. It refers to a process whereby life is engaged in and experienced through the spectacles of watchfulness. This inclusive process *by itself* initiates purification and brings about eventual balance.

One means of steadying this newly found balance in the direction of equalmindedness is through devotion(17). By consciously taking refuge in a reality higher than one's own body ego mind, by surrendering oneself to this as yet unknown and unknowable Reality, the inner emotional and intellectual conviction gathers unto itself more and more energy, more and more power. While witnessing life from the foundation of this inner space, a kind of heat is generated.

Ongoing cooking occurs—that one day, all impressions will melt into pure love.

With this devotion to an ideal around which everything centers, life no longer revolves around pettiness. Rather, the mundane is experienced with a level of attentive awareness that infuses and uplifts all preoccupation with matter. This is akin to redeeming the sparks from matter in the Kabalistic tradition. It could be called uncovering the divine hidden within the world. Daily living takes on a joyousness and meaningfulness in itself. Insights and connections appear. We begin to feel part of something greater than ourselves—like a giant wave that does not stop until it reaches the shore. *The transcendent is becoming immanent.*

Through the ongoing practice of concentrating the mind on the higher, the mind merges into the higher like milk pouring into milk, like water seeping into water. And the degree of absorption increases till one day, the fire of wisdom dawns. The conceptual mind relinquishes her powers of perception and thinking to the total integrated awareness*(prajna)*. Through this ongoing journey toward reality, one day the mind becomes blown out like the flame of a candle. Henceforth, the necessary functions of mind can be rekindled as needed but are no longer mistaken for the main source of light. "Freed from attachment, fear and anger, absorbed in Me, taking refuge in Me, purified by the fire of knowledge, many have attained my Being."

Thus Krishna tells us, the final step in the purification process is experiential knowledge beyond experience; a merging of the individual mind, body ego into the totality, beyond time and place. All paths lead to this wisdom.

Even if a person remains unaware of a higher reality, shows no devotion to nobler ideals, the energy of Reality still serves as the foundation for his desires and actions—with or without his awareness (11,12). If a person worships money, sacrifices his time and energy to gain money he will receive money. From whom? The giver is the unknown power called God, whether it be acknowledged or unacknowledged. Those who work for personal power or acclaim will receive power or acclaim. Whatever we desire and work for in accordance with the intensity of effort put forth, surely will be granted by the gods. But let it be known that sacrifice for material wealth or personal recognition has little to do with ongoing joy, as these are all part of the perishable world of change.

We can put forth our energy in the direction of the perishable or we can expend our energy in the direction of the imperishable. This will be determined by our *vasanas*. But whatever our level of inner development and outer aspiration, the energy of the universe responds to our own expenditure of energy through answering our wish and our effort. *For it is universal law that our energy is not separate from the energy of the universe.* Mutual influences ever abound and intermingle on every level. We human beings are related to the world and events through our thoughts and actions, which are all supported by the higher consciousness.

The Four Types

The fields of endeavor where we choose to put forth our energy will be determined ideally by our natural gifts and inner propensities; by *guna* and *karma*. Originally, the law of Manu divided the occupations of people based on four psychological types, which later came to be called the caste system(13). These types are related to the distribution of *gunas* or qualities within the mind of the person. *Sattva* is peaceful harmony, *rajas* is active passion, *tamas* is inert dissolution.

The four basic classes of activity that evolved from *guna* and inner propensity are: 1) *brahmins*, the scholar-priests who exude primarily *sattvic* tendencies. 2) *kshatriyas*, the warrior-rulers who exhibit a combination of *sattva* and *rajas*. Ideally, their activity is based on nobler ideals. 3) *vaishyas*, the merchants, bankers and lawyers whose tendencies are *rajas* and *tamas*. Their activity is based on bringing weath to the society. 4) *sudras* or hired laborers, whose tendencies are primarily *tamasic* and are based on service.

Originally, all four types had an equally important role to play in the smooth functioning of the society. All were considered parts of one body, the body of God. The thinkers were the head, the warrior statesmen the arms, the businessmen the thighs and the laborers the feet. Human society was considered an expression of the cosmic *Purusha* in life. According to Yogananda, the four orders were revealed as divine knowledge in man(*brahmins*), divine power and rulership(*kshatriyas*), divine production, mutuality and enjoyment (*vaishyas*), and divine service, obedience and work(*sudras*). Initially, caste was a holy idea based on the unity and equality of the whole in conjunction with the dharma of the individual. It was not based on birth but on one's inner being. But as kingdoms became corrupt and the priests and rulers vied for power, the primary intent of the code degenerated into a repressive social structure, similar to other systems throughout the world, which are based on power and economics. Krishna is revealing this fourfold order in the *Gita* based on the original intent of accomplishing a smoothly functioning community where each person works in accordance with his capacities and everyone is respected.

Yogananda says that *brahmins* are God knowers, *kshatriyas* are sense fighters, *vaishyas* serve humanity through mental labor and *sudras* are body-identified persons. "Metaphysically, a *sudra* mentality signifies one who doubts everything except material existence"(p.1055). Our mentality supercedes birth, education and vocation. It is our psyche that determines our caste.

The Secret of Work

Through observing the actions of the *avatar* or holy person working in the world, we come to know the art of *karma yoga*(14-23). The man of wisdom performs no actions for himself alone, no action based on ego needs or personal wishes. He works for the Self in all, for the welfare of the world. *This renders him absolutely free*(14). If we too could work in this spirit of desirelessness, through work we would evolve into our inherent birthright of liberation. Living this way, our every thought and action becomes food for the soul.

> The man who in his work finds silence and who sees that silence is work, this man in truth sees the light and in all his works finds peace. (4:18) JM
>
> He who recognizes inaction in action and action in inaction is wise among men. He is a *yogi* and a true performer of all actions. SwC

For the true *karma yogi*, whether riding on a busy subway racing through Forty-second Street or relaxing on a tropical beach in the Bahamas, the awareness in silence will predominate, no matter what the activity. For silence is the foundation of life, the eternal backdrop against which all the noise and freneticism gathers its incessant energy till it dissipates. It is silence that allows the carousel to keep turning and stop turning. Once we get an inner glimpse of this utter stillness, from being in the presence of a realized soul or through meditation, with practice we can begin to experience it anywhere, under all circumstances. Silence is peacefulness, peacefulness is silence.

As desires are reduced, the mind slows down. Restless activity dissolves. This state of quietude is an initial milestone on the path of any spiritual seeker. It is indicative of the presence of *sattva* within, a steady state of mind beyond the opposites of active and passive, high and low, anxiety and happiness. Imagination and projection no longer hold sway over the psyche. Expectations from others and the world are greatly reduced. Things are seen much closer to as they really are. Nothing external is required for happiness.

> In whatever work he does, such a man in truth has peace: he expects nothing, he relies on nothing and ever has fullness of joy. (4:20)

This person has left behind the animal state and has reached the level of evolution for a true human being. Actions cannot bind him. He lives in freedom and spontaneity.

> Anxiety for the fruits of action, the sense of discontentment and the feeling of dependency upon the things and beings of the world—all belong to the misconceived notion of the ego. The ego in us is the sufferer of all incapacities and inabilities. When the seeker after Truth rediscovers his ego to be the Infinite Truth, the ego ends its career of sorrow and naturally the agony and incapacities of the imperfect ego also end. (Swami Chinmayananda THG p.247)

If we reflect on the causes of our unhappiness and psychological suffering, we will find that it is our expectations of ourselves and life, our preconceived ideas that are the root cause of all unhappiness and disappointment(22). To be glad wherever we find ourselves is to be beyond the sway of the opposites, so that like and dislike become irrelevant. When we can discard disappointment from the past and anxiety regarding the future we are free. Without desire and expectation there is independence. When the myths introjected into the mind can be let go of there is space for freedom. When new myths stop forming we can discover the present. For it is only the concepts regarding what is and what should be that create sorrow. Give up the concepts—sorrow departs.

Sacrifice, Individual and Cosmic

As we begin to speak about surrender we are on shaky ground. For the mind can easily misinterpret, impose its concept of surrender on the projected universe. A concept of surrender also causes new *vasanas*, which in turn lead to further suffering. Our view of "surrender" is molded by our *gunas*.

For example, some beginning spiritual seekers often mistake surrender for not making efforts, while expecting the *guru* to do everything for us. This is not surrender but laziness, an embracing of *tamas*; not using our gifts and talents. Others are convinced their actions are for the welfare of society—no matter how egotistical they may be. Where then is that central point between action and inaction, between living within and giving out, between vibrancy and dullness, between excellence and indolence? The secret seems to rest in being engaged without imposing, learning to *be* without any preconceptions about oneself, others, action or outcome; accepting what comes with alert awareness and relaxed effort.

Can we come to act without imposing our ideas regarding result onto the process of action? For this, we must first taste hints of the joy of just being. In order to be content with whatever comes, we must first be able to receive a glimpse of that bliss which is not dependent on things, people or on anything outside. This is a joy where we feel part of everything. It is a joy without particulars, a joy that knows the inherent equality of every person and everything—that behind every living being rests the One which is the same in a beggar or a prophet, a servant or a king, a student or a teacher.

Sacrifice then is related to surrender. Nobody can live without sacrificing something at some time or other either consciously or unconsciously. Nature compels it. Dissolution, creation, creation, dissolution; sacrifice dissolves that creation can be born. The unborn chick must peck through the shell in order to live. The caterpillar must leave behind the chrysalis in order to become a butterfly. But surrender implies the conscious intention to sacrifice, the willingness to offer one's small ego self to the totality while giving up all illusion of control. The space of emptiness is the starting point for all creation.

> Life by its nature possesses and binds but death makes us free. If we could guard in ourselves the quietness of death we would have access to creative intelligence. We can "build up" all sorts of things in ordinary life but to create we must be liberated by voluntary death in Siva. Creative vision belongs only to him who seeing beyond the dance of life dares to look within himself into the Void. Then what does he see? The beginning and the end, the seed from which life springs and the flowers under which life's adventure ends. He sees the arc of the Void which broods over both. (Reymond, p.218)

The quality of such surrender invokes a partnership, a relationship with the universe and the energy called giving and receiving. Giving and receiving is the basis of creation.

> Those who have can give and such givers are many. The world itself is a supreme gift maintained by loving sacrifice. But the right receivers, wise and humble are so few. Ask and you shall be given is the eternal law. (Maharaj)

One western example of this cosmic interchange of giving and receiving is the sacrifice of Christ on the cross. The sacrifice of His body creates the conditions in human beings for the gift of purification and love in those who can receive it. To take the sins of the world on one's shoulders is within the power of the *avatar*. But in order for the individual to receive a spark of His consciousness, one's yearning and actions must in some way become attuned to the principle of surrender. It does not happen automatically. The connection must be forged.

Individuals make up society, society is part of the nation, nations make up the world, the world is part of nature and nature is reflected through the cosmos. These are all interconnected by the enlivening power that comes into being through sacrifice. *We can each participate in the cosmic sacrifice through severing the illusion of separate self and becoming part of the totality. Sloka* twenty-four, recited before each meal by the traditional practicing Hindu brings the universal ritual of remembrance sacrifice to the mundane act of eating.

> Who in all his work sees God, he in truth goes unto God. God is his worship, God is his offering, offered by God in the fire of God. (4:24) JM
>
> The process of offering is *Brahman*, that which is offered is *Brahman*. *Brahman* offers the sacrifice in the fire of *Brahman*. *Brahman* is attained by the man who sees *Brahman* in every action. EE

This reminder that eating is sacred action helps one experience the enlivening power as One. The power of life manifests itself through the multitude of ten thousand things. There are many names, forms, and actions but all are one wearing a different coat. Without the food of God sacrificing its life, we could not live. The food is *Brahman*, the eater is *Brahman*, the act of eating is *Brahman*. When the consciousness of *Brahman* offers the food to *Brahman*, the balance of the universe is maintained. It is not the person eater consuming the food but the person eater offering the food to its rightful place, unto the higher energy which ever lives in the food, in the eater and in the act of eating. In this way, consumption does not deplete the balance within the totality. Consumption is not *for* me alone but *through* me is part of a process interrelated with all. Through our consciousness, we participate in assisting the freeflowingness of matter-energy by abrogating nothing to ourselves. When we claim anything unto ourselves, we obstruct the free flow of energy everywhere. By claiming it as mine—my food, my eating, new *vasanas* are formed in me. I alienate myself from the totality. Energy whose natural state is freeflowing becomes bound.

Eat and be eaten is the law of life in the world, the law of matter. As our consciousness expands to include the eater, the eaten and the eating, the subject, the object and the process of action all in one, division transforms into unity. It then becomes impossible to harm another being because I am also that being. And actions leave no footprints, as the doer knows he is not the doer but merely an agent through which the process of action occurs. With this quality of awareness, the energy of all action becomes absorbed in *Brahman*.

Though eating I do not eat, though walking I do not walk, though thinking I do not think. In the awareness that He eats through me, that I am both the eater and the eaten, the ego ceases to perpetuate itself as a separate entity. The person can continue to utilize all the instruments of perception and action but now in conjunction with the whole. The food of every impression taken in by the body, emotions and intellect with conscious integrated awareness becomes the opportunity through which the *karma yogi* comes to realize Reality. While working in this way, the person becomes a copartner in the process of creation through helping maintain the balance of universal energies—by accepting responsibility for the consciousness of one's Self.

It is the power of the mind that creates the universe. It is the power of the mind that maintains the universe. It is the power of the mind that dissolves the universe. Our motivation and values will determine how we make use of the mind, how we bring it into action.

> While *karma* in its ordinary form is binding in its form of sacrifice it is liberating. (Swami Chidbhavananda, p.311)

Techniques of Sacrifice

The only genuine sacrifice comes from the heart simply and spontaneously, not based on *should practice* but on *wanting to give.* When we follow this inner prompting, the gratitude of the universe always responds. We might each recall happenings in life when ease and abundance occurred after we gave up something or simply gave up. "That thing which a man devotedly contributes to the welfare of others multiples in him. This is the law."(ibid., p.306)

The forms of sacrifice are many, the acts of sacrifice are one. All self-effort, all effort undertaken in the service of the Self comprises only one sacrifice—a letting go of the ego. In order to gain the technology of knowledge, Krishna delineates twelve different techniques of sacrifice (23-33), which serve as aids in purifying the psyche, unifying the mind around one aim and developing will in the service of the higher. Each is a kind of *tapas* or austerity which, if linked to conscious awareness, offers a means of acting in the world through the body individuality with the prime motivation and prime motivator as the Self.

As in all *tapas*, the emphasis is on purification and developing will as interconnected spiritual power rather than on doing without, or subjecting the body to privation and difficulty in order to gain personal power. With the latter emphasis, will is developed but becomes connected with doing, pride and ego. With the former emphasis, will is also developed but here it becomes connected with the free flow of energy within the universe, called in the Christian tradition, "thy will be done on earth as it is in heaven."

Even on the simple level of conserving physical energy, these techniques can be beneficial. So often, after a hard day's work we feel tired and depleted. Our physical and mental energy is drained. But by performing work as a *yoga*, our fuel of energy becomes more subtle and increases. Something precious accrues; something new is gained.

The first *yajna* consists of an awareness of the "gods" operating through the sense organs and the sense objects. The elemental forces operating in the universe have been personified into perceptual forms called gods and goddesses. For example, the power of desire is called Cupid by the Romans, Kama by the Hindus. The power of mental faculty is called Mercury by the Greeks and Indra by the Hindus. The power of dissolution is called Neptune, the god of the sea by the Romans, and Siva, the god of the burial grounds by the Hindus. Thus, all the powers of life that we encounter living in the world are not claimed as one's own. And they can be mentally offered to the One power higher than each of these diverse forces of vitality(25). For all the gods are aspects of the One.

With this recognition, one is not totally identified with the whirlwind of emotions associated with the vital forces of living. One offers one's music making to Orpheus, knowing well that I am not the creator of this beauty but that music plays though me. One offers one's wealth to Lakshmi knowing I am not the maker of all this money but it has come to me through the grace of Lakshmi. This attitude expressed in *sloka* twenty-five is the antidote against the inflation, which Carl Jung so often spoke about, when powerful energy from the unconscious emerges and we identify with it.

The second part of the *sloka* refers to a deeper level of offering. Here Self awareness is offering the life force to *Brahman* whereas in the first part of the *sloka* it is the mind doing the offering. Swami Chinmayananda says of this *sloka:*

> The perfect masters understand that the sense organs are only instruments of perception and that they can work only when in contact with the supreme, the *Atman*. In this understanding all masters live, allowing the sense organs to sacrifice themselves in the knowledge of *Brahman*. Seekers also are, by this statement, advised as to how they too can gain a certain amount of freedom from their senses by dedicating their sense life in the service of the world. When an individual's sense organs of perception and action are to function not for his own egocentric selfish satisfactions but for the sake of serving the society or the world, then even if such an individual lives in the world of objects, he will not be enslaved by his attachments to his possessions. (THG p.256)

The giving of wealth referred to in *sloka* twenty-eight is not just giving money. It is part of a living charity, a larger giving that everyone can participate in as everyone has something to give if the frame of mind is in this direction. When whatever we do is an expression of sharing love, this is sacrifice(*yajna*) be it in the concrete form of money, knowledge, or expressing artistic, domestic or business talents. When the mental attitude of giving to the Self in oneself and others permeates our actions, this is the sacrifice of wealth.

> To pursue a life of charity, serving the world as best we can with all that we possess physically, mentally and intellectually is the noble sacrifice called wealth sacrifice. Even if we are poor and physically debilitated we can still be charitable because our inner treasures of love, kindness, sympathy and affection do not at all depend upon either our material circumstances or our physical condition. Sometimes a word of sincere sympathy, a look of love, a smile of true affection or a word registering true friendship can give

to the receiver more than a heartless check, even if it be for a very fat sum. (ibid.)

Study of scriptures as sacrifice(28) should strengthen the observation of our motives and lead us toward introspection, detachment and discrimination. Under the gaze of the consciousness within, our weaknesses come out of hiding that under the light they might dissolve. This process helps our inner conscience to emerge. For this inner authority that uncompromisingly knows what is right is the God within each one of us.

The five vital airs or *pranas*(29) have been delineated as five different expressions of life within the human organism. These are: perception, excretion, digestion and assimilation, circulation, and the capacity to reflect. "These activities of life within, about which an ordinary man is quite unconscious are brought under perfect control of the individual through *pranayama* so that a seeker can come to gain a complete capacity to withdraw all his perceptions. This is indeed a great help to a meditator."(ibid.)

Controlling our diet(30) can also be a form of sacrifice. The food we eat affects the mind. If we eat junk food our minds become *tamasic*. If we eat fresh food, this aids the alertness of mind. People with different temperaments and distribution of *gunas* require different diets. Taking in food also means taking in impressions. When we abstain from ingesting negative impressions or let go of painful and pleasurable experiences, the ego becomes gradually purified. With more purity comes less agitation, less clinging. We come closer to a sense of our inner being, closer to independence without separation or alienation.

Each of these forms of conscious sacrifice can serve as a prelude to wisdom. And it is the wisdom sacrifice offered by the saints and sages that is the greatest gift to humanity(33).

These techniques are neither ends in themselves nor a cause of realization. They are a means of preparing the readiness of the mind to engage in contemplation, meditation and *samadhi*, whereby the separate individual mind becomes tranquil enough to let go of its separateness and merge with total Reality. Through these practices, the inner personality becomes more integrated and balanced.

The alignment of the individuality(*jiva*) with the inner Self is not just a personal matter. *It also serves to maintain the balance of energies in the universe.* Without sacrifice, nothing would progress. There would be no change, no evolution; only stagnation. The underlying principle of life that connects us to each other, to the environment and to life is sacrifice. To participate in sacrifice is our attempt to overcome the delusion of egocentricity and separateness that has been programmed into us; to overcome constriction, to overcome death. Sacrifice initiates movement; sacrifice initiates creation. Through this process, a kind of deprogramming occurs. We discover our rightful place in life—spontaneous, natural, organic; an ongoing reciprocity whereby the flowing wave rediscovers itself as the essential material of the ocean.

The principle of creation can be viewed from different perspectives. For example, it can seemingly result from a rebounding of the opposites to discover a new equilibrium. This can be a painful personal process that is not necessarily evolution. Much twentieth century art and literature embodies this form. At a subtler level, creation comes from conscious sacrifice. Here a person is much less under the bondage of suffering induced by the play of opposites. With conscious sacrifice, we are more closely linked to the cosmic nature supporting the individual ego. When we participate in this level of creation we are engaged in evolution, not only for our individual self but also for the universe.

The Power of Faith

Krishna says it is through the experience of Knowledge that we participate in the deepest, most loved, most far-reaching sacrifice(33). With the steady practice of contemplation, Self Knowledge appears. For the person who continues his spiritual practice with even a little spark of faith, realization of Truth *will* come(39). Here Krishna speaks not of an emotional faith which wavers when the going gets rough, but rather of faith based on a combination of reason, love of scripture or teacher and personally verifiable experience. Where the intellect is convinced, faith does not waver.

Initially on the spiritual path, some doubt can lead to healthy questioning and a consequent broadening of mental outlook. But if we are to proceed from mental information to faith, our practice must lead us out of the realm of thought into the realm of experience. Only through experience can we derive enough faith to let go of doubt.

Those who cling to doubt tend to be overly developed mentally and underdeveloped in feeling and intuition. Only through acquiring inner balance can the mental materialists leave their doubting ignorance behind and come to know faith based on experience. By clinging to doubt, our soul becomes buried and inaccessible. For those who doubt but still feel a glimmer of wish deep down to have faith in something other than the ego, there is hope. Begin to be open. Do not close doors by believing the voice that says, "it's ridiculous, it's impossible." Read sacred works. Be in the presence of holy people. And one day, your personal experience will open your heart and bring you faith.

Wisdom is not possible without faith. Our skepticism, disappointment and lack of trust stem from placing our faith in the wrong place. When we put our faith solely in worldly knowledge, we are bound to be disappointed because the ways of the world in this era are not meant to satisfy our deepest questions and silent inner yearnings. Fortunately, hypocrisy and greed cannot possibly gratify our inner longing. Without living examples of the higher, our ideals will be repeatedly crushed. Only through placing our faith in a worthy source can we receive a worthwhile response, an inner abundance that truly satisfies.

Krishna thereby informs us that the secret of life and evolution is sacrifice made firm by faith. For ultimately, when we are able to stop clinging to what does not in essence belong to us—false views, false values, the material world—then all doubts cease. And the joy and wealth of our birthright mysteriously appears.

> He who makes pure his works by *yoga*, who watches over his soul and who by wisdom destroys his doubts is free from the bondage of selfish work. Kill therefore with the sword of wisdom the doubt born of ignorance that lies in thy heart. Be one in self harmony, in *yoga*. Arise great warrior, arise. (4:41- 42)

Sri Sathya Sai Baba says:

> The years of life allotted to man are very short; the world in which he lives is very wide. Time extends far behind and far beyond. What little man has to do here has to be done quickly, at the place that is assigned to him, with the time that is allotted to him. And man has such a formidable task before him. It is to fulfill it that he has come as man, exchanging for this human habitat all the merit he has acquired during many past lives. The task is no less than the manifestation of Divinity latent in man. The easiest and most pleasant means by which this can be accomplished is service—the service of man, done in a spirit of dedication and devotion. (*Yoga of Action*, p.63)

Thus, the fourth discourse reveals the ancient wisdom that through living in the world, performing each action with the true devotion of conscious sacrifice, the mind becomes pure and the individuality gradually merges with our inner divine consciousness. Living in this way, we will surely reach the goal of *yoga*.

Five

YOGA OF RENUNCIATION THROUGH ACTION

Karma Sannyasa Yoga

	Gita verses
Yoga of action*(karma)* and *yoga* of Knowledge*(jnana)*	1–6
Characteristics of the renunciate and *karma yogi*	7–12
Explanation of *jnana yoga*	13–26
Meditation and devotion lead to liberation*(moksha)*	27–29

to truly know
I am not the doer
while continuing to do
wisdom accrues

in joyous equanimity
wherever and whatever
renunciation abides

On the way toward liberation Krishna delineates three main paths, three ways of linking the body ego individuality to the *Atman*, Self, Totality. These are the *yoga* of action(*karma yoga*), the *yoga* of devotion(*bhakti yoga*) and the *yoga* of knowledge(*jnana yoga*). Each of these paths is better suited to a certain type of personality. *Karma yoga* is considered a better starting point for the active person who functions with a combination of feeling and thinking. *Bhakti yoga* is considered more appropriate for the emotional type. And *jnana yoga* is the beginning way for the intellectual, the thinker. At the same time, for every person on the path there is an individual way of working which unfolds as inner practice and outer events establish a partnership. And as we proceed in our spiritual practice, the paths deepen and eventually converge(4).

While an aim of the *Gita* is to bring us to a point where practice is so subtle words are not necessary, in the beginning words are essential and will register differently in our minds as concepts. These concepts will become more fluid, with fewer boundaries as our experience and reflection deepen. Through the beautiful poetry of the *Gita*, we can allow the words to lead us to meaning, to a more total experience. Since Arjuna is a soldier and a beginner in the teaching, the tendency of his mind is to categorize. In an attempt to understand with the intellect, he tries to fit words and ideas into divisions, into either or propositions. His mind requires experience and reflection to be able to integrate seeming paradoxes into one meaningful whole.

The question asked by Arjuna at the beginning of the fifth chapter reveals that his emotional confusion is lifting and he is regaining the use of his intellect. Now he continues to pursue the question brought up in the third chapter about which path is superior, knowledge or action; except here he's asking if its better to give up action or to perform action as a *yoga*. In response to this, Krishna attempts to show Arjuna the interrelationship of action and renunciation, of doing while not doing, all as a preparation to begin meditation, which is the theme of the sixth chapter. So the teachings in the fifth chapter serve as the essential prerequisite and bridge to meditation. Without practicing the ideas expounded in the fifth chapter, meditation would be extremely difficult.

As these ideas become part of the inner aspiration and practice of the spiritual student, the foundation is being laid to banish divisiveness and embrace unity; to view life not as a bunch of separate experiences, but rather to experience life as an interconnected process, a flow ever homogenizing us toward Truth. Our different spiritual practices interlink, separate and merge while the process of evolution continues, supported by events and Reality.

Renouncing Desire

From the beginning, Krishna clarifies that renunciation of action does not mean stop performing action, but rather that in order to be able to reach an inner space of renunciation, much practice is required. Living a full life in the world as a *karma yogi* gives us richness, wisdom and a multifaceted opportunity to know the variegated tastes and textures of humanity—the beauty of creation. As an essential part of life, action is our primary means of purification. The road toward renunciation which begins with action is really only one road viewed as two separate approaches(4). The practice required is: 1) participate in living and working in the world without the desire for results, without the desire to control events; 2) participate in actions in the knowledge that I am not the doer. This body ego mind form is not the one acting. Life is acting *through* me in accordance with my inner world and outer circumstances. My duty and my wish is to be able to serve this life principle with awareness. 3) Keep the mind yoked to the higher throughout all action by dedication and awareness.

In order to be able to live out these three practices, fine-tuning and purification of the psyche is required. It is a gradual process. First the mind must change from its extroverted orientation, its tendency to look outward, to an inner orientation, the tendency to look within. The intellect must begin to reflect on itself, its thoughts and actions, to discriminate right from wrong. Rather than introjecting right and wrong from the society, the media, and authority figures, the one who develops an inward look will be able to know directly from inside what is right action. Insights will begin to occur spontaneously and unmistakably to help the different parts of ourself become united. Through observing ourselves and our experiences, we will begin to see the relationship between our actions, events and state of mind. And if this practice of self-observation is continued, the intellect will soon become convinced of the fact that pursuing extroverted, material desires for their own sake does not bring lasting happiness.

Krishna tells us that if we try to follow this teaching, we will reach a point where the opposites of attraction and repulsion, desire and hatred, like and dislike *no longer rule our psyche*(3). As long as our inner motivation is to go after what we like and avoid what we do not like, to seek pleasure and avoid pain, it would not be possible to work without desire for results or to work without a sense of agency or doership. For to desire something automatically polarizes the psyche and through the workings of the *gunas* and the law of opposites(enantiodromia), the total picture demands to be seen. Love and hate are two aspects of one whole. Every coin has two sides; every stick has two ends. As long as we want one end to the exclusion of the other, nature will demand that the totality be included. This is how life perpetuates ups and downs, highs and lows, successes and failures, belongingness and alienation. As long as we believe that happiness comes from possessing things outside—power, position, "success," sex, or expecting others to make us happy—our emotions will catch us in unending agitation, always wanting more, never being quite satisfied; while the temporary phenomenon of happiness passes like clouds elusively drifting to and fro. Therefore, the true *sannyasin*(renunciate) is he who is free from the pulls of desire—not through lack of opportunity, but through total integration of his body, emotions and intellect with his deepest essence Self.[7]

Action for Integration

To be able to reach that space where there is an ongoing awareness of the presence of the sun in spite of the clouds which cover it, in spite of ups and downs, happiness and sadness, we must come to see the presence of the sun inside us, ever effulgent; that I am the sun and every other living being is also the sun. The sun does not stop shining when it is covered by clouds. To practice working from this center of awareness is to be a witness of our joys and sorrows, our peacefulness and our agitation, until one day the unshakable realization dawns that I am the sun. All joy is inside me and will remain in spite of events, seeming losses, or difficulties. This joyousness, fullness, completeness ever continues, for it is the *source* of all happiness.

> He is known as a perpetual *sannyasin* who neither hates nor desires; for free from the pairs of opposites, O mighty armed, he is easily set free from bondage. (5:3)

First, it must be understood that we cannot just give up our desires. Desires have been there for aeons, our animal heritage preprogrammed into us in accordance with our past tendencies and actions. So it would be a frustrating and unrealistic expectation to think that we could immediately become desireless or give up our craving for results. *The reduction of vasanas takes time*. As our conditioning is gradually reduced through right action and spiritual practices, our self-defeating desires slowly drop away spontaneously or become transformed into nobler desires. We are not now in control of our desires, emotions, speech or actions. To attempt to control directly with the intellect can be both frustrating and futile, as the emotions are too unruly. First they must be tamed. By observing ourselves under the gaze of the sun, in light of our higher ideals, we begin to feel the discrepancy between what we wish to be and how we behave.

This is a crucial moment in our evolution. It must not be glossed over by denial or self-criticism. Beating on oneself is a tricky means of avoiding the emotions involved in the experience of suffering.

Only through our seeing, through our suffering, through our tears, can we be cleansed. By accepting to see ourselves we soften. Harsh judgement of others, as well as ourselves, begins to fall away. There is no blame. We just notice; we just see. And our seeing registers. Sometimes it causes a flood of remorse. Sometimes it causes guilt and shame. Sometimes it just sees. But whatever poison emerges we stay with it and continue our spiritual practice in the knowledge that a connection is being made with a higher source within. For this consciousness energy is overseeing our purification and evolution—like the presence of a good father, who is interested but not attached.

The unnecessary exaggeration of the painful aspects of seeing can be mitigated by our acceptance of pain and willingness to suffer our imperfections. This is one form of surrender. If we can view our suffering as an opportunity to cleanse our former actions, then we are helping ourselves to let go of the past that we might live with a fresh slate in the present. To suffer our imperfections in the awareness of our connection with the teacher, with Krishna, with the higher within is very different from suffering *because* of our imperfections, in resistance and in isolation. For our attempts to cut off our suffering can rob us of its curative effects. Our attempts to link ourselves with a higher power *in the face of suffering* can only induce a healing effect. This willingness to accept is called surrender.

> If you turn your back to the sun, your shadow is in front of you. You can try to catch it but you will never succeed. But the minute you turn to face the sun your shadow is behind you. If you move it follows you. You can make it go where you wish. The sun is Truth, the shadow is *prakriti*. (Swami Rama Tirtha, in Reymond, p.101)

As our *samskaras* diminish, then our efforts become more direct, more like an act of will which is prompted by divine intention. New strategies can be employed to outwit the thief who threatens to rob us of our birthright of bliss. But all in the knowledge that I am not the doer, nothing belongs to me: thy will be done, not mine, not mine. Then one day, after the ocean has spewed forth its mounds of terrible poison under the loving gaze of the sun, the mind becomes calmer and good feelings begin to emerge. Joyousness pours forth, contentment comes, peacefulness peeps up its head, compassion enters. With the advent of this rebirth, something becomes steadier. The nobler desires of the intellect can be put into practice. As our actions begin to reflect our nobler ideals, the head, the heart and the hand come closer to working in unison. The body, the emotions and the intellect gradually are becoming integrated.

> The action of the *yogi*, not being motivated by desire, his understanding gets progressively clarified. As his desires in all forms get liquidated, his self-control tends to perfection. The desirelessness gets transformed into clarity of understanding. This clarity itself becomes the intuition which cognizes the One cosmic consciousness apparently appearing as the multitudinous forms of consciousness. (Swami Chidbhavananda, p.331)

The Joy of Harmony

The person who has attained this inner harmony and integration is called a *yogi(yoga yuktah)*, one who is yoked to the ongoing connection with the higher in oneself and in all. And the practice of *yoga* can be considered both the process and the goal.

> He who is devoted to the Path of Action, whose mind is quite pure, who has conquered the self, who has subdued his senses, who realizes his Self as the Self in all beings, though acting he is not tainted. (5:7)

When the *yoga* of action is practiced with earnestness and steadiness, the senses stop their extroverted orientation, the emotions become purified, the ego surrenders supremacy and compassion becomes steadier. Gradually we come to know there is no separate self, only one Self. A person who experiences life like this lives in love, lives in detachment. His actions cannot bind him. No new *vasanas* are formed because there is no sense of agency, no feeling of an ego doing, no sense of attachment.

to dance through life like the lotus
with leaves untouched by water
all raindrops just bounce off

water neither accumulates
nor makes heavy
nothing sticks

only the essential purity remains
unsullied by surroundings.

This is the quality of joyful detachment, which results from performing actions as an offering, acting in the world in humility as a servant of the higher, without any sense of doership. Krishna says:

> Offer all thy works to God, throw off selfish bonds and do thy work. No sin can then stain thee, even as waters do not stain the leaf of the lotus. (5:10)

The question then arises, how can I get from here to there? If I have no will, if the power of my desires is the primary determinant of my actions in spite of good intentions, realistically speaking, how is detachment possible?

First, we must deeply wish to be transformed. Then we must become truly motivated to discover the connecting link between hearing ideas, reflecting on them and actually participating in practicing them. These three aspects of action—listening, reflecting and practicing are related parts of one whole—just as all opposites are parts of one whole.

Initially, we might try to be as attentive as possible, trying to keep the attention fully focused in an open and relaxed manner on what one is doing, seeing, reading or hearing. When the mind wanders, notice it and return. If we can listen and experience attentively in the present, later we can reflect on the meaning. And much later, reflection is no longer needed, as knowledge of what is required is *revealed* in the present moment with clarity and immediacy.

Action as Duty

The idea of *action as duty* can serve as a bridge between ordinary action and action as *yoga*, between egocentric action and action as surrender. The word "duty" evokes many associations in us. Let's each ask, "what does the idea of duty evoke in me"? To some it might sound like an old fashioned martyr's concept from Sunday school to be discarded like a pair of old slippers. To others, the idea might seem important, as long as it doesn't impose too much discomfort or restriction on our so-called "freedom." And for others it might invoke a very strong feeling of resistance, a sense of being hemmed in where boundaries are too limiting. Ask, "what are my honest feelings about duty"?

Without the knowledge of action as a *yoga*, it is perfectly natural for the idea of duty to evoke enormous resistance and the desire to run, unless the carrot of pleasure is being dangled to ensnare us into duty. Without this carrot or ice cream cone, how many of us would undertake any duty of any kind? How many of us would work for no pay? Or support another person solely out of caring, without expecting something in return? So in western society, duty is considered something we undertake because we have to—either as a bitter medicine we're supposed to swallow or as a result of coming of age, or as an inducer of certain rewards such as position, money, pleasure or standard of living. For us, duty is usually connected with certain results and expectations but rarely is embraced for its own sake.

Duty in *Vedanta* is quite different from all that. It's not something you try to squirm out of or gain something from or grit your teeth and bare it. Rather, the practice of duty is at the heart of action as *yoga*. Remember, Arjuna's heart wrenching dilemna consists of confusion regarding his *dharma*. Having a duty offers us the framework for working in the world and relating to others, without expectation or desire for results. Duty is a means of developing detachment, of accepting what comes, of performing actions without regrets about the past or anxiety regarding the future. Wholehearted performance of duty is also a means of gaining merit. When we undertake an action willingly and wholeheartedly to serve the evolutionary principle within, this has a completely different flavor than undertaking the same task for the main purpose of outcome, income, power, position, or societal expectation. The former motivation leads us to love whereas the latter leads to dissension and ambivalence. With the motivation of serving, actions offer the opportunity to transform competitiveness, hostility and egocentric striving for the benefit of a higher principle.

Then our involvement won't be taken so personally. When the heat to perform for success is gone, the action becomes freer, more spontaneous, more joyful. When we don't expect anything in return, the duty itself offers the framework for eliminating egocentric action in favor of the good of the whole and for the connection with the Self. In this way, all duty as action can be willingly embraced for the sake of the Self within oneself and within the other *equally*.

Action as a *yoga* is only for those who want to evolve and who wish to participate in the giant adventure of *cooperating* with nature rather than resisting nature, or living passively programmed as animals. For nature's plan regarding action is much broader than we know. Nature's plan includes the precursor and the result in an action itself. She works under the extended time frame called the totality. *When an action is performed, the result is inherent in the action.* The action and the result are one and the same, not two separate entities, the way the mind usually divides it up. Thus, to worry about a result is useless. It only interferes with our capacity to perform well. Equally destructive is our trying to manipulate a result by second-guessing what should be said or done in order to seem intelligent or praiseworthy.

These behaviors such as worry and trying to impress, interfere with the flow of nature by impeding the ability of natural law to act through us. This creates blockages and bottlenecks in the body, which nature must compensate for in other ways that are destructive to the individual psyche, as well as to other people. In this way, we cut ourselves off from the aspect of nature that manifests as the spontaneous flow of events. By trying to control, the result is we end up feeling isolated and disharmonious.

In contrast to the typical goal-oriented man of achievement, the *karma yogi* works in the spirit of detachment love, doing what needs to be done in freedom. He lives in the awareness that the body moves, the eye sees, the ear hears, the mind thinks; but all these actions are not me(8,9). It is not I who act but the power of life acting *through* me. With this quality of ongoing awareness, unnecessary limitations and constrictions do not form. Action in itself is freeing and open—a communion with all life.

Just as we can claim a sense of inner responsibility for actions alone and not for results(12), so the Self watches the world as a dispassionate observer without interfering with the results. Here Krishna so gently informs us it is not God's responsibility to interfere with the mess made by human beings, but only to allow nature to proceed in accordance with the lawful blueprint initiated by human actions(14). *The Lord is beyond the workings of the world.* Both individually and collectively, our actions alone are the cause of good and evil. The responsibility for changing events does not belong to God.

Yet at the same time, it is not the human being who is the doer but the ever present enlivening factor within. Ramakrishna says:

> An individual has the delusion, 'I am the doer' as long as the philosopher's stone has not converted the base metal of his mind into the noble one of the divine eye. When he is in ignorance he entertains the feelings of agency such as, 'I am the doer of this virtuous act,' and 'I am the doer of this vicious act.' This attitude is the cause of the continuation of the wheel of birth and death. But when one realizes God, one is freed from the feelings of agency and bondage. One remains convinced in the truth that God is the real doer of everything. (Swami Chidbhavananda, p.331)

The Way of Knowledge

Thus, the *avatar* does not intervene by changing events(15). Jesus did not manipulate events so as not to die on the cross. Krishna did not control events to avert the great destruction of the *Mahabharata* war. Any external manipulation would not qualitatively change anything as before long, human imperfection would repeat and recreate the same difficulties that ever lead to interminable confusion and destruction. Rather, the attempt is to *transform the human heart* so that actions and their consequent results will be more harmonious, more beneficial to oneself and the world.

By accepting responsibility for motivations, actions and reactions, we are participating in life as a *yoga*, thereby contributing to the good of the whole. This responsibility for ourselves is *dharma*; the offering of ourselves to the higher is surrender; the reciprocal relationship with the world is love. All three are part of one thing. All three are connected to remembrance as duty.

> Their thoughts on Him and one with Him, they abide in Him and He is the end of their journey. And they reach the land of never returning because their wisdom has made them pure of sin. (5:17)

Thus, the *yogi* renounces action through merging the mind in the Self. This is the process and the goal. The essence of our entire spiritual work is to link our thoughts, memories, emotions, intellect and ego, all our inner equipment(*antahkarana*) to the love within. Through intentionally focusing on this awareness-love or on the teacher who is the embodiment of love, our heart opens. By bringing this compassionate gaze to our shortcomings in the process of action, we suffer them and they wash away. Through experiencing deeper layers of ourselves, sorrow and joy are experienced together. Now the opposites are uniting, coming closer together.

As the dividing tendency lessens, we begin to get glimpses of the unity of all beings. There is an inner equality in all persons, in all animals, in all nature be they garbage collector, doctor, elephant or blade of grass(18). Everything in nature is permeated by the life principle and is to be treated with *equal* respect and seen as God. The needs of others are just as important as our own. For our words, opinions and level of understanding are all relative. They are merely an expression of our accumulated inner impressions and tendencies. As the sun shines equally on all her children and fries up all impurities, so the light of wisdom once kindled within, burns to ashes the ignorance of separateness, in all its varied manifestations.

The sun is always there inside us seeing, being, pouring forth effulgent rays of light. But His presence will remain unnoticed unless we turn our attention there. Through the practice of attaching ourselves to this inner light, we detach from matter as reality and gradually come to experience the spirit which infuses all matter. We become free from the pull of the opposites. Ramakrishna says:

> *Brahman* is experienced vaguely through discrimination, somewhat vividly through meditation and in its original splendor in *samadhi*.

This experience of oneness loving awareness is the most important purpose in living. Krishna calls it the *victory of life*(19). This is where lasting happiness lies. This is how our *vasanas* diminish and eventually vanish. This experience of peaceful living unity is the gateway to liberation, the place of no return.

> He who on this earth before his departure can endure the storms of desire and wrath, this man is a *yogi*. This man has joy. He has inner joy, he has inner gladness and he has found inner light. This *yogi* attains the *nirvana* of *Brahman*. He is one with God and goes unto God. Holy men reach the *nirvana* of *Brahman*. Their sins are no more, their doubts are gone, their soul is in harmony, their joy is in the good of all. Because the peace of God is with them whose mind and soul are in harmony, who are free from desire and wrath, who know their own soul. (5:23-26)

There's a story from the boyhood of Krishna about a giant serpent Kaliya, who enters the local river and starts killing everyone in sight. Krishna goes after the monster and before long begins dancing on his hoods. Kaliya's wife intervenes and begs Krishna not to kill him. In his compassion, he banishes the snake to a faraway sea where he could harm no living being.

To become the master of desire and hatred is to dance on the hoods of the serpent. Through the practice of spiritual disciplines and love, the archaic, instinctual aspects of our spinal serpent brain become truly sublimated. Passion, rage, territoriality—all enter a realm where *they can no longer harm us.* The snake is not killed. His energies are not cut off from the total scheme of life. He is merely put in his proper place, where he can render no harm.

We each might notice how, in our own lives, emotion or desires dictate our actions. The secret is either to banish the snake by letting go of emotion and desire or to transform them by reclaiming the energy of life in accordance with our nobler ideals.

The reptilian brain is a very real physiological fact in each of us. *Kundalini* is not merely an esoteric concept. It is the powerful energy of life, which challenges us to harness her power for our individual well being and for the benefit of humanity.

> The mind is the axle on which the vast machinery of *samsara* rotates endlessly. When the mind moves, the world moves. When the mind is not the world is not. The impure mind sees the world as a vast battlefield of conflicting passions. The purified mind sees it as *Atma*. The devotee sees the world as the Lord. So the mind should be purified and kept under control by knowing That which is beyond it. (Swami Vidyaprakashananda, p.435)

Beyond Mind

In order to know that which is beyond the mind, thought, word and deed—feeling thinking and movement—must be harmonized within us. The head, the heart and the hand must somehow come to function in unison. Sri Sathya Sai Baba helps us understand the relationship between the partless aspects of a person:

> Truth, bliss, beauty are forms of the divine. These represent the true form of man. Bliss(*sivam*) is that which has no death. Truth(*sathyam*) is that which is not subject to change on account of time, place or circumstance. Beauty(*sundaram*) is the form of the Divine.
>
> Man is described as a lover of food. This gross body flourishes on food. But it is bound to perish some day. And the subtle body, made up of the life force(*prana*), the mind(*manas*) and intellect(*vijnana*) lasts longer. But for how long? Only as long as the mind lasts. When the mind is absent what happens? This state is described as deep sleep state. In this state there is only the causal body. There is no mind. This is a state of bliss.
>
> Hence it is essential to understand the functioning of the mind. Man and mind are not separate. To treat the mind as something apart and becoming subject to it is wrong. It has to be treated as a servant as long as the body-mind consciousness remains. Then the mind obeys you. Today man follows the dictates of the mind.

> It is not easy to subdue the mind immediately. But you must begin to bring it under control. When the mind desires something you must immediately set the intellect at work. Why? So the intellect may give you the proper advice. Examine your desire using the power of discrimination to find out whether it is good or bad, right or wrong. Do not wish to acquire whatever you desire. When you try to teach the mind in this manner, it loses its potency. This intellect is full of intelligence and common sense. It is called Divine Intellectual Will. The Divine Will power has to be acquired by everyone. Only then can they realize their true human nature. It is through this will power that the cosmic divine nature of the universe can be recognized.
>
> If one has the determination anything is possible. If an ant has determination it can travel any distance. But even an eagle, if it has no will to fly, will be confined to the ground. Resolve to accomplish what you want to with firm determination.
>
> Develop the feeling, 'I and God are one.' This should not be purely a verbal exercise. You must realize the implications of the *mantra* you recite such as *'so ham'*, I am He and live up to it. That is true concentation. (*Sanathana Sarathi*, 8-93,p.209-10)

To be detached from the rulership of the mind is not a withdrawn state where we are cut off from our emotions and plod through life like joyless automatons. We are not seeking to separate ourselves from vitality and joy but rather, when we are attached to a deeper level of ourselves, we naturally become detached from the external pulls of the objects of the world. Then we can enjoy the underlying unity of the world from contact with our deeper Self. This brings a steadier, calmer, more secure sense of well being and Self confidence. Through being firmly rooted in our being, in the center of ourselves, we can become an expression of natural enthusiasm and spontaneous joy.

Picture a see saw. When we're at either end it bounces up and down, high low, high low. The closer we come to the middle, the steadier we become. Now picture a circle. If we are at the center of the circle there can be no movement at all. Everything is included in our experience, as the circle has no end and no beginning. Through remaining in the middle we almost become the circle. If we are not in the middle, it's as if we're a point on a line again. The line is the see saw.

When we are linked to the Self, the center of our being, the body, emotions, intellect and thought, word and deed fall into harmony naturally, without our trying. And we live in a contented, inner security that *cannot be taken away*. Through attachment to the point of inner depth, we are not pulled by desire, fear and anger(26). Vivekananda says:

> To live in the world and not be of it is the true test of renunciation. Renunciation and renunciation alone is the real secret, the *mulamantra* of all Realization. (*Pearls of Wisdom*, p.144)

Sai Baba asks:

> What is it that is to be renounced? Are external objects like houses and vehicles to be given up? Or is one to give up kith and kin? No. These things can be renounced easily. But this is not real sacrifice. The real renunciation one has to make is giving up the qualities of desire, anger, and greed. (SS 8-88, p.203).

The Freedom of Meditation

After expounding on the process of renunciation and liberation, in the closing *slokas* Krishna introduces us to the practice of meditation(27). It is not possible to understand liberation without living meditation, both as a discipline as well as an ongoing way of being. Initially, the idea can be introduced to the intellect as a means of quickening yearning, beginning spiritual practice and seeking to unify one's life around higher ideals. But without the actual ongoing practice of yoking the mind to the Highest, the mind cannot merge in God consciousness, Krishna consciousness, Christ consciousness, Buddha consciousness.

The mind can never comprehend the teachings of the great ones. Through living a life of devotion, simplicity and expansiveness, the purified intellect is trained in steadiness, peacefulness and prepared for meditation. Krishna presents the ongoing practice of contemplation meditation(Chapter 6), that realization of the total nature of Divinity can be experienced. This is the ultimate freedom.

Thus, the fifth discourse provides us with the *yoga* of living actively in the world in the spirit of letting go of self-centered will and desire. To truly cherish the essence of one's Self, we must learn to renounce egocentricity.

Six

YOGA OF MEDITATION
Dhyana Yoga

	Gita verses
Attributes of the *yogi* and *sannyasi*	1–4
Characteristics of the sage whose mind rests in the Self	5–9
Practice of meditation	10–26
Bliss and equality of the highest *yogi*	27–32
Mind control	33–38
When the goal of *yoga* is not yet completed	39–47

while moving
train the mind in silence
until wholeness

without movement
train the mind in stillness
until unity

"when he sees me in all
and he sees all in me
then I never leave him and
he never leaves me."

The birthright of being, which is uncovered by the evolution of becoming continues to be revealed to us by Krishna. In order to rediscover the inner sanctum that has existed always, the spiritual work we undertake must gain in intensity and energy slowly, gradually(*sanaih, sanaih*). Step by step we climb the mountain that leads to a summit of silence—a space where agitation ends.

The egocentric will(*sankalpa*), the desire centered strivings which are a manifestation of the life force, must become directed toward deepening one's personal will to include the good of the whole; the harmony of oneself as part of the whole. This broadening of one's boundaries and expansion of one's limitations is the essence of the practice of meditation.

Before we can become calm, equalminded and open enough for the higher energies to reveal themselves to us, we must practice this openness, the dissolution of you and me boundaries through actions in the world. This is one meaning of the *yoga* of renunciation taught in the fifth discourse and the beginning of the sixth discourse(1-9). We willingly participate in the dissolution of the separate sense of self through renouncing actions for oneself alone, actions for the purpose of results gained for oneself. Yet we continue to participate in actions, not as an individual *doing* but as a participant in the process of action, taking our cues from inner feelings, inner abilities and outer requirements regarding what is needed. Through the process of working in the world, little by little we reduce egocentric will. As our self-motivated thoughts decrease, our agitation decreases. And slowly we become fit for the practice of contemplation.

When the wish is strong for knowing the freedom of our own nature, the mind and the will can be gently harnessed toward experiencing that boundless perfection. Just as a wild horse can be trained so that a rider is carried on his back, the egocentric mind can be educated to let go of its conflicting desires by remembering the ongoing supremacy of the higher, by trying to link the inner equipment(*antahkarana*: mind, intellect, ego, outgoing thoughts and memories) to the ideal, and by surrendering our self-centered thoughts to the ideal. With each act of surrender to the Self, our *vasanas* become purified. And slowly, slowly, we make our way up the mountain.

This intentional effort calls forth a lawful response from within and without. The environment responds in some way to let us know our actions are correct and appreciated. *We begin receiving sweetness and joy.* The lumps of sugar given to the wild horse to train him to carry the rider on his back are given to us in the form of inner joy and inner knowing. The *lilas* of Krishna, the sport of Krishna, sometimes in the form of synchronistic events, sometimes as delightful surprise, humorous happenings or loving feelings intervene to show us the way. After a time of conscious practice with surrender, nature always showers her blessings in one way or another. This is the lawful response of the Goddess.

For the outcome is inherent in the action, the effect is part of the cause. As we surrender our unthinking habits, limited ideas and negative emotions, nature establishes a partnership with us, as if to let us know, "this path is right for you, this path helps me, stay with it, continue."

Many of us have been brought up to believe that by competitiveness and assertion we become strong and by getting our own way this will make us happy. Beating the other is sometimes considered praiseworthy while giving in to the other is often viewed as weakness. Actually it's the other way around. Giving in to the other consciously is strength, scoring points against the other is weakness. One ego asserting its opinions or feelings at the expense of another ego—no matter how professionally articulated that assertion might be—can never lead to lasting joy. Small victories gained by perpetuating conflict will always rebound by perpetuating further divisive reactions. Be it in family, workplace, university or spiritual group, the cycle of divisiveness caused by one ego trying to dominate another will not end, until the ego willingly sees that the only way to peace and happiness is to *give up* the pretence of supremacy and make room for all.

For each ego is expressing but a limited aspect of relative truth. It's not a question of becoming a floor mat for others to step on or justifying one's passivity because one can't say no. What is being emphasized here is willingly acknowledging the need to surrender egocentric ideas because these are not in tune with the natural flow of events. Clinging to *sankalpa* diverts the total natural flow of events and imprisons us(4). One desire leads to another and we remain actively going round in circles on the surface of life, never experiencing completion. No one goal ever comes to fruition as our desires continually shift and change while we dance to the tune of *maya*. Exclusively self-centered motivation prevents our evolution.

Why should one remain a prisoner of egocentric will? Only when we see our bondage are we given a choice. We can choose to devote our energy to freeing ourselves by pursuing the highest purpose or we can choose to remain where we are, without deeper meaning pursuing trivia, in bondage to our inner desires and outer circumstances—a slave of *maya*. No matter which path we choose, we can remain doing the same work externally. The only difference lies in our underlying inner motivation, our state of consciousness. This inner awareness can mean the difference between light and darkness, growth and stagnation, life and death. The *yogi* is one who surrenders his egocentric will (2-4). And it is our actions in life, which offer us the opportunity to participate in surrender.

Renunciation of Agency

When we examine what exactly is this construct called ego, we see that it is the sense of I identified with the body, the emotions and the intellect, with time and place and doing. As such, the ego is at any given moment subject to the memories of its joys and sorrows, its victories and defeats, its loves and hates. As every temporal joy contains an equal sorrow, there can be no lasting happiness for a person who bases his life on the reality of the ego. Thus *ignoring* one's Real nature is considered ignorance. Living life as if one's limited reality, the ego is what we are is ignorance. Devoting one's entire energy to perpetuating and feeding the separate existence of this relative reality of the ego and its world is ignorance.

The ego has been conditioned to accept what it has been taught about life from well-meaning persons who were themselves caught by the ignorance perpetuated by their own limited identification with the sense of separateness called the body. How then can a life based on that which is partial, transient, temporary and limited ever liberate us from suffering and sorrow?

In performing action as a bound ego we are subject to our past conditioning—to what our parents and teachers taught us either consciously or unconsciously, our successes and our failures, our fears from the past and our anxieties regarding the future. Therefore, happiness will ever elude us if we identify with the ego. But performing action as a *yoga* is different. We are advised to concentrate solely on the process of acting, without regrets from the past or anticipation of success for the future. By consciously leaving the results to the Higher, we can give up worry, renounce fear, and disregard our relation and excitement, which all tend to interfere with our concentration on the work at hand, thereby detracting from excellence. By thus establishing a partnership with the Higher, we are *invoking* the Higher to enter all our actions. We exert our best effort in the knowledge that all effort is supported by the life force and all is grace, be it called success or be it called failure.

There are two graduated methods of *yoga*(3). The first is desireless action (*nishkama karma*). Through encountering the many difficult circumstances of life, if the mind can remain steadily concentrated on dedication and divine awareness, we are ready to graduate into the second method, called serenity or quiescence(*samah*). When this occurs, we live more deeply in the Self and action tends to drop off by itself.

Self Effort (*Purusharthah*)

How do these two ways occur? Through self-effort. Krishna says:

> Let a man lift himself by his own Self alone and let him not lower himself. For this Self alone is the friend of oneself and this Self is the enemy of oneself. (6:5)

To live one's life in true friendship with one's Self is to follow the path of evolution. In this way, our animal instincts, fears, obsessions and emotional cravings are worked through and left behind with the support of our inner Friend.

> If man wants to exalt himself into the greater cultural and spiritual possibilities now lying dormant in him, he has to raise the lower in himself to the greater perfection that is the true eternal core in himself. The lower in us can ever raise itself to the attunement of the Higher but the Higher can influence only when the power is available for Its influence. To the extent the lesser in us surrenders itself to the influence of the Higher, to that extent It can serve the lower as a great friend. But if the lower refuses to come under the influence of the diviner in us, the divine Presence is considered an enemy of ourselves, inasmuch as the dynamism of Life provides us Its energy both for our life of higher aspirations and the life of lower temptations. Ultimately, *it is for the aspirant himself to accept responsibility for blessing or damming himself.* The potentiality for improvement, the chances for self-growth, the strength to haul ourselves from our own misconceptions are ever open for employment. But it all depends on how we make use of them. (Swami Chinmayananda, THG p.344)

There is no moralistic implication here regarding the "lower" and the "higher" natures inherent in man. For human beings possess three different natures—the animal nature concerned with food, clothing, shelter, mates and dominion; the human nature which expresses through compassion, cheerfulness, forgiveness, straightforwardness, truth and yearns to know Reality; and the God-nature which actually lives in oneness with its own awareness Totality. So the work of climbing the mountain is primarily to transform the animal nature, with all the emotional agitation that arises in the struggle for survival, mates and egocentric territoriality, into the human nature which is basically peaceful and contented through reaping the rewards inherent in living out noble actions.

Preliminary practices of meditation help us go more deeply within. Through these practices, we are guided to a more human level within ourselves, a caring for ourselves and others, alongside a wish to serve the higher within oneself and all. Meditation is the way within, the way to the Self, whether our path is *Karma yoga*, *Bhakti yoga* or *Jnana yoga*. This underlying alchemy brings harmony and integration, that the depths will begin to filter through to our every action, emotion, and thought. Gradually, we become fit for the higher.

Equality, Love and Self Control

Before beginning his instructions for meditation, Krishna specifies the qualities of one whose mind is yoked to Truth and ever emphasizes the importance of self-control(7-9). To this *yogi*, everything in the material world is treated equally, as it is seen simply as a combination of the five elements. Gold is no different than any other metal, stone or a lump of earth. There is no greed or like or dislike for one thing above another. All are equally properties of nature, as the human body is the property of nature and is also composed of the five elements in varying proportion.

Just as the five elements comprise the material world, so the Self is the substratum for every human being. The *yogi*'s role or relationship to one person calls forth no preferences based on like or dislike(9). Once love(*prema*) is born in the human heart, it is not partial, not attached to this or that. The love emanating from the Self is showered equally on all. It exists not *because* of the treatment from the other but is a reflection of the independent, realized soul of the *yogi* which *naturally flows* to whatever is in its path, whether or not the other is capable of receiving it. A friend is treated no differently from a person with enmity; a thief is loved as much as a righteous man, a stranger is given the same love as a family member. This ideal of equality stems from a place of total peace, total harmony and total consciousness, where one sees only the Self in everyone as the true Reality.

This is the vision the spiritual student is being trained to cultivate and experience. Every bird needs two wings to fly. Repeated practice(*abhyasa*) and detachment(*vairagya*) are the two wings that guide the spiritual student on his journey homeward. Then when we reach the summit of the mountain, *karma yoga* is no longer necessary and can even become a hindrance. Activity in the world can gradually subside in favor of sheer meditation, until such time that the realized soul chooses to return or not to return to the world of activity, in accordance with his *dharma,* in an ongoing state of awareness that never departs no matter what. However, Krishna himself is a living example of the path of action.

The Way of Meditation

Through the practice of meditation we can begin to approach this vision of equality, of seeing and experiencing the Self in oneself and in all. While realization cannot occur before living the human values, the practice of meditation can also filter through to influence our daily living by helping us behave in a way that is more human, more sensitive, calm, alert and unruffled. Through bringing a deeper awareness into the process of our daily living, the mentally imposed split between the sacred and the mundane becomes neutralized. *The energy generated from meditation becomes part of our daily relationships and activities.*

In the west, meditation has become a household word, which has been used in a general way to describe certain techniques of calming the body and mind. In the classical tradition of *yogic* practice and Indian scriptures, meditation(*dhyana*) is considered an advanced state in spiritual life that happens by itself after the spiritual aspirant has practiced certain preliminaries for a long time. Meditation is not something that one does; it is not a technique that one practices. *It is an inner state of being.* There are, however, many different techniques that are known to lead to the state called meditation.

Patanjali, in the *Yoga Sutras* speaks of the eight limbs of *yoga.* The first five limbs consist of preparation through right living, noble values, spiritual practices, postures, and sublimation and purification of the thoughts and emotions. These are called:

1. *yama* – developing strong will power from inner motivation, human values and cleanliness. The virtues to be cultivated are: non-injury, truthfulness, not stealing, non-accumulation of wealth, faith in God, celibacy of mind, silence, patience, forgiveness and fearlessness.
2. *niyama* – application of truth through purity of mind and body, self-study or reflection on spiritual texts, austerity, hospitality, worship, visiting holy places, working for the good of others, contentment and service to the teacher.
3. *asana* – physical and mental exercises including posture.
4. *pranayama* – transformation of individual energy, physiological and psychic into cosmic energy through mastery of the five vital airs.
5. *pratyahara* – the process of disidentifying the senses from the sense objects and separating the mind from thoughts.

The last three limbs of *yoga* are specific practices while sitting. These are:

6. *dharana* – concentration.
7. *dhyana* – contemplation, meditation.
8. *samadhi* – equalmindedness; union of individual soul with cosmic spirit.

Technically speaking, our aim in the beginning is to find a quiet, private place and sit, keeping the body still and relaxed with the spine straight to allow a flow of energy(11-13). This helps the mind be attentive, concentrated and open. Concentration can be developed through focusing on a visual symbol, an inspiring spiritual text, a sound symbol(*mantra*), the picture of a teacher, watching the breath, or an inner concentration on energy within the body. Whatever technique has been advised by the teacher can be helpful in stilling the mind, developing attention, concentration and will. But personal transmission is essential, as opposed to mere book instruction.

While in the seat of meditation, the body is to be kept absolutely still and firm, while the wandering mind is to be brought back to its point of attentiveness. The attention awareness is God energy focused on God, both concentrated and expansive. Repeated practice(*abhyasa)* consists of bringing the wayward mind back to its place of concentration. From this effort, will develops.

This is not a will of the ego but is a partnership based on the awareness that the mind can act and the ego can practice, only if it is supported and upheld by the universal energy of the Self(10). So long as this awareness is maintained, the will power and presence that is gained will be in harmony with evolution and self-unfoldment, as opposed to pride, inflation or egocentric will. *All our capacity for spiritual work is the expression of the Self within, which wishes to be known through all creatures.*

At the highest level of Totality, the Self has no wishes. But at that point where the Self enters the world of manifestation, the wish to be known as One and not two makes itself felt within the heart and mind of man. This wish can manifest at the physical, emotional or intellectual level. And it can manifest as the wish for transcendence, the yearning for Realization, for liberation.

The techniques are offered by the teacher, the blessings are given by God, while the fulfillment of the goal rests in the process of practice of the spiritual student. This activates the inner *guru.*

The teacher and the scriptures can inspire us by planting seeds. When we initiate the process of self-effort, the seeds take root. Throughout one's entire life, it is our own responsibility to care for the sapling as if it were our child—to feed it, water it, weed it; to pull out the negative emotions and automatic reactions from the roots; to see that it receives enough sunlight and positive influences, and lovingly watch it grow. Only then can we participate in serving as a vehicle for the higher in us to enter into life. This is the purpose of living.

Through this process, the binding rope of the *gunas* expands unto infinity. There is a story of baby Krishna who was very naughty, continually playing pranks and stealing butter from the *gopis* and cowherds. One day in exasperation, his foster-mother Yashoda tries to tie him up. Whatever rope she uses is never long enough. She ties two ropes together. Still not long enough. *The gunas lose their power to bind us when we try to catch the Lord.* The Lord of the heart is ever free. The Lord of the heart in us can never be bound. And we can surely merge with Him unto infinity.

Through inner acceptance of what comes, our lines of responsibility become demarcated(7-10). Then we are no longer dependent on the responses of others. Clarity of boundary comes from detachment, from experiencing the ongoing support of no boundary. Freedom comes from seeing that the angry response of another need not elicit a hurt or angry reaction from us. Habits and compulsions give way to harmony and moderation. Fears melt, for what is there to fear when I am not the body? Who is there to fear when we are all a manifestation of God?

It is the animal nature, which rightly fears and must protect its territory, as the animal *dharma* is self-protection. It is the human nature, which rightly trusts and wishes to give, as the human *dharma* is compassion. It is the godly nature, which knows itself as the other with the light of loving knowing inherent in the inner eye, which is beyond all modes of knowing. And it is the *Brahman* nature, which is beyond all evolution, beyond all effort, beyond all striving, transcendent and immanent permeating everything.

Through the practice of meditation, the *yogi* in the seat of meditation experiences a stillness, steady like the flame of a candle in a windless place which does not flicker; a stillness resting in the pure *sattvic* state with all restless desires gone(19).

> In the still mind, the Self reveals itself. From the depths of meditation a man draws the joy and peace of complete fulfillment.
>
> Having attained that abiding joy beyond the senses revealed in the stilled mind, he will never swerve from the eternal truth that all life is one.
>
> In this state he desires nothing else and cannot be shaken by the heaviest burdens of sorrow.
>
> The practice of meditation frees him from all affliction. This is the path of *yoga*. Follow it with determination and enthusiasm. (6:20-23) EE

Freedom from Sorrow

Sloka 23 gives another definition of *yoga*. In the second chapter, *yoga* was defined as dexterity in action. Here *yoga* is defined as freedom from pain:

> Let it be known: the severance from the union with pain is *yoga*. This *yoga* should be practiced with determination and with a mind steady and undespairing. (6:23) SwC

Krishna assures us that through the practice of *yoga* we come to let go of our pain (17, 23). There is so much suffering in the world and it seems so senseless. But when we begin to experience our own individual suffering more deeply and reflect on it, we come to see that there is a purpose behind every pain. Our pain offers us the possibility of cleansing our impurity, uncovering its causes in our thoughts, feelings and behaviors that were based on ignorance. *It offers us the possibility of rectifying our past mistakes by learning not to repeat them.* As we become more deeply connected to our inner source, the emotional confusion comes out of hiding and makes itself available to our inner view. Insights appear. Within the backdrop of the eternal witness, our thoughts and feelings work simultaneously thereby allowing us to let go of our past through deeply experienced intuitive knowing feeling. This process cleanses our *vasanas* and allows us to enter the present moment of life with a fresh slate.

Eknath Easwaran has a practical and philosophical perspective on suffering:

> Sorrow is necessary for us only when we require it to grow into our full stature. We can think of the Lord as a phys ed teacher. He looks us over carefully and selects those of us who are drooping with selfishness and self-will. To these he gives sorrow saying, let me give you some special exercises to help you grow as tall and straight as you can. When we have grown to our full height and can push ourselves out of the way to become sensitive to the needs of others the Lord will say, 'You don't require any more sorrow, any more ordeals. You have gone beyond all suffering by extinguishing your self-will and selfishness. Now you are ready to help reduce the

suffering and sorrow of those around you. (*The Bhagavad Gita for Daily Living, Volume 1*, p.359)

We become separated from our pain, firstly by going into our suffering consciously, so that it can become a cleansing, and secondly through allowing the body, mind and intellect to become harmonized by linking them with the higher Reality. This is always an act of grace. It is only when our *vasanas* have been purged to a certain extent that we become able to establish the right conditions whereby the mind can become linked with the Self. Then meditation continues burning the *vasanas*. Swami Chinmayananda says of this *sloka*:

> Detachment from this pain *yoga* is naturally a process in which we disconnect ourselves from the fields of objects and their experiences. A total or even partial divorce from the perceptions of the world of objects is not possible as long as we are using the mechanism of perception, the organ of feeling and the instrument of thinking. To get detached from the mechanism of perceptions, feelings and thoughts would naturally be the total detachment from the pain *yoga*.
>
> Existence of the mind is possible only through its attachment. The mind can never live without attaching itself to some object or other. Detachment from one object is possible for the mind only when it has attached itself to another. For the mind, detachment from pain caused by the unreal is possible only when it gets attached to the Bliss that is the Nature of the Real. In this sense, the true *yoga*—which is the seeking and establishing an enduring attachment with the Real—is gained only when the seeker cries a halt in his onward march toward pain and deliberately takes a right about turn to proceed toward the Real and the Permanent in himself. (THG, p.375)

Much has been said about the monkey mind. Monkeys flit from one thing to another actively pursuing whatever the senses notice. There's a story told in India about a man who was sitting outside listening to a lecture. Monkeys roam freely there and can be very mischievous. While this man was sitting, a monkey came and took his glasses. The man tried to chase him but to no avail. The monkey was just too quick. And besides, the man couldn't climb trees. The lecturer stopped and suggested that the man give the monkey a banana. As soon as the monkey saw the banana he rushed down from the tree and left the glasses behind. In the same way, by giving the mind something more meaningful to hold onto than its roving thoughts, *the mind can be trained* to let go of trivia and cling only to the essential.

Again and again, Krishna returns to the theme of controlling the senses by the mind, the mind by the intellect and the intellect through remembrance of *Atma*, remembrance in *Atma*. This control consists of no violence, no pushing, no struggle, and no judgement. In the beginning it might manifest as struggle. But in essence, it is simply remembrance that calls forth oneself from the depths of oneself. Since the action is from oneself, there is no room for resistance as long as we are in touch with this inner awareness.

And if we help ourselves to keep coming back to this space of awareness silence each time the mind roams, we will reach a place of peace, a space of love within, which is beyond anything that the material world alone can offer(26). Through the material world of our body, emotions and intellect in harmony with the higher, we become vehicles for the divine marriage of matter and spirit to transubstantiate in us. Then in this state, we can reside in the supreme joy of our own Real nature(27).

True Empathy

When we begin to experience this peace and love, this space of calm abiding, we spontaneously share it with others. We exude it from every cell. For it is the nature of love to give of itself by *being itself*, as it is the nature of breath to breathe. Love is the great unifier of all beings. Love allows us to see the other as ourself. Love allows us to see God in everyone. While under the influence of love every being is equal. There is no place for criticism or reactivity to wrongs—only forbearance, compassion, nonviolence.

> The *yogi* who pure from sin ever prays in this harmony of soul soon feels the joy of Eternity, the infinite joy of union with God.

> He sees himself in the heart of all beings and he sees all beings in his heart. This is the vision of the *yogi* of harmony, a vision which is ever one.
>
> And when he sees me in all and he sees all in Me then I never leave him and he never leaves me.
>
> He who in this oneness of love loves me in whatever he sees, wherever this man may live, in truth this man lives in me.
>
> And he is the greatest *yogi,* he whose vision is ever one; when the pleasure and pain of others is his own pleasure and pain. (6:28-32) JM

To be able to live *with* the God in oneself *as* the God in oneself at all times, there can be no room for lack, no room for incompleteness, no space for dissatisfaction. There can be only wholeness—only bliss. According to Ramanuja,[8] *slokas* 29-32 depict four developmental stages of *yoga.* At the culmination, one is fully established in the essence of Knowledge, which brings total equality.

> He who, because of the similarity between his own self and other selves, as they are all constituted similarly of uncontracted Knowledge in their essential being, views the pleasures in the form of the birth of a son and the sorrows in the form of the death of a son of his own and of others as equal, on the ground of their equal unrelatedness to such pleasures and pains to him. Viewing his own pleasures and pains as being not different from those of others of the same kind—that *yogin* is judged as having reached the summit of *yoga.* (Ramanuja, in Swami Addidevananda, p.229)

The highest *yogi* therefore does not hysterically suffer the pains and pleasures of others but rather, compassionately understands the Self is unrelated to the joys and sorrows of the mind, both in oneself and in others.

From another perspective, the sages have likened this quality of total empathy to the relationship of the limbs to the body. When one leg is broken the entire body is affected. In a similar way, all God's creatures are like limbs of His One body, the Cosmic Form. When a person is mistreated, it is as if one's own Self were mistreated; when one is treated well, it is as if one's own Self were treated well, as we are all One Self.

> Man does not differentiate the limbs of his own body as high and low. The *yogi* sees the cosmos as the body of *Paramatma*, himself a limb of the Cosmic person.
> (Swami Chidbhavananda, p.393)

Effort is Never Wasted

When we first hear of this meditation *yoga* it is not easily intelligible. It takes time and practice to distill and integrate. Yet at the same time, it resonates to something truthful within. The difficulty of Arjuna in understanding what in the world Krishna is talking about is evident. Initially his words can be taken in only partially. And again the anxiety and doubts emerge. What will happen to a person who starts this *yoga* and doesn't finish it? Will he end up being unfit for the world of achievement and for the world of the spirit as well?

Krishna reinforces for Arjuna and also for us, the power of yearning, the power of purity, and the power of practice(35). These qualities of consciousness follow us from life to life, ever structuring the nature of our circumstances, offering us further situations conducive to spiritual evolution. For we become what our deepest desire is.

Now that Krishna finds Arjuna ready to practice meditation, he says that when the spiritual student is ripe, meditation is the most important practice as it allows the person to live more deeply in Truth, more directly in his own Self. The paths of austerity, knowledge, and action prepare the way for the yogi to enter the path of practice and meditation. And the fulfillment of meditation rests in one's faithful love for God, which can be experienced in all beings, at all times, in all places. "And the greatest of all *yogis* is he who with all his soul has faith and he who with all his soul loves me."(47)

Reflections on Meditation

Swami Vivekananda says:

> The meditative state is the highest state of existence. So long as

> there is desire, no real happiness can come. It is only the contemplative, witness-like study of objects that brings us real enjoyment and happiness. The animal has its happiness in the senses, man in his intellect and the god in spiritual contemplation. It is only to the soul that has attained to this contemplative state that the world really becomes beautiful. To him who desires nothing and does not mix himself up with the world, the manifold changes of nature are one panorama of beauty and sublimity. (*Raja Yoga*, p.84)

In a talk to his students, Sri Sathya Sai Baba offers some practical uggestions for meditation:

> How is meditation to be done? The first step is concentration(*dharana*). Twelve *dharana*s amount to one *dhyana* (meditation). Twelve *dhyanas* equal one *samadhi*(equal mindedness). *Dharana* is steady, concentrated viewing of an object for 12 seconds. You have to look at an object, a flame, a picture or an idol for 12 seconds with total concentration without blinking the eyelids. This is *dharana*. Practicing *dharana* is a preparation for *dhyana*. The duration for *dhyana* is 12 *dharana*s. This means it should last 12 times 12 or 144 seconds. That is 2 minutes and 24 seconds. It is only after concentration has been practiced that one can do meditation well. Twelve *dhyanas* equal one *samadhi*. This means 144 times12 seconds; that is 28 minutes and 48 seconds, very much less than an hour. If *samadhi* is prolonged, it may prove fatal.
>
> These are the disciplines the *yogis* practiced. If you want to proceed correctly in the practice of these disciplines you have to begin with concentration for 12 seconds a day from now on. This is very important for students. In the past, *yogis* like Aurobindo and Ramana Maharshi practiced these disciplines. Ramana Maharshi used to go up to the terrace and concentrate on a particular star for 12 seconds. There is also an internal method of practicing concentration. When you close your eyes, a small dark spot appears before the inner eye. You may concentrate on this spot for 12 seconds without letting it move. By this practice, the power of meditation can be developed. In that state, the mind is still and steady. By continuing this practice of concentration, you develop the capacity to perform meditation for 2 minutes, 24 seconds. Continuing the practice of meditation in this way, you develop the capacity to be in a state of equalmindedness for 28 minutes and 48 seconds.

> What is the inner meaning of *samadhi*? It is not a state of unconsciousness or some kind of superconsciousness. It is nothing of that kind. That is only hysteria. The correct meaning of *samadhi* is equalmindedness, the state in which the intellect has achieved equanimity. Whether in pleasure or pain, in praise or blame, in gain or loss, in heat or cold, to be able to maintain an equal mind is *samadhi*. That is the real fruit of meditation. This is a sacred day on which you can begin this *yogic* practice, which will enable you to sharpen your mind and develop the keenness of your intellect.
>
> Meditation is an extremely easy process. But merely sitting in the cross-legged posture cannot be described as meditation. To maintain one's calmness and patience during meditation, unaffected by any disturbing elements, such as a mosquito sitting on your nose, concentration has to be practiced. Through concentration, control of the senses is also achieved and purity of mind is secured. Through mental purity the Divine is experienced.

So the *samadhi* of which the sages speak is perfect inner stillness—a stillness that does not identify itself with or react to any stimuli of the senses, emotions or intellect. It is not focussed on one side or the other of the pairs of opposites. It is not concerned with good and bad. The total sphere of cosmic consciousness awareness is perfect equilibrium; an effortless containment of the opposites which allows us to transcend the opposites, a sacred motionless space where the three *gunas* are equal.

Thus, the sixth discourse introduces us to the prerequisites and practice of linking the mind and ego with the all pervasive energy of the innermost Self.

Seven

YOGA OF KNOWLEDGE AND WISDOM

Jnana Vijnana Yoga

	Gita verses
Discriminative Knowledge*(vijnana)*	1–3
Qualities of divine phenomenal nature*(apara prakriti)*, subtle nature and source*(para prakriti)*	4–6
Presence of *Purusha* permeating the entire world	7–12
Ignorant and divine qualities of *maya*	13–15
Four types of devotees	16–19
Worship of the perishable gods	20–23
The supreme Lord, liberation of the highest *yogis*, and bondage of the ignorant	24–30

invisible is
the true foundation of life
One Reality

nature pulsates
exuding loving consciousness
taste it

At the end of the sixth discourse, Krishna teaches that faith and love are the insignia of the greatest *yogis*(47). To inspire love, it is helpful to know who or what we are loving and what is That in which we place our faith. For without knowledge, faith tends toward superstition and love leans toward fantasy or projection. Therefore, to inspire our love and faith, Krishna in the seventh discourse expounds on the nature of direct Knowledge called wisdom. This subjective science is a blending of faith, experience and knowledge.

In the west, science is considered the study of the objective universe and all that's in it. What does the world consist of? From the tiniest quark to the broadest expansiveness of space, how does it work? How does life begin and end? In Sanskrit, the study of scriptures is also called science(*sastra*). This science however is concerned not only with the objective universe, but primarily with the subjective universe. The study of *sastra* is considered the science of our deepest inner subjectivity, the Self, and how this relates to the world, as we know it. It is said that when one has mastered the science of *sastra* one knows everything. There is nothing more that needs to be known(2).

When philosophy became divorced from psychology in the late 1800's, the search for truth was relegated to science. But as science was more interested in phenomenal fact than philosophical Truth, there was no longer a western scientific discipline where reason and heart, logos and love could come together. As philosophy became more speculative and intellectual, science became more technological and factual, until the work of Einstein and other physicists began to revolutionize the way we view matter and energy. Einstein was said to have read the *Bhagavad Gita* daily and was an avid student of *Vedanta*. Now physics views matter not so much as a gross, concrete separate entity measurable by the senses but rather, as unmanifest flowing energy, interconnected with everything else, which dances to the laws of attraction and repulsion, creation and dissolution. In this way, western science is coming closer to the idea of unity as expressed by the ancient sages.

All this is the theme of the seventh chapter. The connection between the Self and the universe is explored. What is the relationship of part to whole, subject and object? On the physical level, the same five elements present in the universe are also the building blocks of the human body. On the psychological level, the world is created by our thoughts, words and deeds. Interactions permeate all levels of existence. Ultimately, the sages say there is no such thing as you and me. There is only "I am that I am." The Self in me is the Self in thee. Nothing is separate. This Self is the universe. *Atman* is *Brahman*. There is only unity. All is one.

The link that interconnects all the varied forms of matter and energy is the atom(*anu*). The atom is invisible and pervades everything, "the smallest of the small and the greatest of the great." The atom has been likened to the *Atma*, which pervades everyone and renders everything equal, permeated by the basic energy of the Self. So in the seventh chapter, we enter the realm of matter and spirit, illusion and Reality, the concrete and the hidden and the relationship between the two.

The science of scriptures is not knowledge that comes primarily from books or university. It is knowledge meant to be lived. The first step is hearing the knowledge; the second step is reflecting on it; the third step is practicing it, experiencing it, entering into it through our daily living. One can give fine discourses on the ideas of the *Gita* but without living the ideas, the knowledge is almost worthless. For the purpose of this science is *to help human beings bring the greatest good into daily living* so that it will benefit us and every being we come in contact with, be it animal, plant or human.

There's a story about an Indian woman who saw her housekeeper reading the *Bhagavad Gita*. She asked the maid, "What good is it for you to read that book? It's nothing but a waste of time. How could it possibly help you in your job, in your life"? The woman replied,

"Before I read the *Gita* I used to vacuum the carpet. Now I turn the carpet over and vacuum the dust off both sides."[9] Whatever way we apply this knowledge to our lives, it becomes useful. It turns into wisdom. And when the wisdom is experienced at the deepest level, Krishna says we become omniscient. We know everything.

Three prerequisites for receiving this knowledge are: 1) having the heartfelt wish to know Truth, 2) taking refuge in the highest Reality; having Truth as one's only authority and protector and surrendering oneself to that Truth—even if we don't yet fully know what this means; and 3) practicing *yoga* or linking the body, mind and intellect to the highest within at all times(1). When these three become our living companions, openness occurs and *the universe becomes our teacher*. But without embracing the prerequisites, our evolution is substantially slowed down, in spite of good intentions.

Otherwise we merely adapt. There is a quantum leap between adaptation and evolution. Life at the animal level adapts to its environment. For the animal, superb adaptation leads to biological evolution. With human beings more is required. Life at the truly human level adapts *and* evolves through conscious yearning for wholeness.

Matter and Spirit

In this science, the material world is called *prakriti*(4). Matter is divided into eight parts—the five elements of earth, water, fire, air, ether; then mind, intellect and ego sense. The number eight symbolizes the world and the number nine signifies *Brahman*, for it is everywhere. Whatever is multiplied by nine adds up to nine.[10] According to *sankhya* philosophy, everything in the physical world is composed of these eight divisions of matter. Our body, mind and intellect are composed of the five elements. When the gross body dies, the five elements dissolve. Permeating all the material world is higher *prakriti* and spirit, called *Purusha*. *Purusha* is the Sanskrit word for Self and is also the name for man. Matter is inert. Only through being infused with spirit are we alive(5). There is no life without *Purusha*. Matter alone is dead.

The problem is we think it is the body ego form that's alive. The body by itself is nothing without the Self, which animates it. Thus our beginning spiritual work becomes the task of separating out the Self from the not Self, spirit from matter, the vital from the inert through observing, which by itself leads to understanding and transformation. We usually spend our lives in a state of identification with our body, emotions, thoughts, and possessions. When this occurs, the life principle in us, the *Purusha* has fallen into matter. The sparks of life have become imprisoned in heaviness. And we suffer.

The Kabalah tells of the *Shekinah*, the female spirit of God, which was enclosed in a vessel. Somehow the vessel broke sending out all the sparks in numerous directions. Soon they became unknown entities hidden in matter. And it is the ongoing task of human beings to redeem these sparks. This is the purpose of life.

> Once the individual comes to understand clearly the distinction between matter and spirit, he will indeed come to understand that the spirit identifying with matter is the cause for all its sufferings and when it is detached from all its identifications, it rediscovers for itself its own essential nature as perfection and bliss Absolute. The spirit identifying with matter and sharing the destinies of the inert equipment is called the ego. It is the ego that comes to rediscover itself to be nothing other than the spirit that presides over matter. (Swami Chinmayananda THG, p.425-6)

God as Nature

In *Vedanta*, nature is considered a friend and not an adversary. It is through nature that we evolve, love and come to know our self. Shankara says that *nature acts for the liberation of souls and not merely to display her own glory* (see *Brahma Sutra Bhasya*, p.516). The question then becomes, what aspect of nature are we identified with? Our animal nature is concerned with mates, money, acquisition and position—with automatic instinct and territoriality; our human nature is concerned with compassion and wishes to give and love; our godly nature experiences the wisdom of knowing and being. So everything we have to work with is nature. Which level of nature are we identified with?

Nature is not considered evil whereas God is considered good. Nature and God are not pitted against each other. The serpent in the garden of Eden is like the awakener to evolution. It is not nature that is to be combated but the identification of the ego with our animal nature—the false belief that I am that person whose life is based solely on job, mate, opinion, status and "mine." This does not mean that animal needs are not important. These can be essential vehicles for our maintenance and growth. But when we believe these externals are "real," or the total human being, we are stuck. And our potential waits on the back burner.

For many of us living surrounded by concrete in crowded apartments, nature deeply inspires the feeling of love, freedom and beauty. She is a living reflection of God in the universe, easily accessible to direct perception and inner experience. *Prakriti* is the body of the Goddess. When we lovingly experience nature, we are experiencing the love of God and Goddess. And through this love, we are actively participating in redeeming the divine sparks from matter. On the other hand, those who strive to control and unconsciously decimate naturc primarily for personal profit are contributing to imprisoning the divine sparks, thereby rendering love inaccessible.

This same process working in the world of nature also applies to the world of the human personality through ongoing creation, preservation and dissolution. For the mind, intellect and ego are part of the eight-fold division of *prakriti*. Brahma the creator, Vishnu the preserver and Siva the destroyer as one unity are ever at work in the world, in man and in the events in life. The ego or human personality is a reflection of the higher nature of God. "Man was created in the image of God." Without life animating, the person would not exist. When there is conscious acknowledgment of life acting *through* me, then for that moment I am no longer identified with the ego. If while thinking I am not identified with the intellect; or while feeling I am not identified with the emotions, then for an instant the sparks have been redeemed. The transcendent is experienced as immanent.

When we observe ourself as an event moving alongside-within the life principle that supports all events, we go from a participant observer ego to a witness. The witness lives in Self remembrance. Through insight that includes sensation feeling energy(*sakti*), lower *prakriti* is transformed into higher *prakriti*. To the degree that we live in acknowledgment devotion ever linking with the *Atma*, the witness and the supreme *Purusha* lose their distinct boundaries. What begins as self-observation from the mind and ego becomes the witness, which is later experienced as the Self. These word categories reveal subtler, finer, more pervasive designations of experience.

Picture a pond. The sun is reflected in the pond. The image of the sun in the pond is like the observer ego. Man was made in the image of God to reflect the image of God functioning through the principles of the material world. The human individuality(*jiva*) is also that. We each have that potentiality. But if we remain imprisoned in matter we don't make very good reflectors for the image of the life principle of divinity to shine through.

Here's what the ex math professor, Swami Rama Tirtha had to say about nature:

> The only right anybody has is to serve. Nature, if allowed to have her free course will never err. The law or God that worked up the evolution of man from the tiniest amoeba to the human form divine can well be trusted. Service and love, not mandates and compulsion is the atmosphere for growth.
>
> Happy is he who turns the whole world into a heavenly garden by seeing the same impersonal breath of life in the throngs of men and women as inspires in the rose garden and oak groves.
>
> So nature is not explained by dwelling on its surface laws and superficial causation but by its becoming the body of man. Unless you feel all you know not all. Diving into the reality sounding below the names and forms, passing free into woods and field, mountains and rivers into day and nights, clouds and stars, passing free into man and woman, animals and angels as the Self of each and all. This is life. This is Self Knowledge. This is practical wisdom.
>
> The whole world is bound to co-work with one who feels himself one with the whole world. (Dayton, p.254, 262)

Atman Transcendent and Immanent

> There is nothing whatsoever higher than me, O Dhananjaya. All this is strung in Me as clusters of gems on a string. (7:7)

All selves are part of one Self. Everyone and everything is part of the body of God. And the Self is the seed in everyone which, if we are conscious of it, can grow into a tree and flower, or if we remain unconscious of it will remain encased in the seed shell, never to blossom, like a divine spark imprisoned in matter. The highest Reality permeates everyone and everything. Everyone and everything are supported by this Reality. "I am not in them. They are in Me"(7:12). Its effulgence will shower blessings on the earth, if it can be but recognized. To open the heart and experience the heart of life, unity is our aim.

> I am the everlasting seed of eternal life. I am the intelligence of the intelligent. I am the beauty of the beautiful. (7:10)

What then prevents us from reveling in the freedom of the Self? What keeps humanity imprisoned in suffering? Why do the ups and downs of life ensnare us like a rope coiled round our necks?

Krishna tells us it is the power of *maya*—a power so strong, so inscrutable, so all pervasive because it was created by God. *Divine illusion is an intrinsic part of divine creation.* As *maya* is extremely subtle it is very difficult to comprehend, almost impossible to grasp. Its power causes us to mistake the unreal for the real(13). It makes us believe that matter is truth; that the five senses and mind know reality. It serves to identify us with our bodies, our functioning, our likes and dislikes. It makes us trust the concrete aspects of life, as if that's all there is. *Maya* keeps us embroiled in the mundane.

There was a great sage named Narada who used to walk through the worlds visiting people and causing trouble, thereby uplifting them from the bonds of ignorance. Even though he was a highly realized soul he was not beyond the power of *maya*, if Krishna so willed it. One day Narada and Krishna were walking and Narada asks, "How does *maya* maintain such power over human beings"? Krishna ignored the question and later asks him to bring a glass of water from the neighboring village. Narada approaches a hut and a beautiful girl appears. He completely forgets about the water. He falls madly in love. They get married. They have children. He ploughs the fields. Everything blooms. He becomes rich. His grandchildren are born. He is very, very happy. And then a flood comes inundating all.

In a flash he loses everything—wife, children, grandchildren, fields, crops, house—everything. Nothing remains. The village totally vanishes. He is the only survivor. In despair he calls on God for help. And who should appear but Krishna, who smilingly asks, "Did you forget about my glass of water, Narada"?[11]

Since *maya* was created by divine intent, she serves some useful purpose for humanity. Just as *maya* keeps us bound to the mundane, *maya* also can free us from the mundane. We must learn how to travel from lower *prakriti*(ego) to higher *prakriti*(witness) to the Supreme *Purusha* which encompasses and transcends both. Until we choose to accept our God given responsibility of *dharma* to struggle against the blinding aspect of *maya*, we are still participating in a divine drama—but as unconscious victims of *maya*. Through accepting the process of spiritual striving, we are being given a choice—to participate in the workings of nature consciously as human beings, or to participate in nature unconsciously, utilizing only the automatic, instinctive, animal parts of ourselves intermingled with our human brains, human functions and human endowments.

Maharaj says:

> "Look at yourself steadily. It is enough. The door that locks you in is also the door that lets you out."

Thus, when we are identified with lower *prakriti*, *maya* appears as illusion. When we have consciously made contact with higher *prakriti*, *maya* appears as a *sakti*, the goddess, the force of creation, an opportunity for freedom. As the veiling power of *tamoguna* becomes lessened through emotional purification, the natural creative power of *maya* reveals Herself in our lives.

> *Maya* is neither illusion nor relativity. *Maya* is free will, the freedom to create. *Maya* is the idea of life giving rise to multiple forms, just as the word flower gives rise to endless forms in the mind.
>
> To which form should one be attached? To none and yet to all. Imagine that you are impartial, not attached to one form or another, not dogmatic about one form or another. Then every form will

delight you for in each you will see the incarnation of a life idea. And *maya* is this exuberance of creation. (Reymond, p.219)

Taking Refuge Within

As part of nature, the workings of *maya* are intertwined with the three *gunas*: *tamas*, lifeless inertia; *rajas*, passionate activity; and *sattva* peaceful actions for the common good(12). As long as the mind is a magnet of the *gunas*, we are under the spell of *maya*. Through purifying the heart and mind, the *gunas* gradually loosen their grip. When realization dawns, the sages say we are no longer under the power of the *gunas* or *maya*.

How then does this miracle occur, the miracle of invulnerability to the *gunas*? Krishna says:

> My *maya* is very difficult to cross. Only those who seek refuge in the higher can leave behind this divine illusion. (7:14)

What does it mean to take refuge in Me? Can we place our trust, our center of gravity, our primary motivation in the highest law of consciousness love, which lives buried inside each of us? Is it possible to just *be* in such a way that all our activities are prompted by, supported by, protected by the Void, that wordless, highest Truth? How can we come to live so that everything we think and do revolves around the belief in the inherent lawfulness of life, that love and knowledge live within us waiting to be uncovered?

Buddhists have an active ceremony called taking refuge. It is a ritual whereby one vows to place one's trust in the Buddha, the higher intelligence; the *dharma*, the laws of righteousness and right living; and the *sangha*, the community of evolved beings and spiritual aspirants. Likewise, taking refuge in Krishna does not necessarily mean worshipping a particular person in a bodily form as God. Rather it refers to a higher, deeper nature that lives within each of us covered by *maya* to a greater or lesser degree. This higher nature has been called pure love, pure awareness, pure bliss, pure Oneness that embraces everyone and everything as part of its totality. First we must learn to discriminate between the genuine and the superficial, the most essential knowledge and concrete information, so that evolution can proceed.

Sri Sathya Sai Baba tells a story about a famous scholar who had to cross a great river to give a speech. Although the boatman was simple and uneducated, since the scholar was bored he began chatting.

"Do you have a newspaper"? he asked." No, I don't know how to read," said the boatman. "Do you have a walkman that we could listen to"? "No, I don't even know what a walkman is," said the boatman. "Do you know the time"? asked the scholar. "What good would it do me to have a watch if I don't know how to read the time"? At this point, the scholar in proud disbelief said, "Living in this day and age, you don't know what's going on in the world, you don't know how to read and write, you don't even know how to tell the time. You're wasting your life. Three quarters of your life is going down the drain!"

The poor boatman said nothing. Shortly after, the wind started howling and the waves became fierce. There was a terrible storm. The boatman asked, "Can you swim"? "No" answered the scholar. "Then *all* your life is going down the drain," he said. And the boat capsized. Sai Baba says:

> When you are travelling across a turbulent river, you should know how to swim. Without knowing how to swim, all your other knowledge of philosophy, physics, chemistry, commerce, mathematics and political science will be of no use. In the journey of life, you are travelling on a rushing, unpredictable river; you should know how to stay afloat and cross that river. To swim safely across you must have the knowledge of *Atma* and you must develop a strong power of discrimination to know that which is useful and that which is useless for crossing this river of worldly life. If you have not developed a capacity along these lines, there will be no way for you to find fulfillment in life. As long as you base your life on wealth, property and worldly things, you will never be able to derive any real joy. There are two things which every person has to attain; one is external freedom and the other is inner freedom. External freedom speaks of independence, being free of external bonds and limitations. Inner freedom speaks of liberation from the

> bondage of the sense organs; having them under your full control. Every individual should realize both these freedoms.
>
> In the external world, as long as you are under the control of other people, such as some foreign king or ruler, you won't be able to get real joy. In the inner world, as long as you are a slave of the various sense organs then also you won't be able to enjoy real freedom. Even for outer freedom, control of the sense organs is important. But for becoming master of the inner world, the single most important faculty that you must develop is the control of the sense organs, by gaining control over the mind. Once you have control of the mind, you will be able to get real joy, both externally and internally, for then you will be able to see the Lord everywhere. (DBG p.137)

So by intentionally taking refuge in this Truth, which is the law of life, we are acknowledging to ourselves that it is possible to gradually peel away the veils that cover Reality from us—all under the protection of natural law that ever guides and guards us, by meting out painful and pleasurable experiences based on our past actions, in accordance with what we need to learn in order to evolve. When awareness is present, these experiences can lead to insight. When we see our failings we can change and grow. Where there is insight we become harmonious. For by seeing ourselves in a new way, our thoughts and feelings come together. Aha! Little surprises, little shocks unite the psyche. Inner dissension in the light of the witness leads to unification. And purification proceeds.

A Function of "Evil"

To believe everything that happens to us is part of this underlying principle of protection, prodding us toward evolution can be comforting. There is a proverb in India, "*Dharma* protects those who protect *dharma*." Sometimes what life dishes out might appear harsh. But in accordance with the science of *sastra*, everything that happens is part of the workings of law to establish harmony within nature. And we are being called to participate. All our suffering is to engage us more fully in redeeming the divine sparks from matter. When we choose to participate consciously, we feel rewarded. When we ignore the urge to cooperate, we become more deeply buried in *maya* and the consequent inevitable sorrows that identification with *maya* brings.

Therefore, in Krishna's teachings, one explanation of evil is based on the degree to which *maya* covers the heart(15). When we have little connection with our own inner Self, Truth or conscience, we cannot help but perform actions that are selfish or harmful to others. When our conscience or inner knowing is less covered by darkness, we will see more clearly in accordance with universal truth. And our actions will reflect that. Since ignorant action brings suffering, as our ignorance comes to light our suffering becomes more intensely conscious so that our ignorance can be revealed. When we are able to feel and see, the compartments dissolve and our pain gradually diminishes. Then we come to know what is needed in each situation as it arises. Through suffering our faults in the presence of the light of consciousness, our imperfections become purified. Our load becomes lighter. Thus, our work becomes seeing our ignorance—noticing how our behavior and motivation are imprisoned by the magnet of maya.

But to suffer without connection to the higher consciousness within, we are neither seeing our faults nor experiencing insight. So we keep repeating the same old mistakes again and again under different guises, as the *vasanas* get stronger. And we become further embroiled in *maya.*

Swami Chinmayananda says, "Sin is not the nature of man. It is only the tarnish that comes to dim the brilliance of the Self due to an error of judgement in the individual." Therefore, let us not get discouraged. In accordance with the evolutionary principles of nature, eventually all beings will be prodded in the direction of realization. Our selfish actions performed because of ignorance inevitably lead to suffering. Our suffering causes us to try to discover an end to suffering. When after much trial and error we come to see that nothing in the material world can be the source of lasting happiness, then we are eventually led to a teaching.

> Evil is the shadow of inattention. In the light of self-awareness it will wither and fall off. (Maharaj)

The Four Seekers

Krishna describes four types of spiritual seekers(16). The first type(*arthah*) is suffering and filled with pain, be it physical or psychological. One might lose a loved one, live in an unhappy marriage, go through a divorce, become ill, lose one's job, wealth or good name. This can happens to anyone during the process of living, at one time or another. For some of us, it takes real trouble to force us to look for genuine help! But not all distressed persons are enough in touch with themselves to seek the higher or to go within. Some turn to drink, sex or drugs instead, until the time is ripe for them to evolve. An example given of this first type of devotee, the one who suffers, is Draupadi, the wife of the Pandavas. And she is a perfect devotee. Even without suffering, Draupadi is the personification of *dharma*. But she suffered a lot.

There was a time in her life when she was subject to a terrible humiliation. As a result of a crooked game of dice, the Pandavas lost every material thing they owned, including their kingdom and their freedom. Duryodhana wished to take Draupadi as a slave. In order to torment the Pandavas, he orders his brother Dushashan to disrobe her. She is dragged by the hair into the court. As the layers of her sari keep unravelling, the cloth miraculously keeps multiplying. After a time, even Duryodhana sensed the presence of the divine. When in her suffering, Draupadi called on Krishna, he was compelled to respond.

The second type is called the intellectually curious(*jignasu*), or the seeker of knowledge. This person might have done a lot of reading, attends lectures, goes from teacher to teacher with the underlying question, "what is Truth and how can I find it"? As he is helped to go more deeply beneath the level of intellectual curiosity to experience his own genuine yearning, he will gradually become a true devotee.

The third category is called the seeker of wealth(*artharthi*). Wealth might not necessarily be money but an awareness of meaning, or divine qualities. To be able to live one's life with an underlying sense of purpose is really the greatest richness. Money and material comfort are unimportant to the one whose life reflects a deeper sense of purpose. As understanding deepens, peace and contentment become an ongoing way of being. This is true wealth.

The fourth devotee is the person of wisdom(*jnani*), the one for whom there is no separateness; there is no you and me, just unity. This devotee sees God in every creature, in every action, in everything that happens be it called good or bad. Mother Theresa exemplifies this type of devotee. When asked about the secret of her success in life she replied that for her, being married to God is Reality. She said something like, "I see Jesus in the face of the beggar dying in my arms on the street or in the eyes of the child. Everyone I see is God. Everyone I love as my Beloved." This is the vision of the man or woman of wisdom.

At different times in our lives, our experiences may reflect each of the first three types. But in the end, in order for us to become liberated, to live that loving consciousness unity, we must each become the person of vision, of wisdom. For it is the *jnani* who lives Truth. He is the true devotee. Thus he is dearest to Krishna.

Worship

Whoever in sincerity looks to the higher or looks within for help will receive it(23). For Krishna loves all beings, as *His nature is love. Prema* is pure love, equal love, not just to those who are kith and kin. Even those who are not devoted to any higher principle will be rewarded based on the quality of effort, for whatever we consistently work on will bear fruit(20). It is a law of *karma*: what we wish and earnestly strive for we will receive. If we worship and work for a paycheck we will receive the paycheck. If we worship and work for wisdom as well as earthly *dharma*, we will receive both wisdom and the paycheck. "Seek and ye shall find. Knock and the door will be open." But how often do our fears of the intangible—all under the guise of skepticism—prevent us from seeking something higher than the familiar?

In the end, everything we work for, everything we receive, is all given by the life energy that supports our capacity to wish and to work(21). It is this life principle *Purusha* that provides, whether we are conscious of it or not. And this divine provider, be he called Krishna, Buddha, Mohammed, or Jesus, is the energy manifesting through these persons fully and is not to be mistaken for a limited form only. For God is infinite pure consciousness without limits of time and place or boundaries of form and locality. This all knowingness is everywhere, says Krishna. If you and I do not experience this yet, this is because of *ahankara*, the limiting nature of egoism.

When the ego becomes freed from the outer forms of worship, be they of work, family, power or fame, the mind leaves its extroversion behind. Our worship soon derives more directly from the source, from the heart, love, consciousness, which dissolves false seeing. Through connecting directly with the inner, the grace of life showers forth. Without this inner connection, we rely on intermediaries; be they called the gods, the powers that be, the system, social structure, logical reasoning, ego effort, past *karma* or influential people. *Maya* is upheld by placing our faith solely in these extroverted pursuits(25). The mind is but a fantasy, a superimposition on Reality. Krishna is teaching that when we wholeheartedly yearn for the life-giving fountain, *the source comes to us*.

> Verily, the fruit that accrues to those men of little intelligence is finite. The worshippers of the gods go to the gods. But my devotees come to Me. (7:23)

The experiences of genuine devotion accumulate and become deposited in the mindbank of remembrance as spiritual wealth. This wealth attracts the love of God. Ramanuja says:

> What is expressed by the term worship is really a succession of memories that becomes the cause of being chosen by the supreme Self and which is very dear because the object of remembrance (the Supreme Himself) is very dear(to the worshipper). (Swami Adidevananda, p.243)

As our inner purification proceeds, we become freer from the chains of like and dislike. To be free from automatically following our preferences is to be free. To be free of partiality is to accept knowingly the destiny we have created for ourselves, as the bondage of our past actions works itself out without causing further bondage. *The more deeply we are able to take refuge in the higher, the more we will be helped to give up our selfishness.* Self-centered focus will gradually give way to motivation for others, for the well being of all.

With this inner intent, purification of "negative" emotions proceeds. As selfishness departs, compassion becomes a way of being.

We come in touch with the Self within. We see the Self in all beings; we begin to make connections, see the workings of universal law. And the more the ego melts away, the more we perceive Truth everywhere, until that's all there is permeating everything no matter what. The atom of *Atma* dispels all divisiveness, all like and dislike, which can be viewed as the result of the *vasanas* or "original sin" called *maya* (27). The *yogi* who is merged with his Self is no longer subject to this delusion of the body ego mind form. He knows his own true nature and the roots of action (29). Through taking refuge in the Self, he lives out the basis of sacrifice. Be it in the realm of sense objects, sense organs or perceptions, he lets go of all identification with the mind and ego(30).

Transforming Levels of Maya

Let's review the ongoing process of the transformation of nature(*prakriti*) toward ever deepening contact with the Self:

1. Lower *prakriti* predominates in the psyche. The ego is ensnared in inertia, identification and ignorance(*tamas* and *rajas*).
2. The ego observes itself and suffers its condition. Emotions come out of hiding and the person begins to wonder, "Is this all there is"? The ego becomes a seeker.
3. Continued self-observation and/or work with dreams, images, scriptures, contemplation or contact with a holy person lead to subsequent insights. This is experienced in the body as energy, emotion, sensation(*sakti*) and in the mind as awareness. This purifies *tamas* and *rajas* and allows more space for the spontaneous flow of creation. Emotional purification proceeds. As the blockages or knots of the heart are cleared away this leads to:
4. Higher *prakriti,* the witness. Now the light of *Purusha* reflects more directly through the witnessing consciousness. The opposites come closer together and shed their power over the

personality. Uncontrollable emotional upheavals, which had been experienced as highs and lows, grandiosity and depression, joy and sorrow, can be consciously experienced under the gaze of the witnessing consciousness, dissolving the veils, bringing balance and equalmindedness. And intuitive inner knowing becomes a way of being. As worship, remembrance and contemplation continue to purify *vasanas*, this enhances our spiritual work and paves the way toward our goal, the goal-less goal:

5. Steady concentration, meditation, *samadhi*, unity, Self realization, liberation.

Swami Vivekananda says:

> At first the goal is far off, outside Nature and far beyond it, attracting us all towards it. This has to be brought near, yet without being degraded or degenerated, until when it has become closer and closer, the God of Heaven becomes the God in Nature; till the God in Nature becomes the God who is Nature; and the God who is Nature becomes the God within this temple of the body; and the God dwelling in the temple of the body becomes the temple itself; becomes the soul of man. Thus it reaches the last words it can teach. He whom the sages have sought in all these places is in our own hearts. Thou art He, O man! Thou art He!

Thus, the seventh discourse reveals the secret subjective science *yoga* that links us to inner understanding, wisdom, and total Knowledge.

Eight

YOGA OF THE IMPERISHABLE BRAHMAN

Akshara Brahma Yoga

	Gita verses
Arjuna's questions and Krishna's answers	1–7
Meditation on the Supreme	8–15
The *yugas*(time scheme) and creation	17–19
The eternal unmanifest and how to uncover it	20–22
Paths of light and darkness during life and death	23–27
The supreme state of the *yogi*	28

there are many worlds
of the living and the dead
pierce them all through love

at the last moment
when the great transition comes
be only in Me

In the seventh discourse, Krishna guides Arjuna toward the experience of the Supreme Self within. Unless this *Atman* is known within, It cannot be known. But at the same time, Self realization is also everything—the supreme *Brahman*. Once the Self is realized, the transcendent *Brahman* in all its unlimited vastness is truly known, say the sages. For this same *Brahman* is called *Atma* or *Purusha* when experienced within the body. So the eighth discourse leads us from the building blocks of the universe toward hints of the infinite and prods the intellect to a point beyond intellect where cycles of time merge into space and causation, thereby revealing a realm beyond change and limitation.

Every phenomenon of the cosmos is *Brahman*; the transcendent totality, cycles of cosmic expansiveness and dissolution, the ever present latency of creation called birth and death—all brought into being by the witnessing action sacrifice of God reflected through the action of man(4). Subtle inner action forges the link between God as Self and God as *Brahman* and reveals that both are One. Real action (*karma*) consists of the spiritual practice that helps the *yogi* rest his consciousness in *Brahman*, worship *Brahman*, love *Brahman*. These practices guide us to a conjunction between the human and divine, the creator and created and all the underlying cycles of the broader manifestations of cosmos, movement, time and Reality.

To speak of the imperishable we must refer to the perishable. Therefore eight, which is considered the number of the perishable is the chapter chosen to designate the Eternal and that which is beyond both permanence and impermanence. "The Yoga of the Imperishable Brahman" conveys not only the vastness of the totality but also what that includes. Part of this totality is time, part is birth, and part is death. The mind is born. The mind dies. The totality remains.

Time rests in the lap of infinity maintained by the mind of events. Death rests in the lap of the creator maintained by deeds and desires. The process of change could not be perceptible without a backdrop more still than change. And the process called death could not occur without the process called birth. Beginnings and endings are impossible without an unchanging substratum. Time is impossible without movement. Time is existenceless without space.

Cycles of Continuity

There is a point(*bindu*) on the "borderline" between the finite and the infinite where death and birth coalesce, where dissolution and creation become one process. This is the realm of the snake biting its own tail to form a cycle of continuity that transcends all beginnings and endings.

Siva is viewed as the god of death and dissolution. His symbol is the *lingam*, the phallic progenitor of creation; and it is also the black cosmic egg, the womb of the universe. He is thus the cause of death and the cause of life as well as the incubating container. And he transcends all these manifestations.

Thus, death is a natural part of change, a natural process of life. It is not an end in itself. Death is not separate from birth. It is a change in the direction of the flow of life, an alteration in the form of consciousness like going from one room to the next in the giant mansion of the universe. Death is like discarding old clothes that have become worn out. It is part of an ongoing cycle that does not end until we wake up to our Reality.

When time and space are perceived as vaster than time and space, vaster than concept, the mind and ego can become naturally merged with the universal mind; that which is, from beginningless past to endless future. The sages say this process is akin to death (*Katha Upanishad*). If we are able to experience the melting of the identification with the ego *while the body is alive*, the process of the death of the body would no longer carry with it the sting of fear. For one who has already died to the supremacy of the body ego has his consciousness grounded in Reality whether his heart is beating or not.

The way we live will determine the way we die. The way we train our minds while living will determine our experience of dying. If daily we work to harness the mind toward Self Knowledge, if we devote our energy to living in awareness compassion, the sages say the mind will be resting in this loving consciousness at the moment of physical agony called death. *And where our mind rests determines our experience after death*(13).

The Indian saint Ramana Maharshi underwent surgery for cancer without any anesthetic. When the Dr. asked him if he felt pain he replied, "when I think of it." For the advanced *yogi*, it is the mind that controls the experience of the body. And even for you and me, it is our perception that determines our experience. As we think so we become. If while living we can train the ego to step aside, the light of awareness will shine through. It is this light which is the bridge from one state to the next. The infant becomes the girl and the girl becomes the woman. This is the natural process of change. Through gradually training the mind to rest in the awareness of the totality, God, love, Krishna tells us we can go beyond the change called death. If we devote our energy to being in full awareness, there will be no division between life and death. For our consciousness is continuous. And change is part of this ongoingness.

Levels of Consciousness

There are different sheaths, coverings, or levels of consciousness which must be disidentified with and transcended if we are to experience the *Atma*:

1. the gross body
2. the subtle body
3. the causal body
4. the bliss body.

When we live with our consciousness identified with the sheath of the gross body, the false belief that I am the body veils the Self from us. When we live identified with the level of the emotions, mind and intellect, ruled by our thoughts, opinions, feelings or quest for knowledge, the subtle body sheath covers the *Atman*. Or we can be under the sway of the causal body, those seed tendencies or *vasanas* either manifested or as yet unmanifest, which determine our habits, ways of being, past and present actions, our imagination and the seeds of our desires. This covering is akin to our fate. The causal body will determine the form of the subtle and the gross bodies. As long as we remain under the sway of the causal body, Reality still remains somewhat veiled from us.

The bliss sheath is the subtlest, closest covering of the *Atman*. The *Brhadaranyaka Upanishad* (4.3.33) delineates several different levels of great joy in the human and godly realms.[12] But only in the perfection of *Atman* do we experience the bliss of our own nature. All else is a covering, which is to be discarded if we are to experience *Atma* directly, Self knowingly and not as something other than the Self. When experienced independent of the senses, external objects and the process of perceiving, then bliss is no longer a sheath but is *Atman*. For *Atman* is the Self Knowledge of *Brahman*, waiting to be revealed through divine human consciousness as the ego lets go of its identification with the sheaths. Through living in this bliss we commune with our true nature.

As our emotions and intellect become purified, the sheaths loosen their grip so that the light of the *Atma* can begin to shine through. As we disidentify from the body, emotions and intellect, the causal body too changes. The *vasanas*, which are the causes of future actions, dry up like burnt seeds unable to sprout. Then the bliss of *Atman* becomes more accessible.

Those places called heaven and hell exist on earth in accordance with the way we live. It is the quality of the mind and emotions that create our heavens and our hells. The sages say the mind continues to reflect the same conditions when the body dies. When the time is ripe to claim a new body, new circumstances and experiences will resume in accordance with the desires of the mind. And the level of the mind's purity at the moment of death will determine our subsequent birth(6).

So life and death are part of one whole. To the *yogi*, death is not fearful and life is not meant for clinging. Just as life has been granted that we might clear away the sheaths that cover our true nature, death too is purposeful.

> Without birth and death, without the perpetual transmutation of all the forms of life, the world would be static, without rhythm, undancing, mummified. Every leaf must fall. If there is a deathless leaf it must be a plastic one. Do you want to live forever in an imitation plastic form of yourself? For what purpose? Death is necessary for the dynamic life to play in all its glory. (Swami Chinmayananda, *The Sages Speak about Life and Death*)

Transcending the Fear of Death

Why then are we so afraid of death? Our fear of death stems from the animal instinct of self-preservation, which is maintained by *identifying our sense of self with the body.* Through detaching the feeling of self from the body and discovering our true identity in the Self, we can discard our fear of death, says Krishna.

But on a more human level, the universal fear of death certainly serves some useful purpose, if we can allow ourselves to face it. Where there is no feeling of urgency or limited time, complacency sets in. And our allotted time here is not well utilized. By masking our fear of death in ceaseless activity and pleasure seeking, we postpone our striving for contact with the imperishable.

It is the feeling knowledge of our own mortality that prods us forward toward an inner realm of permanence, a place beyond decay and perishability, a space beyond death. Seeing the suffering that accompanies disease and death led the Buddha to search for a way that would end all suffering.

When Prince Siddhartha was born, a holy man predicted that the infant would either be the greatest king on earth or the greatest teacher of all the realms. As his father wanted to keep him close to home to rule his own kingdom, he sheltered the boy from suffering of all kinds, including old age, disease and death. His life was filled with beauty, luxury and happiness. But Siddhartha yearned to see what life was like outside the palace compound. One day, he snuck out with his driver to explore.

On the road he saw a sick man, an old man, a corpse and a monk. From that moment on, he searched to find a way to free mankind from suffering. So he left the luxury of the palace, his loving wife, and baby son. And in the forest, the noble prince lived as a renunciate for seven years, till the moment he became the Buddha. Under the *bodhi* tree he sat, true to his vow that he would not get up until full enlightenment. Then, for many years he taught and shared his wisdom, so that others could also be free from sorrow. Through facing death, compassion is born. And a spark of real life is kindled in the heart.

Aspects of Reality

Arjuna begins the chapter by asking seven questions about this Reality(1-2), which Krishna teaches at the end of the seventh chapter. He wants clarification about the meaning of *Brahman*, the primordial Self(*adhyatma*), the primary elements(*adhibhuta*), the total mind (*adhidaiva*) and the first sacrifice (*adhiyajna*). What is action? And how does a person merge in Reality when the body ego dies? The last question is the all-inclusive focus of the entire discourse.

Now Arjuna is beginning to discriminate. His intellect is becoming more open to subtleties. His questions no longer reflect the self-absorption in his own personal issues but reveal an interest in universal Knowledge, in the workings of the cosmos. For natural law, that which rules the life of each individual, is a reflection of cosmic law. The microcosm is but a reflection of the macrocosm: as above, so below. And that which is below influences what is above, as there is in reality no distinct above and below.

In order to free oneself from selfishness, we must first discover our own individual subjectivity. For our own way of seeing is an intermediary step that one day will allow us to let go of self-centeredness and come to embrace the whole naturally, without any pull toward personal merging symbiosis or societal conformity. Experiencing our own inner thoughts and feelings is important. Questions can lead to genuine self-reflection and a wholesome subjective individuality. The atmosphere then becomes ripe for learning, as the student opens to the response from wherever it comes.

Krishna responds simply to Arjuna's questions:

> *Brahman* is the supreme imperishable. His essential nature is called Self Knowledge, the offering. The act of sacrifice that causes the birth of beings is named action. (8:3)

Shankara describes *adhyatma* as "the principle that graces all bodies as their essential Self." And in the fourth *sloka*, Krishna declares that the five elements constitute His perishable nature; that He dwells in the body as the essence and the Lord, who is ever offering and being offered as the Supreme sacrifice. Krishna thus states that He permeates both matter and spirit through the act of sacrifice.

To know the eternal sacrifice, to know that which gives birth to creation is to know all perception, thought and action as sacrifice(4). To fully know all action as sacrifice is to go beyond death; to rest in the middle of creation and dissolution through conscious action. This action is different from automatic action. It is different from *re*action. It is harmonized action; balanced action, participation in life under the conscious umbrella of that which is connected to the life principle.

> The discipline to follow in life is to harmonize the levels of inner being, facing existence without identification, without thought. Then the Void is the return to the beginning, the matrix of Life. (Reymond, p.220)

The familiar western doctrine of Christianity is that Christ sacrificed his body for humanity: He died for us. This belief is reflected here in the fourth *sloka* with a different slant—as universal law in which we all participate.

> Matter is the kingdom of earth which in time passes away. But the spirit is the kingdom of light. In this body I offer sacrifice and my body is a sacrifice. (8:4) JM

This is a quote by Krishna over 5,000 years ago. Here's another translation:

> The *adhibhuta* is the perishable body; the *adhidaiva* is *Purusha,* eternal spirit. The *adhiyajna,* the supreme sacrifice is made to Me as the Lord within you. EE

Nothing can be created without sacrifice. Nothing can be created without dissolution. But it is not life that dies through sacrifice; it is only the *identification* with the body. And matter in the form of the body, mind, and intellect, which is consciously permeated with *Atmic* Reality becomes known as part of the eternal total consciousness that never changes and never dies. When we sacrifice the supremacy of the body, mind and intellect to work for consciousness, the ego gradually dissolves. Ignorance—the veiling power of *maya* and the projecting power of *maya*—progressively departs. And the ever present totality is revealed in all clarity. When we give up self-centeredness, Truth lives through us.

As *avatar*, Krishna has *fully* realized the totality and consequently He *is* that Reality. He is the cosmic mind and the supporter of the cosmic mind. He is the Knower of all, the controller of all, the force behind which life is created and maintained. And through His divine descent He embodies the supreme sacrifice.

Each of us who works toward this ever present perfection is making an offering to aid the cosmic forces that balance the universe. All participants in conscious living do partake of the body of God consciousness and become the collective community of the body of Christ, Krishna, Buddha, Yaweh, and all the unknown souls of perfection throughout the ages in accordance with the particular divine thought form with which they embody. To partake of Christ consciousness, Krishna consciousness, Buddha consciousness is the way to the Father. The transcendent can thus be realized through the ongoing support vehicle of the particular.[13]

Just as the created world in all its manifestations is the sacrifice of the Lord on the total cosmic level, so all our conscious thoughts, perceptions and feelings can also be viewed as a sacrifice by the Lord in us on the personal level. Whereas in Christian doctrine it is Jesus Christ as Lord who suffers and we through our love and identification with Him are redeemed, here it is the Lord in each individual who sacrifices through conscious action—just as the Lord sacrifices Himself through creating and maintaining the cosmos. As action entails a descent into matter, action is viewed as sacrifice. Thus, an aspect of universal law is revealed.

This sacrifice is joyous. For the one who consciously participates in the action of sacrifice, dissolution is also involved in creation. He is connected with the creator as his Self. He is not identified with the sheaths.

Ways of Practice

The practices Krishna offers for the moment of death are to be prepared for throughout life. The primary way of piercing the boundaries that keep sacrifice and dissolution from joy and creation is onepointed attention, "remembering me alone"(5). This remembrance is relaxed, spontaneous, letting go, entering into simplicity. It is attention without tension.

The attention could be focused on the transcendent universal consciousness(*Om*), or on its loving human manifestion(Buddha, Jesus, Krishna, Mohammed, or personal *guru*), or on the inner sensation that serves to dissolve our identification with body consciousness. Whatever way feels right, will clear away the covering of the sheaths, if engaged in with sincerity and devotion. Then consciousness *of* will become sheer awareness—conscious integrated awareness(*prajna*). For Krishna says, if we train the mind to rest in awareness while living, this ongoing *being* will remain throughout the process called physical death.

> Think of me therefore at all times. Remember me and fight. And with mind and reason on me you shall in truth come to me. (8:7)

This is a warrior's fight, the fight to go beyond aeons of conditioning and past tendencies. The battle consists of small, steady efforts; confronting our ignorance, inertia, fear, impatience, anger and selfishness bit by bit, as they arise. By bringing our imperfections to the being-knowledge "I am this *Atma*," we help train the mind to transcend matter without banishment or suppression, in full recognition of its presence, as part of the life principle.

Slokas 8-16 present us with further techniques of helping the mind to rest in *Brahman*(*Om*) throughout life so that at the moment of death this partnership will be second nature. The *yoga* of practice (*abhyasa yoga*), repetition, onepointedness, bringing the roaming attention back to its source of concentration is said to be the means, which can be applied to any *yogic* practice.

One way of helping the mind to live in reality is internal repetition of a *mantra*: "Lord have mercy," "Hear O Israel the Lord our God the Lord is One," "*Om Mani Padme Hum*." There are 1,000 names of Vishnu, which the devout Hindu repeats to train the mind in will, devotion and love. Throughout his life, Mahatma Gandhi practiced repeating the name of God as Rama. When he was murdered by an assassin, the only word he uttered was "Ram Ram." He saw only God. His consciousness was with God. By calling on God, He comes to us, says Krishna.

Another aid for training the intellect is contemplation. Eight indicators of *Brahman* are offered for the student to reflect upon(9,10): "the supreme poet seer, the Self created or most ancient." Everything else is man-made but *Om* is Self created; everything else is an effect while *Om* is the only cause. He is called "the sovereign ruler, subtler than the tiniest particle, while upholding this vast universe, inconceivable, beyond thought, bright as the sun, beyond the darkness of *maya*." We are being invited to allow the mind to rest in the absorption of one of these indescribable descriptions and observe. This is how contemplation can help the mind to overstep the constriction of its present boundaries and expand.

Intrinsic to the way of liberation is self-control, selflessness and freedom from attachment. Long-term training of the senses to be free from the pull of the sense objects is a prerequisite for controlling the senses at the moment of death. The specific instructions offered in *slokas* twelve and thirteen describe the process of spiritual practice at the moment of death.

The Process of Dying

Krishna says that when the life energy of the spiritual practitioner departs, all nine apertures of the body are closed and concentration of mind is firmly fixed in the heart, ever still, never wavering in spite of physical pain, emotional trauma or vestiges of fear. This firmness allows the *prana* to leave the body through the top of the head while the *yogi* remains concentrated on *Om*, which is ever experienced at the time of death as ongoing consciousness-bliss.

> At the hour of death, the doors of the senses are completely closed. If we are to maintain awareness of the Self at that time, nothing can be allowed to take away from the complete concentration within. There is no hearing, no seeing and there should be no desire to see or hear. Everything must be centered on the Self... The only way to be able to still the mind at the time of death is to train it from now on to be filled with love of the Lord who we must see in every creature around us. Then at death there is nothing in the heart but love of the Lord. There is no personal attachment or self-will; there is no conflict, no anger, no fear. The body may suffer but there is no suffering in consciousness for the mind is full only of the *mantram* or holy name.
>
> For the great mystics the *mantram* has taken root and become established in this consciousness. The holy name echoes continuously in the depths of the heart. In sickness and in health, in favorable circumstances and in times of turmoil the *mantram* continues to fill the heart and mind. When this happens we are so established in God consciousness that death loses its terror. At the time we shed the body there will be no break in consciousness for we have become continuously aware of the Lord who dwells within.
> (Eknath Easwaran, BGDLv2, p.108-9)

Another account is given in "Talks on Samkhya":

> At the moment of physical death or of passage to a lighter density, *Purusha* is perceptible in the vibration of *sakti*. It is a moment of transubstantiation, a function of the spirit informed by sensation. When you are face to face with death, do not struggle. Let yourself glide. The impulse that will carry you away is cosmic. It is not comparable to any life force. It is written that 'Death is the last of sacrifices.' To reach this point, the sacrifice of life has to have been made long before. Then in the last sacrifice, there is not even the waiting for death. It is simply the life-death state.
> (Reymond, p.220)

Lama Sogyal Rinpoche of the Tibetan Buddhist tradition describes how our level of spiritual attainment during life reflects the way we die. He tells of a time during his childhood in Tibet when he witnessed the death of two lamas:

> The death of Samten taught me the purpose of spiritual practice. Lama Tseten's death taught me it is not unusual for practitioners of his caliber to conceal their remarkable qualities during their lifetime. Sometimes in fact they show them only once, at the moment of death. I understood even as a child, that there was a striking difference between the death of Samten and that of Lama Tseten and I realized that it was the difference between the death of a good monk who had practiced in his life and that of a much more realized practitioner. Samten died in an ordinary way and in pain, yet with the confidence of faith. Lama Tseten's death was a display of spiritual mastery. (*The Tibetan Book of Living and Dying*, p.7)

By offering Arjuna all these techniques what is His purpose? Out of sheer love for his friend, Krishna sees that Arjuna is capable of living out the perfection within himself. And we too are being offered ways to become one with our Real nature—to embrace Truth, to consummate the mystic union with the imperishable. Krishna is ever encouraging us to believe in our Self and the ease of spiritual practice. "I am easily attainable by that ever steadfast *yogi* who constantly remembers Me and thinks of nothing else."(14)

Cycles of Time

The discourse continues by revealing the ongoing order of the cosmos called time(*kala*,16-20). Time can be viewed as coexisting with creation. Where there is only one there is no time; where there is two, there is a *second*. Time is born. Thus the interval between one thought and the next creates time. *Without thought there is no time.*

Time manifests through creation and dissolution repeating its cycles of day and night over and over again as the manifest world continuously expands and dissolves into the unmanifest. The order of events called time is divided into *yugas*. We are now living in the *Kali yuga*. One meaning of *Kali* is violence. This *yuga* is said to last for 432,000 years before dissolving into a new order, the Golden Age.

The traditional division of *yugas* into that unit of time called years is as follows:

1. *Krita* or *Sathya yuga*(Golden Age)-1,728,000 years;(4 times *Kali yuga*).
2. *Treta yuga*-1,296,000 years;(3 times *Kali yuga*).
3. *Dvapara yuga*-864,000 years;(2 times *Kali yuga*).
4. *Kali yuga*-432,000 years; total 4,320,000 years =1 *mahayuga.*

One thousand *mahayugas* comprise a day for Brahma, one thousand *mahayugas* make a night. Three hundred sixty-five such days make a year and one hundred such years constitute the lifetime of Brahma. Therefore the creator, Brahma is limited by time. This implies that the ancients believed in a semi-finite universe, but a universe so expansive it would boggle the mind toward the infinite.[14]

The night of Brahma is the time of dissolution when matter changes its form, sheds its skin and remains as a kind of latent energy called the unmanifest. Just as a human being dissolves his outer form from life to death by shedding the body, so the cosmos changes form by shedding visible matter. It is said in the *Puranas* that during the time of dissolution the serpent Ananta (without end) sleeps on the ocean of milk and serves as a couch for Brahma the creator, who takes a long nap during this night of dissolution. So too, our own *vasanas* or unconscious tendencies remain latent until time and circumstance offer us the opportunity to live them out.

After this deep sleep of one thousand *mahayugas*, Brahma is somehow awakened. He yawns, stretches and the latent energy becomes manifest once again, allowing creation to proceed. It repeats and repeats all over again. The nourishing ocean of milk is stirred to action. Evolution proceeds. And the cycle of life informs the universe of its existence as creation continues; projects out of *Brahman* under the administrative helper Brahma. At the end of the lifetime of Brahma(100 Brahma years or 311,040,000,000,000 human years) all beings of *Brahma loka* are said to merge in the infinite Lord. Matter is dissolved back into its total oneness with spirit. And a new creator is born. Like the snake biting its tail, the process is continuous.

Creation is also said to be simultaneously occurring at varying stages of evolution, repeating itself ad infinitum throughout the cosmos until full realization. The wise ones say this cycle of creation and dissolution takes place in the seat of meditation, as worlds dissolve and come into being.

The cosmic theory of the *yugas* is not so ethereal as it might appear. Dealing with such large numbers could become numbing if the process remained abstract but inherent in the science of Reality, the transcendent abstract is the support for the immanent concrete. The two are partners. *Purusha* and *prakriti*, which must first be separated out from one another in our consciousness are really One.

Each *yuga* is said to reflect a different quality of humanity as a whole.[15] The *Sathya yuga* is the age of Truth. Here *dharma* is represented by the symbol of a cow, which stands on four legs. This is the golden age of peace and righteousness, where love for all is a way of being. Evil exists in some faraway world. In the *Krita yuga* the cow of *dharma* stands on three legs. A little bit of selfishness has crept in. But the motivation of the average person is basically just. Evil exists in some faraway country. Next in the *Dvapara yuga*, the cow stands on two legs. Corruption and lying increase. Values disintegrate. Selfishness prevails. Evil exists within the same family. In the *Kali yuga*, the age in which we are now living, violence, lawlessness and greed have become a way of being. The demonic qualities of lust, power and possession are considered admirable. The society is ruled haphazardly, egotistically, by men of little wisdom. Corruption, jealousy, and hatred abound. Evil exists alongside good within the same person. With the descent of the *avatar*, the end of the *Kali yuga* is said to usher in a golden age. And the cycle begins again.

Love and Devotion Beyond Time

This schema can also be viewed as existing within the hearts of human beings at all times—from the unmanifest to the manifest, from the manifest to the unmanifest. While we sleep all our actions are unmanifest. When we awake they manifest. The thoughts and deeds will remain in seed form until the right conditions arise for them to emerge. Back and forth we go within the oscillations of time and change, until the process of purification erases the effects of our past motivations and helps us reach our true home(21).

Our home is the abode of peace, that place within, which is beyond both the manifest and the unmanifest. This home is the place of eternity, which is no place and everywhere.

> This spirit supreme is attained by an ever living love. In Him all things have their life and from Him all things have come. (8:22)

The love that begins with a personal God expands to include all. Through opening the heart we find our home. Through devotion, by devoting ourselves to the Self within us and in our fellow creatures, we come to abide in that which is beyond the unmanifest. Through living the love that is ever within, we come to serve as vehicles for eternal love to permeate life.

This love(*ananya bhakti*) means devotion without any otherness —loving only That, thinking only of That, seeing That everywhere and in everyone. The more fully, the more deeply our love is experienced, the more identified we become with the experience of love and the object of our love until one day, the sages say, there is no longer a subject and an object. There is no lover and no beloved. The Self of one is experienced as the Self of the other. The Self in one is the Self in all. There is only One, the ongoing source of all life.

> The heart with compassion is God. If one has no compassion his nature is devilish. Compassion is the most essential quality of a human being. Without compassion, man is inhuman. A compassionate heart reflects divinity.
>
> God has no birth or death. He remains an Eternal Witness. How to realize such an entity who is beyond description and beyond proof? He responds only to love. You should understand God through love and spend your life with love (*prema*).
> (Sri Sathya Sai Baba)

> Thou shalt love the Lord thy God with all thy heart, with all thy soul and with all thy might. (Deuteronomy)

> Love thy neighbor as thyself. (Jesus)

> That highest *Purusha* is attainable by unswerving devotion to Him alone, within whom all beings dwell, by whom all this is pervaded. (BG 8:22)

Swami Chinmayananda reveals the difference between ordinary love and devotion:

> When you're in love you *fall* in love. We fall in love. Love is a fall. When we are in devotion we *rise*. We soar beyond all limitation of body and mind. We become inspired. In devotion we are raised up, in ordinary love we are brought down. In devotion, we would sacrifice anything for an ideal, for a loved one, for God. In ordinary love, our ideals often fall away.

Indian culture has a wonderful way of bridging the gap between falling down into love and aspiring upward toward devotion. By truly seeing God in the other, our relationships can become spiritual practice. In India, the husband is consciously seen as a manifestation of God. The wife is seen as embodiment of the goddess. Through enlarging our vision we can work toward eliminating attachment, egoism and selfishness. It is much easier to surrender to God than to another person. In this way, through seeing God in the other, we can practice vanquishing self-will. Without this, serene happiness remains impossible.

With our experience of total devotion, all feelings of loneliness and alienation cease. There is no separation. For true independence and self containment consist of experiencing oneself simultaneously as part of the whole, interdependent with the whole, and the whole itself (*dvaita, visisthadvaita* and *advaita*, respectively). Most sorrow and disappointment in relationship stems from segmenting oneself and the relationship from the totality, be it in the form of superimposed expectations, clinging, idealizing or merging with that which is perishable. Most unhappiness with oneself stems from cutting off our Self from the natural, total fluid scheme of things of which we are each a part. This yoga of nonseparation*(ananya bhakti)* does not allow us to merge with anyone or anything but the Highest. Neither one's husband, wife, child, or friends are worshipped at the expense of the whole but rather, are seen as a manifestation of the divine. Through living in devotion without any otherness, all seven aspects of life in this Cosmos become connected with one's Self.

We now begin to see that the opening questions asked by Arjuna about the seven aspects of existence are all interconnected by the thread of devotion. The transcendent *Brahman* from which the primordial individual Self(*adhyatma*) is projected seems to become ensnared in *maya*. Through conscious, detached action (*karma yoga*) in the elemental world of *prakriti*(*adhibhuta*), and in the realm of the gods, mental functions and sense organs(*adhidaiva*), this Self can be redeemed from separateness and experienced in totality as *Brahman.*[16]

Paths of Light and Darkness

The *Gita* speaks of two paths we can follow—the path of the sun and the path of the moon(23). The sun illumines with direct light. The moon shines with reflected light. Thus the path of the sun is the way of spirit. The path of the moon is the way of matter. The moon is the way of darkness, the way of mind. The moon superimposes concept onto Reality. The sun is the way of direct illumination.

Those who are spiritually evolved follow the path of the sun. They have utilized their innate intelligence and love for liberation and Self realization. They have followed their deepest inner yearning. Those who place all their eggs in the basket of material life and tangible pleasures follow the path of the moon. They tend to have little faith in the inner depths and therefore limit themselves to the concrete; to the senses and that which can be seen, heard, tasted, smelled and touched. They imprison themselves in what their own minds can conceive of. Their interest is primarily in the external world and in controlling the elements through science or ritual(*karma kanda*). Unlike Arjuna, those in the second group might at present be unwilling to go beyond what the personal mind already believes because something about the unknown seems too threatening. This reflects spiritual immaturity. Others who follow the path of the moon might still be evolving but as they have not yet reached wholeness, they must return again.

The *Bhagavatam* tells the story of a man who was destined for death and the path of the moon. At one time, Ajamila was a pious *brahmin*; but then he became infatuated with a selfish, sensuous woman who took over his mind and common sense. In short, he becomes her slave. He started gambling to support her greed and he lost all self-control. They had ten sons and his favorite was Narayana. At the moment of death, he lovingly calls out to Narayana. As Narayana is the name of the Lord, He responds to Ajamila's call and would not allow Yama to claim his soul. *To repeat the name of God with love at the moment of death calls forth God's unswerving protection no matter what!*

Then there's another story about a boy named Markandeya who follows the path of the sun. His parents are very pious. They are childless and greatly long for a child. They perform many prayers and austerities. Soon Lord Siva appears and tells them they will be granted a son. The boy will be very pure and devout. But he will die on his sixteenth birthday.

Too soon his sixteenth birthday is here. The heartbroken parents tell Markandeya to prepare for his death. The boy begins to worship and meditate for hours, until his soul leaves the body and merges with Siva. Parvati then feels compassion for his parents and asks Siva to intervene. He brings Markandaya back to life—eternal life.

Those who have merged their minds with consciousness, experience the eternal while living, says Krishna. The source of all consciousness is known within. They are untouched by death.

In India, when the sun is travelling toward the north vis-a-vis the earth(*uttarayana*), this is considered an auspicious time for the soul to leave the body, for it represents the way of light. When the sun is travelling south, this time of death is considered inauspicious. Great *yogis* such as Bhishma have been known to postpone their time of *mahasamadhi* to coincide with the northward path of the sun.[17] It would however, be more practical for us to view these two paths symbolically.

Krishna here reiterates a *Vedic* cosmology of departed souls. Those who have practiced spiritual discipline to a high level of purification but who have not yet merged fully in the love of God while living go to the highest heaven called *Brahma loka*, the place of the creator. This is called the path of the sun, the path of the gods. Here under ideal conditions they dwell and proceed on the way of gradual liberation (*krama mukti*) . Then when the *mahayugas* of Brahma come to an end, these now purified souls merge in God; liberated and eternal they return no more(24).

All other aspirants who perform good deeds, but are still attached to the mind and senses follow the path of the moon. This heaven is called the world of the ancestors. When their merit is exhausted, they are said to be reborn on earth in accordance with their desires and vasanas—again and again and again—until total purification is achieved (25).

Both paths are continuous. Both paths are eternal. The *yogi* with the knowledge of both ways is being offered an opportunity to choose. Krishna tells us that after we have prepared ourselves through study, sacrifice, self-control and charity we will be ready to practice the way of meditation, which will bring us to direct realization of Truth (28).

Thus, the moment of death is considered the most important moment in our lives. All spiritual work and inner purification help prepare us for this moment. All mathematical calculations of the beginning and end of *yugas*, all creation, dissolution, sleep and waking, all life, death, matter and spirit—all are layers of consciousness, accessible to each of us. All are supported by that subtler than the subtlest, which is beyond ordinary consciousness, but very reachable. And when we experience That while living in this body says Krishna, there are no *yugas*, no creation, no dissolution, no sleep, no waking. There is no matter, no spirit. There is no where to go. There is nothing to strive for. We are home (21, 28).

This everlasting home is the primordial essence available throughout all the aeons. But we need a human body to be able to work, to practice, and evolve into our ongoing presence. We need ordinariness to be able to be. Sri Sathya Sai Baba says:

> Death is an event that is the very nature of the body. Men seek the cause for death but no one seeks the Divine Source of Life. Be engaged during the brief span of life in glorifying God and in doing God's work. Never be afraid of death. Never forget God. Never take this world as real. (*Digest 2*, p.82)

Thus, the eighth discourse teaches the *yoga* of the eternal, imperishable *Brahman*, the true consciousness, the ever present link between before and after, above and below, birth and death throughout the aeons.

Nine

THE SECRET KINGLY YOGA

Rajavidya Rajaguhya Yoga

	Gita verses
Dharma and the direct formless Knowledge	1–6
Origin of the universe	7–10
The natures of ignorant and godly persons	11–15
Universal presence and subtle form of God	16–19
Results of action with and without desire	20–25
The power of devotion, surrender and desireless action	26–34

all beings are in Me
the Source of all that lives
worship Me with love

The ninth discourse reveals the royal science that can enable us to experience the secret knowledge and inherit our rightful kingdom. This is not a secret words can convey. Though unhidden, it is accessible only to a select few. The mystery manifests as a way of seeing, a way of being, a means of penetrating to the essence of things.

It can be seen in the sparkle of melting ice and the silence behind noise. It is the ongoingness behind creation and dissolution, and the love behind hatred and destruction. It rests within our own bodies. Beyond cause and effect, beyond the reasoning mind, this elusive secret you and I cannot begin to fathom until we want it so badly we begin to work for it, pray for it, *live* for it. The prerequisites for receiving it are purity of heart, truthfulness and freedom from ignorance(1). Only then will it begin to trickle into our lives. And we cannot grasp it because it is so subtle.

The sacredness of life, our own sacredness and the holiness of every living being filters through to us from a foundation of ingenuousness, openness and spiritual work—a work that is a joy to seek and easy to follow(2). Through motivated spiritual effort our density becomes more subtle, our thick skins more permeable; our brittle hearts soften. So throughout this discourse on *raja yoga*, Krishna offers Arjuna exercises in contemplation, verses that will help him attune his mind to the expansive knowledge of Reality and gradually purge the *vasanas*.

As we each ponder these stanzas and allow the hidden, intuitive meaning to permeate our consciousness, we too can be helped to link our subtle energy and our minds with Truth, that one day we each might *be* That. For this secret becomes accessible through an inner knowing or direct intuitive knowledge, which appears when we live with the faith and openness to seek it. It is the faith to pursue Truth, the essence behind appearances, which delineates the living from the living dead, the perishable from the imperishable(3).

Dynamic Divine Cosmology

In verses 4-10, Krishna further elucidates the cosmology of origins, creation and the relationship between the eternal infinite *Brahman*, the creator God of the universe and the created world of names and forms. These are three ways of contemplating the divine:

1. as infinite, eternal, all inclusive *Brahman*(*nirguna*, without form)
2. creator of the universe of names and forms(Ishvara, with form)
3. the total universe with all its manifest names and forms, including the subtle transcendent.(*Paramesvara*)

Throughout the chapter, Krishna speaks of this relationship in different ways at different times—ways that might appear contradictory. Let's keep in mind that these seeming contradictions occur because He is explaining this complex relationship of God to the universe from different angles. And each is true at its own level. In reality, the three are one, but the intellect requires this division to aid understanding. In *sloka* four Krishna says:

> All this world is pervaded by Me in My unmanifest form. All beings exist in me but I do not dwell in them.

This is similar to his previous statement:

> Whatever beings that are pure, active and inert, know them to proceed from me. Yet I am not in them, they are in Me. (7:12)

Swami Chinmayananda has called this idea the relationless relationship. It is not the relationship of part to whole. It is not the relationship of cause and effect. That which cannot be seen by the eye as material form or conceived by the mind as thought is present nonetheless as an undifferentiated form of *prakriti*, subtler than concrete matter. In the realm of the invisible: the more subtle, the more pervasive, the more in everything. The subtlest is all pervasive—all in everything.

> As all limited things must have forms, the all pervasive alone can be eternal and infinite. All forms are perishable. Thus the Self, in its essential unmanifest nature must be pervading everything as mud pervades all forms and shapes in all mud pots. (Swami Chinmayananda, THG p.522)

Let's stop for a moment and picture the clay that pervades all pots: yellow clay, tan, brown and gray—all formed by the pervasiveness of Godstuff. Picture the pots being shaped and painted, baked and fired; many different shapes and colors and forms; all clay, all God. Chinese, Indian, Black, Caucasian; all clay, all God. Rock, sand, lettuce, ant; all clay, all God. This eternal life substance of the five elements, located in the human body, the earth body and the cosmic body is everywhere, unmeasurable by our gross instruments. Awareness knowledge of its pervasive omnipresence helps us link the mind to God.[18]

Another image used in *Vedanta* to elucidate the relationless relationship is gold. Picture shimmering gold. Gold is the stuff out of which all jewelry is made. Gold pervades all bracelets, necklaces and earrings. This same gold can be used to fashion a sculpture of the gods or be shaped into an ashtray for holding refuse. In the same way, the divine pervades all human beings, all life forms.

In the beginning level of worship and understanding, God and humans are linked but are distinctly separate from one another like father and son, master and servant. Man is said to be created in the image of God, with the potential of becoming like God. God and his creatures are two separate entities(dualism). But here in this stanza there is no separation, no segmentation between the universe and God. There are no energy divisions and limits from thing to thing, from creature to creature. The fourth *sloka* reflects the philosophy of qualified nondualism(*visisthadvaita*), for differences are acknowledged while unity is seen and worshipped as the support and Reality for all the varied names and forms.

> All beings exist in me but I am not rooted in them. I in my unmanifest nature am the substratum for all the manifested chaos of names and forms but neither in their joys nor in their sorrows,

> neither in their births nor in their deaths am I sharing their destinies because I do not dwell in them. (ibid., p.523)

There is no two in Reality, no dualism. There is only one—only unity. Thus the science of the unity of mankind and nature and all and everything is expressed by this *sloka*, "All the world is pervaded by me in my unmanifest form. All beings exist in Me but I am not placed in them." *The infinite cannot be delineated by forms.*

Now in the fifth *sloka* this idea is further clarified. In Truth, all beings do not exist in the infinite for there is nothing finite in the infinite. The only Reality is *Brahman*. This is the philosophy of nondualism (*advaita*).

> From the ordinary dualistic point of view, the world has existence as it is touched and confirmed by the senses. So it is said to exist in and be sustained by *Paramatma*. From the standpoint of unity, nondualism(*advaita*), the world does not exist at all in the same manner as water does not exist in a mirage. The seen world does not exist in Him nor He in the seen. The man who has awakened from dream comes to know that he never existed in the dream, nor the dream in him. The cosmic illusion appears to exist but really does not exist. (Swami Vidyaprakashananda, p.614)

The example used to illustrate this point is when we see what we think is a snake but it's really a rope. In India there are many snakes, some quite fearful to behold. After a few scares by the real thing, it is very easy to start projecting. We see a rope and think it's a snake. This *Vedantic* analogy of Shankara from the eighth century is still very much alive today in snake infested India.

The same principle of displacement and projection takes place on a personal psychological level as well as at the cosmic level. For example, if I'm angry at my boss but I unconsciously suppress that anger for fear of getting fired, I may come home and be angry at my husband or wife. If the emotional *vasana* of anger is very strong and clouds my self-observation and subjective discrimination, I may try to justify why I'm angry at my husband and attribute it to some cause or other that feels true—all because I could not acknowledge my anger towards my boss. In a similar way, I attribute absolute Reality to the physical world, which exists only as relative reality, supported by absolute Reality. I project absolute Reality onto relative reality. I project the snake onto the rope. So the world appearing to exist really does not exist in and of itself. All this is nameless, infinite *Brahman* and nothing else. Thus, *Brahman* (the God principle) pervades everything, every single thing but is not affected or influenced by anything.

> Though wind carries the good and bad odor alike it remains unaffected by both. *Parabrahman* is in this way unaffected by the phenomenal universe. (Ramakrishna)

In order to bring this intellectual knowledge into our lives as understanding, we can begin to cultivate the attitude of the witness (10)—connect with an inner view, a part which is separate from all the comings and goings, joys and sorrows, emotions and thoughts. This diffuse awareness of oneself in the environment is not meant to distance us from living or from other people but to help us participate with an ongoing perspective, with detachment. As the creations and dissolutions dance through our lives, there is this perpetual awareness, this inner look, like the uppermost point of the Egyptian obelisk, looking upward in stillness being, ever connected to the base, overseeing oneself and everything.

This all pervasive, unifying principle then, can be understood through the combined workings of nature and scientific law within the universe and the individual. Whereas the physicist might call its physical manifestations energy and matter, the *raja yogi* would call it the interaction of *akasha*(omnipresent existence space) and *prana*(life energy).

> At the beginning of creation there is only *akasha*; at the end of the cycle, the solids, the liquids and the gases all melt into *akasha* again, and the next creation similarly proceeds out of *akasha*.
>
> By what power is *akasha* manufactured into this universe? By the power of *prana*. Just as *akasha* is the infinite, omnipresent material of this universe, so is *prana* the infinite, omnipresent manifesting power of this universe. At the beginning and at the end of a cycle, all tangible objects resolve back into *akasha* and all the forces that are in the universe resolve back into *prana*. In the next cycle out of this *prana* is evolved everything that we call energy,

> everything that we call force. It is the *prana* that is manifesting as motion; it is the *prana* that is manifesting as gravitation, as magnetism. It is *prana* that is manifesting as the actions of the body, as the nerve currents, as thought-force. From thought down to the physical force, everything is but the manifestation of *prana*. The sum total of all forces in the universe, mental or physical, when resolved back to their original state, is called *prana*... The knowledge and control of this *prana* is really what is meant by *pranayama*. (Swami Vivekananda, *Raja Yoga*, p.34-5)

Mastery of one's own individual *prana* is likened to mastery over the universe:

> This body is very near to us, nearer than anything in the external universe; and the mind is nearer than the body. But the *prana* which is working this mind and body is the nearest. It is a part of the *prana* that moves the universe. In the infinite ocean of *prana*, this little wave of *prana* which represents our own energies, mental and physical, is the nearest to us. If we can succeed in controlling that little wave, then alone can we hope to control the whole of *prana*. The *yogi* who has done this gains perfection; no longer is he under any power. He becomes almost almighty, almost all-knowing... All manipulations of the subtle forces of the body, different manifestations of *prana*, give a push to the mind, help it to go higher and become superconscious from where it acts.
> (ibid., p.37-8)

God and Nature

In *slokas* 7-10, we see that God as creator works always through nature—be it on the time scale of the birth and death of a *yuga* or of an individual life(7). Beings are ever coming and going, dissolving from matter at death, created from matter at birth, and dissolving again into the subtler *prakriti*, the finer formless substance of the body of God. There is no inherent antagonism between nature and God. Nature is the instrument through which God's creation takes place. Nature is the means whereby God's miracles occur. When the Red Sea parted and the Israelites crossed to safety while Pharoah's armies were drowned, God worked through nature as the controller of nature. This aspect of God in Hindu cosmology is called Ishvara. Ishvara as Lord of the Universe is the controller of all things and beings. But he does not control at whim like Zeus, who uses humans as his playthings. Rather, the rulership of Ishvara is fully lawful, based on the motivation and behavior of humanity as a whole and individuals in particular.

He always administers in *partnership* with the world in accordance with our individual and collective *karma*, whether or not we are aware of it. Only when we acknowledge this partnership do we vivify the relationship and keep our part of the pact of entering into a human body at birth. A more equitable meaning of the "chosen people" is that this chosenness is open to all without any distinction regarding the particular form of God that we follow. Be He called Christ, Buddha, Mohammed, Jehovah or Ishvara doesn't matter. Only when *we* choose to accept this divine relationship are we truly chosen.

Divine protection through nature is always earned through devotion and action in accordance with *dharma*. Thus, there is no inherent antithesis between religion and science, as miracle and divine law are expressing the same thing. It is only a compartmentalized view of Ishvara *versus* nature, which feeds this perceived division. Whether He sends down hailstones or frogs, destroys cities or makes deserts bloom, cures the crippled or infuses the empty heart with love, it is always through nature. And prakriti as God is controlled by *the action and desires of the devotee*, not through technical manipulation or through the desire to control but in accordance with the deepest wishes of the soul and one's corresponding behavior. But once these forces of nature have been set in motion, we are bound within that particular level until we are able to evolve toward other levels of nature, ad infinitum until liberation.

So fundamentally, this is not a philosophy of helplessness or divine punishment but rather, a partnership between the actions of human beings and divine will—which ultimately resides within the person. Thoughts, actions and events are all connected both on the individual and cosmic level. We are therefore far more responsible for our personal outcomes and for the outcome of events in the world than we could ever imagine. Herein rests the *urgency* of developing a broader view, a deeper view and a more reflective view that includes the interactive partnership presence of the totality. This is the true creative aspect of *maya*, the only "free will" whereby human action interacts with divine intent. However, ultimately, from the perspective of Reality, it is not a question of relationship. *It is the Self in us that chooses to acknowledge the supremacy of its own Infinite Self.*

Action as Creation

When our actions are pleasing to God, fertility and rain result. Ritual *yajna*(sacrifice), *Vedic mantra* and positive motivation for the well being of all have been traditionally utilized to uplift society. In the same way, on the individual level, our motivation, speech and action create our destiny.

The threads of *karma* with all its manifestations are very complex. Shankara delineates three types of *karma* based on the time frame for working through their fruits:

1. action which causes an immediate reaction in the present and thereby exhausts its future potential
2. the consequences we reap from a past action
3. *karma* we are able to create now.

In the first instance, an action produces its effect immediately. Through suffering we pay back our debt to nature. This can repair the future, especially if there is detachment. Then there are no repercussions. As suffering is immediate, no lingering debt remains.

The second example can be more persistent, as this deeply entrenched *karma* travels with us from life to life. It may remain unmanifest until the right circumstances appear that will allow it to come into being. Then when it does manifest, if we are aware, this is an opportunity for us to experience the event in such a way that it will no longer bind us to its spell. This can only occur through attaching oneself to Truth and detaching from matter. Or to put it another way—to experience the suffering or joy in the light of Self, with compassion and God consciousness as our witness. When we suffer the results of past actions as a limited ego disconnected to larger consciousness, this suffering is sometimes useless as it can lead to the formation of more deeply entrenched *vasanas*, new bondage and further *karma*. But even unconscious suffering can somewhat cleanse our *karma,* depending on our motivation.

The third instance is the *karma* over which we have some control. Through conscious striving to watch our thoughts, words and deeds, through awareness of non-doership and service, through meditation and purification, the deposits from the past dissolve and the slate is washed clean.

Swami Chinmayananda says that the *karma* from the past *vasanas* (*sanchita*) and that which is yet to come(*agami*) are both destroyed at the moment of Self realization:

> They can no longer affect the individual because he has transcended his little indentification and has experienced the Bliss beyond. The individuality which is responsible for past *karma* is no more in that equipment. It has dissolved itself in the transcendental experience of infinitude. (*Vivekachoodamani,* p.522)

Shankara further clarifies that *prarabdha karma*(the *karma* responsible for that particular birth) continues even in the realized soul until the natural effects of past actions are exhausted:

> That work performed before the dawn of Knowledge and because of which this body is conjured up is not destroyed by Self Knowledge without yielding its fruits—just like an arrow shot at an object." (*sloka* 452, ibid.)

Thus, even the realized soul must witness the results of his past actions with loving detachment. Yes, we are bound by the works of creation and are rendered helpless by the forces of nature(8). But when we begin to practice linking our awareness with God remembrance, we come closer to merging with the Lord of Creation, that we might participate in co-creating our own destiny(9). "I am not bound by this vast work of creation. I am and I watch the drama of works." To the degree we can be led by our dharma as inner divine will, we become increasingly liberated from the bonds of maya, which manifest through nature.

Through the living process of *dharma* and evolution, the eternal witness becomes more accessible. While the worlds are seemingly spinning round and round, we can choose to *consciously co-participate* in turning the wheel of *dharma*. When we are aligned with a higher energy, the conscious turning of the wheel produces a qualitatively different outcome than the wheel that spins automatically to the tune of lower prakriti.

> One who controls, regulates and orders everything in the cosmos is called Ishvara, the Lord. He is the Lord in each one of us. Our own *vasanas* determine, order, regulate and control our lives. Hence our *vasanas* are our Lord.
>
> This Truth can be experienced only by the student who has done spiritual work for a sufficiently long time. He who has created spiritual *vasanas* can bless himself. Such an individual crosses *samsar*(illusory existence) by his own illumination when he studies and thinks independently and is helped by his teacher from time to time. (Swami Chinmayananda, ibid. p.546)

Ignorance and Knowledge

In the eleventh *sloka*, Krishna encapsulates the cause of all the religious persecution and "holy" wars that have ever been fought; he delineates why human beings remain stuck on the same rung of the ladder. He calls us "fools" or spiritually immature, when we live on the level of concreteness. In this psychological space, one might think there is no God, it's all nature, all science all biology; or one might believe, "only my God is the true God, all other Gods are false." This latter group mistakes the form for the real thing. The real thing is the experience of Truth, Infinity, *Brahman*, the Way, Eternal Law, Love, the nameless. The form of God is merely the vehicle through which we can contact His essence, His love, that His teachings might flower forth into our lives.

There is a definite leap to be made from the psychologically immature level of literalism and dogmatism to the more aware and flexible view of openness, which acknowledges the workings of the transcendent divine in all of us and in the whole universe. For this we must look beyond physical appearance and the senses. We must go within. This can occur through grace invoked by purity and self-effort.

> The mystery will always be that 'all' is discovered by coming back into oneself and not through the process of exteriorization. Within oneself there is no longer any surrender to outer will but an immersion in the principle of a higher will. One returns from it a different being even if one cannot make the experience last. It is illuminating. That is all. Intellectually one invents means to reach it, whereas it is rather a question of chemistry, of transformation. If you could understand that, the transformation of one element into another would passionately interest you—earth into water, water into fire, fire into air, and so forth. These words are only the keys to understanding what takes place in us at different densities of being.[19] (Reymond, p.177)

Even if you and I are the fools about whom Krishna speaks, there is hope if we can allow our love to manifest. Love of God in one particular form is a means through which the teachings of the master can later be expanded and transferred to humanity as a whole. Jesus said, "Love one another as I have loved you."

In the beginning love for our God may be mixed with clannish suspiciousness or hatred for others of a different ilk. All fanaticism and sectarianism is the desire to assert the individual ego under the false name of truth. As we become more purified, more onepointed, the dogmatic edge to our love, which tries to control and impose our views on others slowly softens. There is a gradual transition from hatred and competitiveness to tolerance to universal acceptance to love. But in order to reach a higher rung on the ladder, we must first practice forbearance for difference in those we care for. Our families, friends, coworkers, neighbors and teachers serve as the raw material out of which our egotism, our wish to impose our own views, can develop first into tolerance and then into love. *Our daily relationships can become our spiritual work.*

All the *mahatmas* or great souls of the world possess the universal vision of love and knowledge in action (13).Through total devotion to the One in all, they love God in everyone, they love everyone in God. These *mahatmas* show us by their presence, the meaning of devotion through their work of uplifting humanity. All genuine work for humanity is work for God. And devotion without any otherness(*ananyamanah*) means keeping the mind steadfast, with onepointed remembrance concentration in everything we do, say or think.

> They know me to be the origin of all beings. Those who know the mud to be the origin of all mud-pots cannot fail to see the mud in all pots. So too, those who understand the divine principle as the source of all beings, cannot but respect every other member of the society as they would respect themselves.
> (Swami Chinmayananda THG, p.535)

> There are some great souls who know me. Their refuge is my own divine nature. They love me with a oneness of love. They know that I am the source of all. (9:13)

In *slokas* 14-15, Krishna reveals the taste and texture of devotion to help us quicken our own depth of feeling, mindfulness and love. Through glorifying and praising God we are filled with awe; we become imbued with a sense of *mysterium tremendum* that draws us in and helps to make our aspirations viable, emotionally alive and charged with energy. Without this sense of wonder, spiritual practice is mechanical and empty. Firm resolve requires the participation of the emotions and body as well as the intellect in order to bring the harmony and consequent identification with Truth that will purify. Worship is an expression of feeling that invokes more feeling, work is carried out with the physical equipment, and the wisdom sacrifice, the sacrifice of spiritual vision (15) is primarily an act of the purified intellect, which serves to bring together all three parts. Swami Chinmayanda says:

> The wisdom sacrifice is a constant attempt to see the expression and vitality of the One Conscious principle, the Self, in and through the experienced names and forms, situations and conditions. The seeker here, practicing wisdom sacrifice has understood that the immutable Self pervades all, penetrating everything and in Its homogeneous web of existence It holds together the phenomenal multiplicity and their variegated interactions.
>
> In the sparkle of the eyes, in the smile of a friend, in the grin of an enemy, in the harsh words of jealousy and in the soft tones of

> love, in heat and in cold, in success and in failure, among men, among animals, amidst the trees and in the company of the inert, everywhere he successfully gains the auspicious vision of the supreme either as existence pure or knowledge absolute or bliss infinite! To watch for and discover the smile of the Divine through the trellis of names and forms is to live in the constant spirit of wisdom sacrifice. To adore Him in all visions, to recognize Him in all situations, to feel Him with each thought is to live in a constant remembrance of the Self and therefore such people worship the Self through the wisdom sacrifice. (ibid., p.539)

Narada once asked Krishna to reveal to him the deepest truth. Suddenly he finds himself in the midst of a village carrying a begging bowl. In every home he enters, he sees one person with the same smiling eyes of Krishna. The dancing eyes of a child, the detached, loving eyes of an old person, the warm dazzling eyes of a beautiful woman—all exude the love of Krishna.[20]

> Whatever be your concept of God, be it with form or formless, hold fast to it and ardently worship Him. But be not conceited that your concept alone of Him is the finale. In the course of your *sadhana* you will come to know by His grace that His attributes and forms are inexhaustible. (Ramakrishna)

Worship and the Wisdom Sacrifice

In the sheer poetry of verses 16-19, Krishna offers us specific pointers through which to heighten worship and experience the divine source in every thing—food, fire, mother, father, friend, universe, *tao*, stillness, striving, silence, giving, peace, change. All are sacred. All are an expression of Him, of his Love:

> For I am the sacrifice and the offering, the sacred gift and the sacred plant. I am the holy words, the holy food, the holy fire, and the offering that is made in the fire. I am the Father of this universe and even the Source of the father. I am the Mother of this universe and the creator of all. I am the highest to be known, the Path of purification, the holy *Om*, the three *Vedas*. I am the way, and the master who watches in silence; thy friend and thy shelter and thy

abode of peace. I am the beginning and the middle and the end of all things; their seed of eternity, their treasure supreme.

The mother and father of the universe is this all pervasive energy which is our own real mother and father(Sakti-Siva). The cosmic parents support and allow our own parents to give birth to us; they allow us to give birth to our children. All love, all healing power stems from the love of the cosmic parents. The act of creating a child is made possible by the cosmic parents. The love we feel for our parents is this universal force of love that manifests through our individual parents. No matter how ignorant the personal parents might be, the child can experience gratitude to them for serving as vehicles for his entry into life; all in the knowledge that behind the concrete love which gets experienced in a particular name and form called mother and father, lives the force of divine love, which is all pervasive. It is this divine love that allows mother, father and child to participate in the ongoing mystery of creation. In ever-continuous rhythm, the child is father to the man.

That which makes us feel so deeply by invoking in us the power of love is in fact the power of God. Through the force of love we touch this mystery. It is only when such deep feelings are made concrete or are dedicated to the ego, name and form of the particular person rather than the eternal depths within the person that we become disappointed because we are allowing ourselves to become limited and encapsulated by *maya*. To see God *in* the other is Truth, to unconsciously see the particular person as the god image is idol worship. To idealize the ego form of the person can only lead to false expectation, frustration, and consequent disappointment. To consciously see God as the foundation of oneself and the other can lead to mutual appreciation, tolerance and respect.

Relationship offers the opportunity for sorting the seeds into their rightful place for planting. Human love offers a priceless opportunity for letting go of egotism, opinions and ways of doing things by practicing caring for the other, doing what is pleasing for the other and seeing God in the other. Through awareness connection with the divine inside oneself and the other, the seemingly impossible becomes possible.

There's a story in the *Yoga Vashishta* about the power of the mind, especially the power of the mind in love:

> Ahalya is a beautiful Queen who falls in love with the leader of a gang. She even leaves the palace to live with her beloved. When the king finds out he is furious and condemns the couple to torture. He puts them in icy cold water in the middle of winter. But all they do is smile at each other. Then he throws them into a big frying pan on the fire. They remain unhurt and say, "O king. We rejoice at the delight of our souls thinking of each other." Then they are trampled by elephants but they remained unruffled and say, "O king, we feel intense joy at the remembrance of each other." They are severely beaten with rods, straps and hammers. Even then they simply smile and laugh. The king is utterly amazed. He asks Indra and Ahalya: "How is it that you both do not experience any pain when you are tortured"? Indra replies.
>
> "O king, the entire universe to me is nothing but my beloved. It's the same to Ahalya. So we are unaffected by all this. Sir, I am only mind and mind alone is the individual. You can punish the body but you cannot punish the mind, nor bring about the least change in it. If the mind is fully saturated with something, whatever happens to the body does not affect the mind. The mind is unaffected even by boons and curses, even as the firmly established mountain is not moved by the horns of a little beast… The body does not create the mind but the mind creates the body. The mind alone is the seed for the body. When the tree dies, the seed does not, but when the seed perishes, the tree dies with it. If the body perishes, the mind can create other bodies for itself."
>
> The furious king then approaches a sage and asks him to curse the couple. Though his curse destroyed their bodies, their minds remain forever with each other and they are continuously being reborn in different forms and species as loving husband and wife.[21]

Devotion

The remainder of the discourse culminates in devotion, not only as poetic inspiration but as a means of helping each of us develop devotion to That which is truly meaningful and makes our lives worthwhile. Through love, worship and giving, through seeing the

Self in all, the *prana* circulates, *sakti* rises—we expand our consciousness. The cells in the body take on a glowing quality. Warmth exudes from the eyes and the heart.

> I am the goal of life, the lord and support of all; the inner witness, the abode of all. I am the only refuge, the one true friend. I am the beginning and end of creation and the receptacle for the eternal seed. (9:18)

Here Krishna is not suggesting that we withdraw from human friendship but that we see divinity in every friend and come to treat every person as the divine friend. And if we can each turn to the Lord in our own heart as the only refuge, the one true friend, our sorrows, disappointments and "negative emotions" will always have a comforting place to be brought, shared and left behind. Our loneliness and alienation will always melt into the light of His presence. To bring God down to earth, converse with Him and offer him a place at the dinner table or a chair in the playroom does not demean Him. Rather, to treat God as friend can only help divinity enter into every simple aspect of our lives, without any trace of split between the sacred and the mundane.

The wonder of being in the presence of a genuine saint is the power of his seeming ordinariness. Whether bantering, joking, playing or working, the human quality of the holy man is more human than in you and me. Genuine holiness is living and laughing. It is never masked in the mold of stolid seriousness. Genuine holiness is lightness supported by equally loving detachment; solidity of purpose supported by purposelessness.

The sages reveal that all relationship, no matter how meaningful—be it friend, mother, father, husband, wife, lover—all our relationships are temporary with only one exception: our relationship with this energy called Truth, God, Krishna, Jesus, Buddha, Allah. It is this relationship that remains with us from life to life(17). It is this relationship that can never leave us *no matter what*. It is this relationship that is eternally present waiting to be discovered. This is the relationship of heart to heart existing in Truth as one heart.

Our relationships to objects are temporary. When we take refuge solely in a career or home or in our capacity to make a living as our main security, we are selling our birthright for a bowl of porridge. According to *Vedanta*, even working for good deeds to accumulate merit and go to heaven (i.e. work for happiness through goodness) is inferior to working for liberation. Heaven is just an important step on the way but even that is perishable(21).

Krishna makes a monumental pledge to his devotee: we need not worry about centering our lives around acquiring and preserving material things. One cannot be a true spiritual aspirant if his major motivation in life focuses on working for material things. *This is placing one's refuge in the wrong place.* The only way to be a sincere spiritual student is to take refuge in Truth, in divine protection, while working and putting forth one's best effort. Krishna promises:

> Those who worship me and meditate on me constantly without any thought of their own welfare, *I will provide for all their needs.*(9:22) EE
>
> To those who worship Me alone thinking of no other, to those ever self-controlled, I secure for them that which is not already possessed by them(*yoga*) and preserve for them what they already possess(*kshema*). SwC
>
> There are those who, excluding all else, think of Me and worship Me, aspiring after eternal union with Me. Their prosperity and welfare are looked after by me. SwA

For one who is devoted to the highest in oneself, there is no place for worry. Worry is only for those of us who place our faith in the perishable and in our own control over events. *Work well for the sake of evolving into our inner God nature; dedicate all our actions and thoughts to This and leave the results to Him.* Put forth our effort in the knowledge I am not the doer and all that is needed will come. This is universal law. It is not Pollyanna thinking but rather, an expression of cause and effect. It is the lawful working of the science of the universe.

> When the devotee takes one step towards the Lord, He takes ten steps towards that devotee. Such is His grace. (Ramakrishna)

When we can link our hearts to that which has been called the First Cause, the causeless cause, the way, It will carry the momentum of our lives toward the direction of ultimate fulfillment. This is faith based on scientific understanding. This is Krishna's promise to the person who surrenders his ego will to the will of the higher, be He called Krishna, Christ, Buddha, Yaweh, Self or *Atman*. To live one's life on the foundation of this secret brings true Self confidence.

> To be free in the world you must be free *of* the world. Otherwise your past decides for you and your future. Between what had happened and what must happen you are caught. Call it destiny or *karma* but never freedom. First return to your true being and then act from the heart of love. (Maharaj)

The Yoga of Giving

The enlivening force of life is always with us and expresses itself in different ways in accordance with our *vasanas* and what we need to learn in order to evolve. At one level, the divine *sakti* is the sheer power of sex, at another time it is maternal instinct, creativity, love of beauty, or working for a noble cause. Later, it might appear as symbolic understanding or descend as the shocking power of meaningful coincidence; or an ongoing mixture of all these. This same force of life is the momentum for our lower nature as well as our higher nature. When we begin to experience this inner energy as awe and gratitude, loving appreciation for the gift of life, we yearn to share this wonder somehow by living the love inside. *This loving gratitude is the expression of a natural, informal devotion, which spurs us on to give.* The spirit of genuine giving is the spirit of loving. If we want to forge a link with the love hidden inside, the best way to coax it out of hiding is through giving.

Krishna needs nothing because everyone and everything is His. Although we might not be aware of it, we also own nothing. Everything in Reality is He. When we are mentally aware of giving to Him, the love that is latent within comes to life. *His loving consciousness comes to life within us*. It is a universal law that by giving we receive.

> He who offers me with devotion only a leaf, a flower or a fruit, or even a little water, this I accept from that yearning soul because with a pure heart it was offered with love. (9:26)

If every time we drink water and we mentally give it to God, the act of drinking water becomes loving and holy. It crosses the bridge from biological need to holy offering. Everything we do is like that. Every breath has the potential of infusing sanctity into our lives. Through giving, we become linked with Him to whom we are giving. If our gift is mentally to God we come closer to God. This is why in vernacular life it India, it has been suggested not to give others gifts because through the gift the *karma* of the recipient and the giver become intertwined. To be able to give and receive from the Self to the Self, we participate in the cosmic exchange and cosmic sacrifice.

To live with the awareness that even our suffering serves some purpose we can learn to link our suffering with consciousness(27). The process is multifaceted and entails an acceptance of all aspects of life as a gift.

> Whatever you do, or eat or give or offer in adoration let it be an offering to me. And whatever you suffer suffer it for me. Thus thou shalt be free from the bonds of *Karma* which yield fruits that are evil and good. And with thy soul one in renunciation thou shalt be free and come to me. (9:27-28)

When we are no longer under the sway of our conditioning and our karma we are free. The stark simplicity of this inner freedom offers space for the light of conscious presence within to make itself felt. Through giving comes love. Love purifies. And then fullness consciousness appears within the heart that is empty—empty of all baggage. When we live in this loving devotion says Krishna, I am in you and you are in me. There is no difference between us(29).

This love is present equally within every heart. But it manifests differently to each of us, in accordance with the degree of covering. Ramakrishna says, "God is in all beings; but all beings are not in God. And that is the cause of their suffering."

All electricity behind the bulbs is the same but the voltage in the bulb is different. Likewise, all sin is never inherent in the core of a person. The worst criminal, be he a Hitler or a Stalin or a bin Laden has the same universal life force within his heart, inaccessible though it may be. The author of the *Ramayana* named Valmiki was once a murderer and thief. After he turned his mind to God, his past actions became so purified that his former way of being was left behind totally. And he became the creator of one of the most sacred texts of ancient India.

This lord of forgiveness can purify any soul no matter how black, as long as we turn to Him for help with deep remorse(30). For it is His wish to manifest, to come out of hiding and become apparent to all through our treatment of our fellow creatures. We are each His potential manifestation. This is the purpose of our presence on earth. And when after many lifetimes of intentional striving, this partnership with the divine presence shines through, even the most tortured characters among us will find lasting peace through merging with our inner divinity.

> Having come to this world of sorrow which is transient love thou me. Give me thy mind, give me thy heart, give me thy offerings, give me thy adoration. Thus with thy soul in harmony, making me thy goal supreme, thou shalt in truth come to me.
> (9:33-34)

So it seems this royal secret is ultimately a secret of the heart. Through seeing God in all and experiencing all in God, the effulgence of loving feelings harmonizes the heart—helps it beat to the One vibration of the universe(*Pranava, Om*). No longer a physiological entity, the subtle heart, the secret heart(*hrdaye guhayam*) becomes the sacred heart. Sri Sathya Sai Baba says:

> Spirituality is the spirit of oneness. It is the spirit of oneness that constitutes the real spiritual endeavor, the right devotion and the correct wisdom. (*Summer Showers, '93*, p.3)

> Man's native characteristic is divine love, his nature is divine love, his breath is divine love. God is the source of all love. Love God; love the world as the vesture of God. Through love, you can merge in the ocean of love. (*Digest 2*, p.192)

Thus, the ninth discourse reveals the living vision of secret loving unity that supports and pervades all seeming diversity.

Ten

YOGA OF DIVINE SPLENDOR

Vibhuti Yoga

	Gita verses
The source and powers of the divine	1–6, 8
Devotion and the effects of knowing these powers	7, 9–11
Arjuna asks to see the divine glory	12–18
Krishna reveals the ongoing infinite powers of existence	19–42

unborn I manifest
the essence of everyone
everything I am

Krishna has been expounding the science of Knowledge and God's relationship with the universe to help Arjuna differentiate Reality from unreality, leave his confusion behind and proceed toward liberation. By the end of the ninth chapter, it is clear that this Knowledge cannot be experienced without the prerequisite of devotion, love and a means of expressing this love called worship. Worship serves as the means of unification—linking our inner feeling and thought with our actions in life, with whatever happens and whomever we meet.

Ramanuja says:

> Fix your mind on Me uninterruptedly like a continuous stream of oil; on Me, the Ruler of rulers antagonistic to all that is evil, the sole abode of auspiciousness, omniscient, whose resolve is always true; the sole cause of the entire universe; the supreme *Brahman*, the supreme Person, the ocean of infinite mercy, affability, beauty, sweetness, majesty, magnanimity and parental affection; on Me the refuge of all without exception and without regard to their differences; on Me the Lord of all.
>
> What is called worship is the conduct of one who realizes that he is absolutely a subsidiary of God(*sesa*). Offer things of enjoyment. Do services which are incomparably dear and animated by an experience of Myself who is dear, unlimited and unsurpassed. Bow down to Me in utter humility regarding Me as the supreme goal. You will thus, through love which is unsurpassed and incomparable obtain a mind fit for experiencing Me. You will then realize Me alone.
>
> With this mental outlook of pleasing Me alone, carry on your secular works for bodily sustenance and *Vedic* activities, regarding them as activated by Me and finding sole joy in absolute subservience to Me. You shall ever engage yourself in praising My names with love and endeavoring to serve Me. You shall contemplate on the entire universe as being under my rule and subsidiary to Me. Contemplating on the multitudes of my attributes,

> which are exceedingly dear to you and practicing everyday this worship, you will reach Me alone. (Swami Adidevananda, p.323-4)

The framework has thus been presented for living life in all its diversity, motivated solely by our loving knowledge of the One—even though this love and knowledge are not yet fully experienced. Now in the tenth discourse, Krishna proceeds to elucidate His nature and His powers that we might be further awed and inspired to *know Him, love Him, see Him everywhere, and come to connect with His essence and His will.*

His will manifests as the life force or enlivening factor within each of us. This force is not to be confined to any religion or philosophy. It does not refer to a specific God of a special people living in a particular time and place. Rather, all its varied manifestations express its universal nature. All concrete forms and happenings are but different possibilities to lead us to the center of ourselves. This is the purpose of the world. This is the purpose of life.

> I am the soul which dwells in the heart of all things. I am the beginning, the middle and the end of all that lives. (10:20)

The title of the tenth chapter is "*Vibhuti Yoga.*" *Vibhuti* means kingship, lordship, ultimate power. Everything and everyone is an expression of the sovereign power of the Lord. This glory is all pervasive and everywhere: in matter, energy, the five elements, the atom, time and space. It is in all creation, preservation and destruction. It is the seed of all beings. The subtlest of the subtle, it transcends the man made boundaries of past, present, and future, of here and there, of all kinds of category, causation, and explanation. It simply exists in the ever present now awaiting union with our experiential perception.

From time to time in moments of inspiration, we are offered intuitive flashes into this realm of love, this space of ongoing unity. Steadiness in motivation is needed to deepen momentary inspiration into the continuous vision of persistent consciousness, that we might ascend to another rung on the ladder, through descending into a deeper layer within. It is this steady descent, devoted to finding our home in the center of the earth, that will enable us to perceive the splendor pulsating immanent in all things, in all beings, in all events, in all actions.

Arjuna knows that hearing about this as concept is not enough. He wants to experience specifics direct from the mouth of his God friend teacher *avatar*. For through specifics, the mind in each moment can become linked to understanding, to actions, to practice, to love, to everything and everyone. Through deepening experiential intuition and consequent understanding, the false sense of ego melts away and the person comes to occupy his rightful place as part of one whole. *The dual eye of maya gives way to the unified eye of wisdom.*

So the tenth discourse expands upon the themes of the seventh, eighth and ninth chapters by bringing together the specific and the universal, the individual and the totality, the archetype and that which is the unifying enlivener of the archetype. According to Shankara, the entire tenth discourse expounds *sarva loka maheshvara*, the Lord of the whole universe. This *sarva loka maheshvara* can be known only through Knowing(3). Just as we can learn to love only through loving, we can learn to know only through Knowing. And the Lord of the universe, Who is immanent in all things, is in fact the entire universe called Ishvara.

The Lord alone within each heart knows Himself with a thousand arms and faces everywhere. He is everywhere, forever omniscient. He was never created. Unlike human bodies, He is without beginning. Even the liberated Self, which is no longer subject to birth and death is said to have a beginning because at one time it was identified with matter. Only the Lord is without beginning and has existed always, without any form or modification.

It is only the coverings, defilements or unnecessary mental and emotional baggage that prevent our knowing His(Our) nature. When these are diminished, the divine auspicious attributes emerge. Clarity ensues, initiating the presence of devotion within(7). The stronger and steadier the devotion, the closer we come to experiencing His presence in everyone and everything—That which has existed always. Therefore, says Krishna:

> He who knows Me as unborn and without a beginning as the great Lord of all the worlds, he among mortals is undeluded and is released from every sin. (10:3)

The Origins of Individual Functioning

To help Arjuna proceed to a space before the origin of creation which is not then but *now*, where only primordial unity exists, Krishna poetically elaborates a symbolic explanation of the origin of the world from the seven seers(*rishis*) and the four founders of the human race, the eternal youths. To understand how the mind creates the world can lead us back before the beginning to always. When this search is undertaken with steady devotion that combines action and knowledge with ongoing loving practice, Krishna calls this process the "tremorless *yoga*"(SwC), or "the oneness of unwavering harmony"(JM)(7) This is pure devotion born of the knowledge that He is the source of all things. *Our own Self within is the eternal primordial beginning, ever fresh, ever new.*

Through practicing this *yoga*, through seeing with the vision of loving consciousness (*bhavasamanvitah*) the loving consciousness everywhere, the shower of grace descends. This fertile spring rain is the gift of *buddhi yoga*, the *yoga* of vision or discrimination(10-11). The gift is effortless, though this grace comes only from effort: a loving awareness that knows the origin of Itself and everything because It alone *is* the origin. It alone exists before the inception of anything. It alone is before the cell divides, before the egg hatches, before the division of time, before day and night, before the separation of conscious and unconscious. And It continues to exist after the dissolution, decay and death of everything. Through being in touch with ever finer levels of mind, ever purer levels of intellect, this awareness is gradually revealed.

From a symbolic perspective, the seven seers(*rishis*) relate to the seven planes of consciousness(2,6). In some philosophical systems, this has been called the ray of creation (Ouspensky). The great mystery of how the One seemingly becomes many has been expounded by the *Vedic* seers throughout the millenniums.

The transcendent Absolute, beyond time, substance or attribute, through an act of sacrifice, seemingly takes on form, intertwined with the subtle substance of matter itself (*pradhana*). And the huge cosmic egg, Hiranyagarbha, becomes the seed of all future manifestation. As the Word of God *Om* rings forth, time enters the arena. The descent of the Word of the Absolute can exist through us, when our body, emotions and intellect are in harmony.

Creation continues. First as an idea in the mind of God(*Mahat*), or an archetype of the collective unconscious,[22] this subtle form of preduality further differentiates into the individual form level of body, ego, mind, senses and sense objects. And the worlds are born. Intuitional glimpses into the process of creation, as experienced by the *rishis* in the seat of meditation, are also possible for us. Following is a schema of these seven levels:[23]

Cosmic Levels of Creation

0. beyond all levels, the Absolute, *Parabrahman*
1. Self, *Atma*, pure Consciousness, *Svabhava*
2. the root seed out of which matter evolves. *Mula prakriti*, unmanifest object, *Avyakta*
3. collective unconscious, causal body, *Mahat,* cosmic ideation, *Adhi daivata*
4. the light of pure intelligence with direct perceptual knowledge of the first three, *Buddhi*
5. individual ego, *jiva, Adhiyajna*
6. lower mind, mind united with desire, *manas,* senses
7. outer world, objects of outer senses, *Adhibhuta.*

These "stages" all exist simultaneously in *Brahman*. They interact and influence each other in mysterious ways, which can become partially accessible in accordance with our level of consciousness. It is all one giant play, the play of the Lord. And in actuality, Krishna tells us, nothing is moving or proceeding. There is only stillness eternity.

But as the Lord of the universe has created this partnership system, whereby we could coexist in matter in active participation with Him, it is only through dissolution and creation that we can work our way up to progressively higher levels of evolution, and ascend the seven steps of matter energy to the Absolute. Then we can serve as vehicles for the Absolute to descend into the world. The Word of God descends into our world as presence, dissolution and right action effort. When our thoughts, words and deeds are integrated, our inner personal dissonance no longer blocks out the harmony of the spheres or the universal vibration(*Om*).

Through living Truth(*sathyam*)—when we *feel* what we *think* and we say only what we knowingly feel—a power reveals itself. This power is a manifestation or *vibhuti* of the Lord. With each experience, a little ignorance is dissolved and we are brought closer to living in devotion. At the moment of liberation, all the "lower" levels lose their separating potency and are subsumed in the Absolute.[24]

On the collective level, great nature requires dissolution in order to maintain her creation. Esoteric teachings reveal that when the vibration of the Total Mind is not fine enough to provide the food nature requires for her sustenance, she demands her nourishment in the form of living beings(Gurdjieff). The wars that result from individual human greed, hatred and attachment are according to natural law, the inevitable consequence of the impoverishment of the Total Mind. *When the life principle called Kali is not worshipped with love as the Great Mother, she exhibits her terrifying aspect in the form of earthquake, flood, famine, bomb and the effects of ozone depletion and global warming.*

The process is ever ongoing. Where there is balance, there is no need for destruction. Dissolution comes only where there is imbalance, as nature's way of bringing harmony to nature. Thus, the quality of life for each of us depends solely on our level of consciousness, or on which rung of the ladder we exist. And the mind of each human being determines the quality of life in the world as a collective whole.

The mind creates the world, our perceptions create the mind, and the sense stimuli that enter the mind create our perceptions. If sense objects do not enter into our mind, it is as if they are not there. Therefore, our active participation in creating our own lives and contributing to our spiritual growth begins at the level of controlling the sense organs. Through learning to keep the senses inside(*pratyahara*), to oversee the senses that they not compulsively run after sense objects, we work to prevent the lower level of sense objects and material desires from controlling our mind, our actions and our lives.

Through this practice, we establish a *partnership* with Vishnu Krishna Self as *sarva loka maheshwara*, the Lord of the entire universe. For to be king of oneself requires balanced, just, and harmonious rulership. As each of us is a universe unto ourself, we are also but a cell in the body of the whole. So our spiritual work is to become Lord of ourselves and thereby king of the universe. To illustrate the point, Swami Chinmayanda says:

> We know that when thoughts rise in us they are capable of disturbing us. At a certain moment some desire in us gets concentrated and identifying with it we maintain it in a steady stream of dynamic thought. Thus dynamized, the initial thought becomes mighty and powerful enough to destroy our peace and tranquility and projecting itself creates the perception of and our reactions to the world of the five sense objects. The thought stream and its projections together supply us with both the material and efficient causes for our own tiny world of joys and sorrows, victories and failures, yearnings and fulfillments. (THG p.591)

This demonstrates simply how a thought actually provides the emotional, intellectual and material content of our world and thereby *creates our universe.* In the same way, the quality of our perceptions will determine where we stand on the ladder of creation. Total identification with the body, senses and concrete consciousness, for example, places us on a "lower" level than when we receive glimpses of an expanded awareness of the enlivening force of life within all.

> United to the lower levels, the Self flows outward into forms and dies as it were with them. While united to the higher, it is carried homewards by the inflowing cosmic tides. (Sri Krishna Prem, p.93)

Until consciousness unites the different archetypes, the diverse gods, the human individuality remains split off from the totality of world experience as well as from interactive connections between different qualities of individual experiences. Energy is energy; *prana* is *prana*. This subtle unifying thread of consciousness can be experientially felt throughout each archetypal theme and variation of living. As more and more people experience this consciousness, the balance of power in the world shifts from evil to beneficence.

The Tremorless Yoga

Swami Chinmayananda helps us further understand and experience this knowledge:

> When the Self detaches itself from both the individual mind and the cosmic mind it comes to revel in all its absolute glory. Identifying itself with the cosmic mind it becomes the creator(Ishvara) creating the universe and identifying with the individual mind it becomes the limited ego suffering the limited world. To know this implication and to live up to this is the tremorless *yoga* wherein a permanent and steady establishment in the experience of the Self is assured. (THG p.593-4)

So the "oneness of unwavering harmony" is a steady awareness of the infinite playing through the world of names and forms, equally present in the ant and in the human being, in the murderer and in the holy man. This awareness induces love, increases love *is* love. *It is this awareness which supports all evolution beyond the automatic biological level.*

The process can emerge when we allow ourselves to observe and experience that which is most primitive within us—when we embrace a voluntary return to Siva, the auspicious, dissolver aspect within. When we are drawn into anger, passion or passivity, we are being called upon to make efforts of awareness. For there is a power in these raw energies, which can be transformed by the light of awareness into the light of Consciousness. When we begin to worship the One by trying to link our emotions and actions to center around this One, we are putting forth the effort of ascent that will allow grace to descend in the form of *buddhi yoga*, the *yoga* of vision.

> In my mercy I dwell in their hearts and I dispel their darkness of ignorance by the light of the lamp of wisdom. (10:11)

Emotions are not just emotions
Stones are not just stones
People are not just people

Thus, Krishna teaches Arjuna how:

> The Divine pervading powers are to be looked for in the things below. By constant meditation, the disciple must sharpen his intuitive perceptions to clearness until outer forms seem unreal things through whose translucid shells the wondrous powers shine in their gleaming splendor. As he proceeds, a change will overtake his vision. Not only will he see the spiritual power in each form but since these powers are united in a loving whole, he will begin to see what before he could but think; the vast interconnections of all things. (Sri Krishna Prem, p.98)

Let's pause and review the different definitions of *yoga* we've already encountered:

1. *Yoga* is dexterity in action(2:48).
2. *Yoga* is evenness of mind(2:50).
3. *Yoga* is severance from the union with pain(6:23).
4. The tremorless *yoga* is seeing the Self pervading all at the individual as well as the cosmic universal level(10:7).

Again and again we are faced with the teaching that each of us is the architect of our own life, in accordance with the workings of the mind. Yet, at the same time, we are not free to create our life in accordance with *dharma*, as long as our desires, mind, and actions pursue imprisoning ways of living. So the dilemna is we are absolutely free and we are fully imprisoned by the shackles of our past impressions.[25] What is the way out?

The sages say, the way is to work on *transforming the quality of the impressions* we receive. We can choose to place ourselves under influences that will bring new impressions, finer impressions to our inner equipment. This descends to the subtle body in the form of finer feeling and sensation.

Everything in the world exists as a reminder to bring us back to the One. Beauty opens the heart to the One. Suffering opens the heart to the One. Sacrifice opens the heart to the One. Potentially, every moment, every movement is but a ripple in the body of the whole, which beckons to purify all that prevents our connection with the One. *Evolution itself can be considered a process of purifying the mind or inner equipment that veils our perception of the One.* All this comprises the tremorless *yoga*.

Devotion and Buddhi Yoga

The One is the power of love. Love is the cohesiveness that holds together, embraces and permeates every level of being in the universe.

> I am the source of all. The evolution of all comes from me. Understanding this, the wise worship me in loving consciousness. (10:8)

From an external standpoint, the world is the same to a wise person or a fool. But the wise one sees the workings of the law of love in everyone and everything whereas the fool takes things at face value, paying attention only to the outer aspect. The spiritual student sees the continuous sweetness of being and the purposefulness behind everything, although it cannot often be articulated. The fool sees only the concrete thing or happening. The aspirant lives life in the graciousness and gratitude of ever receiving what belongs to the Lord alone, as everything and everyone is only He. But the fool is ever grabbing for more, craving for more, clinging to this or that as his own, unable to revel in the moment of the natural wonder of existence. The fool is unable to receive. The world is ever permeated with effulgence but the radiance remains unknown to us as long as we expect material things and egocentric striving to make us happy. When we consciously begin to perceive and suffer our own shortcomings, there is a purification of *prakriti* within; we begin to participate in a kind of shedding process under the jurisdiction of the One. The suffering entailed in this process can be joyful.

Once we take a stand in favor of uncovering Truth, it is helpful to join energies with other like-minded people(9). Sharing group energies serves as a more powerful inspiration in our individual work and makes daily life lighter, more meaningful, more vital. Others serve as a mirror of our own love, our own faults. They bring out our reactivity, our unthinking reactions, that this automatic mechanicalness might be brought under the gaze of the inner witness for purification. When the vital energy becomes more fully centered on the ruler of the heart within, we begin to experience love for others that is not based on personal relationship. There are flashes of perceiving a level where there is no difference between oneself and others. Through communal work, through giving to each other, the inner vitality quickens, becomes more tangible.

The more steadily we are able to give love and calmness of presence in whatever we do, the stronger these qualities become. Or the more acutely we experience our own lacks based on observing our behavior, the closer we come to rooting out the impediments to devotion.

Our life is a practice in developing love and service not just by doing good deeds but by integrating the mind, the heart and the hand in ongoing loving presence. After many years of this practice, through stillness meditation in action, *Krishna promises his devotee that his grace will descend.* There is no more need for effort.

> Out of compassion I destroy the darkness of their ignorance. From within them I light the lamp of wisdom and dispel all darkness from their lives. (10:11) EE
>
> In my mercy I dwell in their hearts and I dispel their darkness of ignorance by the light of the lamp of wisdom. JM
>
> Out of mere compassion for them, I dwelling within their heart, destroy the darkness born of ignorance by the luminous lamp of knowledge. SwC

Arjuna's Faith and Understanding

Now when Arjuna speaks, the deepening power of his faith is evident(12-18). He is no longer the skeptical doubter. Krishna's words have entered his heart and he deeply wishes to understand, to be shown through personal experience the depth and breadth of God's sovereign splendor. Arjuna is now able to pray to Krishna to help him transcend the limitations of his name, form and function in the society. He no longer wishes to worship Krishna's form alone in a dualistic manner, in an I-thou relationship. His aim is to know Himself with Himself; with the spirit within himself he wishes to know the spirit within the universe. And he asks Krishna to help him unite His energy with the energy of the world filtering through the spirit in all, that he will be able to touch that spiritual essence in himself and in all things. Arjuna is devotedly asking Krishna to help him experience God immanent in the universe of names and forms.

> Only thy Spirit knows thy Spirit; only thou knowest thyself.
> Source of Being in all beings, God of gods, ruler of all. (10:15)

Consciousness and the Total Mind

From *sloka* nineteen onward, Krishna reveals to Arjuna some of the archetypes of life in this world, as we know it. He is not merely listing concrete things in a poetic manner. He is responding to Arjuna's underlying question of how to meditate on God in life. He is describing the ever living, ever expanding, ever continuous faces of God in the world. *Vedantins* call it Ishvara, the Total Mind. Carl Jung calls it the collective unconscious.

Behind each statement a Platonic idea is revealed, an archetype that exists continuously, as long as the universe exists. To perceive the image of the archetype induces a subtler form of perception than experiencing the concrete image from the sense organs. In one schema of cosmic creation, the Total Mind has been placed third in the continuum. Whether the archetype is perceived as image in dream or seen as existing now from another era; whether felt as a moment eternal or experienced as part of the Totality, this form of perception can serve as a shock that inevitably expands our limited sense of self, so that *we no longer remain under the total domination of the sense organs and lower mind.* Although macrocosmically, each stage is viewed as a total level of evolution, we can also receive partial and momentary flash impressions from this level without yet experiencing it totally. Thus to perceive the inner, which also appears to be outer, one comes to question the boundary between inner and outer. "Am I a butterfly dreaming that I'm a king or a king dreaming I'm a butterfly"?

In this realm there is an ongoingness throughout time, a fluidity which transcends any category the mind might create, such as beginning, middle and end or past, present and future(32-3). There is a cohesiveness of existence, which is sustained and supported by the subtlest of the subtle called consciousness love. Without this loving sustainer called Vishnu or Buddha consciousness living within each heart, which pervades all existence in all three realms of time, there would be no world. In the same way, when consciousness is withdrawn from the world of plurality to Vishnu there is no world. Our thoughts and experiences rise from the sea supporting them and return again to the sea, to the Total Mind where they interact with, influence and create life on earth.

Behind each image presented, there is a story with which the average person of Arjuna's time was quite familiar. Each image is an expression of life that can invoke wisdom. Krishna begins with the Self, the essence, the enlivening factor of everything(20). This is reflected in the cosmos and symbolized by the sun, the giver of warmth and radiance, without which there would be no life, heat or movement(21). The sun has been worshipped as the center, as God by many ancient peoples, including the authors of the *Vedas*, who revealed the ever ancient knowledge that is always preserved within the human soul and can never be destroyed(22). The *Vedas* then, serve as a link between the Self, the cosmos and the inner equipment(*antahkarana*) through which we process knowledge.

Consciousness is not the mind, it is not the ego. Consciousness is simply the *light through which the mind and intellect feel and think.* Like the sun that illumines everything, consciousness supports and pervades everything. This is beyond Indra, who is often viewed as the chief of the mind, that part of us responsible for perpetrating our thoughts and desires. Clearly, this light of consciousness is not to be equated with ego functioning but exists as the "essence of all beings, the beginning, middle and end of all that lives."

Sri Sathya Sai Baba says:

> There is an atomic particle subtler than the atom.
> There is something vaster than the vastest you can imagine.
> The atom is in the immense and the immense is in the atom.
> The *Atman* is in the atom as the Spirit. (SS3-95, p.57)

There's a story told in the *Bhagavatam* about Indra who becomes jealous of the child Krishna gaining such unbounded love and worship from all the people. In envy, he pours down torrents of rain to reveal his power. At the time, Krishna is a boy of about seven. With one finger he lifts Govadhara mountain, which serves as an umbrella to shelter everyone from the rain. Then his foster mother Yashoda becomes worried because she thinks of him as her seven year old son, even though she has seen over and over again manifestations of his divinity. The literal perceptions of body consciousness are so deeply entrenched because of attachment, that even the impact of miraculous experiences can be forgotten in an instant of anxiety. As the protective umbrella of Krishna continues to shield the people of Brindavan, Indra is forced to capitulate and worship Him. So he stops the treacherous rain.

This tale tells that in our arrogance we come to feel the mind and ego are supremely powerful, but their actions are nothing compared to the power and radiance of being-consciousness, as represented by Krishna. When pride motivates us to reveal our power, destruction results. What we considered to be *our* power is inevitably taken away. For the right flow in the natural order of things both individual and cosmic, the ego, mind and intellect must pay homage to the Self. *And the Self is everywhere.*

The Ocean of Milk

The *Puranic* story of the churning of the ocean of milk is the prototype for spiritual evolution(27). It tells of a time of stalemate in the fight between the gods and demons. The only way a new world order could be formed would be for the gods and demons to cooperate with each other and start churning the ocean together so as to receive the nectar of immortality, *amrita*. This teaches that our positive and negative qualities, the energy of "lower" and "higher" *prakriti* must both be acknowledged and utilized for spiritual work.

Manthara mountain is used as a churning rod with the snake Vasuki wrapped round it. While the *devas* and *asuras* are carrying the mountain to the ocean, it falls and crushes many people. Then Garuda, the great eagle vehicle of Vishnu comes to the rescue and helps them. The *asuras* don't want Vasuki's tail because they think it's dirty so they grab the head, not knowing this is where the poison would later emerge. Clearly it is the mind, the subtle and/or causal body that is the original carrier of our inner poison and not the physical body.

When the poison starts pouring out, fear and panic are everywhere; it kills everything in sight—snakes, fish, people. But the unleashed power of our passions, rage and "negative emotions" must emerge in the light of consciousness for a rebirth to occur. The gods pray with all their might for help till Siva appears and drinks the poison of the world. He lets it remain in his neck and does not swallow it. His neck turns blue. By taking on the poison of the world without digesting it, Siva as Neelakanta(blue-necked) becomes the prototype of sacrifice. This serves as an example for the true spiritual aspirant—to participate in dissolving one's own poison as well as the poison of the world—without being inundated by it.[26]

After all the poison vanishes, wondrous and useful things begin emerging from the ocean, such as the white winged horse Ucchaisravas and the elephant Airavata. These symbolize pure intuition, grace, and the power of overcoming obstacles. They are given as gifts to Indra. Other fantastic objects emerge: a wish fulfilling cow(Kamadhenu), a youth with all knowledge of medicine, a beautiful enchantress Mohini, and finally the *amrita*. Of course there is a fight over the nectar and the *asuras* steal it away from the gods. When the situation is most desperate, the gorgeous Mohini appears. She is none other than Vishnu in disguise. She entices the *asuras* to follow her, which enables the gods to possess the nectar.

Anyone who spends time delving into the essence of the tale is given guidelines for his own process of evolution, which demonstrates how the universe is created. It shows how the raw energies of *prakriti* become transformed through meditation, how *kundalini* transmutes the serpent of desire—dissolving and transforming self-centered desire into beneficent, universal love. Sri Sathya Sai Baba says:

> When the ocean of milk was churned, a pot of poison arose first. Undismayed by this, the *devas* and *asuras* continued the churning and thus obtained many priceless and valuable gifts and finally the nectar of immortality. Similarly, in spirituality when the heart is churned with the rod of wisdom, we may meet with many losses, disappointment, pain and blame. But if continued with undaunted courage and faith, we will reap kindness, sympathy, tolerance, forgiveness, forbearance and other such virtues. Rather than succumbing to disappointment, man must face life with courage and self confidence. Without faith in one's own Self, nothing can be achieved.

Story of Prahlada

The story of Prahlada reveals the life-giving strength of faith and devotion against seemingly impossible odds(30). Prahlada is a devout boy whose father Hiranyakasipu is a powerful king of the *asuras*. The *asuras* are those who worship gold or material things. Hiranyakasipu feels very threatened by anything spiritual and is interested solely in power, in being worshipped as God. In other words, he believes that his own actions and accomplishments are the measure of all things. And he insists everyone else follow his beliefs.

Since Prahlada's birth, the name of Vishnu reverberates in his heart. His father tries everything to reeducate him to adopt material values but to no avail. As a young boy, he is kicked out of school for teaching the other boys to take the *mantra* of Vishnu. He is then given a tutor who has the sole task of molding Prahlada's mind to conform to his father's beliefs.

When Hiranyakasipu realizes that reeducation is impossible, he tries to kill the boy. First he is thrown off a high cliff. But he remains unharmed. Then he is given deadly poison. He recites Vishnu's name and drinks it. Nothing happens. No matter what the demon king tries, his knowledge and power cannot circumvent the boy's protection by Vishnu. *How many fathers today strive to educate their sons to be an extension of themselves—either knowingly or unknowingly?* This insensitivity is akin to murdering the Self of the child.

The *asura* became so powerful and haughty because after performing *tapas* he was granted a boon—not to be killed inside or outside, in daytime or night, nor by any weapon, man or beast. Thus he was seemingly invincible, or so he thought.

One day in the courtyard of the palace, Hiranyakasipu challenges his son:

"Where is this God of yours"?

"Father, he is everywhere," replies the boy.

"How can he be everywhere if I can't see him"?

Now that's the argument of all concrete people who believe the real world consists only of matter.

"Is he in that pillar there"?

"Yes father."

"Then show him to me," says Hiranyakasipu, making fun of the boy.

Suddenly during dusk(neither day nor night), in the breezeway between inside and outside, out of the pillar emerges a creature called *Narasimha*, half lion half man, neither man nor beast. This creature is one of the ten *avatar* incarnations of Vishnu. He proceeds to claw Hiranyakasipu to death. No weapon is used. All the conditions of his boon are rightly met.

This story reveals the power of devotion and purity is ultimately stronger than the power of materialistic thinking and military might. To know that the power of God lives even in stone is to be protected by the inner strength of the lion. Evil might gain the upper hand for a time, but ultimately it is doomed to failure. And even if we're born into a highly materialistic society, in a family with few spiritual values, it is possible to follow our inner prompting, our inner conscience and develop our own character in a way that feels right inside. All the past conditioning we receive from societal and parental values that are not in accord with our deepest wish, with Truth, *need not bind us.* It is always possible, even in the *Kali yuga* to search into our heart and live out our spontaneous essence, uncovered and uncluttered. This alone makes life worthwhile, purposeful and joyful, that we might each become a blessing unto ourself and every one we meet.

On a deeper level, the sages say that Prahlada saved his father from the curse of his demonic birth. Because of his death at the hands of the lion avatar, Hiranyakasipu became liberated.

Psychology of Alchemy

Everything in the world of matter from the human body to the tiniest cell is composed of the five elements. And each of these elements—ether, air, water, fire, and earth, offer us their own mode of purification. Any transformation from one level of functioning to another must reflect itself within the body, which also includes the psyche. The body then serves as the alchemical vessel.

Purification by fire(23) especially relates to work on the emotions, passions, explosiveness; the tendency toward *rajas*. Whenever the *rajas* of passion arises, the element fire, or god Agni is offering the opportunity to transform our volatile energy into Self. By heating us up we get melted down. That which is hard and constricted becomes fluid, while all that is unnecessary gets burned to ashes. Through heating, base metals are transformed into gold. Through melting and burning, the human personality is transmuted. Lust becomes luster. Shining radiance emerges.

The element water(24, 29) purifies by cleansing and dissolving. Our fixed attitudes and disappointments are washed away through tears of depression and pain. The "terrible powers," the eleven *Rudras* are the aspects of Siva related to different kinds of suffering(23). Purification by water forces us into receptivity. Here the *guna* of *tamas* predominates, causing us to wait, to float, and wallow in inertia flooded by emotion and confusion till we seem unable to function. We might feel overwhelmed or even useless for a time, until we are forced to develop patience. When under the influence of the water element, if we are able to look within and develop faith, we will come to see that our impurities are being cleansed and dissolved, paving the way for the baptism of rebirth. Then we might truly learn to swim across the ocean of *samsara*.

For the element ether, the attribute of sound predominates(25, 26). Repetition of *Om* serves to purify the mind and the environment. Three letters of A-U-M relate to the three states of consciousness—

the waking, the dream and the deep sleep state; while that which supports them is considered the fourth state(*turiya*), which includes and transcends the three (see *Mandukya Upanishad*). Through the practice of concentration on *Om*, one attunes his mind to a state of remembrance of the higher.

Purification through earth takes us through the reptilian, snakelike energies of physical needs and physiological functions. These influence our emotions and actions. Our instinctive energies can be directed primarily toward living an animal existence and propagating the human race or some of this snakelike earthiness can be utilized for evolving *kama* or desire into *kundalini*, the upliftment of animal energy toward Truth. Everyday our bodies offer us this opportunity. Be it in the realm of food, sex or hormonal responses, the choice is ours. Each time we consciously refuse to capitulate to an ice cream cone, we are giving reptilian energies an opportunity to become separate from the mind, not to overstep their sphere of influence. Again and again in our upward ascent we are thrown down into the *prima materia* of earth energies, which demand to be accepted but need not be acted out, that we might participate in liberating a chunk of spirit from the clutches of *tamas* and *rajas*, from matter.

A timeless image for the transformation of snake energy to spirit energy is the Buddha sitting under the *bodhi* tree. To shelter the meditating Buddha from rain and sun, the cobra stands erect, making use of his hood as a protection from the elements. When the mind radiates harmlessness, even the most harmful cobra will not attack. When the Buddha mind radiates love, the serpent responds with love. When we can respond with detachment kindness to whatever seemingly negative thing happens, we are no longer under the grip of the lower instinctive energies. *Then the powers of life bless us. And the divine presence acting through us, in turn, blesses all life.* Another name for this "reciprocal maintenance" is *dharma*.

Purification through air or wind(31) can be viewed as a drying off process after the tears of dissolution. When old hurts and attitudes are let go, the capacity to be blown by the wind, to give up the need to control and to experience oneself and one's life in partnership with external happenings and inner prompting relates to the capacity to surrender. To be open to whatever we meet along the way stripped of all preconceived ideas, to live fully in the present moment is to follow the way of the wind. This leads us to our Self. When we bring inner presence to whatever comes, the wind will bring us freedom.

As we proceed on the path, transmutation of the elements occurs at progressively subtler levels. For example, with the element fire at the grosser more extroverted level, the task might be to transform the eruptive heat of emotion and passion into steady, sustaining warmth. As a person becomes more introverted and further evolved, the task would be to generate an inner heat or electromagnetic energy. The subtler the energy, the closer we come to God. The practice of *tapas* and meditation serve this alchemical function.

> If the spirit can become malleable matter and matter made supple become spirit, spiritual experience will demonstrate that it can transform the behavior of the individual. This transformation—spirit-matter and matter-spirit is true spiritual existentialism, the consciousness of *sat*(existence). (Reymond, p.179)
>
> All spiritual experiences are sensations in the body. They are simply a graded series of sensations beginning with the solidity of a clod of earth and passing gradually in full consciousness through liquidness and the emanation of heat to that of a total vibration before reaching the Void. The road to be traveled is long. (ibid. p.192)

The *Chandogya Upanishad* says:

> Oh amiable one, with the help of this sprout that food is search out its root that is water. With the help of this sprout that water is search out the root that is fire. With the help of this sprout that fire is search out the root that is existence. (VI, 8:4)

Death too is a transformation, an integral part of life whose function is to destroy, that something new can be created(34). All existence is dependent on the power of death to dissolve whatever has outlived its usefulness, that *prakriti* be given another opportunity to create and construct in added purity.

The Seven Female Qualities

Krishna then lists the seven female qualities, those goddesses or powers who are aspects of the Lord (34). Recognition of these universal aspects of the goddess are found throughout the ancient texts of India(for example, see *Devi Bhagavata Purana, Book III*). These are: fame based on *dharma*, beauty or prosperity, perfect speech, memory, intelligence, firmness or loyalty, and forgiveness. Here the goddess is worshipped as the divine mother, the mother of the universe—one who gives birth to love, poetry, music, creation, right speech, science, knowledge, invention and all that helps humanity come closer to Self Knowledge (*Atma vidya*). *This mother nourishes us with the food of finer impressions, the basis of love.*

The beauty of which Krishna speaks is called *sri*. This is the *inner beauty* of the goddess—potentially accessible to all. It reflects an internal glow, which shines through the eyes and skin, posture and deportment. It is far more subtle than external appearance and has little to do with age, sex or physical features. Rather, it reveals gentle compassion, grace, gracious living, vitality: a life quality ever radiant. *Sri* is personified by Lakshmi, the goddess of beauty, harmony, wealth, abundance, and radiance.

The goddess Saraswati embodies another aspects of *sri:* the beauty of noble speech, intelligence, music, poetry and the science of scripture. This includes the quality of firmness, persistence in spiritual practice and the ability to stand behind what's right, to speak up justly, without hostility or judgement. This is an intelligent firmness that participates in creating positive conditions for daily living. *She is the muse yogini who graces us with Self Knowledge.*

Forgiveness (34) is a prerequisite for love and growth, for letting go of the ego. Without forgiveness we remain attached to our anger, hurt and confusion. This attachment is like armor that covers the warmth and fluidity of the heart.

Ultimately, the female qualities are not only the domain of woman; nor are they culturally determined. All qualities of the gods and goddesses are part of one self-contained, androgynous whole—a whole that transcends gender and matter. Siva is depicted as hermaphrodite, part man part woman called Ardhanarisvara, the

Lord whose half is woman. In the *Bhagavata Purana*, the *Parabrahman* or transcendent God is described as:

> The lord of Sakti and Siva are the womb and seed of the universe who, like the spider forms his web in sport through the agency of Sakti and Siva (who are one with himself) preserves and reabsorbs it. Sexual biunity is beyond the duality of Siva and Sakti(his active power) for both are within him. Through the seed and womb of the universe together in one, the great god playfully creates, preserves and reabsorbs the universe.
> (Stella Kramrisch, p.18)

Incarnating God Energy

Another form of beauty is called *tejas*(36). This is an inner splendor related to the five *pranas*, the subtle energy that circulates and reflects the subtle body. When we live in *brahmacharya*, purity or pure *sattva*, our thoughts, feelings and actions shine forth as a shining radiance of being. This glow is the light of God, which is very bright and tangible.

The scriptures speak of three levels of energy that comprise human radiance, perfection and beauty. These are:

1. physical health and virility due to perfect balance in the constituents(*tattvas*) of the healthy body(*ojas*)
2. the shine of an individual(*tejas*) when *ojas* has been conserved, disciplined and trained through meditation and personality integration
3. beauty or the aura of divinity(*dyuti*)

> When a *yogi*, through intelligent living and a devoted life of continued meditation has gathered to himself sufficient *ojas* and *tejas*, in time he grows to become an experienced saint of divine realization, a Buddha. The enchanting atmosphere of irresistible peace and compassion, love and perfection, knowledge and strength such a man imparts around him is called the aura of divinity. (Swami Chinmayananda, *1000 Names of Vishnu*, p.87)

In this way, the mind and body interact. *As finer levels of soul energy manifest, the physical body actually changes.* The resultant glow(*dyuti*) is a lawful physiological process.

> I am the cleverness in the gambler's dice. I am the radiance of all things beautiful. I am victory and the struggle for victory. I am the goodness of those who are good. I am the scepter of the rulers of men. I am the wise policy of those who seek victory. I am the silence of hidden mysteries; and I am the knowledge of those who know. And know Arjuna that I am the seed of all things that are; and that no being that moves or moves not can ever be without me. Know that whatever is beautiful and good, whatever has glory and power is only a portion of my own radiance. But of what help is it to know this diversity? Know that with one single fraction of my Being I pervade and support the universe. And know that I Am. (10:36-41) JM

The energy of love is the support for every aspect of manifestation, both good and evil. But *the good* is a direct reflection of and participation in the divine. Qualities that spread love and uplift consciousness are part of the divine descent. Qualities that spread material values and hatred are also supported by the divine but at a more distant and impersonal level. The unmanifest *Atma* is the same in everyone but where there is evil action, divine support has not yet permeated *prakriti* in the field of daily living; divine energy has not yet incarnated. This breeds confusion and suffering. *A real human being is needed to become the carrier of divine energy, so the greatest good can enter into life.*

Yet in nature and in the workings of the cosmos, the divine is equally present in all. To live in this level of being existence I AM, where the individual I knows itself as formless I(Self, *Atma*) is the practice and goal of all spiritual work. To approach this aim, we must first pass through the portals of the good.

Through practice, divine distance ends in presence. To ever strive toward manifesting through our thoughts, perceptions and behavior the perfection that is inherent within is the task of the spiritual seeker. We can connect with this divine glory in myriad of ways, under varied circumstances. But no matter how different the manifestations, it is all One, all unity, all blessing, all love. May our every perception, our every intuition, our every thought come to reflect and radiate this divine love. Sri Sathya Sai Baba says:

> God is the eternal witness with no attributes or form. He can take any form at will. Though attributeless, He is in all attributes. Divinity is everywhere in the form and the formless, in the attribute and the attributeless. (Discourse, 2-28-95)

> Look upon external nature as the vestment of God. It is the expression of His will, the manifestation of His glory, His Power, His Might and His Majesty. See this in every blade of grass, in every petal, every fruit... The universe is the universal principle manifested in multifarious particulars. Man is God in miniature. (*Digest*, *v2* p.138)

Thus, the tenth discourse reveals the *yoga* of the descent of the Absolute into all levels of life where His/Her power and beauty and glory can be seen everywhere by our purified consciousness. By experiencing the divine presence in our daily lives, we participate in uplifting the world.

Eleven

YOGA OF THE COSMIC VISION

Visvarupa Darsana Yoga

	Gita verses
Arjuna asks Krishna to show him the cosmic form	1–4
Krishna reveals the beginningless universe	5–8
Sanjaya describes the cosmic form to Dhritarashtara	9–14
Arjuna's loving gratitude	15–22
Arjuna's fear inducing vision	23–31
Krishna as Lord of time inspires Arjuna to fight	24–34
Arjuna's universal prayer and request for forgiveness	35–45
Arjuna's wish for the familiar form of God and Krishna's response	46–51
Single-minded devotion alone*(ananyabhakti)* qualifies one to see the cosmic form	52–55

with the divine eye
see My presence continuous
beyond the realm of time

worlds of dazzling splendor
black holes and jaws of death
I maintain them all
ever peaceful

The eleventh discourse in a flash dispels all notions of God, annihilates all concepts of God, dissolves all preconceived ideas about God. Even the atheist has some belief about what God is or is not, but every opinion is subjective. Reality cannot be conceived by the mind. Every attempt to think about God is an expression of duality. Contemporary theoretical knowledge of physics as energy interconnecting all things in total time can actually be *experienced* as the universal, cosmic form of God. The only way to know God, the sages say is to *be*. Be your Self. Live the God-nature.

There are three graded steps in the process of dissolving the veils that prevent us from living our God-nature: 1) to know, 2) to see, 3) to enter into(54). In the tenth chapter, Krishna helped Arjuna to know, to feel and understand this Reality by enumerating the one pervasive power inherent in all the variety and multiplicity of gods and archetypes, names and forms. Now in the eleventh discourse, Arjuna wants to *see* this Reality(4).

This is a seeing that comes not from the eye of the senses but from the divine eye(*divya chakshu*), the third eye, invisible to sight, located between the eyebrows. This eye of wisdom sees with the subtlety of the purified intellect. It sees all. It knows all.

When Arjuna asks his teacher friend Krishna to let him see the cosmic form, little does he know what seeing God entails. But he trusts Krishna so completely that he asks in the faithful knowledge that Krishna will reveal what is right for him to see. To ask and articulate what we wish is essential for spiritual growth. It helps us clarify what is needed so that the unconscious can respond. "Ask and you shall receive. Knock and the door will be opened." At some point, it is essential to ask.

Now what exactly did Arjuna ask for and what did he receive? Sanjaya reported it all to the unseeing king. Whereas Dhritarashra was too blind mentally to comprehend what was being shown to Arjuna, you and I are given an opportunity to penetrate our darkness and experience a tiny fraction of this Reality. Reality is always here. Truth is ever present. But we must be open to be able to receive it.

By revealing some of the glories of the cosmos, Krishna shows Arjuna how the subtlest seed of divine energy is the essence of life that permeates and pervades everything. Chapter ten teaches the One in the many, the sacredness immanent in every atom of the universe, in every cell of the body. Chapter eleven depicts the many in the One. Here, every aspect of the cosmos, matter, time and space are all viewed together as the body of God, Truth, Reality, *Paramatman*.

Whatever we see as creation, growth, preservation, decay and death are all part of the body of God. *These are one simultaneous process*. They are not segmented. All are part of God's play, the *yoga* of God. Just as a cell is seen to move and pulsate under a microscope, so Arjuna sees the body of God moving and pulsating as one immense, infinite cell, ever changing within its changelessness.

This macrocosmic body is One. It includes past, present and future as One. Time and space are One—the U.S. and India, ocean and land, sky and earth are One. All the earth changes and continental drifts from unfathomable millennia are ongoing parts of this wholeness. In Reality, time, place and space are all part of One body, One *Purusha*, One *Brahman*.

What is it then that prevents us from experiencing the eternal continuity of Reality? What causes us to segment, divide and separate? We see you and me, here and there, yesterday, today and tomorrow. Arjuna knows that this partial view is his perception of life. He knows he wants to penetrate behind the barrier of individual separateness to break down the brick wall that prevents his experience of Reality. Now he is at the turning point. By asking for the Real he has acknowledged that his perceptions are not Real. On the battlefield before the war, Krishna shows Arjuna the vision of the body of the cosmos as One limitless entity; where past, present, and future are perceived at the same time, and there are no barriers of time and space.[27]

Without the concept of time and space everything is One. No divisions exist. What was once perceived as diverse becomes united. Just as the different limbs and organs comprise the human being, so too the different planets, suns and life forms are all part of the body of God. When our vision is no longer attached to the physical eye and the little I, *we begin to see.*

What exactly is Krishna revealing? He is showing Arjuna Himself as the God of Time(*Kala*)(32). And how can we view time? The sages say, from a wider perspective time does not pass; time as we conventionally view it does not exist. When there is only One there is no time. When there are two, then time is; a second enters the arena of life. A second is born from a thought. Where there is no thought, there is no two. And there is no time.

Time is infinite. Time is God. Time is composed of all space and all the names and forms that live in this space. It is composed of all sounds that vibrate, all movements that dance in this space. And what do these movements consist of? Birth, death, birth death, coming and going, going and coming, all to make room for the new forms that are entering be they suns or stars, planets or people, ants or amoebae, we are all ever moving as part of the wondrous eternal that never changes.

this dance of Siva Nataraj
ever flitting through all
names and forms and circles of fire

every standing still
on the chubby infant of desire
who recreates the universe again and again

as worlds come and go in the game of life
danced by the Lord in myriad forms
under the silent gaze of the seed
of cause and effect

while universal law in its essence
never changes
from beginningless time

For all effects are nothing but the cause in different forms. And Arjuna is hereby a witness to the eternal continuity of consciousness, witnessing the energy called Krishna as the uncaused cause, radiant behind all causes, effulgent behind all effects.

> I see in thee all the gods, O my God; and the infinity of beings of thy creation... All around I behold thy infinity: the power of thy innumerable arms, the visions from thy innumerable eyes, the words from thy innumerable mouths and the fire of life of thy innumerable bodies. Nowhere I see a beginning or middle or end of thee, O God of all. I see the splendor of an infinite beauty, which illumines the whole universe... How difficult thou art to see. But I see thee; as fire, as the sun, blinding, incomprehensible. Thou art the Imperishable, the highest End of knowledge, the support of this vast universe. Thou, the everlasting ruler of the law of righteousness, the Spirit who is and who was at the beginning. (11:15-18)

Cosmic Splendor and Destruction

Now the beauty, the power, the wonder of it all is easy to appreciate. Radiance uplifts, inspires and makes us part of a realm of bliss. Arjuna sees the dazzling stars all together as if they are one—radiance brighter than a thousand suns. This beauty would be too bright to bear had Krishna not deemed it. He reveals all the forces of nature, the gods, the forces good and evil; all wealth, all joy, all sustenance, the power and the glory and all that is bliss. All the archetypes of existence combined into one, Krishna reveals to Arjuna. And Arjuna is breathless, in a state of wonder and awe.

Nature in her beneficent aspect fills us with ongoing peace and joy. Sounds and smells of beauty, pleasing visions of perfection offer an inner wealth to which we are most receptive. But the body of God contains more than just goodness, more than joy, more than beneficent power. *It contains a terrifying aspect as well.* For every heaven there is a hell. For every joy there is a sorrow. For every creation there is destruction. When Arjuna is shown the horrific aspect of the body of God, he trembles in fear(25-31).

> Dead to all worldly things, standing outside himself the disciple sees the great expanse all blue with quivering supernal light like lightnings massed in some world-ending cataclysm, the storm-tossed ocean glittering with souls, dizzily spinning in the dread vortex whirl, the terror of the Sound, throbbing in awful power through the vast space like some great engine pulsing forth the cosmic tides to ebb and flow throughout the universe; and yet beyond the storm the changeless peace, massively shining in a bliss beyond all words.
>
> All this he sees and more that none can tell, sees with a vividness past all mere human seeing; yet all are symbols cast on the background of the fathomless, wherein is neither sound nor space nor sea nor vortex whirl, nor any form at all.
> (Sri Krishna Prem, p.103)

Remember, Arjuna is being shown Reality through the divine intervention of Krishna. This capacity to see is within him just as it is within each of us, but Arjuna might not yet be quite ready to perceive it solely in accordance with natural law. And it can never be received by the ego. As his preparatory *tapas* and meditation had focused on specific worldly goals, such as obtaining powerful weapons from the gods for strength in battle, it was not yet pure *dhyana*—for its own sake, for the sake of the Self. This gift from Krishna is now given under highly unusual circumstances. It is awe inspiring but also terrifying. For a spiritual student who has prepared himself gradually over many years, the vision might come at its own natural pace and have a less frightening effect. Here Arjuna sees it all at once, through the blessings of Krishna. *To the ego, the vision of destruction is always terrifying.* To one living as the Self, only loving bliss encompasses everything. Whether it be called creation or destruction, there is the loving certainty that all creation, all destruction equally is nothing but the body of God, the will of God. Where then is the space for fear?

The fear of surrendering structure, the illusion of false control, the feeling of giving up the "solid" ground beneath our feet, our smallness, our helplessness, our seeming insignificance in the face of the gargantuan forces that move us is something each one of us might experience at some moments in our life. All these perceptions and manifestations are fearful to an ego that wants to hold on to its dominion and cling to the familiar, to life as we know it. Confrontation with the Void can be frightening.

Even at later stages of spiritual development, one can still fear absolute surrender to the Higher, either in the flesh and blood form of the external *guru* or the internal form of the voice of God. Until we can trust completely, until every trace of doubt is gone, all our experiences occur to teach us what medieval astronomers were burned at the stake for believing—that the earth revolves around the sun; the sun does not revolve around the earth. Humility is a prerequisite for liberation. Until we can *meet* the void rather than *confront* her, experience her as the Great Goddess of justice as opposed to the killer, there will be fear and trembling. This is a natural, rightful step on the evolving road to consciousness. Gradually, through allowing these experiences to be deeply felt under the divine gaze of the witness, we come to see the whole as one giant tapestry—interconnected cells pulsating with the force of love.

Dissolution on a Personal Level

Sri Aurobindo describes the experience of the cosmic form as transforming one's limited personal consciousness into an expanded awareness of cosmic consciousness:

> The cosmic consciousness is that in which the limits of the ego, personal mind and body disappear and one becomes aware of a cosmic vastness which is or is filled by a cosmic spirit and aware also of the direct play of cosmic forces, universal mind forces, universal life forces, universal energies of matter, universal overmind forces. But I did not become aware of all these together. The opening of the cosmic consciousness is usually progressive. It is not that the ego, the body, the personal mind disappear, but one feels them only as a small part of oneself. One begins to feel others too as part of oneself or varied repetitions of oneself, the same self modified by nature in other bodies. Or at least as living in the larger universal self which is henceforth one's own greater reality. All things in fact begin to change their nature and appearance. One's whole experience of the world is radically different from that of those who are shut up in their personal selves. One begins to know

things by a different kind of experience, more direct, not depending on the external mind and senses. (*Letters on Yoga*, p.316)

In order to be ripe for spiritual experience one must be relatively free internally. Many things that we cling to both inside and outside must go—body armor, emotional barriers, concepts—all must go. This is the meaning of being open, not being weighted down by emotional and intellectual paraphernalia, not being identified with customs or actions, being able to let go of known structures and expectations. This allows us to be open to the present moment, open to the energies of the total mind, that we might experience directly what has been called the will of God, the law of life unencumbered by like and dislike, impermeable to desire. However, being open too soon can present a problem.

First one must be well-grounded in relative reality, in time and space, in duty and daily living with virtue. Through the process of action in the world in the conscious knowledge of higher, subtler energy as the center and support of all life, our body, emotions and intellect become harmonized. Only when this balance has appeared is it fitting for the grace of the cosmic form to manifest. Developing balance is a preparation for realization. With harmony comes openness. The task is to integrate our thoughts, words, feelings and actions. This occurs through incremental awareness love.

Prior to Arjuna's crisis of ambivalence induced by attachment under extremely trying circumstances, he was well harmonized, super successful in the world, and an impeccable practitioner of *dharma*. In addition, he lived with much devotion in his heart. But the years of spiritual practice and meditation required he did not undergo. Krishna however, reveals the destructive aspect of the body of God for a reason. His revelation is not premature. Before the battle, Arjuna needed to know that his enemies would all be swallowed by the jaws of death (26). The greatest heroes with magnificent powers, who seemed totally invincible would be chewed up by Yama, the god of death. Now Arjuna could enter the battle utterly fearless. He would know for certain that he was not responsible for their deaths. He was merely serving as an instrument of divine will. Krishna was gracing him with the gift of Self confidence.

One of the most powerful spiritual teachings is the living certainty that each of us will one day die and death could come at any moment; we know not when. To allow this experience of our own mortality to sink in can change the way we live our lives. We begin to let go of false ideals, grafted on expectations and live what is truly important. There is a traditional Indian proverb, "When you meet a person, think as if you are meeting him for the first time. And when you are eating or enjoying something, think that you are enjoying it for the last time." How beautiful to live this way!

But here, Arjuna is not seeing his own death but the death of his enemies. He needed to know that he could fight and win. And again Krishna reiterates; *you* are not killing these men; it is their actions which compel *Me* to kill them. You are only serving as My instrument. You are not the doer, you are not the killer(32). This experience knowledge ever prods us toward purpose, toward the rediscovery of our own divinity. When we can live in the awareness of the jaws of death waiting to close shut, our lives, actions and thoughts all take on a different meaning. *We deeply wish to make use of our allotted time here and serve as vehicles for the manifestation of the Self to enter into life.*

The equilibrium of nature is maintained through eating. Throughout the eco-chain, one life form feeds upon another: bug eats leaf, spider eats bug, bird eats spider, hunter eats bird. And who, pray tell, eats the hunter?

The law of the jungle, of eat and be eaten operates from the lowest to the highest. The Buddhist painting of the wheel of time aptly demonstrates time devouring all things, all people, all time itself. Ignorance, attachment and hatred perpetuate the repetition of this divine meal unto eternity. Just as the tiger devours the wildebeest, so time continuously devours the person who is identified with his body ego mind form.

Because of our ignorance of Reality, we fear death. This fear causes us to block out its presence from our lives until one day we are suddenly caught unaware, when the inevitable death comes to seize us or our loved ones. How strange that we are surprised by death when the only certainty in life is death. Death and destruction on a cosmic scale are occurring all the time but we don't experience the impact. Cyclones, earthquakes, floods, famine, all the wars we study about in history, plane crashes, death camps, bombs—all part of the destructive aspect of the body of God. But here, the awesome difference is that Arjuna is forced to see it all instantaneously, as one ongoing happening ever revolving through beginningless time.

Karma and Cosmic Action

According to Krishna, none of these destructive events is preordained by God but are fulfilled as a result of man's actions. *All destruction is caused by man, not by God.* The way people treat the earth, the earth treats people. There is no respite from the law of *karma*, from action and reaction. Rivers can no longer give fresh water if they have been polluted by man's greed. The ozone layer cannot protect us from harmful radiation if it has been dissolved by chemicals. In accordance with eternal universal law(*sanatana dharma*), Krishna (as Ishvara) is compelled to proceed based on the actions of human beings. Arjuna is bearing witness to the unfoldment of universal law in accordance with the actions of man. Sai Baba asks:

> How do we identify Divinity? The heart or *chitta* is associated with *chittagupta* that is the one who is hidden in the heart. (He is the record keeper of our good and bad deeds who sends us to our respective places after death). All our deeds, good and bad are recorded in the heart. These recordings are given form and we receive them as consequences of our deeds.
>
> God does not give what is not there. Nor does he nullify what is there. God merely gives what is already there. He gives the entire authority of creation(*sristi*), protection(*rakshana*) and destruction (*layam*) to the administrators. As He righteously administrates, He is known as the form of righteousness(*dharma svarupa*). He does not interfere in their respective territories. He is merely a witness. He is known as the form of Truth(*Sathya svarupa*).
> (Discourse, 3-95)

According to esoteric teachings, the quality of human beings as a whole affects the cosmos by emitting a corresponding vibration. If the quality is fine and loving, the birthrate and death rate remain low. If the quality is crass and selfish, the earth does not radiate the vibrations necessary to maintain the cosmic order. So more deaths are required as food to uphold the total cosmic nature and sustain the universe.

In the Kabalah it is said that thirty-six wise men uphold the world. Without their living presence, the world would collapse. The interrelationship between human actions and the fate of the cosmos is also reflected in the beliefs of many native peoples throughout the ages, especially the native-American. And in Indian mythology, the Goddess Kali in her horrific aspect is depicted holding a skull and drinking blood. The cosmic earth mother seems to require some form of sustenance to help maintain order. The purpose is not for revenge or even punishment but to maintain the earth. *The universe cannot be smoothly maintained until all false values perpetuated by the ignorance of mankind have been annihilated.*

With the creation of human beings in the world, a partnership was established between the higher energy and man, a covenant between God and human beings. Those who yearn to evolve beyond the animal level feel a natural urge to participate in this partnership that upholds and sustains the world. Anyone who truly wishes to participate can learn to do so. But right education is required. In today's society, too many extraneous influences take us away from the core of ourselves. We need loving exposure to follow the heart, follow our conscience and discover the still small voice within, that we might come to act from that and that alone. Then universal balance is restored.

There is thus a collective cosmic *karma* to which *each of us contributes* either knowingly or unknowingly. "You cannot pluck a flower without shaking a star." And here Arjuna, stripped of his defenses, is staring this Reality in the face. And the ego experiences terror.

After Death Experience

The experience of Arjuna's vision of the cosmic form reflects the flavor of *The Tibetan Book of the Dead*, as well as the research reported on the near death experience, such as in the work of Dr. Raymond Moody. The person who returns from death seems to be experiencing on a total individual level what Arjuna experienced on a total collective level. Although the content of the imagery may vary in accordance with cultural familiarity and personal experience, the underlying principle is similar. When the senses and physical body are no longer the filter through which we perceive life, the imagery from the subtle and causal body predominates. In cases of near death experience, many people report seeing their entire life flash before them in an instant, knowing all at once with utter clarity what was right action and what was evil action; as well as the implications and long term effects of their thoughts, words and deeds. "You see the ripple effects of your actions, how we're all interconnected," said one person.

Many people report experiencing a sense of purpose in life they had not known existed. Most have lost their fear of death, through discovering an inner strength to which they formerly had no access. They see life as infinite. "We cannot die because we were created to live forever. Death is a doorway." This is all indicative of the transforming effect of contacting a deeper layer of consciousness; or to use the language of the *Gita*, of establishing contact with the cosmic form, which lives always within the purified mind of each of us.

Arjuna's experience is therefore universal. It transcends culture, time and place. Whereas the faithful Christian at death might see St. Peter or the angel Gabriel ushering him into heaven with Jesus, the Hindu might see Garuda, the eagle of Vishnu taking him to *Brahma Loka*. The shape the image takes results from the patterning of one's mind—the form through which the symbol expresses a very deep feeling. But the love and security behind the image is universal law; a Truth that transcends culture, time and place, that is constant for everyone, *that can never be taken away.*

The images in the dream seem different. Your life and my life appear to be different. But the forms and happenings in the dream all depict the material of the mind. No part of the dream is anything but reflections of mind. My life and your life are patterned by the beliefs and motivations of mind. The events and thoughts in my life and your life are made of the same stuff as the dream. Both the dream and the waking existence are equally unreal. And both are equally Real as part of the Total Mind that is supported by the Absolute. All the images of dreams and dreamers and the events of wakers and waking minds are but fractions of the Totality called the cosmic form of the Lord.

Arjuna's Loving Gratitude

The hymn of praise(36-46) is a most beautiful universal prayer which reveals Arjuna's love, gratitude and awe. It also reveals his understanding.

> It is right O Krishna that the world delights and rejoices in thy praise. The *rakshasas*(demons) flee in fear in all directions; and all the hosts of *siddhas*(perfected souls) bow to thee. (11:36)

This verse contains several powerful seed syllables (*bijaksharams*), and it is said that by repeating it in Sanskrit *the vibratory power of the word will render evil harmless.* When the unthinking qualities of our lower nature are guided to acknowledge the Self within, their autonomous power is dissipated.

> You are the primal God, the ancient *Purusha,* you are the supreme refuge of this universe. You are the knower, the knowable and the abode supreme. By thee is the universe pervaded, O Being of Infinte forms. (11:38)

Arjuna now knows with total certainty that God is everywhere, God pervades everything, God is boundless—"in front of me, behind me, on all sides of me, God of all"(40). Through living the experience of the subtle formless God, Arjuna has been reborn into a deeper level of faith.

With the advent of new understanding, we see how ignorance prompted our past actions. It is not uncommon for a naive person to view a friend or teacher like himself—in a familiar way, without awe and respect, not comprehending the God nature behind the friend. This is true of all our relationships as well. We forget that all human beings are carriers of the divine. As we mature spiritually and psychologically we begin to appreciate the value in others and gain discrimination. We stop judging another based on like and dislike, or level of ego functioning, or compatibility with our own intellectual or emotional expression. We see the God nature shining through ourselves and others. This evokes love.

So here Arjuna is deeply apologizing(41) for what is natural to all of us functioning in a particular stage of ignorance—when we identify our Self with our role, our emotions and thoughts. On the brink of light, we feel shame for having perpetrated darkness. And the experience of shame serves as a kind of healing and cleansing that leads us to the experience of remorse. *Then we can let go of that level of ignorance forever.*

Since the cosmic dimension seems without limits, without the label of friend or teacher, it remains too frightening for Arjuna in his present condition and psychological level. He needs the familiarity of a loving brother and friend, a God with human form. At a certain stage of development this is true for all of us. It is extremely difficult, if not impossible, to relate to an impersonal God without having experienced the love of a personal God. This is why there are so many skeptics and agnostics in today's western world—because the forms through which to mobilize the experience of the love of God and the love of man are lacking. The love lies latent inside all of us. But access to the vehicles that would bring it to life in the world today is sorely lacking.

The compassionate Buddha, Christ, St Francis, the Hassidic Masters, Sufi Saints, Indian holy men and women such as Mother Theresa, Sai Baba, Amachi, and Karunamayi are all examples of love that can inspire and uplift us. But how many of us feel it is possible to make a connection with these ever living souls who are divine representatives of God on earth? It is extremely difficult to feel linked to their love and the love within, without some corresponding connection to their physical presence, without being part of a living community, or at least experiencing some concrete demonstration of this love in our life. This quality of love (*prema*) is clearly not supported in our society. *Therefore, we must accept individual responsibility for actively seeking it.*

God with Form

Arjuna feels very lost in the realm of the impersonal God(46). Without known structures, without the four directions, without day or night, without the orientation of time and space, how can a body ego live? In order to live in this world, a body ego is necessary. We must allow the body ego its rightful place as a trusted servant of the inner divine Will.

The human form of Vishnu is the representation of God as the all pervading principle on the personal level. The rulership and authority implied by the crown, scepter and circle is comforting to Arjuna. The four arms of Vishnu carry the lotus, conch, mace and discus(*cakra*). Each is a symbol of the workings of His Law. In one hand, He holds the lotus, which represents purity and the goal of spiritual work. The lotus is born in the mud and with every sunrise, her bud opens anew. Neither water nor mud can affect her pristine purity.

Another hand carries the conch. This symbolizes the call to Knowledge and awakening. To become a spiritual student, it is essential to hear the silent inner vibration of the conch. In his third hand he carries the mace, the emblem of kingly rulership.

> He uses his mace to give merciful knocks in life. Still, if an individual or a generation is not listening to His kindly warnings, He has the discus in hand, which totally annihilates the existing forms and recreates.
> (Swami Chinmayananda, *1000 Names of Vishnu*, p.105)

Until we experience unity, our inherent birthright of inner perfection, there is a need for a beneficent ruler-teacher who can help us unify ourselves and quicken our love. There is a need to believe in God as something similar to oneself. Thus the kingship of Vishnu as Lord of the Universe, *sarva loka maheshwara*, can be brought inside as lord of the senses, emotions and intellect. In this way, He is more pleasing to Arjuna than the Lord of time who beams forth blissfully unbearable light, who swallows all and creates all. The love of the *avatar*, who descends to earth in human form to help his devotee is a comfort, inspiration and joy.[28] To worship this God of love, a personal God who gives his love to everyone, offers a great sense of peace to Arjuna.

True Spiritual Experience

What then is the psychological effect of Arjuna's meeting with the vast? To perceive the oneness pervading all things, as in discourse ten, brings clarity and discrimination(1). The unreal can never again be viewed as the Real. To see all the archetypes of existence at once, as in discourse eleven, sweeps Arjuna out of his limited skin and introduces his individual mind to the expansiveness of eternity. Never again can his narrow personal viewpoint dominate his intellect and emotions. Never again can his personal attachment induce fear. For he knows what is and what is not. *When the tiny discovers itself as part of the infinite, one no longer experiences himself as the tiny.*

In the last four *slokas*, Krishna imparts to Arjuna the secret of spiritual life—all spiritual practices are but the most elementary forms. *They are merely a preparation for the heart to open and experience love.* It is only a living love that liberates, that elevates, that connects us with our fellow creatures and makes us one with the cosmic form.[29]

> Perfect purity of mind, stainless devotion and an entire submission of the human personality to the Lord—these are the essential conditions to see the Lord in His cosmic aspect... When the mind is not distracted by anything material it acquires divine power and thus attains the Lord.
> (Swami Vidyaprakashananda, p.754-5)

Sri Sathya Sai Baba says, "Start the day with love, live the day with love, end the day with love. Love is the form of God." This love is not attachment but rather, is an energy that permeates everything and everyone. It is all-inclusive. Love is the true form of God, the formless. And this is present everywhere.

> Not by the *Vedas*, or an austere life or gifts to the poor or ritual offerings can I be seen as thou hast seen me. Only by love can men see me and know me and come unto me. (11:54)

Once the spark of love is awakened in our heart, we know the value of this inner wealth. And it can never be taken away. This wealth we never lose. Little by little it accrues until it becomes permanent and self-evident. Never again is it to be traded in for tinsel: for attachment, sex, success, or material desires. With the experience of *prema*, love from God, love of God or pure love, we come to know our true worth. *We come to live in Self confidence that nothing can shatter*. And this can occur only from wanting That and That alone, from knowing This and This alone as the basis for all.

The way entails knowing about truth from scriptures and teachers (*jnatum*), to seeing Reality directly (*drashtum*), to entering into this Reality as God (*praveshtum*). One instant a star is seen in the sky above the distant mountain. Then its radiance beams forth from our eye until we freely become that light. The initiation of Arjuna into the vision of the cosmic form invokes a love that is a primordial penetration entry into his own God-nature, initially reflected through Krishna and his total surrender to Him. As all natural life is surely annihilated in the sacrificial fire of the mouth of God in eternal recurrence again and again, *the only security rests in conscious sacrifice*. The gratitude, bliss and love expressed in Arjuna's universal prayer is a wondrous testament to his surrender, as the path and the goal become one. Surrender the ego in the sacrificial fire as Arjuna surrendered to Krishna, saith the sages.

Through fully returning to our inner nature there is no fear, as there is no separation. Fear stems from difference. As our love unites us with all humanity, this is the beginning of a process that will gently allow us to surrender and eventually to enter into that Reality, to become That which we truly are.

> He who works for me, who loves me, whose end supreme I am, free from attachment to all things and without enmity towards anyone, he in truth comes unto me. (11:55)

All our action, all our work when performed with remembrance can be seen as work by the Self for the Self, for the universe, for the cosmos.

> Wherever there is an incentive to act or a capacity to achieve, it is all a ray of His infinite potentiality. (Swami Chinmayananda)

> True action does not displace; it transforms. A change of heart is action. Activity is not action. Action is hidden, unknown, unknowable. You can only know the fruit. (Maharaj)

> If you want God you will have to develop the sacred quality of love. Only through love will you be able to experience Him who is love itself. (Sri Sathya Sai Baba)

Thus, the eleventh discourse reveals to Arjuna the *yoga* of the total experience of cosmic matter and energy within the vast expanse of time without end in all its radiant splendor and explosive darkness void. Upon seeing the cosmic form, one can never again return to the limited ego, which places its faith in the sense perceptions of the finite.

Twelve

YOGA OF DEVOTION
Bhakti Yoga

	Gita verses
Yoga with form*(saguna)* and without form*(nirguna)*	1–5
Excellence of single-minded devotion and meditation	6–7
Spiritual practices for different people	8–12
Qualities of the devotee *(bhakta)*	13–20

I love them all
who worship Me with devotion
or dispassion

love only Me
in all creatures and happenings
with faith in My eternity

From the vast immensity, intensity and all inclusiveness of the eleventh chapter, Krishna guides us to the human godly warmth, wisdom and sweetness of the twelfth chapter. Here is a love that is accessible to all, a compassion that empathizes with every aspect of the human condition, a knowledge so precise and practical that we are drawn into the still perception of love underlying all knowledge and knowledge underlying all love. *When love is the basis for knowledge, the greatest good results.* When knowledge exists without love, egoism and confusion reign.

At the close of the eleventh discourse, Krishna informs Arjuna that the energy perceived as the cosmic form of the universe can be known only through unswerving devotion. "By single-minded devotion can I of this form be known and seen in Reality and also entered into"(54). When a person becomes truly motivated to know, to see and to merge with the highest consciousness that has been called God, the prerequisite and the process is single-minded devotion(*bhakti*).

What then is devotion? Devotion entails steady application of the mind toward a particular underlying motivation, object or goal. Devotion is that quality and practice through which the mind becomes *onepointed.* As it stems from a deep wish inside the person, it is considered a simple path. Nothing extraneous is added, nothing is superimposed. Practices are geared toward uncovering the love that lives within the heart. Devotion is sustained with joy.

Bhakti can be considered a giant melting pot. What does it melt? It melts our stodginess, our exclusivity, our invisible categories regarding what belongs where and the "way things should be done." It also dissolves our knowing into unknowing so that our unknowing can in turn be replaced by genuine experience. Devotion gathers all our wordly wishes unto itself, pulverizes and dissolves them into sweetness, into ongoing flowing joy. With the blowing of the breeze of *bhakti*, our longing has been transformed forever. There is no turning back. Fragrance now resides in our homes and lives in our hearts.

> Devotion is the expression of love. The emotion which is called love emanates from the *Atma*. Love is synonymous with *Atma*. Love has nothing at all to do with worldly feelings and secular things. Love, which is just another word for devotion is the very name of *Atma*. This principle of love emanating from the core of the heart must saturate every action, word and thought. This will happen when you think that everything you do, say or think is for the satisfaction of the Lord alone. (Sri Sathya Sai Baba)

Great devotees such as Kabir, Mirabai, Chaitanya or Ram Prasad felt compelled to express their joy in poetry and song. Mirabai left her palace and roamed anonymously with her inner Krishna throughout the countryside, filling the land with the sounds of her bliss. Other lovers of God such as the *gopis* lived solely for the moment they could be with their beloved Krishna, feeding him butter, tending the flocks, enjoying his pranks or listening to his flute. When Krishna left Brindavan forever, the *gopis* continued to keep his presence always in their hearts. And the sweet sadness remains. The sweetness deepens. Attachment to the physical form of the *avatar* is forced to transform into something more subtle, more lasting.

There is a song sung by children and devotees in India, which reflects the essence of *bhakti*. These are the words:

> You are my mother, you are my father, you are my nearest kin, you are my dearest friend. You are my treasure, you are my wisdom, you are my everything. You are my Lord, my loving Lord.

Through this song, we see that the idea of the "Lord" is not fixed, not tied to one form or one thing. It lives through love. It permeates all. Devotion alone supports and deepens all our practice. *Bhakti* bestows upon us the living experience of love.

If we begin as a *karma yogi*, there will come a time when we graduate to *bhakti*. Once we have experienced love *of* the divine and *for* the divine, our actions become more pure. Now we can proceed on the path of *karma yoga* in a new way, carrying the bliss of divine *sakti* into life alongside our actions.

If we begin with study and contemplation, the experience of *bhakti* deepens our knowledge and helps integrate it into our lives. Feeling and thinking unite. Now our contemplation is also loving, as opposed to distant and removed, dry or intellectual. Once a person on the path of knowledge has experienced divine love, he comes to see there is no need to withdraw from life. Renunciation is not necessary. Is not everything in this world a manifestation of God? When the whole world evokes such love, what sense is there in becoming a renunciate?

If our starting point is from the rituals of *bhakti*, such as worship or singing *bhajans*, these actions magnetize our love within and serve to connect us to a deeper layer of love within ourselves. For we are all not born as *gopis*. Through continuing our practice and meeting the teacher, our inner experience deepens and intensifies. When the vibration is powerful enough, God will in some way reveal Himself.

Eventually, all three paths are necessary for integration because they are the living expression of a means of focus for the three parts of a person; the body, the head and the heart. At different times in our *sadhana*(spiritual practice), one approach will prevail over another until the personality becomes harmonized and integrated. But in all honesty, the *gopis* who ever live in *bhakti*, have no interest in integration, self-effort or ideas. They simply surrender. They just love. They live absolutely for the ongoing presence of their beloved—nothing more and nothing less. That's all that's really important. *All our practices and integration are to bring us to a space of total surrender!*

In the west, the need for *bhakti* is particularly pronounced. Although devotional expression is evident in some fundamentalist Christian groups, Hasidic Judaism and Sufi groups, the mainstream of westerners do not find vehicles through which the depth of love inherent in every human heart can readily be shared. With the breakdown of family and community many people feel alienated, lonely, and starving for love. This very condition creates an entry point for longing—provided one allows oneself to experience the need and view it within its rightful perspective. Many people confuse the deep-seated need for love solely with the need for mate and family. When after marriage, children and career this deep longing remains unsatisfied, the cause need not rest with the marriage or career but with one's misconceptions regarding how our *deepest* needs are to be met. The sages say, the world by its very nature of change can never be a source of lasting happiness. If our disappointments can lead us to an opening and a search, life will always present us with new possibilities that can offer the potential for genuine satisfaction.

There is however, some initial discrimination required between acknowledging love as a source, a force of universal God energy, and the varied expressions of love on the personal level. The universal *force* of love can be experienced inside directly, or through our contacts with other people. But in close relationships with others, the pure power of love is often mixed with mental expectations and emotional needs, be they issues of attachment, dependency, desire, dominance, submissiveness, competitiveness, self worth, egoism and self expression. So for the spiritual aspirant, the way of *bhakti* can be viewed as *forging a link with the force of love*, either directly in an inner nonattached way or through loving a teacher who embodies the highest ideals and thereby serves as a conduit for the energy of love to be experienced.

> Each member of all living species has many-sided love towards offspring, parents, comforts and guards, its food and drink, its joys and plays. Each of these types of love or attachment has a distinct name suited to the objects on which it is fixed. It is called affection when directed towards offspring; it is named infatuation when it is directed to the mate; charity when directed towards persons who are less fortunate; comradeship when flowing towards equals; attachment when extended to goods or places. It becomes fascination in some cases, friendship in others. When it is directed towards elders, teachers and parents it becomes reverence or humility.
>
> But *bhakti* is a word that is used only with reference to love as directed to the Lord. When this love is broken up into many streams

> flowing in many directions towards many points it causes only grief for it gets fixed on mortal things of the moment.
> (Sri Sathya Sai Baba, *Gita Vahini*, p.184-5)

The underlying implication here is not to stop loving people or things but rather, to help us recognize that all our loves are simple reflections of a tiny fraction of the dazzling light of highest consciousness that yearns to reconnect with its *source* and be complete.

In order to evolve on the way of devotion, everything and everyone who invokes our love must at some point become connected to the source of love and be acknowledged as a vehicle for Love itself. All our relationships are a reflection of the love of the creator for his creatures. Through our personal love we can come to see God in all.

After exposure to right Knowledge, the various practices involved in developing devotion can help us become onepointed; that we might gather together the many fragments which have become shallow and attached primarily to ego needs. We can learn to dig deeper, direct to the source of the spring, so that what had formerly been sipped in tiny glasses of water that is easily depleted or spilled can now be experienced as an *ongoing spring which never runs dry*. Through reconnection to the spring, the causes of suffering become superfluous.

A story from the *Puranas* reveals a secret of *bhakti*. Krishna once rescued 16,000 maidens from imprisonment in the dungeon of a powerful demon. Then he marries all of them, gives them separate homes and spends every evening with each of them simultaneously in marital bliss. True devotion elicits such closeness and intimacy with the devotee, it's like a marriage, but closer and more permanent. God is your husband, your wife, your best friend, your teacher, your lover, your mother, your father, your child, your very own Self. He is nearer than your eyelash, dearer than your lifelong passion. He elicits heart to heart communion that never leaves you no matter what.

Levels of Devotion

The different modes of expression of our *bhakti* are dependent on our emotional and intellectual makeup as well as on our inner purity. We pass from one level of devotion to the next on our way to liberation. Different steps on the ladder of devotion are:

1. very strong love for one's own God(*asakti bhakti*).

   At this level, narrow intolerance leads to divisiveness and war as only my God is true and yours is false. We are unfortunately, all too familiar with this narrow, fanatical form of devotion. On the personal level, it is analogous to the narcissistic parent who loves his child only when he sees him as a reflection of himself. This is how love manifests when there is a lot of inner emotional impurity.

2. loving God and sharing that love freely with others(*prema bhakti*).

   Here love begins to expand and include various religions such as those who worship differently from us and come from other places, other socioeconomic groups, other races, other creeds. The realization is developing that God is One. He is not only limited to form but the form is an expression of His limitlessness. On the personal level, it is analogous to the parent who also loves other people's children and not only his own.

3. loving one's Self and the Self in others equally(*parabhakti*, supreme devotion).

   When inner development reaches this stage, one sees God always, everywhere. There is no difference between self and other. Love is all. Peace and contentment can never be taken away, as bliss is not dependent on anything external or material. One lives out the purpose of one's birth.

In *Vedanta*, just as faith is not blind but is the result of a well-tuned intellect functioning in harmony with the heart, so too devotion is not blind; surrender is not blind. Unlike the contemporary cult, *Vedanta* entails training in discrimination through questioning and independent reflection. There is no group pressure toward conformity. Monetary payment is not expected, as this knowledge happiness is viewed as the inalienable right of all who are ready to discover it. It is the *dharma* of the teacher to teach and practice, just as it is the *dharma* of the student to receive and practice. The basis is mutual trust.

Surrender to the teacher is viewed as an intermediary step to help us give up attachment to the ego, to the beliefs, conditioning and primal ignorance(*maya*) that has been grafted on to our essence. Through connecting with the presence of the realized soul, the tenacious grip of the ego can be released. Through infusion with the consciousness of the master, we come in touch with the inner voice, enabling us to surrender directly to the highest divine will within. When we are fully realized, our surrender to God alone is total. Maharaj says:

> God gives the body and the mind and the *guru* shows the way to use them. But returning to the source is your own task.

Love for the master develops organically through contact with his/her loving compassion functioning through his/her actions and pure motivation. It is not the body of the teacher that is loved. It is *Brahman* in the master that inspires love and elicits the desire for perfection love in the student. As the student already possesses the same perfection essence as the teacher in latent form, through experiencing the love of the realized soul, the veils covering our love gradually dissolve. Connections are forged with the core of oneself. The teacher's love and our love are gradually experienced as one Love. The surest sign of this comes when we begin to feel unity with all our fellow beings without distinction. This is one aspect of contentment, of feeling at home anywhere, with anyone(19).

The hallmark of wholesomeness and healthfulness is the natural and spontaneous being expression of the innate capacity for love. As the force of divinity, love is the oneness essence of life. Love is the individual universal awareness merging with infinity.[30]

When love becomes confused with sex, one is under the influence of the lowest *cakra*(*muladhara*). The majority of humanity is identified with the body and a slave to the promptings of the three lower *cakras*(sex, food and egocentric will). When the *muladhara* center is fully awakened by the spiritual energy of *kundalini*, one is no longer a "prisoner of sex." Then, the *yogis* say we too can come to understand the language of animals[31] like King Solomon and Saint Francis.

Including and Transcending Personal Form

The beauty of the physical form, the mind's feeling of total protection and confidence, the adoration by the intellect is meant to inspire us to the deepest intensity of love beyond the physical. We travel from the concrete to the universal, from love of one person to love of all persons as an expression of His form of love. For unless we can discover the Truth behind the level of individual form, religion or opinion there will be divisiveness; there will be war. All disharmony between people is a reflection of idolatry; worship of one god, one power, one opinion in a concrete way that does not include the whole.

Psychologically, it is an example of the inability to proceed from the concrete to the ideal behind the concrete. The purpose of the idol is to invoke the ideal so that the idol or the teacher will no longer be needed in that form, as the *guru* is discovered within oneself and all beings. But without first loving the living guru or God, tolerance and humility is difficulty to develop.

One aim of spiritual work is to be what we are: wholly Self contained, independent and interdependent, wholly one with all and all with one. Then we can function freely, unfettered by the attachments of body, mind and intellect. While all thought is said to be but a disturbance in the mind of God, our instinct for love, our capacity for compassion is an expression of the *highest* within us, a manifestation of divine expression. When it gets fixated primarily on the concrete level of body, family or clan, it loses its inherent free flowingness and bondage is created. The divine power dissipates.

Just as the *gopis'* love for Krishna is an expression of Love itself, so our love for family, friends and pets is a means for uplifting personal love and attachment to its universal dimension. Thus, an important function of relationship is to help us learn to surrender the ego with all its imprisoning limitations. Through clinging and craving we lose, through surrender and sacrifice we find. And we are found. The universal law of love descends into our lives.

When the inner energy of loving becomes more accessible as a natural way of being, the expression of our love becomes less dependent on a particular person or condition. All life is a reflection of us and we are a reflection of all. We travel from a tiny street within a certain family in a particular time and place into the home of the universe. No longer imprisoned by attachment under the guise of love, *we discover the freedom of the bond, a life of purity, love without attachment.* In this way, loving others in the world serves as a link to God's love, as all love is God.

bhakti is sweetness
bhakti is butter
bhakti is the land
of milk and honey

Arjuna's Question

Arjuna asks, "Which way is nobler, the path of form or the path of the formless"? In the last chapter, Arjuna has received a taste of the transcendent immutable formlessness that supports the cosmic form. He has also experienced the cosmic form as the personal, immanent, comforting Vishnu Krishna God *avatar*. From early childhood, he had been educated to value the formless transcendent God. But now he knows from his own experience that God is also with form. And the overflowing love he feels for this form induces a level of trust and faith that is like an anchor, his only security, his one great joy.

Arjuna also knows his spiritual work must continue; that the experience of the cosmic form is not synonymous with realization but is a precursor, a gift to help him on his way. Now he must know more precisely how to proceed. So again, in an attempt to reconcile a seeming paradox, he asks Krishna which path is better—the way of love or the way of knowledge, devotion to a form or the aspiration toward the formless, seeing the divine in every human being and every aspect of nature or training the mind to go beyond the visible world—which way is more efficient? Should the world of the five senses, emotions and intellect be included as the raw material of the training, or shall everything but the transcendent be negated so as to focus our entire attention on the unmanifest? Which of the two is the most direct road to liberation?

Krishna tells his disciple that both ways undoubtedly lead to liberation from the bondage of ignorance or *maya*. However, the way of *bhakti* is simpler for most people. Nothing special is needed: no gifts, no talents, little intelligence—just a good heart. *An open heart is the most important thing.* Only those with a highly developed intellect are suitable for *jnana*. And the way of Knowledge is fraught with difficulty, as it requires quiet and peaceful conditions, lack of interruption and dependence on the good will of others for physical sustenance. *Bhakti* on the other hand can be practiced anywhere, under any circumstance. We can have a family and work and still glorify our love for God in everything we do and everyone we meet. The important part is, "set your heart on me, remember me." In *bhakti*, remembrance is usually on an inner image of the physical form of God or awareness of the universal cosmic form. The form induces love. Love burns away our *vasanas*.

In *jnana*, remembrance comes from keeping the mind steady in concentration and contemplation. This also leads to love. This also purifies past actions. When practiced steadily over a long duration of time, both ways lead to Self realization. Both paths lead to liberation.

> Set thy heart on me alone and give to me thy understanding. Thou shalt in truth live in me hereafter. (12:8)

As we listen to Krishna, keep in mind that on the path of devotion, inner feeling evoked is more important than the particular form of the teacher. We proceed from love of the teacher to love of God to love of Self within, to love of Self in other, to the *Parabrahman*, the formless transcendent. The process of love itself becomes formless. Through the act of loving, we become an *expression of the body of God,* a living community of evolving beings. And it is love of the master, love for the *mahatma*, which initiates the grace of our inner purification of emotions and agitation. Until the ego is calm and unconflicted, our attachment to it cannot be transcended. So spiritual work is a process of harmonizing conflicting tendencies and letting go of agitation(4).

For the true devotee, practice or *yoga* entails three things: remembrance or place your mind in Me and have Me as your only motivation; worship Me and my ideals or express your love for Me through every aspect of your living and giving; and develop unshakable faith, a faith that will not crumble in the face of misfortune or suffering, a faith that expects nothing in return(2).

For the contemplator endeavoring to attune his intellect to the formless, eight pointers for contemplation are given as an aid to practice(3). These so called characteristics of That which is without any characteristic have often been repeated by the great sages, authors and commentators on the Upanishads. To bring each word within, helps us attune the mind with the infinite: *"Imperishable... Indefinable... Unmanifest... All pervading... Beyond thought... Unchanging... Immovable... Eternal."*

In order to have enough concentration for meditation, we try to develop three qualities within: the ability to restrain the senses, the capacity to maintain equanimity, and the intention of working for the good of all beings(4). These qualities help to harmonize the body, emotions and intellect, thereby paving the way for steadiness. If our *vasanas* are not in control, pure action is impossible. We do not act—we *re*-act. Only when our past conditioning diminishes can the mind become clear enough to allow loving reason to support our actions.

No matter what the path, the goal is the same. Both devotion and knowledge are equally effective for the person with that particular disposition. The criterion for choice depends upon our own nature. For the emotional type, devotion is initially more conducive and it begins with faith. For the intellectual, contemplation is the way and it begins with enquiry. But for the average aspirant who is still identified with his body and the material world as reality, devotion is the easier path. And eventually, the paths converge.

Shankara, one of the greatest *Vedanta* scholar saints of all times possessed the purest intellect and the highest contemplative faculties. At the same time, he was an ardent worshipper, a superlative devotee who performed all the rituals with love. Ultimately there is no split between the two. Spiritual work that incorporates form is the practice toward realization of the formless.

Krishna strongly reiterates that what is important is the sincerity and motivation behind the practice. *He who yearns only for the highest and centers his entire life and actions around this ideal will reach Truth*, will leave behind the world of change, will merge with the imperishable(6,7). Everything we do, feel and think, from the mundane to the ethereal is to be saturated with *bhakti*, with remembrance, with love.

Techniques of Devotion

In *slokas* 8-12, five techniques of spiritual *sadhana* are emphasized as conducive for different kinds of students. Swami Chinmayananda has expounded these stanzas as a scientific process of spiritual work in accordance with the quality of the mind of each aspirant. For the person whose mind and emotions are calm, whose concentration is steady, direct contemplation meditation is the path(8). This way is natural and easy for the aspirant, if most *vasanas* have already been purified. His total thought forms based on past conditioning, both personal and societal, would be about 20%. He is no longer interested in anything other than God. He knows the falsity of egoism and is able to live in attunement with divine will. Through years of resting in this contemplative state, total merger with God can be experienced. The son and the father become One. The spiritual seeker becomes the sought and there is no longer a seeker or a sought.

But as we well know from our own attempts at meditation, and from chapter six, it is extremely difficult to keep the mind focused in the direction of the highest. Extraneous worldly thoughts and feelings constantly seem to be intruding at the most inappropriate moments. Hence, Vyasa coined the term *abhyasa yoga*, the *yoga* of practice or repetition(9). This consists of bringing the mind back to the focus of concentration whenever we notice it wandering. Each time we are aware of the wavering and act on the awareness, the witness is strengthened. Steadiness develops. This practice is conducive to those with 40% *vasanas*. As the effort becomes second nature, the concentration, steadiness and readiness occur to remain more consistently in a contemplative state.

If the body ego identification is so great that the mind and senses go out into activity and leave the awareness behind, then Krishna says that it's okay for now to go with it. Just dedicate all your activities to me(10). This practice is suited to the extreme extrovert who is burdened by 60% *vasanas*. Be it washing your face, driving a car, preparing dinner, teaching children or attending a board meeting, before starting an action offer it to God. This requires the intellectual appreciation that everything is not in my hands. My capacity to think and act and speak is because of Thee. You are my support. With recognition and gratitude I pay homage to Thee in every act I perform. This is one form of selfless service.

But if one's mental energy is too scattered even to remember to dedicate an action, there is still hope for spiritual practice. Even for those of us who are functioning out of past conditioning 80% of the time, there is an easy way. Simply give up the desire to control a certain result. Do your best and leave the rest to Me, says Krishna(11). Surrender the result to Me. Surrender the fruit of action to Me. This doesn't mean don't wish for a certain result. Just let go of attachment to a wish. This doesn't mean don't plan. Just maintain flexibility. Just give up worry.

Worry is based on the illusion of control. *When we give up the illusion of control there is no room for worry.* Establish a partnership with the forces of events from a place deep down. When we are able to turn to our inner, unseen support for help we invariably notice a response. We come to know there is a greater power helping us always, if we can but make contact with it. Through this experience of surrender, faith deepens. Our actions become more efficient, our minds more calm, more clear. We are less defensive. As a portion of our conditioning dissolves, we soon become fit for the other practices as well. Surrendering the false notion that I am the doer leads to peace and fulfillment. The simplest is best, says Krishna(12).

But surrender is only simple when we are in touch with our own lack and own our utter neediness, our total inability to go it alone. Surrender cannot be contrived. When we feel totally impotent, like a little child, helpless, lost, afraid, screaming for his mother, only then is the condition ripe for surrender. *The Lord of love who lives within the heart is compelled by the workings of universal law to help the child who asks.* Whereas there is no space in the kingdom of heaven for the rich man who thinks he knows, there is always a space when the cries of the helpless are directed to the right place. The master will always respond.

In this way, we come to know through vivid, visceral personal experience that we are utterly dependent on God, the Law of life. Once a connection is forged, He can be fully relied upon to teach us and shoulder our burdens, if the ego can but give them over to Him/Her. Thus the root of all devotion is surrender, total refuge—*saranagathi*. Surrender evokes love. Love invokes healing. Healing brings wholeness.

There's a story told in India about the power of surrender to the perfect master:

> A realized soul once came to a town. Many inhabitants went and prostrated to him and asked for his blessing. In this town lived a thief who wanted God's help in his chosen profession. When he prostrated to the master the *guru* said, "I know you are a thief but I will send you the blessings of God on two conditions. The first is that you treat others with compassion. The second is that you always tell the truth." The thief agrees to follow these conditions and receives the master's blessing.
>
> Confident in his newly found source of strength, the thief decides to rob the royal treasury. He sneaks into the palace and easily finds his way to the safe. As he walks out with a sack of gold, he's discovered by a guard. A fight ensues. The thief gains the upper hand and begins choking the guard. When he sees the face of the guard, compassion dawns; he loosens his grip. After escaping with the treasure, he hides for a time in an old lady's hut. She is so poor there is nothing to eat. He feels compassion for her and secretly leaves a gold coin under her bed.
>
> While walking down the streets of the town, he encounters the destitute, the crippled and the homeless sleeping in the gutters. His heart wells up with compassion. He slips each of them a gold coin.
>
> The king is amazed that the royal treasury has been robbed but knows that before long the thief would be discovered. His spies are sent out to the shops to await the discovery of the coins. Soon the poor old lady spends her coin and is brought before the king. When she tells him her coin appeared under the bed, he would never have believed it had not all the beggars in town repeated the same tale. Finally the thief is arrested. "Did you break into my safe"? asks the

king. "Yes, I did, your majesty," comes the reply. The king is flabbergasted. He had never before met a thief who told the truth.

"How did the beggars get the coins"? asked the king.

"When I saw them sleeping on the street my heart felt such compassion that in secret I slipped them each a coin."

The king couldn't believe his ears. He began to feel enormous remorse. As a king, it was his job to take care of his subjects. Here all these homeless people had been sleeping on the streets and he never thought twice about it, until this thief felt such compassion for them that he gave them the coins from the royal treasury. The king proceeds to thank the thief for teaching him that he has been negligent in his duty and showing him how to solve the problem. He then offers the thief a position as his prime minister.

Now the thief is dumbfounded. "O king, I am but a thief. I went to the *guru* to receive his blessing for help in my profession. He bestowed his blessings on two conditions: that I have compassion and that I never lie. If a thief can become a prime minister by following only these two conditions, I want to know what will happen to me if I surrender completely to the *guru*. Thanks for the offer, but I cannot be your prime minister."

So the thief goes back to the *guru* and surrenders completely.[32]

No matter what stage of the path we are on, to be in touch with the childlike openness humility which initially invoked our devotion is essential if we are to serve without egoism as a vehicle for the power of love to enter into life. Faith based on experience is the mighty force that impels us to serve. And surrender is the most essential foundation, as well as the culmination of devotion. Krishna says:

> Better indeed is knowledge than mechanical practice. Better than knowledge is meditation. But better still is surrender in love, because there follows immediate peace. (12:12)

When we truly put forth our best efforts, our surrender can ripen to fullness, as the embodiment of ongoing devotion. Then the sweet ripe fruit ready to be eaten falls from the tree of its own accord.

Avoiding Pitfalls in Spiritual Work

The beauty of adhering to this graduated method relayed by Krishna(8-12) rests in its ease and naturalness. When we try to force meditation prematurely, the result might well be suppression of certain tendencies that could be more wisely worked through by action and emotional understanding. For suppression makes itself felt in the physical body through illness and in the mind through agitation in some other area. Therefore, trying to meditate without engaging in service in one's life can be self-defeating. For the serious aspirant, technique, motivation, understanding and actions all go together. Purification is a joint venture.

Just as it is possible to push meditation too soon, so it is also possible to remain stuck in some method too long believing it is spiritual work when in actuality one is merely going round various aspects of the same circle in the wheel of time. For example, one can acquaint oneself with the different archetypes of existence ad infinitum without ever living true compassion or experiencing the ongoing unifying force behind these varying changes. Evolution is both change and stillness. Stillness is eternal awareness. When we focus primarily on change we are in the realm of nature, the realm of the growth of the body, mind and intellect and not in the realm of genuine evolution that connects us to ongoing unity.

An experience of the archetype can evoke deep feeling but in order for that feeling to be lived as compassion, *devotion to the highest is required.* For love itself is the form of God. Arjuna's experience of the collective unconscious in the eleventh chapter does not suffice to create a wholesome *human* being. For this, it is necessary to internalize the twelfth chapter with its instruction on how to invoke this ongoing love in one's life. Then the *cakra* of the heart remains open—not only with awe but with love. It is also possible to get stuck in a technique, mistaking the technique for spirituality. Not all techniques are meant to take us directly to the goal but only to a new rung on the ladder. Many methods that are called "spiritual" are merely a bridge to the spiritual and must be let go of in due course if we are to uncover the ever living presence that is our true nature. Purity of motivation, consistency of practice, knowing when to let go, are all essential parts of the process. And developing the ability to discriminate the Real from the unreal is said to be the key.

The True Devotee

Slokas 13-20 are the most beautiful description of the sincere lover of God in the entire *Gita*. They are comparable to the description in chapter two(*slokas* 55-72) of the man of steady wisdom. This person reveals love for God through his very being, her every breath, his every action. In turn, this evokes the love of God. So this love is mutual. Whether or not we can receive it is dependent on the quality of our minds; the degree of agitation which veils our inherent nature. *The act of loving is itself God loving us*. Whether our love is evoked by a formless God or a God with form doesn't matter. One's entire life is an opportunity for living this love and earning the love of God. And love itself is the greatest purifier.

As we read the description of the true devotee, a natural response might be to question whether this level of perfection is possible for the aspirant. It sounds more like a description of the perfectly realized saint rather than an ordinary mortal like you and me. Krishna keeps reiterating that he loves the devotee with all these wonderful qualities but what about you and me?

Therefore, rather than giving up on these attributes as being impractical and out of reach, it would be really helpful to allow the essence of each quality to permeate the psyche. Be as open as possible to the meaning. See the ideal, what is my present relationship to it and how can I come closer to living out this perfection? Like a seed waiting to blossom within the soul, the potential for the ideal exists inside each of us as our true nature. Since we are not trying to impose anything foreign or learned upon the psyche, there is an ease of acceptance. But the connection must be formed between the ideal and the intellect(*buddhi*). *Transforming the ideal into practical reality requires exposure, as well as our active wishing participation.*

A simple way to begin is to concentrate on one of these *slokas*. Memorize it. Try to get beneath the surface of the words. Then focus on each quality at a time. See what comes. At first, possibly an intuition, insight or thought. Then while observing our actions during the day, a subtle link can be established with the ideal. In this way, it becomes related to us and slowly the effort evolves from a seemingly impossible utopia to a very practical way of being. The sages say, if we can learn to put just one of these ideals into practice with ongoing vigilance, the rest will soon follow.

Where the opposites have found their harmony, the middle way becomes a way of being. Neither this nor that, neither inner emotional disruptions nor outer material things can interfere with the peace and love which characterize the person whose entire being is devoted to Love itself. There will be no favoritism, no desires, no enchantments, no injustice—only equalmindedness in the face of every situation, no matter how unjust or provocative. No person or animal will be afraid of the person who exudes gentleness and good will for all. What others say about him doesn't matter. Be he greatly praised or wrongly accused his joy remains.

He neither takes credit for his "successes" nor tries to fix the world. His "failures" are not seen as his own. Whatever comes becomes his *dharma*, to be acted upon without any sense of doing. For all his emotions and actions are simply the energy of God playing through him. With no desires of his own, whatever happens be it called good or bad is accepted in total faith in the lawfulness of life. One is merely a servant of God's law of creation and destruction. There is no blame. In this way, the entire world of actions and events, emotions and knowledge are linked to Love.

When one's entire life is dedicated to living these thirty-five qualities, agitation ends. Energy is conserved. Our very life then becomes our spiritual food. And Krishna promises that the lover of man and the lover of God will shed his mortal nature and embrace the eternal, that one day the perceived boundaries between oneself and God will surely vanish.

> He who hates no creature, who is friendly and compassionate to all, who is free from attachment and egoism, balanced in pleasure and pain and forgiving.
>
> Ever content, steady in meditation, self-controlled, possessed of firm conviction, with mind and intellect dedicated to Me, he My devotee is dear to me.

> He by whom the world is not agitated and who cannot be agitated by the world, who is freed from joy, envy, fear and anxiety, he is dear to me.
>
> He who is free from wants, pure, alert, unconcerned, untroubled, renouncing all undertakings. He who is devoted to Me is dear to Me.
>
> He who neither rejoices nor hates nor grieves nor desires, renouncing good and evil, full of devotion is dear to Me.
>
> He who is the same to foe and friend, and also in honor and dishonor, who is the same in cold and heat and pleasure and pain, who is free from attachment.
>
> To whom censure and praise are equal, who is silent, content with anything, whose home is not in this world, steady-minded, full of devotion. That man is dear to Me.
>
> They indeed who follow this Eternal *Dharma*, endowed with faith, regarding Me as their Supreme goal, such devotees are exceedingly dear to Me. (12:13-20)

The sages say the true task of the devotee is to go from loving God to having God love you. This comes about through trying to live an impeccable life. The highest aspirations of the intellect and the most compassionate feelings of the heart are to be expressed through our actions. This is our aim, our striving toward perfection. We live out our *dharma* through the integration of thought, word and deed, ever supported by the subtle energy of ongoing remembrance. Through our steady effort to approach this ideal *in the face of all our failings* we become dear to our Self, the Lord of our heart. "He my devotee is dear to me." And as His grace pours forth through us into life, we come to serve as vehicles to consummate the divine partnership.

Reflections on Love

> If a man loves me he will keep my words and my father will love him and we will come unto him and make our abode with him. (John 14:23)

> To act from desire and fear is bondage, to act from love is freedom. (Maharaj)

Love is not selective, desire is selective. In love there are no strangers. When the center of selfishness is no longer, all desire for pleasure and fear of pain cease; one is no longer interested in being happy. Beyond happiness there is pure intensity, inexhaustible energy, the ecstasy of giving from a perennial source. (Maharaj)

Bhakti yoga is a real, genuine search after the Lord, a search beginning, continuing, and ending in Love. One single moment of the madness of extreme love of God brings us eternal freedom... When a man gets it he loves all, hates none. He becomes satisfied forever. This love cannot be reduced to any earthly benefit—because so long as worldly desires last, that kind of love does not arise. (Swami Vivekananda)

The only medium through which spiritual force can be transmitted is love. God is love and only he who has known God as love can be a teacher of Godliness and God to man.
(Swami Vivekananda)

Lord created this world that his creatures may live in the cohesiveness of the embrace of love. The Lord in our heart is the very center of all love. Hence we express, in all our love outside, only our love for our own Self. The outer world is but an expression of the One Self which is in all.

Until we discover this spiritual center in ourselves we will be confused, unsatisfied, an enigma to ourselves and to others. Love alone is the path. It alone has the necessary penetration to reach the required depth to rediscover the real essence in us and others around us, the One Infinite Self. (Swami Chinmayananda)

There is love and Love. You love your family but you do not love your neighbor. You love your son or daughter but you do not love all children. You love your father and mother but you do not love everyone the way you love your father and mother. You love your religion but you do not love all religions. You may even dislike those of other faiths. Likewise, you have love for your country but you do not love all countries and may feel animosity towards different people. Hence, this is not true Love; it is only limited love. The transformation of this limited love into Divine Love is the goal of spirituality. In the fullness of Love blossoms the beautiful, fragrant flower of compassion.

When the obstructions of ego, fear and the feeling of otherness disappear, you cannot help but Love. You do not expect any return for your love. You don't care about receiving anything; you just flow. Whoever comes into the river of Love will be bathed in it whether the person is healthy or diseased, a man or a woman, wealthy or poor. Anyone can take any number of dips in the river of Love. Whether someone bathes in it or not, the river of Love does not care. If somebody criticizes or abuses the river of Love it takes no notice. It simply flows. When that Love overflows and is expressed through every word and deed we call it compassion. That is the goal of religion. A person who is full of Love and compassion has realized the true principles of religion.
(Sri Mata Amritanandamayi Devi)

The *gopis* prayed to Krishna, 'Oh Krishna, if you are shining like a flower, I shall go round you like a bee. If you are a tree, I shall go round you like a creeper. If you are the infinite ocean, I shall join you as a river. If you are Mount Meru, I shall be a waterfall on that mountain. If you are the vast sky, I shall shine like a small star.'

Thus the *gopis* developed the kind of relationship with Krishna that said, 'Without you, we won't exist. You may exist without us, but we can't live without you.' They grew up with this kind of discrimination. Whatever they did was Krishna's work. They never entertained any difference between themselves and Krishna. Everything was Krishna for them. They had this quality of oneness.

This is the type of love you should develop today. In this loveless world, we have to sow the seeds of love, we have to water it with love and experience and enjoy this love.
(Sri Sathya Sai Baba)

Love more and more people
Love them more and more intensely.
Transform the love into service.
Transform the service into worship.
That is the highest spiritual discipline.
(Sri Sathya Sai Baba)

Thus, the twelfth discourse teaches the *yoga* of devotion, which reveals how we can bring sweetness, love and God realization into our lives. Through linking our individual love with the perpetual love of the divine, egoism gradually ceases. And we come to experience the beneficent power of true devotion.

Thirteen

YOGA OF THE KNOWER AND THE KNOWN

Kshetra Kshetrajna Vibhaga Yoga

	Gita verses
The field*(kshetra)* and the knower of the field*(kshetrajna)*	1–7
Qualities of Knowledge, which the *jnani* embodies	8–12
That *(Brahman)* which is to be known*(jneyam)*	13–18
Knowing the distinction and union of matter*(prakriti)* and spirit*(Purusha)* leads to liberation*(moksha)*	19–35

to know the field
and the knower of the field
is to know Me

beyond beginningless nature
beyond pleasure and pain
beyond matter and feeling consciousness
Know Me

Life has been called a game(*lila*) by the seers and a drama by the bards. But this is no ordinary play. For in a drama, the actor knows he's playing a role. The script has already been written. He simply follows the lines and plays his assigned part to the best of his ability. In the play of life however, we often forget that we have been assigned a role. The ego forgets that the role is not real; that this particular stage is not necessarily located in a theater named reality. Rather, the entire play exists in a state called *maya*.

This is a magic place ruled by the director, the divine magician. Our parts have been assigned by our *vasanas*. Somehow we have been tricked into viewing the whole thing in a very strange way. How can we escape from our particular maze of divine illusion? How can we come to participate in Reality?

Our task is to see ourselves as actors, our particular stage in time and place as the field of experience, and the process of action as the link between the two. Gradually, these three aspects become differentiated from each other. Through self-observation, detachment becomes a natural way of being. Then the three can become reunited once again in a new way—as one special unity. But this seeing cannot be accomplished by the mind. For that would prevent our natural participation. Something more is required for true detachment to promote wholesome integration.

Another way of putting it is to compare the play to a dream. I dream a dream. It seems very real. I do not even know that I am dreaming. So how can I know where the dream began? The dream state seems like an ongoing way of being; it is beginningless. Only when I wake up do I know I was dreaming. And when I wake up, the dream ends.

The process of waking up consists of knowing that we are dreaming. At first we become dissatisfied with the dream. It can be painful, sometimes boring and might seem superficial or repetitive. "Is this all there is"? we ask. As we begin to turn within, soon we see flashes of ourselves dreaming. I am separate from the dream. This glorious process of life is something far deeper than it seems from the surface. Different facets of the process begin to unfold—cause and effect, interrelationships, meaningful coincidences, the birth, growth and decay of happenings and many other events experienced by the dreamer. The more deeply we consciously enter into the subjective realm of the dreamer, to separate out the dream from the dreamer, the knower from the known and from the process of knowing, *the closer we come to the invisible, all pervasive core that supports all dreams and dreamers*.

This is the theme of the thirteenth chapter. It is a continuation of *jnana yoga* and *sankhya* philosophy expounded in chapters seven and nine. Although the emphasis is on understanding and the subtleties of intellect, contemplative idea and logical discrimination are never divorced from devotion of the heart. Devotion to the inner ideal is a precondition for true Knowledge. The motivation to live *jnana yoga* stems from devotion.

In some later editions, an initial question has been added to the original text for cohesiveness. Arjuna asks Krishna to explain what is matter(*prakriti*), spirit(*Purusha*), the field(*kshetra*), the Knower of the field(*kshetrajna*), Knowledge(*jnanam*) and the thing to be known (*jneyam*). The entire chapter centers around the answers to these questions.

The place of the battlefield in this war is Kurukshetra, an ancient holy site, which also has the potential of becoming *Dharmakshetra*, the field of *dharma*. *Dharmakshetra* has been called the vale of soul making. We are each participating in a battle in our own life-space field based on the perceptions and experiences that influence our thoughts, emotions and behaviors. When one's ordinary battlefield becomes a field of *dharma*, every aspect of life becomes an opportunity for allowing transformation of lower *prakriti*(the body ego mind form) into higher *prakriti*(the unmanifest). As we pluck the weeds from the field, our "negative emotions," automatic instincts and unthinking conditioning are all gently enticed toward perfection under the jurisdiction of the inner eye of the witness and the sacred heart of devotion. What begins as inner conflictual tendencies and the divisiveness of battle can be transformed into peaceful coexistence and love. *The field can bloom and bring nourishment.*

To participate in the battle with awareness is to experience the *Knower* as we play our different roles in life, that we might come to discriminate between the multiple aspects of the field—the experiencer, the experienced and the process of experiencing; the subject, the object and the active processing link between the two. As our spiritual practice intensifies, the observer becomes a seer, while the knower of the field one day melts into a Knower.

The Field

The body is referred to as the field. Another literal translation for field(*kshetra*) is "that which is protected from perishing." This body encompasses far more than the mere physical body. It is the material body of the world, an environment of experience from beginningless time—our values, our *karma*, the situations that come to us and actions that serve as causes for our future situations, the way we take in and process our lives. It is science and scientific theory. And it encompasses much more that remains hidden. The subtle root of matter(*Mula prakriti*), from which the universe seemingly emerges, is the foundation for the personal field, which is always changing, as it is ever involved in creation and dissolution.

How is one's field created? Simply stated, if I look at an object, my eyes take in the imprint which travels through pathways to the brain for physical processing; then through association a link is formed with memory, like and dislike and other mental or emotional phenomena. If the object elicits past attachment, then emotional reactions occur and connect the object with old desires and past *vasanas*. The old conditioning gets strengthened and further bondage results; all from simply seeing something and being drawn into it, by eliciting memory, desire, action and emotional responses.

When a sense object appears within one's scope of vision it is not necessary to be drawn out into it. The mind can be trained not to slide into the object but to remain linked to a more inner part of oneself(*pratyahara*). *I can learn to see without fully looking out and losing myself.* In the untrained person, the object draws in the eye of the seer, as part of the process of seeing. The mind is then also drawn in to associations and bondage ensues. For the person whose mind is linked to the higher, there is remembrance of a higher support, which serves to prevent the senses from automatically being pulled into the sense objects. This explains why control of the senses is such an essential component of spiritual work. To the degree that we are connected to consciousness, the true Knower, the senses lose their automatic power and we become free from the unaware form of bondage. But in order for this quality of experience to occur, we cannot be identified with the body, emotions and thoughts. We cannot take refuge in the world as our primary support. We cannot follow the senses or the mind.

The body or the field is all this. It is the object, the eye that sees the object, and the mind which integrates the object with all its associations and memories. The field of experience also includes all the processes involved. In this sense, the field is subject and object, the person and the environment. But that which is the true subject—deep and all pervasive—is the *Atman*, the Self. The real *Purusha* as opposed to the person identity *purusha* is the true Knower of the field. All else is mere reflection, which does not exist in its own light, through its own power. Permeating and supporting all bodies is the *Paramatman.*

The ego personality that reflects, processes information and thinks it knows is not the true Knower, but is part of the body or the field of *karma*, be it the gross body, the subtle body or the causal body. That which is truly omniscient throughout all the different fields of experience, the three states of consciousness(waking, dream and deep sleep) and the three periods of time (past, present and future) is the true Knower. The Knower remains unaffected by all *karmas*.

> Know that I am the Knower in all the fields of my creation; and that wisdom which sees the field and the knower of the field is true wisdom. (13:2)

All else is but a covering. *I am I am.* All else is knowledge *of* and not Knowledge *Itself.*

Just as the *Atman* is qualitatively distinct from the material world while pervading it, so *prakriti* Herself as the external world is not distinctly separate from the inner person. All matter consists of interaction. All life consists of atoms and the five elements. Sense objects and sense organs are part of one whole. The kind of sense apparatus a being has determines how he sees the physical world. What is felt is determined by the kind of mind a person has. The personal mind and inner psychology influence the senses as well as the body, thereby creating its own distinctive environment.

Various levels of matter with different densities of fineness are ever interacting, as physical reality is not independent of the subtle body of the person and vice versa. All of matter, everything in the world of change is *interdependent* on each other and *dependent* on the *Atman.* Only the true Knower is fully independent and not subject to change while pervading all, transcending all. If we could live in this knowledge, a kind of detachment from our usual perceptions, reactions and confusions would develop.

Contemporary science has demonstrated the interpenetration of matter and energy, element and form with all pervasive subatomic particle as the substratum for star, planet, person and ant. When we think of it, we know the thing called table is a series of moving particles, which make up the form called tree. Color, sound and heat are merely vibrations of energy of different frequency, which get projected from the senses to the brain to create a richly fictitious dream world. We know nothing exists as it seems. And yet—our perceptual apparatus has still not caught up with contemporary physics. *We still view distinct forms as being more real than unity.* Our senses have programmed us for dualism(*dvaita*). This is the power of *maya.*

Millennia of reliance on the external senses cannot shift gear based on scientific theory. Not even a belief system can alter the basic quality of our perception. Only the Knower of the field can see the unseeable!

Everything in the field of matter is ever in movement, always changing. To be able to see these ongoing transitions from a point of stillness and know them for what they are, to participate fully in happenings without getting involved in them, to discriminate between the changes and that which helps us to detach from matter, thereby allows us to be the witness—the Self that one *is*. Through knowing participation in our total interdependence, we approach Self containment.

In verses five and six, the body of the ever-changing field of experience is again enumerated through the twenty-four principles (*tattvas*) of *sankhya* philosophy. These demonstrate stages in the evolution of *prakriti* from the gross to the subtle, and they pervade cosmic as well as individual levels of creation. By Herself, *prakriti* is insentient; it is *Purusha* that infuses the principle of consciousness. The field consists of:

1. *Mula prakriti,* the matrix or support of all matter
2. five elements
3. ego
4. intellect
5. five sense organs(eye, ear, nose, tongue, skin), five organs of action (hand, feet, mouth, anus, sex organs) and the mind that oversees them
6. five sense perceptions that correspond to the sense organs and the five actions that correspond to the organs of action.

Also included in the field are:

7. the opposites; love hate, pleasure pain
8. the capacity to evolve, to harmonize and integrate the opposites so that we will not be subject to their unrelenting, instinctive pull
9. intelligence(*vritti jnanam*), which is the vehicle through which *Purusha* is reflected in our lives
10. courage, determination and fortitude, which allows us to persist in the process of our evolution, and detachment in the face of all the changing modifications of the environment.

What is called the ego in *sankhya* philosophy is more expansive than our individual, psychological understanding. In chapter three, we spoke of ego(*ahankara*) on the personal level as "I doing." But according to *sankhya*, ego derives from a cosmic manifestation called *mahat*. *Mahat* is viewed as a source from which the projecting power of *maya* emerges. The subtle, root source of all cosmoses becomes the total mind, the cosmic ego. This all inclusive cosmic ego can be viewed as total consciousness, or God the controller. It is said that the universe originates from the mind of God or the Word. And there is an ongoing interconnection between the creation of the physical universe, happenings and the motivation, thoughts, and discriminative understanding of human beings. Swami Chidbhavananda describes how this cosmic process becomes limited or personal:

> Egoism is the cause of the five elements. The Self projects the non Self and identifies Itself with it. This identification is egoism. When the pure consciousness thinks of Itself as the materialized consciousness it is egoism. Intellect is the *tattva* or principle of determination. It is from this principle that egoism emanates. (p.678)

How then can we utilize the gift of life with all its changing modifications of the field? *The enlivening principle must be separated out from its manifestations.* We must learn to return to the source of creation.

We can be battered by the waves in the ocean or we can learn to navigate and swim. We can come to understand something about the changing conditions of the tides and the cycles of storms or be drowned by them. Or we can transcend them while fully engaged in living.

In addition to the scientific detachment and alertness of the weatherman, who is able to predict the next hurricane or tidal wave, the spiritual student can also render the turbulence personally harmless by identifying with a higher level of reality than the physical world. Storms will always come and go. If we cannot escape them, we can at least seek the proper protection to render them harmless. *Through discovering the inner witness, the illusory power of maya is conquered.*

Aspects of Maya

Maya can be viewed as having four aspects. The first three indicate how our true consciousness becomes merged in *maya*:

1. the veiling power of *maya*(*avarana*). Our impurities cover the Self so we are unable to experience It.
2. the projecting power of *maya*(*vikshepa*). Our basic ignorance regarding Reality causes us to see and think concretely and accept what the senses tell us as if it were Truth.
3. the creating power of *maya*. The multiple forms of *prakriti* are in an ongoing state of flux in conjunction with our *vasanas*. We mistake dynamic movement, time and change for existence, for that which *is* and remain unaware of the true stillness eternity behind all change.
4. the revealing power of *maya*. Through inner awareness linking with all creation, the revealing power of *maya* emerges. Joseph Campbell viewed genuine art, scripture, ritual and meditation as vehicles for the revealing power(See Diane Osbon, p.242). *Here is the link between prakriti and Purusha "within" and "without."*

Simply stated, one function of the field is to offer us the possibility of enjoying the game, playing it well, learning from it and then through steady training and practice, reach a point where we can begin to transcend clinging to the field. Through our capacity to participate in transforming tiny bits of this field, the quality of our experience changes. We proceed on the ladder of evolution toward realization.

The capacity to detach from the field and transcend our identification with matter does not imply a rejection of life, relationships and work. The dilemna of Arjuna is that he could not *discriminate* what his true *dharma* is. His confusion stems from his emotional attachment to his relationships. So here, Krishna is emphasizing that from the perspective of the higher Intelligence, as opposed to ordinary thinking processes,[33] the task is to separate out the field from the Knower of the field. This practice can occur on all ten levels of the field just listed. It is a simultaneous alchemy of separation, purification, and attaching to the Real.

Behind the twenty-four principles of *prakriti* rests the supreme *Purusha*. Sri Sathya Sai Baba says:

> *Paramatma* is latent in *prakriti* as oil is latent in seeds, as fire in wood and as fragrance in flowers. *Paramatma* is the cause and *prakriti* is the consequence. *Prakriti* is not separate from *Paramatma*. It is nothing but the physical form of the Lord.
>
> The *sankhya* system held that creation cannot be made from one entity alone and that it is the union of two entities—nature and God. One cannot clap with one hand. One needs two hands to clap. Similarly, *prakriti* and *Paramatma* are essential for creation and without them creation is impossible. The *sankhya* system held that Divinity runs as an undercurrent everywhere in *prakriti*.
> (*Summer Showers in Brindavan, '93,* p.82)

Thus from the outset, we see that initially the mind must differentiate *prakriti* from *Purusha* to avoid confusion and identification. But ultimately, through the presence of the witness, mental knowing transforms into experience. As *Paramatma* pervades every aspect of matter, through conscious integrated awareness, *prakriti* and *Purusha* become detached and reunited in our consciousness in a fresh, new way as part of one whole—as they always have been, shall be and are.

Although the process occurs gradually it is also direct and instantaneous. Effort over time is required to reach depth, intuition and eventual transcendence. But through grace, this occurs in an instant.

Psychotherapy and Purification

Whatever the individual aim in therapy, the process well-done consists of purifying different aspects of the field. This was vividly brought home to me in the middle of my personal analysis. I dreamt I was singing in a chorus of little children and the conductor was my analyst, Edith Wallace. We were singing a song from Handel's *Messiah*, "And He Shall Purify."

What does purification consist of? Transforming *tamas* into *rajas* and *rajas* into *sattva*. The latent energy locked into inertia, repressed or split off emotions and emotional reactivity must be made accessible to the person in the form of positive energy, which is already there but covered through the veiling power of *maya*. By exposing and processing our emotional pain, fear and negativity, a cleansing of *tamas* and *rajas* occurs. The precious energy that once went into "protection, defense and offense" can then be utilized for *discovering our inner dharma and living it.*

Each theory or school of therapy can potentially provide a framework for purification, provided the motivation of the therapist is pure. However, if the therapist unknowingly imposes on the client material values and attachment to the field, then purification cannot effectively proceed. A major distinction between eastern and western schools of psychology is that in the *Gita*, for example, the direct focus is on the *highest*. The preparation and aim is to experience life directly with an awareness link to the highest consciousness. On the path of devotion(*bhakti*) this occurs through love; attaching to God and then later, seeing God immanent in all. On the path of knowledge(*jnana*) this occurs through contemplation and bringing the ongoing presence of the witness into action. The goal is to live our inner perfection, our spontaneous inner joy, our total consciousness love. The first step of the process consists of discriminating, through practice and understanding, the highest consciousness within from every aspect of the field.

Under the gaze of the sun, the darkness of the earth is illumined. Whatever emerges is experienced in the moment. Every role the ego plays is feelingly known as a role and not the essence of oneself. Under the eye of the witness, all levels of the field become purified. *Prakriti* becomes separated from *Purusha* experientially. Identification with the unreal ceases.

It is therefore essential to know the difference between the field and the Knower of the field, through establishing a conscious link with the ongoing inner presence. Without this process, further attachments and false values will continue becoming imprinted on the psyche and serve as causes for future suffering, no matter how much purification of past emotions has taken place. The deeper the level contacted by consciousness, the more pervasive the purification.

Without some conscious link to the highest, attachment to matter and ego functioning is reinforced, which cannot but lead to further bondage and suffering.

Until one's philosophy of living catches up with one's inner purification, attachment remains. Arjuna is the perfect example. He is not troubled by rage, fear or envy. He is devoted, just and brave. But due to delusion, or lack of discrimination between the field and the Knower of the field, he was attached to the body form of his relatives, as well as to his own body ego in the form of identification with the doer. *Only through transcending the belief in the ultimate reality of the field, is suffering left behind.*

Although the aim of psychotherapy is far more limited than that of spiritual work, both can lead to personal harmonization and relative integration. Therapy can provide a contained focus for experiencing emotions and working through parental and societal conditioning. Rightly experienced, it can be a great purifier and initiate adaptation based on a more inner orientation, thereby bringing us closer to our essence and more authentic self-expression. Awareness and acknowledgement of the archetype, supporting the dreams of life, can help us forge a link with the depth and breadth of the universal. But only steady spiritual practice leads to liberation—provided the basic purification has occurred.

However, when spiritual work ignores dealing with emotional issues, it can serve as a defense that prevents a person from facing problematic developmental and psychological factors. This avoidance tends to reinforce our inner rigidity and egoistic need to control. By sidestepping inner emotional purification, the law of karma requires extra external difficulties to initiate the necessary cleansing.

To bring our deep idealism into daily life through action is a major task of the spiritual student. We are each carriers of God energy that yearns to manifest. But when we identify with this energy in the wrong way, the end result is grandiosity. Carl Jung spoke of inflation as identification with the archetypal energies of the unconscious. In this day and age, some spiritual students also identify with the *guru* and spiritual collective in a way that is self-defeating. For example, when a person mentally merges with the *guru* to unknowingly prop up his own ego, this can serve as a crutch to narcissistic practitioners, who are prevented from facing their own suffering and inner emptiness. *Atman* and ego become confused.

Many a well-meaning idealist maintains the prop of grandiosity through an unconscious spiritual support system based on merging. Only through integrating "positive and negative," "good and evil," can the true idealism of God energy rightly manifest. Practitioners who remain stuck in this maze may require therapy.

From one perspective, the entire battle of the *Gita* took place because a number of good people could not confront and integrate their own tragic flaws. For example, Bhishma was a very great soul, a wonderful *yogi*. He had the moment of death under his command. Because he loved his father so much, he sacrificed marriage and kingdom so his father could marry a beautiful fisherwoman, whose father insisted that her son be king. This blind sacrificial love led Bhishma to support Duryodhana, in the knowledge that he was evil—all because he had promised his father he would support the throne of Hastinapura. Each great hero and heroine of the *Mahabharata* has a similar tragic flaw, which if acknowledged might have prevented the war. For misguided judgement fosters confusion, and confusion leads to harmful effects. *When "evil" is not openly confronted on an inner level, it ends up being fought externally, through argument and war.*

Prerequisites for Knowledge

Once some weeds have been removed from the field and the soil has been tilled, new seeds must be sown. *Slokas* 7-11 enumerate the twenty values of life which are the prerequisites for Self realization, That which is to be known. Living these values offers nourishment. Through cultivating these qualities in ourselves we uncover the innate wisdom inside that is veiled.

> Absence of self glorification, absence of pretence, non-injury, fortitude, uprightness, service to (the values of) the teacher, purity, firmness, self control, dispassion toward sense objects, absence of egoism, remembrance of the evil and sorrow of birth, death, old age and pain; nonattachment and nonidentification with son, wife, house, possessions; constant equalmindedness during desirable and undesirable occurrences; unswerving devotion to Me by the *yoga* of nonseparation, retiring to solitary places, avoiding the noisy multitudes, constancy of Self knowledge, perception of the true end

> of Knowledge: all this is *jnanam* and what is opposed to it is ignorance, *ajnanam*. (13:7-11)

Until we live by at least one of these qualities, we cannot come to know consciousness, our true nature, our real destiny as human beings. By noble living, the inner equipment becomes further purified and one day we will live as godly human beings on this earth. We leave behind completely the hold our animal nature has over our actions. Through meeting the difficulties and successes of life with the ever present eye of the witness, conscience appears; the motivation for the greatest good presents itself and these qualities intensify. As we aspire more and more to embody humility, service, devotion and purity, we discover our true support. Only when our practice becomes total can we be called a *jnani*, a person of wisdom.

It is worthwhile to note that the moral and spiritual qualities needed for Self realization are called *knowledge*. The sages say that without perfect command of these attributes no one can experience Reality. When the mind becomes purified by living these qualities, *Paramatman* is revealed spontaneously. From the flower of devotion, the fruit of knowledge grows.

The genuine experience of each of these qualities leads to detachment; to shedding identification with body ego consciousness. If, for example, one truly lives in humility, one does not mistake the false sense of I for reality; I know I am not the doer. Through knowing our place within the universal scheme of birth, life and death, we become linked to the inner source of all life. *When connected to this source, it is impossible to hurt another person in thought, word or deed.* Likewise, through the process of striving to remain linked to the One throughout all personal attachment to loved ones, we come to shed our attachment by seeing the One in all. To make this connection requires some inner solitude, whether one is physically alone or in the midst of a crowd. Until we are able to reflect upon the imperfection and sorrow inherent in our present state of functioning, there will be no motivation for change.

> Unless a seeker is fully conscious of the inward personal shackles in himself, he will live on in his own ditch of sorrow, never striving to get out of it. Both the human mind and body have a

> tremendous amount of adaptability. They can adapt themselves to any condition and even come to enjoy it.
>
> Unless a seeker is constantly conscious of the evil of the pain in his present stage of existence, he will not discover the necessary spiritual urge, intellectual dynamism, emotional enthusiasm or physical courage to seek, to fight for, to win and to possess the divine fields of perfection. (Swami Chinmayananda, THG p.777)

Through the intense desire to contact the highest within, a process is set in motion. Thus, these twenty attributes are not just to be considered a mental construct called moral qualities but insead, serve as a *dynamic* bridge that links us to our inner Self, to Reality. Once this connection has become ongoing, there is no longer a need for effort. The sages say, with realization all the positive qualities shine through the light of consciousness naturally. This is a state beyond all qualities, be they positive or negative. But to abandon the practicing aspiration for positive qualities prior to realization would send us tumbling into identification with the field, and kill our possibilities for evolution.

Thoughts and actions that are inherently good also serve to protect us from the negative effects of other people, as well as from negative thought forms of the collective unconscious. *Dharma protects those who protect dharma.* As positive qualities are lived, the mind sheds its agitation and becomes fit for contemplation.

Intimations of Brahman

In *slokas* 12-18, Krishna offers exercises in contemplation on That which is to be known. To describe what is beyond qualities is not possible. Yet, through these practices in contemplation, the mind of the spiritual student is being led toward the state "beyond what is and beyond what is not, beyond the manifest and the unmanifest (*sat* and *asat*).

> His hands and feet are everywhere, he has heads and mouths everywhere. He sees all, he hears all, he is in all. And he is. The light of consciousness comes to him through infinite powers of perception and yet he is above all these powers. He is beyond all

> and yet he supports all. He is beyond the world of matter and yet he has joy in this world. He is invisible; he cannot be seen. He is far and he is near, he moves and he moves not, he is within all and he is outside all. He is One in all but it seems as if he were many. He supports all beings. From him comes destruction and from him comes creation. He is the light of all lights, which shines beyond all darkness. It is vision, the end of vision, to be reached by vision, dwelling in the heart of all. (13:12-18) JM

As we repeat these words with inner silent speech, the meaning enters a deep space within and resonates, reconnects us to something hidden, silent, changeless, eternal, invisible, transparent not only within us but within everyone and everything—all pervading light, beyond wisdom. When a person knows this knowingless space, says Krishna, he is liberated from finite identification with the body ego mind form. His God is without form as he is without form. He lives forever in liberation(*moksha*), free from the limitations and imperfections of matter.

Although this state might feel far away now, it is also very near. Each little flash of insight or experience of depth accumulates slowly. Relatively real experiences compound and serve to support us as spiritual power develops. Gradually, subtlely, an ongoing link to our inner Self is being formed.

There's a story that beautifully illustrates the subtle supremacy of the loving heart over the entire field:

> Once Krishna asked Narada, "What is the greatest thing in the world"? He thinks for a moment and answers, "The earth is the biggest." "How can the earth be biggest if water covers three fourths of the earth"? So he had to agree that water is greater. Then he was reminded that Sage Agasthya once drank up all the oceans and now he's a star in the sky. Narada then agrees that the sky is the biggest. When he was told that the *avatar* in his incarnation as the dwarf Vamana traversed the whole sky with one step, he finally realizes that the Lord, in whatever form, enters the heart and resides there.

Therefore, *the heart of the devotee and lover of God is the grandest, greatest thing in all creation.* The five elements and the entire field of creation cannot be compared to the heart of the devotee.

The true witness of the *jnana yogi* is akin to the heart of the devotee. In loving consciousness, the secret heart of the devotee becomes the Totality.

Relationship of Matter and Spirit

Slokas 19-23 expound the interrelationship between matter and spirit, the field and the Knower of the field. Both are said to be without beginning and ongoing(19). The question asked is, when does darkness enter the cave? It has always been there says the sage. But the domination of *maya* over the psyche does have an end. The dominion of *prakriti* ends when the dream ends. And the dream ends when we are no longer identified with the gross, subtle and causal bodies of matter. Light then illumines the darkness of the cave.

Prakriti is said to be the raw material in all cause and effect, as the groundwork of happenings. But as this principle is inert, without sentiency or consciousness, she must unite with *Purusha* in order for perceived experience, thought and feeling to occur(20). Although in pure form, *Purusha* remains actionless and unidentified with the experience, His presence is necessary for a perception to occur. Without the light of consciousness enlivening the inner organs there can be no experience. Thus both *prakriti* and *Purusha* are needed for a world to enter into existence, for life to function. And when in the seat of meditation, the field is withdrawn from the world of experience, the sages say, only the supreme *Purusha* exists.

> Know that the modifications of desire and hatred which cause bondage, and the qualities of humility and modesty...which cause release originate from *Prakriti*. *Prakriti*, having no beginning develops into the form of the body and conjoint with the Self causes bondage through its own transformation as desire and hatred. The same principle through humility and modesty...causes liberation. *Prakriti* subservient to the Self alone is the causal factor.
>
> The Self in its pristine nature experiences Itself by Itself as nothing but joy. When conjoined with a body It becomes the cause of experiencing both pleasure and pain derived from sense objects and experiences qualities born of *prakriti* which are effects of the *gunas*. The Self existing in the body becomes the spectator and

> approver of this body by means of will in consonance with the functioning of the body. It also becomes the experiencer of pleasure and pain resulting from activities in the body. By virtue of ruling and supporting the body, by making the body completely subservient, it becomes *Maheshvara*, the great Lord in relation to the body, senses and mind. (Ramanuja, in Swami Adidevananda, p.450)

When a person is attached to the different happenings of *prakriti*, he is entangled in *maya*. His life is determined solely by his fate, his past actions and his desires. He suffers the sorrows that nature metes out to him. But when a person begins to observe the whirling of *maya*, he separates his ego *prakriti* self from *maya* and becomes the witness, connected to *Purusha*. A choice now presents itself. To the degree that he connects himself to *Purusha* throughout the levels of experience, he disconnects from the laws of fate(23). He *transcends* fate. He transcends birth and death. Be he householder, contemplative, a man of action or a *sannyasin*, a meditator, a *karma yogi*, a listener or a faithful devotee, the law of the witness applies *equally* to all(24-5).

Through non-identification with the body, the inner witness blesses *prakriti*, disperses positive feelings to everything in the field—initiates *prakriti* into the conscious realm of spirit. Through connecting with inner loving feeling, the divine union of matter and spirit occurs. *Spirit infuses matter through love.* Without this union, matter and spirit remain united unconsciously. Spirit is lost in matter through identification and a person lives a mechanical life as an automaton. With this union of inner feeling flowing freely to all creation, the inner field and the outer field become permeated with new energy and different possibilities. Ongoing "peace on earth, good will toward men," can occur only from the conscious participation union of the field with the Knower of the field. All good intentions that stem from the ego are only temporary and cannot be maintained. *The quality of the field is dependent upon whether human beings serve consciously as vehicles for the infusion of spirit into matter or whether it just takes place mechanically, without one's conscious participation.* Herein rests the difference between war and peace, destruction or creation, joy or sorrow. The choice is ours.

We can unknowingly slay the Self by the self(28) through perpetuating our separateness and identification with the body mind form by living in the misconception that our ego, thoughts and senses are real in themselves. Then we are caught in the mire of the mundane. Or, on the other hand, we can see that this way of living is a reflection of ignorance, of being stuck in *prakriti*. Each time we feel angry, anxious or hurt, each time we deny, project or overcompensate, we are identified with the field. We can watch our misconceptions, desires and false identifications unfold. These are merely the play of our *vasanas*. The more we observe our participation in life with the detached eye of the witness, the more the field is subsumed into spirit. This perception is nurtured and supported by Self awareness until the destructiveness of negating one's Self and the Self in others *ceases*. The unmoving realm of *Purusha* consciously linked with *prakriti* seemingly expands His dominion until the Totality is experienced. *And the heart of the devotee then becomes the greatest thing on earth.*

> I adore Him as *Brahman* who is all awareness, unaffected by activities such as creation, preservation and destruction. I adore Her as *Shakti* or *Maya* or *Prakriti* who carries on all these activities regularly in the proximity of the actionless *Brahman*. (Ramakrishna)

In genuine spiritual work, *Purusha* is not to be favored over *prakriti*. Both are equal and all pervasive. There is nothing intrinsically "higher" about spirit than matter. It is rather our *identification* with matter that drags us down, not the qualitative presence of matter. For matter itself offers us the precious opportunity for liberation.

> And when a man sees that the God in himself is the same God in all that is, he hurts not himself by hurting others. Then he goes indeed to the Highest Path."(13:28) JM
>
> He who sees the same lord everywhere equally dwelling destroys not the Self by the self. Therefore, he attains the highest goal. SwC

Five Steps Toward Discrimination

In summary, following is a review of the sequence of the process:

1. The power of *Purusha* seems automatically buried in *prakriti* through *maya* when one's conscious ego mind thinks, "I do this and I do that. How great I am, how bad I am."
2. Through purifying the inner equipment and approaching Knowledge, the light of consciousness becomes accessible. This helps the person separate out *Purusha* from *prakriti*. The process of separation takes place alongside the experiential knowledge, "I am not the doer. *I am*."("Know that I am the knower in all fields of my creation.")
3. As one persists in bringing the witness to all fields of experience, including meditation, compassion lives. This is the conscious union between the field and the knower of the field. Compassion unifies.
4. Through performing all action as service in the state of ongoing witnessing compassion, past *karmas* are burned to ashes. The twenty values for which we have been constantly striving are naturally lived. No new *karmas* are formed. Meditation becomes more ongoing.
5. The continuous capacity to discriminate the Real from the unreal becomes a way of being.

Ever part of the One, the forms divide, separate and grow, ever moving and intertwining like the molecules of one giant cell swimming toward its destination without knowledge of its destiny, till it returns again to its identification with the One. The sages say the entire universe that appears to exist, projects out of *Paramatman*, merges in *Paramatman* and returns to *Paramatman*. All the lawful permutations undulating like waves in the sea discover their source as unity.

That which has no change has no beginning, no cause. When we rediscover our identity with unity, there is only qualityless perfection purity existence. In a flash there is only love, only everything, only One(30).

Whether we see the body dance or stumble there is always stillness, always unity. The seer within is fully free from all the permutations of the field. Worry, anxiety, joy, attachment, earthquake, blizzard, the seer is free from all the modifications of matter which are equally *prakriti*—be they called good or bad(32). To periodically return to this rock of awareness is spiritual work. To live in this ongoing awareness is liberation.

The sages say there is a point when the *sadhaka*(spiritual aspirant) becomes the *sadhu*(holy person).

> When a man sees that the infinity of various beings is abiding in the One and is an evolution from the One, then he becomes One with *Brahman*. (13:30)

The light that lives in the heart as the Knower of the field also lives equally in all other hearts and in all things animate and inanimate. As we experience the distinction between the field and Knower of the field ongoingly, throughout the daily joys and sorrows, we will come to serve as vehicles for *Purusha* to infuse the *prakriti* of our lives. When this way of being becomes permanent, we know Truth. We are fully free.

Liberation

What then is liberation? At this juncture, the aspirant has the knowledge and resources to view liberation as more than freeing oneself from a personal rut, hang-up or repression. Liberation does *not* exist in the false security of feeling more on top of things under the illusion of being in control. Rather, liberation implies surrender—surrendering the illusion of control itself—and witnessing the dream of the world go by, not from the vantage point of ego but as one whose sense of individual self is part of the total mind and the highest consciousness. The liberated soul is no longer bound by his senses, thoughts, memories, desires or past conditioning. He lives the ever-continuous stillness presence of the Real.

Lest we become intimidated by this lofty ideal as being out of reach, Sri Sathya Sai Baba says:

> Liberation is just the awareness of Truth, the falling off of the scales of delusion from the eye. It is not a suburb of select souls. It is not a closed monopoly of expert *sadhakas*(aspirants). Like the river losing its form, its name and its taste in the sea, liberation dissolves the names and forms, aptitudes and attitudes. You are no more a separate and particular individual.

Thus all striving to feel important, to feel like *somebody* or to legislate equal rights is not what the science of Reality would call liberation, because these are based on identification with ego body consciousness. Yet they can all be part of the raw material, so long as we realize that genuine liberation does not come from changing one aspect of matter for another aspect of matter. Political rights and external freedoms have their rightful place within the world of *karma*. But if we wish to transcend our fate with all its limitations, then all sense of isolated individuality must be separated out from the particular as well as the collective.

This does not imply uniformity of personality—just the realization that individual expression is part of one whole. The realized souls are more individual than you and me. But their individuality exudes compassion and universality. Some play the role of the noisy rogue, others are silent. Some teach through humor, others seemingly through logic. Some evoke awe, others instill love. Their personalities might appear utterly distinct but in each of them, the personal mode of expression is secondary to the effect produced by just being in their presence. For it is never the personality that creates or uplifts the atmosphere but simply the indescribable stillness loving presence of Brahman, which is the hallmark of the liberated soul.

Liberation requires a change in our basic orientation and motivation. All the time and energy that goes into survival needs, self expression, and attempts to change the external environment and our place in it, need to be *redirected* toward helping the ever present witness be attentive to the play of life in all its manifestations—while fully participating in the task at hand. Then we neither sleep nor dream. Ever alert to the drama of *prakriti* and *Purusha*, the field of *maya* becomes the field of liberation.

> Those who with the eye of inner vision see the distinction between the field and the knower of the field and see the liberation of spirit from matter, they go into the Supreme. (13:34)

Thus, the thirteenth discourse teaches the *yoga* of the separation of the objects of consciousness, thoughts and feelings from the experience of pure consciousness, that *prakriti* and *Purusha*, the field and the Knower of the field can be reunited as a state of ongoing awareness in the omnipresent supreme witness.

Fourteen

Yoga of Dividing the Three Qualities

Gunatraya Vibhaga Yoga

	Gita verses
Supreme wisdom and origins of the universe	1–4
Nature of the three *gunas (sattva, rajas,* and *tamas)*	5–13
Effects of the three *gunas*	14–18
Way to liberation *(moksha)*	19–20
One who has transcended the *gunas (gunatitah)*	21–27

three ropes of matter
ever bind us to the world
cut them

with the scissors of consciousness
know and feel and see
in utter detachment

In the fourteenth discourse, Krishna continues to elucidate the nature of the field from a psychological perspective. If all human beings are inherently equal as the Knower of the field or supreme consciousness, why then is there so much diversity between us? Our intelligence, talents, morality, motivation, character and actions are very different. Some are smart, some seem dumb, some are creative, others dull, some are open, others rigid, some are active, others passive, some are happy, others unhappy. Can we understand these individual differences in a way that is more profound and specific than explanations based on heredity, environment, conditioning or personality? Is there perhaps some underlying principle inherent in the transformation of matter itself which determines how nature(*prakriti*) will express herself through different people in different ways, or through the same person under different circumstances? And can knowledge of this law help us proceed in our evolution toward Truth?

This chapter thus goes directly to the source of all human psychology. In a terse and straightforward manner, it cuts through all theories of personality, both conscious and unconscious, direct to the source of creation where matter and energy are known as One. This is the spot where universal law enters into manifestation. It elucidates how the law of dissolution, preservation and creation underlies the human psyche and seems to produce all undertakings, all aspirations and all the actions that structure, define and determine our lives. By observation comprehension of how the three *gunas* bind us, we come to remove ourselves from their power. Through understanding the workings of this law, we are given a means that will help us evolve, discover our essence and eventually free ourselves from being ensnared by the net of *prakriti*—to end the cycle of birth and death (2).

From the outset, it would be easier to comprehend the law of the three qualities if we could view creation and change primarily as precipitated by the mind and occurring within the mind. *What we call the external world results from the contents of our consciousness.* When we are identified with the mind and the five senses, we view *prakriti* or the external mechanism of the self/world as real. We view our thoughts and emotions as material, as possessing an intrinsic beingness. We view the ego as concrete, solid, existing within itself. But when we take refuge in this Knowledge and begin to receive intuitions, insights and sparks of light from a higher source, we are no longer identified with *prakriti* as her unconsciously bound victim.

Rigidity gives way to fluidity, as the purifying effect of receiving this knowledge, in whatever form, leads us to a finer space within matter and beyond, until eventually there are no more thoughts to create our world, no more emotions to dissolve our world, no more *vasanas* lurking round the collective unconscious waiting for an opportunity to manifest and create new worlds, new births, new deaths. For the realized soul, only the Knower of the field exists; that which we call creation and dissolution is but a lower form of perception superimposed upon Reality.

In order to transcend this superimposition of all the extraneous levels of perception, Krishna offers us insight into the workings of the *gunas* and how they rule our lives. This leads to supreme wisdom(1), the undifferentiated source from which all springs, an awareness of origins before the superimpositions and agitations of mind veil Reality from us.

From *Mula prakriti*, the subtlest womb of total creation, the enlivening seed of pure consciousness (*Paramatma*) seems to descend(3), like a ripple on the waters of the lotus, which awakens Brahma the creator from sleep. It differentiates into the total *vasanas* or collective unconscious, which is seemingly controlled and directed by Ishvara, under the power of *maya*. The three *gunas* together constitute *maya*, the total cause of all creation. Inherent within the cause is also the effect, the universe. When the three rest in a state of equilibrium as one, there is no movement, no action, no time. When the three become unequal in proportion, the world is created. Movement and division occur. Heaven and earth, light and darkness, dry land and water, conscious and unconscious—all become separate. Since the total *vasanas* are inherently dynamic, further differentiation appears to form an ego and populate a world, as the seeds of "past" thoughts and actions create our "present" conditions. Behind all the activities of the ego are the three *gunas*(4). And behind the three *gunas* are *prakriti* and *Purusha*, which can be viewed as two aspects of the aspectless *Brahman*, the mother and father of the universe. Like a spider that weaves a web out of itself, the universe seemingly emanates from the immovable *Brahman* until compelled to imbibe the web and dissolve into the invisible *Brahman*.

Description of the Gunas

Nature can be viewed as consisting of three principles—*sattva*, *rajas* and *tamas*. As an ever present constituent of matter, *rajas* can be considered the active force, *tamas* the passive force and *sattva* the neutralizing force. On the macrocosmic level, the root of subtlest matter(*Mula prakriti*) can be understood as the aspect of total receptivity(*tamas*, or Siva the dissolver); as the seeds of all actions(*rajas* or Brahma the creator); and the connection between the two, which incorporates both as the controller of all our thoughts, feelings and actions(*sattva* or Vishnu the sustainer); all pervading as a manifestation of the One, ever present in the dynamic process of the whole universe.

The workings of the *gunas* can be perceived in every field of knowledge. For example, in historical events these patterns have been viewed as thesis, antithesis and synthesis by Hegel; in science they are reflected as proton(positive force), electron(negative force) and neutron(neutralizing force). And in daily life this principle can be called yes, no and the ongoing recognition of both, which leads beyond ambivalence and resistance toward unification. The *gunas* have been called the ropes that bind us to joy and sorrow; alternating, undulating, in all manner of permutation until their lawful, universal secret is discovered and conquered.

Sattva is the principle that absorbs and reflects the light of *Brahman.* This appears as silence, subtle vibration, purity, clarity, intelligence, goodness, justice, harmony, peacefulness, intuition, positive values, altruism, compassion and the striving for perfection in oneself and others. It can be active or inactive in accordance with the rightness of the situation but its primary mode is inner stillness. Its color is white.

Rajas is the principle whereby the light gets fueled into extroverted action and fiery emotion. It manifests as dynamism, desire, passion, agitation, incessant activity, restlessness, the capacity to do, egoism, greed and the striving for acquisition—primarily for oneself and one's clan. In some societies, these active attributes have been likened to the male principle, but not in India. Its color is red.

Tamas is the principle that absorbs the light, so deeply unto itself that it remains buried, unable to be seen or experienced. This leads to misperceptions, confusion and ignorance. It appears as inertia, heaviness, sleep, laziness, lack of reflection or insight, extreme attachment or merging, fear, delusion, insensitivity, automatic instinctive reactivity and passivity. It can also bring great depth and is a vehicle of receptivity or a sponge-like taking in of vibrations and impressions without any filter.

In some cultures, the more receptive attributes have been likened to the female principle. According to *Vedanta* however, the total female principle known as *maya sakti* encompasses all three *gunas* as the active aspect of the Godhead; that power through which all things and beings enter into manifestation. For creation requires dissolution, and activity requires passivity. *In order for conscious action to occur, these three aspects must be identifiably present as one.* And action under the gaze of the witnessing consciousness is like no action. It is only when societal conditioning programs a person to lose touch with his inner sense of *being* that the dichotomy between the female "*being*" and male "*doing*" becomes the norm. Inherent in the Self is the unification of being and doing. The color of *tamoguna* is black.

The three *gunas* rarely appear in the average human being in pure form but are found in varying combinations in different people at different times. The ideal combination of the *gunas* is seventy percent *sattva*, twenty per-cent *rajas* and ten per-cent *tamas*. Each of us is ruled by a primary *guna*, which determines our motivation, character, life's purpose, happiness or suffering as well as our degree of evolution. Anyone who wishes to work directly on transforming his personality into greater efficiency, depth, compassion, joy and wisdom can be greatly aided by assessing and observing the workings of the *gunas* within.

This process can bestow the knowledge that leads to liberation (2). Through a gradual or immediate process, *tamas* is transformed into *rajas*, *rajas* into *sattva* and *sattva* into detachment. When *sattva* is experienced in its pure and natural state, the Self can shine through any *guna* directly without covering or reflection. Our *conscious* participation leads to evolution. Whenever detachment occurs, or Love or the witnessing consciousness, even if only momentarily, we enter a higher state of being, which influences our actions.

If one wishes to approach the root space where matter and spirit coalesce to shape personality, observation of the workings of the three qualities can be helpful. For this is the beginning point of creation and dissolution, birth and death. *By seeing, we are offered the opportunity to participate in the creation of our lives.*

Without this seeing knowledge, our actions proceed in an automatic way based on fitting in present events with past conditioning. Then the *gunas* serve as ropes that bind us by attaching the body ego to functioning in a rigidly prescribed manner, in accordance with the propensity of the predominant *guna*. Without seeing, there is no freedom to act differently from what the *gunas* have programmed for us. For the *gunas* are the influences under which the thoughts function to produce actions. Any attempt to change our actions directly *without* understanding the underlying principle would tend to lead to resistance or the need to control.

So we behave like automatons under the decree of the three-fold aspect of nature, which binds spirit to matter and brings experiences to us in the alternating round of joy and sorrow, attraction and repulsion, birth and death. Only by seeing-understanding can the ropes be loosened and separated out from the Self, that the beauty of our true identity be experienced at the core and lived(5).

Effects of the Gunas

In *slokas* 5-9, Krishna explains how the different ropes bind us. *When we are tied to anything whatsoever, we are not fully free.* We can be attached to something "good" as well as to something "bad," bound to heaven as well as to hell, fated for a "moral" and peaceful lifestyle or an "immoral" and raucous lifestyle, wedded to happiness as well as to sorrow. All these alternatives are still bondage from the standpoint of liberation. Being tied to the good is still not good from the perspective of Reality.

For example, the predominantly *sattvic* person is bound to knowledge and happiness(6,9). This means he is still dependent on certain external conditions to produce happiness in him. These conditions ensure contentment when he's in a nice clean, quiet atmosphere surrounded by beauty, intelligence, culture, nature, in an environment where decent values are espoused, where he is free to study, create and live a life of virtue with minimal external disturbances. And the *sattvic* person will often find himself in such a peaceful environment because he has earned it as a result of his past thoughts and actions. As his *vasanas* are few, his interests are noble; this attracts to him the external conditions that correspond to the *guna* of his internal nature, as outer and inner are one.

But since he is not yet *pure sattva*, problems arise—especially when he finds himself rubbing shoulders with "cruder" types. He can be somewhat self righteous and rigid. His preconceived ideas about what is spiritual and what is not can be insufferable. He can exude the pride of scholarship and plenty. His sensitivity and openness can cause him to feel terribly imposed upon or invaded by the emotional ugliness around him. And he can be equally imposing on others who are not quite yet ready for his wisdom. Until his attachment to goodness, peacefulness and happiness is severed through experiential knowledge of Reality, he will remain bound to nature by seeking his perception of the good and avoiding or condemning his perception of the inferior. Although his mental perception is acute and his assessment of most situations is valid, he is still attached to propagating his views. His happiness usually occurs by being able to be contemplative, creative and live out his introverted nature. As long as happiness is dependent on anything external to produce internal well being, this is not liberation.

The Pandava King Yuddhisthira is an example of one who is sometimes attached to *sattva guna*. Although he is a *yogi* with impeccable purity and much detachment, he still has faith in the external forms of *dharma* and in the authority figures of his elders. Had he not been attached to the rules of right conduct, he never would have prevented Bhima from fighting with Duryodhana when Draupadi was humiliatingly dragged into court by the hair and disrobed as a slave. When one relies on anything external or superimposed one has not yet transcended the *gunas*(*gunatitah*).

The person whose actions are *sattvic* has inherent righteous intelligence, or has been a practitioner of spiritual discipline and/or has been brought up by parents who embody ideal values, aspirations and wisdom. As his temperament is basically peaceful, he would be attracted to modes of living that are free from agitation. But if he has no contact with the values that would allow him to create a link with his inner Self, then he might internalize the prevailing *gunas* of the parents. Adaptation to an environment that is foreign to his nature would result in an inner hunger and feelings of alienation from himself and deeper relationships with others.

For example, if a child's nature is basically *sattvic* and his parents impose a *rajasic* lifestyle on the child, he will never feel at home with himself until he is able to free himself from his parental internalizations and rediscover his natural essence. For living one's inner nature requires time, ease and spontaneity. To be free, to be, to play, to create things within the natural cycle from beginning to end, not as structured activity but as a *way of living* is an important precondition for the formation of independent initiative, competence, self esteem and the capacity to enjoy being alone with oneself comfortably without boredom or restlessness. The excessive imposition of entertainment, structured activity and rushing to meet it interferes with the organic pace that is essential for the *interrelationship* between inner feelings and external actions to occur.

Imaginativeness, being, contentment, depth, ideals, feelings, communication as an ongoing part of life become stunted as the pervasive teaching of our "affluent" society unconsciously promotes *reliance on externals*. This all pervasive influence leads to greed, egoism, feelings of dissatisfaction, seeming loss of Self and lack of inner rootedness. Parents need not impose this contemporary, heedless, commercial tendency on their children if intrinsic human values can be incorporated into life.

Although the *sattvic* person has transformed a good majority of his passions, bad habits and negative emotions, he remains attached to his sexual instincts and "lower" knowledge, both secular and spiritual. An artist, poet, scientist or healer needs to experience the joy of creation, discovery or healing in order to feel whole. In spite of the fact that it remains a very fulfilling form of bondage for oneself and the society, nonetheless it cannot prepare us for liberation—unless the underlying motivation is for one's inner evolution and the well being of all. It has been said that the *sattvic* person remains attached to the joys of a life fully and wholesomely lived. The *boddhisattva*, on the other hand, sacrifices happiness and liberation for himself alone to participate in the healing of the human race.

If the attachment is to spiritual knowledge, this means that intellectual understanding has not yet deepened enough to become integrated into practice. Doctrine, ritual and literalism still prevent the soul from soaring into the flight of oneness. But if practices are adhered to steadily, the narrow aperture will widen. As purification proceeds, liquidity of light will erase all compartments, loosen all attachments and the *sattvic* person will come to see how all forms of technique in spiritual work, which have a definite time and place are but a means to an end and not the end in itself. Nothing is to be identified with.

So the person evolving on the ladder of *sattva* receives much gratification from the process of living with faith in the guidance of Intelligence higher than his own ego. Life's simple happenings become very interesting as he learns that all life is a university and the process of mindful living will bring him to his goal. This quality of life is inherently joyful. As surrender, detachment, compassion, flexibility and onepointed devotion become his steady companions, he can transcend the binding influence of *sattva* and approach Self Knowledge.

Rajas, on the other hand, binds one to suffering(7,9). When actions are primarily for oneself alone, the end result can only be suffering. When we step on other toes, those toes eventually stomp on us. When our primary motivation grabs for power or praise, sex or wealth, the end result is bound to be sorrow. For all these things perish as part of the world of change. The pain of loss is the inevitable other side of the coin of gain. To be dependent on the way others view us, on our paycheck or our friends and family for our happiness is a set up for misery. Value relationship, value work, a good source of livelihood, value a good name but do not *depend* on them for your sense of well being.

The *rajasic* person lives under the misconception that people and things will bring him happiness. So all his energy is directed toward the pursuit of incessant activity to possess and acquire. *He has adapted all too well to the prevailing values of our present society.* He worships the idol of work, toils hard for things, not realizing that things are a poor substitute for genuine feelings, communication and simple time shared with friends and family. For *rajas*, the ego is the measure of all things. He feels if he doesn't constantly compete and assert his prowess, power and territoriality, he will fail. He will perish. He mistakenly equates self-centered aggression with survival. To live under the domination of this coping mechanism induces enormous anxiety and stress.

When not working and running he keeps himself so busy there is little time for relaxation or reflection. Relaxation becomes a chore to fit into his schedule. His body and mind dart from thing to thing, unaware of the stress he inflicts on himself and his family. His attachment to incessant activity serves to veil the inner thirst that lurks below the surface. But the only drink that can quench his thirst is to allow his essence out of hiding. As long as agitation, surface emotion and movement dominate his life, his satisfactions will remain superficial, temporary, basically unsatisfying.

The compulsive nature of his actions renders him an unconscious victim of alcohol, cigarettes, overeating, advertising, the media, consumerism and conformity to the prevailing values of the times. Though he is often quite capable and successful in his chosen field, he can never really enjoy it as he somehow negates his inner self in the process. He tends to treat himself and others like objects, things to be manipulated, controlled and fitted into his schedule of incessant activity. Rarely does he ever listen to another person. And as his sexuality is often split-off from feeling, he robs himself of the possibility of inner growth through relationship, as a cooperative undertaking. The quiet sharing necessary for a real relationship feels too threatening. The so-called narcissistic character disorder is one form of the contemporary prototype for the *rajasic* temperament.

Some characteristics of the "narcissistic character disorder" are:

1. extreme rushing and busy-ness. Always *doing*, never just *being.*
2. little self-reflection. reliance and focus on externals with avoidance of inner feelings and sensitivity. As one's depth remains hidden, the result is confusion, misperception and covering over the Self.
3. emotions such as rage or envy very easily erupt—especially when another doesn't fit into his belief system or lifestyle.
4. excessive need to control and impose one's opinions and lifestyle. Mistakes his subjective preferences for reality.
5. treats others as objects or extensions of oneself. Can be very manipulative to ensure that others—especially children—are a reflection of him.

Of course, there are many different individual scenarios dominated by each *guna.* These are determined by the encrusted configuration of our past thoughts, memories, level of evolution and actions over many lifetimes. In the case of Duryodhana, for example, the passionate driving force behind his insatiable need for power and control was envy. His nature was inherently generous and brave but the tragic flaw of envy compelled him to sacrifice his life, his sons, his kingdom and all the warriors to annihilate the Pandavas. *He knew they were the embodiment of dharma yet he was completely at the mercy of his envy.* Why was he not able to work it through?

There was a crucial moment in the life of Ḍuryodhana when there was an opportunity for change. He had entered the forest hoping to humiliate the Pandavas and gloat over their exile. But instead of making them jealous, he was captured by local warriors who intended to kill him. Rather than allowing their evil cousin to die, the Pandavas fought for him and set him free. Duryodhana felt humiliated, broken down, despairing—on the brink of conscience. He wanted to kill himself.

At that crucial time, if he had sought the help of a teacher *avatar* such as Krishna, or a wise man such as his uncle Vidura or great-uncle Bhishma, the possibility for change might have occurred. But instead, his friend Karna comforted him and prevented him from killing himself by propping up his pride and reinforcing his familiar egoism. Karna's attachment to his friend, prevented Duryodhana from remaining sensitive enough to his suffering to benefit from it. Only this life-giving sensitivity allows our false pride and envy to crumble. *Only then can conscience emerge.* How often does the seeming "help" of family members and loved ones at a time of crisis serve only to reinstate the known and prevent the potential growth that could occur from encouraging openness to the realm of the unknown?

Whereas in Duryodahana's time, the *rajasic* temperament was confined to the warriors(*kshatriyas*), in the contemporary person, the compulsively *rajasic* temperament is universally reinforced as the norm by our societal values, which place little emphasis on spontaneous being, quietness, self-reflection and genuine feeling caring for oneself and others.

When the *rajasic* type compartmentalizes by becoming compulsively extroverted, it is because he is running away from feeling pain and disappointment. He unconsciously believes his world will fall apart if he sits still and faces himself. When finally he is forced to experience his inner sadness and suffering, he comes to find it is not so devastating but rather, is nature's way of forcing him to grow and participate in life in a more meaningful way. With this realization comes a newly found freedom.

No longer is there a need to run. No longer is there a need to control. No longer is there a need to manipulate. *With the acceptance of his own feelings, love can be received.* Now he can begin to redirect his wonderful energy and suspicious vigilance, that has been scattered into a hundred directions, to become focused on his own inner growth. He begins to participate gently in creating things—music, plants, painting, cooking, nurturing children and pets, allowing time for relationship with natural cycles of completion. He participates in activities that benefit others. And if he becomes more open, his suffering might lead him to a genuine spiritual teaching. As he allows himself to discover his inner sensitivity, he becomes self-reflective, less egotistical and grows into a positive dynamic force, a well meaning man of action, a loving leader who accomplishes good things for himself, his family and the society.

The great *maharajas* of ancient India, who were known for their courage and skill in warfare as well as for their just governments reflected temperaments that combined *rajas* with *sattva.* As the *rajasic* type evolves, he finds his life far more fulfilling. When he allows his feelings to exist, he is no longer bound by the desire for results which stems solely from mind based actions. To let go of the need to control, to soften and permit the presence of finer feeling to combine with reason makes for a far more fulfilling and sensitive life. Black and white gives way to a many colored spectrum, as stress and agitation decrease and the light of *sattva* enters.

Soon the motivation of the *rajasic* person changes, that his actions might serve the welfare of the whole. As his orientation embraces the common good, his self-centered passions decrease, his desire, thirst and hostility become transformed. Through his innate intelligence and creativity, he begins to express himself in more fluid ways. As he becomes genuinely appreciated, he comes to value himself as well as others. No longer needing the crutch of compulsive activity, he embraces the essentials of living.

He begins to enjoy his innate competence. His anxiety decreases as he approaches the threshold of self confidence. Slowly, nature leads him from materialism to faith, *to the belief that he is in fact part of the larger scheme of things.* As intelligent motivation and caring gradually become the basis for all his actions, his restlessness subsides. Compulsion and emotional avoidance are no longer the driving force for his actions.

Whereas *rajas* is unthinkingly attached to action, *tamas* is unconsciously attached to the path of least resistance, the easy way out(8,9). "What does it matter," is his motto. "If I don't do it today, it'll get done tomorrow. Its not really important." This attitude is not detachment but rather an unconscious merging with a state of sleep, dullness and inertia, which is often the result of defending against anger, fear or excessive worry. For the individuality of the *tamasic* type has not yet differentiated itself from the clan or the collective unconscious; and though seemingly awake, he floats through life merged with the waters of accident, bringing tiredness, confusion, miscommunication and delusion wherever he happens to be.

It would be fine for him to stay in bed and watch TV for hours on end. Feeling comfortable close to home, he thrives on video games and entertainment systems that require no effort. He feels so heavy and weighted down by suppressed emotions that movement is a chore. He passively pampers himself, utterly insensitive to his own real needs and the needs of his children, family and friends. His home usually reflects his inner mental sluggishness—sloppy and dirty. Even while cleaning, dust is often swept behind the bed as his desires and emotions are swept under the rug. Likewise, he denies and blocks out his sadness and hatred, which remain unconscious until life forces him to begin his inner cleaning, that he might one day claim his immaculate human heritage.

Most *tamasic* types feel more comfortable holding jobs where they are taken care of and little independent initiative is required. Whereas *rajas* often fights acknowledging his dependency needs, *tamas* revels in them. A child who has not received wholesome nurturing or has been prevented from developing a sense of separateness because of too much attached nurturing will remain fixated in *tamas* until the inescapable suffering eventually initiates the time of ripeness for his growth to begin. Then the seed of *tamas* will sprout and an individual person will be born.

The prototype of pure *tamas* is not to be found in the human realm but in the plant kingdom. In the human and animal realms, *tamas* and *rajas* usually interact with each other thereby producing different patterns of personality. For example, the compulsive activity of *rajas* can be viewed as an instinctive spurt of energy to free oneself from the clutches of *tamas*. Without the externally imposed structure of activity, he would slip back into the inertia of *tamas*. As his inner feelings begin to be taken into account in formulating his activity, purification occurs and his actions become more inner directed; stem more from discriminating feeling and less from the automatic compulsion of rage, fear, greed and envy. The crutch of external structure for achievement to occur becomes less necessary as the reflectiveness of *sattva* enters.

Psychopathology and the Gunas

A contemporary prototype for the psychopathology of *tamas* is the borderline personality. Although his body may be active, his finer feelings and intellect, as well as the connections between the two are fast asleep. He functions primarily through a symbiotic merging with others. Then when others do not fulfill his unstated ideal he becomes explosively enraged or coldly hostile, avoiding and withdrawn. He is unable to participate in a back and forth, give and take relationship. His seemingly individual thoughts and opinions stem directly from some external authority such as "shoulds," "isms," or from what he thinks is "normal." This leaves no room for question. Any discussion that pricks the bubble of his cherished opinions or severs the symbiotic merging is responded to with rage. For this is a rage that accepts no responsibility. The other person is always to blame for doing or saying something unthinkable.

This explosiveness, hostility and avoidance, coupled with a lack of self reflection characteristic of an unformed ego, causes him to latch onto others and rule them or be ruled by them. As a parent, this person is totally dominating, controlling and possessive. He might be able to "love" his children as an extension of himself but never for who they are. To reinforce their emotional dependency and symbiosis, he possessively guards them from close relationships with others, thereby promoting the "dysfunctional family." And he will always manage to find a scapegoat, so as to avoid accepting responsibility for his own feelings and actions. The degree of attachment, merging, denial and manipulativeness reflects the degree of pathology.

Some elements of borderline attachment are evident in Dhritarashtra's relationship with his son Duryodhana. But since Duryodhana was given the subconscious message that he should be king, his envy, rage and hatred for the Pandavas is very conscious, unlike the unconscious acting out behavior seen in narcissistic borderline disorders. Although Dhritarashtra knew his treatment of the Pandavas was unjust, his fear of losing Duryodhana served to reinforce his psychological blindness, greed and attachment.

The more passive *tamasic* type is a running target for cults and psychics, as these require giving up one's own reflective discrimination, which the *tamasic* person has yet to develop. Invasion by spirits, possession by entities and external thought forms of darkness can occur to a person who is so open without the protection of a healthy ego or the direct intervention of divine grace. Due to the abundance of darkness and confusion, one's faith and trust is often placed in the wrong place, thereby leading to a long series of disappointments and disasters.

As *tamas* yearns to evolve, nature obliges. The volcanic emotions that have been dormant within the unconscious for aeons begin to spurt. If they remain undirected or proper guidance is lacking, their legacy can bring massive denial, delusion, splitting of personality or paranoia. The fire of self-hate can scorch oneself and others; and the perpetuation of denial, projection, and splitting off of feeling serves only to intensify the rage. Unfortunately, the inner need to "be right" alongside "acting out" behavior often prevents this person from receiving help, and loved ones are sometimes forced to withdraw. Until one can acknowledge one's suffering and seek guidance from a rightful source, the transition from pathological *tamas* to *rajas* inevitably leads one through a veritable inferno.

But if a person can find a real teacher, or at least an honest and competent helper, then his inner receptivity can be a genuine support in assuring his progress. As he becomes more able to trust his helper, he can start feeling safe enough to own his own emotions, experience remorse and thereby lessen his projections. He can begin to participate in life and discover his talents or vocation. He can involve himself in spiritual work, which strengthens his sense of purpose and belonging. If he is blessed enough to find a teacher, the love of the teacher can help heal his early wounds. Through the grace of love, his confusion decreases, faith and trust deepen. As he learns to participate with right effort and connect with his inner essence, the cloud of ignorance begins to fade. Since the core of each human being is God, no matter how deluded or rageful a person might seem, his true Self is sheer love, perfection, consciousness—covered over by conditioning. Through experiencing the living support of this feeling knowledge, the diseased mind can be cured.

The psychopathology of *rajas* and *tamas* occurs primarily in cases of extreme imbalance between the three parts of the brain, which function through the body, emotions and intellect. For example, the mind may be very active while the feelings are cut off; so there can be no genuine self-reflection—as in the case of Dhritarashtra. Or, where *tamas* rules certain emotions in a rigidly fixed manner, the free flow is blocked, insight is prevented and the physical body, such as the endocrine system or heart, become overly taxed and stop functioning naturally. When certain emotions such as sadness or suffering are repressed, other emotions such as rage or anxiety are often experienced *in the body* in an exaggerated way. This undue stress can lead to a variety of physical and psychological symptoms from heart disease to delusion.

The three *gunas* as psychological types can be viewed as three stages of ego development. *Tamas* is the undifferentiated matrix of consciousness where the ego as part of the collective is fast asleep to its individuality. *Rajas* is the emergent ego that attributes actions and power unto itself; the prototype of pride and the attempt to control. *Sattva* is the self-reflective ego that seeks to disidentify with the sense of agency and reconnect with the source of light, the inherent unity of all humanity. If a person is fortunate enough to encounter and practice a spiritual teaching while enmeshed in *tamas* and *rajas*, his evolution, sense of well being and quality of life can be greatly enhanced. Those around him will also benefit—especially his children. As parents free themselves from the compulsive influences of *rajas* and *tamas*, their children will tend to suffer much less, for they will not be as burdened internally with the conditions that program them for present and future pain.

When we differentiate and completely disidentify the Self from the body ego mind form, we have transcended the *gunas*. Only through detaching from the *gunas* do we transcend the grip of the ego, which has become encrusted by the *karmic* patterns of many lifetimes. *It is identification with the ego that prevents us from living in the ongoing state of liberation.*

Observing the Gunas Within

In the "average" person, the primary *gunas* are perpetually moving and changing(10). Sometimes we are caught in inertia, sometimes in action, sometimes in reflectiveness. A task for the spiritual student is to observe oneself in action as the movements of the three *gunas* flow through our thoughts, feelings, words and deeds. For a person to be happy and wholesome, the qualities must be in relative harmony. This occurs through three different aspects of oneself: the body, emotions and intellect. When the intellect is noble and the emotions are repressed, there can be no unity of thought, word and deed. There can be *no Truth.* By open seeing, harmonization occurs. We come to know what is needed.

The aim is to be able to participate in the gradual transformation of *tamas* and *rajas* into *sattva*. Always and everywhere the spiritual student is vigilant, ever alert to embodying a *sattvic* mood. This is not necessarily achieved by "doing" but by "being." As one practices observing oneself in the moment, a ray of *sattva* is brought to the situation. This quality of seeing in itself brings about the potential for change.

For example, a person who speaks in *sattva* thinks before opening his mouth and his tone is soft and sweet. When he walks, his gait is smooth and his body is connected with his awareness. Whether he brushes his teeth or combs his hair, the light of awareness is present. When we catch a glimpse of our voice tinged with the strident harshness of *rajas* or the lifeless dullness of *tamas* we are given a choice. Either we can remain in unconscious action, lessen the raucous tone, or we can play the role of the strident one with some degree of consciousness. And when we notice ourselves feeling sluggish with a dullness in the eye, we can remain so consciously or unconsciously; or else get up, go for a walk and repeat a *mantra*, or perform any other action of remembrance that can help us link the body, mind and intellect to the higher.

So it is for all our thoughts, feelings, words and actions. To notice when the body, emotions and intellect are functioning under the influence of which mood of the mind is the beginning of a training in developing the ongoing companionship of the observing witness, that a more subtle aspect of oneself can enter into life. When witnessing action exists on a conscious inner level, it need not be *acted out* on an outer level and lead to further vasanas and deeper entrenchment in bondage(16). In this way, we approach the ideal of seventy percent *sattva*, twenty percent *rajas* and ten percent *tamas*.

The effect of inner purity is far reaching. Nonverbal exposure to the presence of pure being is the most powerful teacher. Right action can occur through sheer detachment without any accompanying external action, as in the case of the true *sannyasin*; or it can occur through external action based on feeling compassion, as demonstrated by the genuine *karma yogi*. But as long as the motivation is selfish, the effect of seemingly right action can produce harmful results. Maharaj says, "The mind must know itself in every mood. Nothing is a mistake unless repeated."

The *rishis* of India have advised a simple general approach for evoking the *sattvic* mood—control your diet, control your impressions. Eating junk food and taking in junk impressions produce a comparably junky character. And a poor character is programmed for unhappiness.

There is a lawful relationship between our diet and our character. Eating fresh vegetables mildly prepared makes it easier for us to participate in cleansing the mind of its confusion and aggressive tendencies, thereby giving us energy for *dharmic* action and allowing the *prana*, subtle energy, to flow more freely. And by not imbibing the violence and base values of the mass media or the negative influences of other people, impure *vasanas* are prevented from forming. For we are influenced by what we come in contact with. When we surround ourselves with *sattvic* influences, this tendency takes root within us.

Continuity of the Gunas

As the *gunas* are behind the formation of our *vasanas* and our *vasanas* underlie the subtle and causal bodies, which travel with us from life to life, it is the primary combination of *gunas* within that leads to our future; not only in this life but in all future incarnations(14,15). *The way we live creates the composition of our minds at the moment of death.* And the moment of death is viewed as the most important moment of life, for this determines the quality of our *bardo* state(the level of the subtle body after death, which can be called heaven or hell), as well as our next life.

Like attracts like. The law of cause and effect is a function of the subtle and causal body. *It does not stop with the decay of the physical body*, says Krishna. It is right that the person whose mind is *tamasic* be born into a *tamasic* environment. For this is the perfect place for him to live out his *tamasic* desires. Without this opportunity, he would be unable to evolve, unable to contribute to and participate in the scheme of Great Nature in maintaining and balancing the cosmos. Likewise, the person with a restless mind will be attracted to the womb of a restless mother, bound by greed and incessant activity. And the aspiring spiritual student will be born into an environment conducive to continuing his spiritual work.

Whatever circumstance is most suitable for our individual tendencies and growth is where we find ourselves. Though it may not necessarily be what the conscious ego would wish to choose, nonetheless we are each in the perfect place to work through our negative tendencies and be prodded toward perfection. As this present era demonstrates far less goodness, homogeneity and unity within families than at the original time of Krishna's teaching, it is now even more essential for persons to comprehend, confront and transcend our parental and environmental conditioning if we wish to live our true nature and approach freedom.

Evolutionary Potential of the Gunas

When viewed from the perspective of what is needed, the three *gunas* are to be evaluated equally. Only when viewed from the ladder of evolution is *sattva guna* considered closer to the goal. But when we consider the *gunas* as forces, psychological constituents of nature that give rise to behavioral qualities, then no one *guna* is better than another. For example, *tamoguna*, which has acquired a negative connotation when it becomes imbalanced and fixed as the foundation of character, can be highly auspicious as the dissolver of our negative emotions and impurities. The force of involution or divine descent is a primordial visitation of God depicted in the form of Siva, through whom the prevailing universe is destroyed to make way for the rebirth of a better world.

The "dark" aspect of god and goddess is essential for life as we know it to evolve. When the forces of dissolution are experienced in direct connection with the power of God, suffering is experienced at the same time as deep joy. "O death, where is thy sting"?(Corinthians 15:55) Intense suffering and intense joy are no longer divided as they are the same unity, the same bliss, the same *Brahman*—for one who is not identified with the body. This is the auspiciousness of Siva as exhibited through the conscious principle of *tamoguna*.

To be able to abide in *sattva* and evolve, we must practice the development of will through training the intellect in awareness, presence and concentration; steering the body toward simplicity and wholesomeness; guiding the mind in austerity and sense control, and transforming the emotions through creativity, giving and devotion(18). Through this ongoing training, one need not sink into the heedless mire of *tamas* or the agitated battlefield of *rajas*. Through maintaining an ongoing awareness of our aspirations—good, bad and indifferent, the sages say we prepare ourselves for pure *sattva*, a spaceless space beyond all attachment, beyond all *gunas*.

> When the seer beholds no agent other than the *gunas* and knows that which is higher than the *gunas* he attains to my Being. (14:19) SwC

> When the man of vision sees that the powers of nature are the only actors of this vast drama and he beholds that which is beyond the powers of nature then he comes into my Being. JM

Way to Paramatma

Thus the *gunas* serve as the foundation on which the multiple dreams of existence are created, upheld and dissolved. Through experiencing the intangibility of all seeming constituents of this spaceless dream, the way is cleared for ongoingness, wholly unattached to movement, thought or quality.

who is the doer?
where is that which is done?
what sees?
what strives?
who? who?

When the dream has ended, the conditions of the dream are each equally untrue, according to the waker(20). It makes no difference to the waker if he was a homeless alcoholic or the President of the U.S. in the dream. For both roles are only a dream. Likewise, it makes no difference to the realized soul whether *sattva*, *rajas* or *tamas* is exhibiting through him. He watches them from the vantage point of divine indifference and remains unaffected like the waker who knows the dream is not real.

To live a life immersed in matter is like living a dream. To leave the dream state forever is to transcend the three qualities of nature, which comprise the limited ego. When the cause is removed there is no effect. When the *gunas* have seemingly surrendered their binding power, there is no world, no birth, no death. There is no mind. It appears as if nothing has changed. But everything has changed. And nothing has changed.

Now Arjuna wants to know how to identify the person who has transcended the *gunas*(*gunatitah*)(21). What does the process consist of? Krishna responds with a description reminiscent of the person of steady wisdom(2:55-72). Now however, the mind of Arjuna is better prepared to receive the essential meaning and practice the ideas(22-27). No longer do they seem so out of reach like an unapproachable fantasy. In chapter two, the seeds are being planted; in discourse fourteen, the seeds are beginning to sprout.

When we are able to accept everything that happens simply as a happening that is not part of us, and not care if it is ugly or fine, agitated or peaceful, destructive or constructive—because we are so rooted in the being conviction that it is not Real, it is not I, it is but the conditions of nature and I am *Brahman* I am I am; I am *Brahman* I am—then we have transcended the *gunas*.

When we are not the least affected by wanting anything, by doing anything, by praise and blame or loss and gain, by love and hate or light and shame—because we are so firmly rooted in the being conviction that it is not Real, it is not I, it is but the conditions of nature and I am *Brahman*, I am I am, I am *Brahman* I am—then we have transcended the *gunas*.

And when we love God with all our heart and see him within ourselves and within others everywhere, our only aim is to serve Him, to surrender to His will, to work for Him with an ease that is not work but is our very breath—that His being be lived through all in love forever and ever as the ongoing dissolution of all universes while participating in this life—then we have transcended the *gunas*. We are fit to revel in the loving consciousness I am I am I am I am, I am *Brahman* I am. This is the deepest *dharma*, which transcends all *gunas*.

So here, Krishna approaches the all encompassing One Truth from another perspective, offering us further spiritual practice, deeper understanding and a new way down into the depths of the Self, whose center is everywhere and whose circumference is nowhere.

Summation of the Three Qualities

In summary, here is a teaching on the three *gunas* by Sri Sathya Sai Baba:

> The entire world is a form of the three *gunas*. As long as these take up residence in your heart, beclouding your understanding, you remain in bondage. Among the three *gunas*, *rajas* and *tamas* are responsible for all the sorrows, grief, troubles and problems that you experience. Whenever fear, rage, laziness, inertia, drowsiness or sleep manifest, then you are overwhelmed by *tamoguna*. When *rajoguna* holds sway, your true human nature is forgotten. *Rajoguna* brings out the animal and demonic nature. A person filled with *rajoguna* will always be hasty in everything. He will have no patience or forbearance. He cannot be steady for even a moment and he will exhibit a great deal of anger. He will also have unlimited desires.
>
> As long as the two *gunas*, *rajas* and *tamas* are in your heart, the heart will remain impure. These two *gunas* continuously pollute and dirty the heart. As long as it is dirty, divinity will not enter your heart. You will not be able to perceive its presence there. Therefore, you must first remove *tamoguna* and then *rajoguna*. Then *sattvic guna* will shine. Start now by making every effort to remove every bit of dirt that has accumulated in your heart.
>
> What is the best way to remove the *gunas*? If a thorn were to enter your foot, you need not take a big sharp knife to remove it; you just take another thorn and remove the first with the second. Once this has been accomplished you throw away both thorns

without making any distinction between them. In this way, you have to remove *tamoguna* with the help of *rajoguna*. Then you have to remove *rajoguna* with the help of *sattva guna*. Finally you give up *sattva guna* also.

Before you can enter into the kingdom of God realization, you have to cast out all three *gunas*. If any *guna* remains it will keep you out of this kingdom of liberation. That is why Krishna commanded Arjuna to transcend all three *gunas*. He warned Arjuna that he will have to make maximum effort and take great care to permanently rid himself of these three *gunas*.

The primary cause of these three *gunas* is the mind. It is impossible to transcend this human nature and realize your divine nature until your mind loses its waveringness and becomes silent. Therefore, the first step is to offer your mind to the Lord. *After you have offered your mind to Him completely, God will take care of you in all respects*.

You should become mind-less. Only when you have a mind with pleasure and pain, happiness and sorrow will all other pairs of opposites be present. If you want to be free of these opposites and treat all things equally, you have to offer your mind to the Lord. That is why it has been said in *Vedanta* that it is the mind that is responsible for liberation and bondage. As long as you retain the mind, *rajoguna* and *tamoguna* will not leave you. Krishna explains many ways in which the *gunas* can be conquered. You can transform yourself into one who is steeped in the highest wisdom. (*Digest 2*, p.143-4)

Thus, in the fourteenth discourse, the *yoga* of the three *gunas* offers us the possibility of viewing the fluctuations of matter within and without, that these might gradually be transformed into their most refined possibility—pure *sattva*. As internal awareness dissolves the dichotomy between subject and object, matter and spirit, the link between *guna* and *karma* is severed. In this state, there is nothing left within the mind that could prevent us from serving as a loving embodiment of Truth.

Fifteen

YOGA OF THE SUPREME SELF

Purushottama Yoga

	<u>*Gita verses*</u>
The tree of illusory existence*(samsara)* and path to *Paramatma*	1–6
The person as the Self*(jivatman)*	7–11
Infinite existence and omnipresence*(Paramatma)*	12–15
The perishable, the imperishable, and the highest Self are One*(Purushottama)*	16–20

the tree of life
with root beyond the firmament
eternal essence seed

enmeshed in the tree we die
discover the root
and live

Visualize a tree; a giant healthy tree that fills the whole universe, our entire range of vision. See it expand. The trunk is very thick, the roots are very deep, the leaves are very lush. The branches are labyrinths leading to everywhere. Many secondary branches descend as if desiring to form roots. Down and straight they go intermingling with leaves and twigs creating a most miraculous maze of *maya*—a haven for children of all ages to play hide and seek, unaware of where the giant tree begins and ends.

The most unusual thing about this tree is that *its main root is above*. From our special space of seeing, we notice the root above spreading life, love and consciousness to everything below. There would be no tree of life without this primordial root above, ever nourishing the entire universe, feeding it with everything necessary for life on earth to emerge and continue. Thus the Absolute, which is beyond all change and changelessness, beyond all motion and immovability, seems to enter into manifestation and descend into life.

The fifteenth discourse weaves the tale of the tree of life and demonstrates how its supreme root above, which symbolizes the highest Reality, intermingles with our perishable body and our relatively imperishable soul to bring the Absolute directly into life.

The *asvattha* tree in India is similar to the pipal tree(1). *A shva stha* means "not standing till tomorrow." *Ashva* means "horse," symbolic of the restless mind of desire, which can be tamed. Tree(*vriksha*) translates as "that which can be cut down." This ancient tree seems to last forever, offering shade and shelter to people and horses from generation unto generation. But actually, the tree is always changing, growing, losing leaves, forming new roots, becoming more entrenched in the soil. When we become aware of the presence of the Absolute, this knowledge can enter the world, uplift human beings and bring something of value to the society. Like the leaves that offer shade, right Knowledge can be a fertile oasis in the scorching desert of *samsara*(1), the illusory world of change. But without awareness-experience of this Knowledge that is ever accessible, we become enslaved by the concrete understanding of the mind and senses and remain roped by the three *gunas*.

Thus new buds form, new roots strengthen and *karmic* tendencies reach fruition, causing new *vasanas* which lead to pleasure or pain(2). The downward root of our past conditioning and personal collective heritage ensnares us in the illusion of reality. And actions for one's ego self alone enlarge the roots, entangling us in identification with relationships and bondage.

Sometimes it is difficult to distinguish the reflection of the tree in the pond from the actual tree itself. Likewise, it is difficult to recognize the body ego person as but a reflection of the universal *Purusha*. To discover the downward root is to discover our personal heritage, our personal roots, an aspect of nourishment that can also be a cause of our personal stuckness and separateness. To discover the upward root is to discover our divine heritage, our inherent unity, the place where we are all one.

To know the whole tree we must know both roots as one. Who am I? What is life? What is the purpose of my life are some of the questions this knowledge elucidates.

Without living awareness of the upper root, attachment and selfishness, clannishness and divisiveness, egoism and intolerance rule our existence, in spite of all our good intentions and positive actions. The more entrenched the ego becomes, the stronger the root of our bondage. As this bondage strengthens, the more difficult it then becomes to detach ourselves from suffering. When we comprehend the downward root only, this can help free us somewhat from the slavery of our personal past and cultural conditioning, but this understanding in and of itself cannot offer the knowledge that will prevent us from being imprisoned by our present and future actions. Self Knowledge alone dispels ignorance, repels bondage, invites liberation.

Until we can detach ourselves from the illusion that the reflection is real, there can be no freedom. Detachment comes from dispassion, from viewing oneself as a part of total life, like segments of film on a movie screen. All the shots are part of one whole, which could not exist without light. Through watching our emotions as they froth and bubble, through seeing our likes and dislikes without capitulating to either, through attaching ourself in knowledge to the Self alone, the reflection can be revealed *as it is.*

> Men do not see the changing form of that tree, nor its origin, nor its end, nor where its roots are. But let the wise see. And with the strong sword of dispassion, let him cut asunder this firm rooted tree. Then that goal should be sought where having gone, none returns again.
>
> I seek refuge in that primeval *Purusha* from which streamed forth from time immemorial all activity or energy. (15:3-4)

The Secret of Nonidentification

This stark and practical example of detachment can help us notice and cut asunder our unconscious merging identification with *prakriti:*

> The world of matter is inert and insentient. The experience of life gained through it is known and lived only because of the play of consciousness upon it. As long as the wheels of a car are geared onto the machine, the vehicle moves. If we can clutch the motive power off from the moving wheels, the vehicle must come to its own motionless condition. Similarly, if consciousness is withdrawn from the body mind intellect vehicle, its play of perception emotion thought must necessarily halt. This clutching off of consciousness from the inert matter vehicles is detachment. With the ax of detachment, Krishna advises Arjuna to cut down the tree of multiple experiences. (Swami Chinmayananda, THG, p.888)

Krishna is not advising us to kill the tree of life. Life is meant to be lived in joy, but in the joy of *nonidentification* with the shell of things. For shells so easily crumble.

We experience an ongoing joy in life when we see the upward root permeating all, including oneself. This is the steady source of living in loving consciousness. The happiness of the downward root is based on our identification with the perishable positive, which is always changing into its opposite—loss and suffering. Only through identifying with the *source* of life can we be flexible enough to embody the origin of joy itself, present everywhere, in everything. When our identity with the depths of the vast ocean is established, the waves pounding on the surface can neither bother us nor erase our true identity. Once we know our true identity as the ocean, there is no return to the coming and going of the separate existence of the wave.

In the fifth *sloka,* Krishna reveals five conditions that are a prerequisite for the immature and foolish state of nonapprehension of Reality to leave forever. These conditions are also a process of spiritual work, which guarantee purification and consequent steadiness in contemplation. As we observe ourselves walking through the day, we can be alert to moments when feelings of pride emerge. It lifts its head under many guises: self-righteousness or comparisons, ambition or lack of ambition, pride in spotting pride in others. Or sometimes even under the guise of humility, arrogance lurks as the flip side of the coin in all feelings of inferiority and fear of success. To spot the subtle guises of pride weaving through our psyche is a very useful *sadhana* that hastens purification.

When the quality of watchfulness is present, alert to the thrust of desire and the various means employed for procuring and clinging, when mindfulness sees the habitual, unconscious motivation of seeking what we like and avoiding what we don't like, then we begin to approach a new degree of freedom. *To see our functioning with clarity keeps the mind balanced between the opposites*. Alert attention is the greatest ally in helping us form the link with Self. After many years and many lifetimes of reforging this link, the sages say we come to know we *are* this consciousness. Then no more links are needed. No longer is it necessary to find light from secondary sources. The moon, the sun, the stars and fire, are all but reflections of that One light inside.

Nothing external, no outer illumination is required—no practices, no teachings, no scriptures, for there is only One, only indefinable ongoingness Being(6). Everything is. Nothing is. Neither nothing nor everything is. And once this source is experienced, there is no falling back to the error of mistaking the reflection or the reflector for the omnipresent, prime illuminator.

The Source of Birth, Death and Action

Slokas 7-11 demonstrate the immanence of this supreme *Purusha* as it manifests through different developmental stages of growth of the person from birth to death, from death to birth. What begins as a tiny sperm seed swimming to unite with the ovum is enlivened by the upward root only, "an eternal ray of Myself." Without that spark of eternal spirit, there could be no life. At this stage there is no ego, no sense of I or my. Only later when the five senses and the mind repeat their seeing, hearing, thinking and grasping, which become programmed onto the mind, does the feeling of "I" and "my" take root below in the waking state consciousness, thereby creating the world of multiplicity.

It is the combination of the activities and thoughts of these six senses[34] that form the subtle body, which travels with us from life to life. This is the world of dream—as real or unreal as the waking state. In this world of inner perception, mind predominates, weaving its fantasies, emotions and mysteries into symbolic messages that can be decoded. This is also the stuff from which *vasanas* are made, based on what the mind processes and identifies with. In *Vedanta*, the five senses are not considered part of the gross body because of their direct connection with the mind. Until total identification with the subtle body based I-ness is severed, we will be ever travelling on the ocean of *samsara*, enjoying its fragrance, suffering its garbage, without any known captain or anchor.

Of course the anchor is always there called "Lord Ishvara," or no subtle body could exist. Krishna says it is He that obtains the body and draws the senses to it as we travel from life to life. Without that eternal spark, the *vasanas* could not form and the individuality(*jiva*) would not be drawn into the world, attracted by desire into a particular environment to act out its joys and sorrows. But until we become conscious of the "Lord" functioning through us, we can never become Him, even though we already *are* Him.

It is not *we* who die but *He* who remains in the body and enjoys through the mind and sense organs and then travels on. When the pathways to the eye of Knowledge become cleared, our ignorance of Reality falls away. The pathways clear when the multiplicity of intellect becomes *onepointed* and the agitation of emotions becomes transformed, through ongoing devotion and loving action for the benefit of others. When the body, emotions and intellect become integrated, the meditator can approach the goal. When the three parts of the person remain dis-integrated, meditation by itself can never take one to the Self(11). Agitation will always interfere.

Whenever we are exiled from our true nature of peace and joy, it is because we are identified with the downward root and not the upward root. *We mistake our self to be the ego.* Whenever we are anxious or aggravated over some seeming injustice, there is always an attachment or identification with the unreal that robs us of our peace and joy. Freedom comes from severing our attachment with the matter envelopments. We must attach to the Real and detach from the unreal. Right attachment is to be accomplished directly, through devotion. Right detachment entails long work with transforming the emotions.

In addition to observation and feeling, sometimes this requires taking action in a forthright manner, dedicating the results to Him, and articulating our dissatisfaction and prospective remedy without hostility, in a language that can be understood. For even if the right thing is said with hostility, it will always produce the wrong effect. The emotions and speech must be harmonized in accordance with the highest ideals of the intellect, for the right message to be communicated. Otherwise, only confusion will result.

At other times, this requires turning the focus of the mind to the Atman and letting go of everything else—not caring about injustice, not trying to explain, maintaining silence and forbearance in the face of false accusations. The latter way is for *sannyasins*, the former is for the *bhakta*(devotee) or the *karma yogi*(person of action). Both ways entail ascent and descent, remembrance and dedication. Both are needed at different times throughout our spiritual *sadhana*. For when *bhakti* alone remains fixated on the form level, it can lead to attachment and overly reactive emotions. And when action oriented detachment leaves out love and devotion, this can lead to egoism or the compartmentalization of spiritual practice *versus* life.

A third way of removing obstacles to our joyful nature is through the realization that the other is also *Atma.* When we can offer love *to* the *Atma from* the *Atma*, we see the shortcomings of the other are only the shell of ignorance, as is our own ego's reaction to the other. All shells must be discarded if we wish to live in freedom.

In *slokas* 12-17, the transcendent cosmic Reality is elucidated as part of an interconnected whole, a kind of ecological food chain of seemingly separate things which affect each other and are Him alone. Just as the arms, legs and head are part of one body, so the different parts of the cosmos are part of His Body. But our vision is too constricted to perceive this expansiveness as one.

The sun, moon and stars, all sources of light and fire are *Brahman*. Without the sun and moon there would be no earth, no life, no plants. *Brahman* alone, through love supports all things on earth. From this perspective, *Brahman* is the fire of desire, which perpetuates the species and moves us forward to action. Behind all life lurks the fire of desire. We need food to give us energy for life, and *Brahman* supports the digestion of food and excretion of food, the taking in of impressions and letting go of impressions, the breathing in and breathing out. *The nature of the food we eat and the impressions we imbibe will determine the ongoing quality of our lives.* All this is Brahman. As a reminder of this all pervasive actionless action of *Brahman*, the fourteenth *sloka* is recited before eating.

> I enter each living creature and dwell within as the life-giving breath. I am the fire in the stomach which digests all food. (15:14)

Once impressions and information are imbibed, they are processed and linked with what is already known, which then becomes digested as one's knowledge(15). This too is food—food for thought. Some impressions are rejected, some are altered. If emotions and memory color these impressions, they become *samskaras* and serve as part of the veil of *maya* that covers the light of the Self. As inner emotional reactions become purified, identification dissolves and the veiling of the Self departs. All knowledge, all capacity for memory, all capacity for forgetting is supported solely by this life-giving love.

For ultimately, in order to be connected with the source, we must cross the threshold of the end of knowledge. True Knowledge enters when the irrelevant departs. As in Dante's *Inferno*, we must cross the river Lethe and leave all memory behind. When we can let go of our emotional reactions and forgive, the veiling of the source vanishes, that love might reveal herself. Likewise, even the greatest knowledge, created by Krishna Himself beyond creation and offered to mankind through the *Vedas*, can become hardened if we cling to its form or if we are attached to the mechanism through which it is received, such as words, technique or the intellect. The aim is to go directly to the subtlest, to the space of the end of knowledge, the true meaning of *Vedanta*.

> And I am in the heart of all. With me come memory and wisdom and without me they depart. I am the Knower and the knowledge of the *Vedas* and the creator of their end, *Vedanta*. (15:15)

Approaching the End of Knowledge

In the "Karika" of the *Mandukya Upanishad*, Gaudapada gives a focused method for reaching the end of knowledge. He distinguishes four modes of motivation and action that can be applied to spiritual work or any worldly endeavor.

> The four things to be known in the very beginning are: l) the things to be avoided, 2) the object to be realized, 3) the things to be attained, and 4) the thoughts to be rendered ineffective. Among these four, all except what is to be realized exist only as imagination. (p.405)

In his commentary, Swami Chinmayananda says:

> In order to achieve any secret aim in life—whether domestic, political, economic, national or international, the individual or community will have to have a good grasp of these four items. They must know their goal. They must know what values are against the achievement of their desired goal; what values they must develop in themselves to fulfill their ambition. And they must also know definitely for themselves what are the false traits of culture in them at present to be made ineffective through diligent practice. All schemes of living, charters of freedom, programs of growth and constitutions of government will have to consider these four items...

> The things to be attained are wisdom, childlike innocence and silence. The thoughts to be rendered ineffective are the animal instincts such as attachment, hatred and fear. The things to be avoided are identifying the ego with the three states of consciousness; the waking state, the dream state and the deep sleep state. The goal to be reached is the fourth plane of consciousness called the Self. (p.406-408)

From the standpoint of Reality, *the entire existence of the tree is imagination*—the projecting power of maya supported by the root of the Absolute, sustained by the mind. Nonetheless, as long as we find ourselves part of this relatively real illusion, our work is to proceed with the equipment we have been given and the life circumstances in which we find ourselves, to purify the emotions and dispel all identification with the body ego mind self, that we might live in full connection with the Real. This is the gift of life, the abundance of *maya sakti*, which lovingly prods us toward the goal. When we realize the upward root, the sages say there is no more tree, no more desire, no more effort, no more transmigration. "All except what is to be realized exists only as imagination."

Three Aspects of the One

Slokas 16-19 elucidate the three *Purushas*: the changeable self (*kshara*), the changeless self(*akshara*) and the Absolute Self (*Paramatman*). The first consists of the gross body, which is inert and decays and perishes when the enlivening factor leaves the form. But that self within the body which experiences a continuity from youth through middle age to old age, which watches the comings and goings and changes that are incessantly taking place around it is called the unchangeable(*kutasthah*). It is relatively permanent with regard to the body. This is the transmigrating soul, which has been likened to the anvil that serves as a steady support for all transmutations of metals during the process of shaping, pounding and creating. This is the unmanifest, the seed from which the world of creation emerges, into which all creation dissolves. It has been loosely called the total mind, which consists of the subtle and causal bodies. Ramanuja calls the changeless the liberated soul.

Then there is that which has been designated as the supreme *Purusha*, beyond all opposites of change or stillness, life or death, world, heaven or eternity. The sages say it is around you, inside you, above you, behind you. It pervades all. It has been called ongoing objectless awareness, beyond all word, beyond all description.

On the macrocosmic level, the changeable consists of the world, the universe; the changeless is of the archetype, such as *gandharvas* (divine musicians), *apsaras*(divine dancers), gods, and other heavenly beings; and the absolute is ever the same, ever one, without form(*nirguna*), permeating both the changeable and the changeless.

> When the perishable is transcended, what remains is not the imperishable but that which played as the perishable *purusha* as well as the imperishable *purusha*. This pure spirit is spoken of as the supreme Self who pervades and sustains the three worlds... They are not three different types of *Purushas*. According to the limitations and conditions around, the Spirit appears different in its manifestations. The infinite consciousness is itself the perishable field in another form, and as the Knower of the field, the same consciousness is the imperishable Reality in the perishable conditionings. But when the conditionings are transcended, the same Self is experienced as the supreme Self.
> (Swami Chinmayananda, THG, p.912)

It is relatively easy to understand Jung's concept of persona—that we each play different roles in life in accordance with the conditioning received from external situations. We can be an obedient child, a stern taskmaster, a passive mother, a harried executive, or an intelligent teacher. When we become identified with the external mask, we unnecessarily stifle our self-expression by preventing the free flow of life from the outside in as well from the inside out. But it is more difficult to understand that the ego is also a kind of persona, a shell that keeps Reality from us. What has been masking as a concrete thing called person, born into a particular time, place and society, is actually the supreme Reality wearing the mask of the *limitations* of a particular body, emotions and thoughts.

Thousands of years of habitual repetition developed each mind and intellect to function as it does today. And all this subtle body is nothing but a role of the Supreme Self. The way we take in the world, think about it and feel its manifestations is only a kind of shell, which hides the Self from us. We are being called upon to refine our emotions and intellect, that we might disidentify from these matter envelopments, consciously *play* the role of the ego person and claim our true identity as the highest Self, which functions through everyone and everything.

The fairy tales and myths about the princes and princesses, who know nothing of their royal birth, are tales of you and me estranged from our true Self. Many clues are offered to help us regain our royal heritage. Sri Sathya Sai Baba says, "God seeks man with greater anguish than what urges man to seek God. For man is but God playing a role, but too struck with admiration for the costume he wears." (Kasturi, p.252)

This ego believes himself to be awake, while in actuality he is really asleep. The ego presumes herself to be dreaming, when in reality she is wholly awake. And the ego enmeshed in deep sleep knows nothing, although everything is always knowing and known and beyond both. So behind the three states of consciousness of waking, dream and deep sleep remains the highest Self, supporting all, transcending all. Behind the past, present and future rests the highest Self, supporting all, transcending all. Alongside here, there and everywhere lives the highest Self, transcending all, supporting all.

> This is the inner controller. This is the source of all. And this is that from which all things originate and in which they finally dissolve themselves. (*Mandukya Upanishad*:6)

Thus, what begins before birth in the pre-uterine stage as a process of undifferentiated I-ness seems to become an ego. On the personal developmental level, the separation of ego-self from not-self seemingly proceeds to enhance ego identity and functioning in the world. And on the level of spiritual *sadhana*, the separation of Self from not-Self seemingly evolves to elicit the *realization* of Truth.

That inner work is truly therapeutic which leads to the realization of *Atman*. Other forms of therapy are incomplete, so they can never bring genuine self confidence and ongoing happiness. For lasting and spontaneous self confidence relies on nothing external, as it stems only from an experiential knowledge of the Self, or from the feeling links, rays, and pathways to the Self.

When the Self is known totally in every cell, through all our parts, the witness is no longer composed of the stuff of the subtle body consciousness, but comes under the direct jurisdiction of supreme Reality and eventually becomes merged with it. Then, the sages say there is no longer a need to discriminate the real from the unreal, there is no longer a need to evolve. For only Reality *is*—beyond that which is and that which is not, including and transcending both.

Therefore, total devotion with all parts of oneself, with body, mind and intellect throughout the three states of consciousness results in *forging the link between all three Purushas, that the three become One;* that all living beings at all times in all places be experienced as One. The witnessing awareness is the precursor for the unification of the trinity. The Father, the Son and the Holy Spirit are One. The three *gunas* are One. Vishnu, Brahma and Siva are One.

When all boundaries between oneself and God are dissolved, we become what we are—pure auspiciousness, pure sattva(*visuddha*), *Purushottama*, the supreme Self. Krishna says we fulfill the purpose for which we have taken birth in life after life and death after death. What begins as *acquisition* of knowledge becomes the *process* of consciousness, until we know all that we know and all there is to be known(19).

> He who, permeating the three worlds, sustains them; who is different from the perishable and the imperishable, who is the indestructible controller of the universe is called *Paramatma*, the Supreme *Purusha*.
>
> As I transcend the perishable and am higher than the imperishable soul, for that reason I am declared the highest *Purusha* in the world and in the *Vedas*.
>
> Thus, he who undeluded knows Me as the supreme *Purusha* knows all there is to be known. He worships me with his whole being. (15:17-19)

With the completion of the fifteenth chapter, we see that devotion is also to the formless *Brahman* as well as to the loving Krishna; that Krishna himself is called *Purushottama*, the highest Self. And the highest Self cannot be a person yet is a person, cannot be a god and yet is God. What the mind has divided up into *saguna Brahman*(with form) and *nirguna Brahman*(without form) is created by the realm of concepts. Krishna as *Purushottama* includes both and is beyond both, as you and I are also potentially both as well as beyond both.

> All the Deities of the Hindu pantheon, who represent the infinite aspects of the One Supreme Being, exist within us as well. A Divine incarnation can manifest any one of them for the good of the world by mere will. The Divine mood of Krishna(*Krishna Bhava*) is the manifestation of the *Purusha* or pure consciousness aspect of the Absolute. (Mata Amritanandamayi).

The focus of *sadhana* for the *jnani* (person of knowledge) is a kind of dispassion, detachment beyond the forms of the intellect. And yet, that very detachment from the world of forms, both internal and external is what induces love, unity, and a space where there are no theories, no distinctions, no need for separateness. *Total detachment induces love. Total love induces detachment from the unreal.* And to go beyond theory, beyond philosophy, beyond debate, both devotion and detachment are needed and none is needed. All seeming paradoxes melt as clarity, love, duality, totality, shed the significance of words to entice us into Reality.

> All entities are by their very nature beginningless and unattached like space. There is not the slightest variety in them in any way at any time.
>
> All egocentric entities are by their very nature illumined from the beginning ever immutable in their nature. He who with this knowledge, rests without seeking further knowledge is alone capable of realizing the highest Truth.
>
> All egocentric entities are from the very beginning and by their very nature all the same, unborn and completely free. They are characterized by sameness and are nonseparate from one another. Therefore, the separate entities are in Reality nothing but *Atman*—unborn, always established in sameness and purity.
> (*Mandukya Upanishad with Gaudapada's Karika*, SwC, p.412)

Affirmations of Brahman

With the culmination of the fifteenth discourse, the highest philosophy has been succinctly expounded. In order to help us realize this knowledge in practice, Sri Sathya Sai Baba offers five great Truths(*mahavakyas*) for us to contemplate and repeat as prayer and *mantra*:

1. I am God, I am not different from God.
2. I am the indivisible Supreme Absolute.
3. I am *Sat Chit Ananda* (Being, Awareness, Bliss).
4. Grief and anxiety can never affect me.
5. I am ever content. Fear can never enter me.

Sai Baba says:

> As the physical body is maintained healthy and strong by the five vital airs(*prana*), these five prayers will endow you with the awareness of *Brahman*, which is the same as the status of *Brahman* itself.

Thus, the fifteenth discourse discloses the knowledge of the three levels of manifestation of the one *Atman* in the world. Through awareness of the supreme Self, we approach the highest knowledge, which severs the root of the tree of *samsara*, that the tree of life will no longer entangle us in the bondage of identification with cyclical existence.

●○

Sixteen

Yoga of Discerning the Light and Dark Paths

Daivasura Sampad Vibhaga Yoga

	Gita verses
Qualities of the divine nature	1–3
Qualities of demonic nature	4
Respective results of both natures	5
The demonic nature and its consequences	6–21
Freedom from the three gates	22
Laws of the science of spirituality *(sastra)*	23–24

divine wealth
leads us to our Self
the path of light

the way of ignorance
haphazard and entrenched
perpetual darkness

become fit
to transcend
endless cycles!

In any discussion of "positive" and "negative" qualities, it's very difficult not to have the feeling that one is moralizing, condemning, criticizing or passing a value judgement. This can sometimes lead to an automatic turn-off. Therefore, if we are to comprehend the enormous significance of the sixteenth chapter, it would be helpful to approach Krishna's discourse not as moral judgement but as a scientific, intellectual evaluation of two opposite ways of living; two different philosophies of life that inevitably lead to very different results. Krishna's intent is not to condemn but to enlighten. He wants Arjuna to comprehend what's at stake, what the battle consists of and *how it can be won.*

As we come to understand the foundation of the game of life, we will be better equipped to participate with an informed view of the rules, their order and changeability as well as the purpose of the game. Without knowing the object of a game, we flounder and fall again and again, bewildered, ignorant, unaware of our true objective and why we fall. We are like sailors afloat at sea without a compass or a map.

So in the sixteenth discourse, Krishna continues the discussion of the *gunas* in terms of their behavioral effects. What are the beliefs, character structure and actions of the person whose mind is predominantly *sattvic*(the *deva*)? And what kind of philosophical basis leads a person to behave in a way that is primarily a mixture of *rajas* and *tamas* (the *asura*)?

Those who yearn for freedom need the utmost clarity regarding the difference between the two. For in today's society, there is much confusion within the minds of people regarding what is "good" and what is "evil." That which is harmful and creates bondage is often viewed as good while that which is potentially freeing is seen as bad—especially if it is not in accord with a materialistic ethic.

In His boundless love, Krishna is trying to quicken our reasoning capacity to help us clearly comprehend the relationship between our philosophy of life, our actions and what happens to us. In the realm of *karma*, for every effect there is a cause. And the consequences of actions go much deeper than our actions. If with a noncriticizing eye, we can hear what Krishna is trying to impart, we will understand that results stem not only from our actions, but from our understanding of life; its source, laws and purpose. Happenings also originate from the ideals that comprise our philosophy and determine our motivation and intentions. These in turn lead to our thoughts and actions, which can be accidentally acquired based on our environmental conditioning, or can stem from a deeper foundation—the fountain of Truth.

The crucial question then is: do our ideals come from the Self or do they originate from the automatic, unthinking, popular current of the times? Our way of living, the quality of our life and death depend upon our ultimate response to this essential question.

Let's keep in mind that both "educated" and "uneducated" persons are living a philosophy of life, either consciously or unconsciously. The quality of our actions has little to do with literacy or formal schooling, but rather is based our inner sensitivity and what feels important to us. Have our values been consciously reflected upon and applied to our lives or have they just been internalized automatically from parents and society, or mechanically rebelled against? Krishna is hereby offering us the opportunity to contemplate these issues so *we can have a choice.*

Introversion and Extroversion

The underlying basis for these two psychological types, the *devas* and *asuras* is *nivritti* and *pravritti*. *Nivritti* is a kind of introversion, an inward movement whereby one's life energy is experienced within.

This inward movement is the source of contemplation, reflection, worship and meditation. It is a process of evoking and connecting with the divine, one's inner essence, a state of loving being. Then the task is to function from this inner space no matter what the activity. In this way, the inner energy of life radiates out to others, evoking an atmosphere of the greatest good.

Pravritti is the movement of energy outward, a dynamism or extroversion whereby one's life quality goes into outward activity and doing, desiring and acquiring, achieving, possessing and controlling. It can also refer to creative and beneficial action with a positive spiritual connotation. Both *nivritti* and *pravritti* are essential for a well functioning society. And sometimes one's own energy needs to go out in order to return to the source. However, when *pravritti* becomes split off from *nivritti*, then action is not based on inner conscience or the domain of the Self but becomes oriented to the ego, which has formed as a result of external demands and inner instincts coupled with the *gunas* of the mind. *The further away our actions from the source of Truth, the more split off pravritti is from nivritti.* This leads to lack of love, competitiveness, hostility, violence, war and destruction in the individual, the family and the society.

For spiritual evolution to proceed, the inward movement is essential. To learn the technique of turning our attention within through contemplation, meditation and devotion can initiate a rebirth, which allows us to enter a very different *loka* or psychological space. Then our actions come to reflect our inner wisdom. (In Sanskrit, *loka* means place and refers to the fourteen different heavens and hells.)

The *Vedantic* concept of introversion and extroverson might on the surface appear similar to Carl Jung's understanding of the phenomenon, but there is a crucial difference. In *Vedanta*, introversion is considered a more positive and fundamental force than extroversion, as it is essential for conscience and evolution. The capacity for genuine love and compassion is a function of living within. An aim of spiritual work is to live in a deep inner space while serving others without losing one's Self; without going outward from the senses or organs of action. Hence, the emphasis on sense control, being, contemplation and meditation can all be viewed as a training in *nivritti*. The primarily *sattvic* person lives in *nivritti* whereas the predominantly *rajasic* person functions from *pravritti*. The *asura* is one whose actions have become split off from *nivritti* due to the compulsive, outward orientation of his mind. In more complex situations that require direct contact with inner conscience, this renders him incapable of *pravritti* as right conduct.

Materialistic Values of Contemporary Society

One great difficulty for the contemporary person of the *Kali yuga* is the wide gulf that separates the Self from the popular current of the times. Knowledge and practice of the universal laws of life, which had been incorporated into past cultures, are no longer carried on through society. What had been unconsciously preserved through family love, communal caring, customs, religious ideals and education based on communication and reflection has largely been replaced by "education" based on materialistic goals, egoism, "survival needs," argument and competitiveness under the guise of "individualism." In short, the total person is no longer engaged in his life, as only the more surface aspects of living are emphasized.

People today are thus faced with a dilemma of unprecedented proportions—that within the social fabric of life, the majority of our "authority figures" do not embody either selfless knowledge or the values that lead to Knowledge. Many teachers, clergymen, politicians, judges, psychotherapists, scientists and physicians, well meaning though we may be, are basically functioning under the veil of *maya.* With so few pure and genuine authority figures, how can trust develop? How can people thrive and live in peace? As long as adaptation to contemporary societal values dominates our philosophy and actions, we will be passing on to others a self-centered approach to life that is doomed to failure. As long as we live under the illusion that our survival and security primarily depend upon our adaptation to anything but the *highest Truth,* we are headed for destruction. For those already living in Reality, Truth requires no adaptation.

Therefore, the present age more than any other time in history invites us to develop *discrimination* and not cynicism, *idealism* and not nihilism, *competence* and *love in action* and not conformity to the prevailing path of least resistance, which is intrinsic to a self-centered life. Because of the nature of the times, this work is very subtle. And more than ever, it requires the capacity to seek a competent source of authority both within and without that will help us to nurture and uncover the genuine *authority* that lives within each of us. This difficulty in finding one's true center is the reason for the *Gita's* insistence on utilizing the scriptures as one's authority(1, 24). What is meant by this is not necessarily accepting someone else's interpretation or memorizing concepts but through self-study (*svadyayah*), finding the depth within to comprehend, contemplate and verify directly the nonmediated, immediate Truth, as the authors of the scriptures have done.

The Purpose of Suffering

The scientific basis of these laws is simple. We can either go up or go down. The force of gravity applies to the psyche as well as the body. We can either evolve on the path toward liberation or devolve on the path toward destruction—destruction of the sensitivity of the soul. This leads to inner death and is referred to as "hell." Hell is a space of intense physical and/or psychological suffering which results from our thoughts and actions. But unlike Dante's *Inferno*, this hell is not a place from which there is no return. It is a psychological space where more cooking is required before we reach rock bottom and thereby become ready to go up again. This occurs back and forth in stages. When we are burnt and pulverized by the suffering of cyclic existence(*samsara*), there comes a moment when the shell of the ego cracks and makes room for light to enter. We are broken down for a mind-boggling purpose—liberation—the opportunity to encounter a path and begin the long and arduous and satisfying journey toward freedom.

The issue then becomes a matter of readiness. Among the three categories of humanity taught in the science of spirituality, the most demonic(*rakshasas*) are not yet ready to find a path; the demonic materialists(*asuras*) are capable of personal growth and eventual evolution under certain conditions, and the gods(*devas*, or good ones) are well established on the way to liberation. The sixteenth chapter can benefit the *devas* and *asuras*, not the *rakshasas*.[35] In addition to being two distinct psychological types, these categories include qualities that are found within the heart of each individual. Where conscience and good intentions have not yet totally atrophied, evolution is possible—provided one can encounter and receive the help of a genuine teacher and/or teaching. To proceed alone without the help of this positive energy is far more difficult.

True Wealth

Krishna begins the discourse by elucidating what constitutes real wealth and enumerates the twenty-six qualities of the *devas*. *Deva* stems from the root '*div*', which means to illumine. The *devas* then, function from a space of inner clarity and light, devoid of the cloudy confusion of *vasanas*. True wealth is experienced as fullness—fullness to which nothing can be added and from which nothing can be taken away. This completeness could also be called emptiness. The twenty-six virtues are prerequisites for the path of wholeness. These embody our aspirations and provide a focus for our *sadhana*. They are called wealth because *they bring happiness through creating the causes for positive actions to happen to us.*

The most important is the first: *freedom from fear*(1). All the mental effort and maneuvering of the *asuric* mind is based on fear—fear of poverty, fear of illness and old age, fear of being alone and unloved, fear of death. As long as insecurity dominates the psyche, we embrace many false gods to prop us up and protect us. We look for security from external sources such as money, position, family, success, good marks, good health, praise; to the very things that are *impermanent,* we look for happiness. It is undoubtedly true that friends, family, talents, money and jobs do help us feel more secure in the world. But are these the *source* of our security?

Thus, the *asura* is one who places his trust in the factors of the material world for his feeling of security.[36] The more material things he gains, the more bound he becomes, the more driven are his actions. And as these factors are all subject to change, consequently he can never possibly expect to feel secure. Beneath the surface, fear lurks everywhere—fear of loss, fear of death, fear of not being on top of things. This fear pushes him to possess and acquire, as well as to be possessive; clinging, guarding and worrying about his relationships and acquisitions. He is not a "bad" person. But in the process of trying to protect himself from the pain of loss he loses his own Self, his sensitivity to people, his own real needs, simplicity, what is fundamentally important for life to be satisfying. As an insurance against pain he has sacrificed his precious life energy to appearances, to the trappings of life, to the multiplicity of surfaces. He is not aware of what he is doing. *He is killing his soul.*

Fear is a powerful animal instinct that is necessary for the care and survival of the body. It can also be an important factor in the initial stages of soul development—to fear God can serve as an inducement toward moral living. However, when fear dominates the mind and convinces us to adopt values that are not based on our *deepest dharma* but on social norms, we unknowingly become solid citizens of a totalitarian regime. We relinquish our right to liberation.

> Fear is the expression of ignorance. Where there is Knowledge there is fearlessness. (Swami Chinmayananda)

When a person does not know about the workings of natural law, about the force of *maya sakti* and how she operates, it is difficult to have faith in the partnership between external events and deep inner yearnings. One is afraid to allow his deeper yearnings out of hiding. "It's no use, why subject myself to disappointment? I'm a realist. I trust what I see." This is how the fear manifests. As we acquire the faith to risk allowing our deepest wishes and feelings to emerge, we are creating conditions to live in relationship with nature. The course of events inevitably deepens in response to our internal yearnings. We come to know the power of desire when allowed its deeper expression. We begin to relax, become more open, and enter into partnership with life. The external environment responds to the yearnings of the soul in her time. *No longer alienated or isolated, we become cells in the body of humanity.*

Thus out of fear, the *asura* is in deep-freeze. Through allowing a dethawing to occur, the parameters of his vision expand and a new world appears. Fear creates one world, faith and feelings create another.

It is fear and fear alone which maintains the branches, leaves and roots that perpetuate the tree of life, the tree of *samsara*, *maya* (see chapter 15). Fear and other emotions lead to blockages in the *cakras* of the subtle body, which can create obstacles to our experience of Reality as well as present opportunities for purification. The process and implications of cleansing oneself of fear is illustrated by the following dream:

> A woman dreamt she was sitting peacefully in meditation. Her teacher walked by and asked her about being unemployed. Suddenly she found herself totally fearful; frantically cleaning out dirt, twigs, branches, leaves and roots from a space within his heart. And simultaneously, her own heart was also being cleansed of all this natural debris.

Through acknowledging and working with our emotional reactions, they slowly dissolve. They relinquish their power over us, so that we can participate in cleansing the subtle body and proceed in our evolution. The dirt that gets projected onto others must be seen as one's own. For the dreamer, the cleansing was occurring naturally through her deep connection and identification with the teacher. As the tree of life becomes detached from the subtle and causal bodies, *prakriti* releases her grip on the soul. And the heart can open.

Sri Sathya Sai Baba says:

> When you have steady faith and an integral vision, when you constantly think of the indwelling divinity, you will not become elated by joy nor shrink away from sorrow. It is only then that you will become completely fearless(*abhaya*). Becoming subject to fear and then becoming free from fear are both momentary experiences. They come and go. Fear is only a delusion created by the mind. Lack of fear is also a delusion created by the mind. *Abhaya* is not associated with these two at all. Fearlessness is a permanent state where there is no question of ever experiencing *any* fear. A person with *abhaya* is continuously aware of his own Reality. For him to become subject to fear would be impossible.
>
> In fearlessness, one is not aware of any second entity. One experiences fear only when there exists a second object, but for one who has *abhaya* there is never any second object at all. Therefore,

> fearlessness is associated with unity consciousness. It refers to nondualism(*advaita*), where there can be no two but always just one. Only when you are in such a state of *advaita* will you be truly fearless. (DBG, p.207)

Another quality of divine wealth is *ahimsa*, translated as nonviolence, which means not causing harm to another living being either physically, verbally or emotionally. All forms of abuse, be they personal, political, economic, or unconsciously abusing one's Self, are an expression of the aggression, competitiveness, reactivity, self-centeredness and hatred which underlie the rampant violence of our era. But on a more subtle level, *ahimsa* refers to nonviolence in our *thoughts*. As long as hatred and ill will exist in the mind, they are bound to find expression in some external form through the law of *karma*, sooner or later.

The direct root to *ahimsa* then, is to work on purifying the mind through the various techniques of *sadhana* so that we can truly love. Then violence will gradually be rooted out *at its source*. This is very different from "religious" techniques that unknowingly induce guilt and can lead to suppression, repression, projection and splitting off of "evil" tendencies. It is also different from acting out sexual and emotional behavior as encouraged by quasi-psychotherapy. Rather, the energy behind the emotions is seen and experienced as the life force, *maya sakti*, which can be viewed as the dynamic aspect of *Brahman*. As this energy becomes reconnected with its source, transformation ensues. This leads to love, detachment and equality. Through the process of receiving positive energy, sharpening awareness and developing totality connected will, as opposed to self-will, *we can learn to create conditions for a more peaceful and joyful quality of karma in the present and future*. This is very different from suppression.

On the societal level, Gandhi's political movement of *ahimsa* was far more than just a shrewd tactic. It was successful in toppling the might of the British empire because it was based on the natural law of cause and effect. When Martin Luther King adopted the principles of nonviolence, the success of the civil rights movement ensued. When we do not return hatred for hatred, something changes. Qualitatively new conditions enter. Two aggressive forces fighting each other lead to more of the same for generation unto generation. When one force is peaceful and connects inside with the force of love, the force of hatred is *forced* to change. One mind works on another mind. Our thoughts constantly influence whatever and whomever we come in contact with. Our foolish fears often come true. So do our deepest dreams. Where to focus the mind and what to work for is *our choice.* The result follows the lead of the mind.

Ahimsa leads to compassion and compassion leads to *ahimsa*. It is extremely difficult for the ordinary person to show compassion for all beings, in spite of good intentions; especially to those who treat us with rage or injustice. This quality uncovers itself after long spiritual training in detachment, fortitude and forgiveness. When we ourselves feel fully loved, we spontaneously give the wealth of love to everyone, *irrespective of how they treat us*. For we see beyond appearances. This quality of love is the embodiment of the ongoing, gentle, force of subtle energy. Experiencing compassion can become like breathing. Being in the presence of a person with full compassion is the greatest healing. Swami Chinmayananda says:

> In society in general, it is not reasonable for a seeker to expect that all will keep up to the ideal that he himself entertains. There will be imperfections around. But to recognize in and through those imperfections the infinite beauty of life expressed is the secret of enduring tenderness in all saints and sages. *Love alone can discover an infinite amount of tenderness in us.* Unless we train ourselves to see the beauty of life pulsating through even wretched hearts and ugly characters, we will fail to bring forth tenderness to sweeten life within and without. (THG p.925)

The twenty-six qualities of divine wealth are:

> Fearlessness, purity of mind, steadfastness in knowledge and concentration, charity, self-control and sacrifice, study of scriptures, austerity and uprightness, nonviolence, truth, freedom from anger, renunciation, tranquility, aversion to fault finding, compassion to living beings, freedom from covetousness, gentleness, modesty, straightforwardness or absense of fickleness, vigor, forgiveness, fortitude, purity, and freedom from excessive pride. (16:1-3)

When these virtues are developed and lived, the mind becomes calm and energy is conserved. No expenditure of effort gets wasted defending against inner emotional issues or external attack. With the conservation of energy(*tapas*), comes an inner glow(*tejas*), a give and take with others without resistance, a self contained mass of peaceful light which shines through the eyes, through every pore of the skin, through the melody of the voice. By practicing these twenty-six virtues at the level of body, emotions and intellect, we not only conserve energy, but also allow it to develop and intensify. This illumining energy gradually accrues and brings a person unshakable contentment.

Thus, what has been called "morality" on a surface level that differs from culture to culture and from age to age, is found in the *Gita* to have an objective, lawful basis when viewed at its profoundest level. *Through contacting inner conscience, which is deeper than all the surface introjects from parents and society, our thoughts and actions become linked to the unfoldment of the Self.* The purposiveness of life and our place in it becomes apparent, as through understanding this inherent order, our lives become joyful, steady and calm. Through developing these virtues, our very presence becomes a source for good. And we come to know it is a scientific law that happiness and liberation cannot be experienced until we consciously embody virtue(5).

Divine wealth also aids the earth on a collective subtle level, as well as helping the individual approach perfection:

> From the vibrationless region, through a cosmic rhythm of ordered activity, the Spirit brought into being all vibratory creation. Man is a part of that vibratory cosmic activity. As an integral entity in the cosmic plan that all creation, projected out of spirit, must evolve back into Spirit, man also must ascend through activity in harmony with the divine schema. (Yogananda, p.327)

The Asuric Mentality

The primary inner attributes of those with a demonic nature are: ostentation, arrogance, excessive pride, deceitfulness, extreme anger, harshness and ignorance(4). In *slokas* 7-18, Krishna paints a further portrait of the person of *asuric* mind. One meaning of *asura* is he who takes away life. *Asu*(life) means the real nature; *ra* means to take away. The *asura* pays no attention to his innate inner nature. He does not live in accordance with the light of inner clarity. Though he may be highly intellectual and able to spout forth many spiritual and psychological teachings, he has no genuine knowledge, little self-reflection and is devoid of the inner knowing that keeps one in tune with life. Conditioning, egoism, insatiable desires and lack of purity cloud the inner connection. *All ambivalence and conflict stem from lack of contact with the innate spontaneity of inner knowing.* The *asura* ignores his real inner life.

living imprisoned by
external surfaces
the perpetual life force
is covered by
the bricks of ignorance.

The *asuras* know not what to do and what to refrain from doing. Neither purity, right conduct, nor truth is found in them.(16:7)

He lives in a universe where things just seem to happen mechanically without any perceived connection to each other, to his own actions or to the source of life. As he believes the foundation of creation is lust (8), his sexual and gluttonous instincts dictate his behavior. There is no knowledge of universal law, cosmic order, cause and effect, and how these relate to one's own actions. His understanding remains fixated on the level of matter. Hence there is no long-range sense of consequence or acceptance of responsibility for one's actions and their effect on others. He does not wish to discover why his intimate relationships have failed or acknowledge his ongoing fear of caring. Unknowingly, he maintains a close affinity with the "six enemies" of desire, attachment, anger, envy, egoism, and confusion. Though he might have a high IQ and be considered a "success" in his chosen vocation, Krishna calls him one of "little intelligence"(9).[37]

> Once a person refuses to recognize the divine presence of Truth embracing and underlying life, he will function as a self-centered, selfish entity endlessly striving to eke out his own personal satisfaction from the material world. Seeking complete fulfillment in sensual gratification, he strives hard but discovers only a carping disappointment, a burning hunger and a sense of defeat in life. Krishna, in his infinite kindness sympathizes with such men and calls them men of small intellect.
> (Swami Chinmayananda, THG p.938)

This philosophy based on insensitivity is an accepted norm of our culture, both on the personal and national level. For example, children are brought into the world without providing for them the necessary conditions for their wholesome nurturing. Parents of both sexes are rarely at home and are therefore unable to offer the foundation of a steady, loving environment that is essential, if a young child is to grow up with the self confidence of feeling truly worthwhile and appreciated. Time spent in the presence of love and acceptance—not attachment—instills love. Time spent in the presence of TV, video games and babysitters engenders feelings of alienation, space-out, and expediency.

As children are unknowingly taught to be dependent on things, entertainment and structured activity, they become easily bored with themselves and others. They lose their innate sense of play, spontaneity and feeling. Parents who are unreflective products of this age of narcissism are the innocent perpetrators of the seeds of this discontent.

Material acquisition is a poor substitute for the security that comes from growing up in the presence of peace, open listening, truly human values and unconditional love combined with limit setting. *When thought, word and deed are not in harmony in the parent, the child is not given an example of Truth.* Without living Truth, one is lost.

Although the average *asura* basically means well for his children, as he is insensitive regarding what constitutes steady, joyful living, he passes on his own blindness and conditions them to accept a way of being where surface substitutes become indistinguishable from the real thing. By living intrinsically false values and not providing the ongoing security of an honest and tangible loving presence, the *asura* unconsciously teaches his children to bury their own *deepest feeling needs.* This attitude is a soul killer.

On the macrocosmic global scale, the same insensitivity operates. We all know the fresh air and waters of this beautiful earth are still being decimated, in spite of feeble attempts to offset greed and ignorance. We all know about global warming, chemicals and carbon emissions that deplete the ozone layer, which was created to protect our glorious planet. We clearly see how hypocrisy rules the political fabric of our lives. We are all too familiar with the deadening effects of media violence on the human soul. We repeatedly experience how computer quickness leads to impatience, frustration and the expectation of instant gratification. We readily observe how commercial consumerism intrudes into our homes and our minds, ever encroaching on our privacy, quietude and humanness. As bigness and impersonality invade the world, the hydra stretches forth her many heads, bringing in her wake a deadly, new form of destruction and colonialism worldwide. The *asuric* mentality does in fact now rule the world.

> These men of dead souls, of truly little intelligence, undertake their work of evil. They are the enemies of this fair world, working for its destruction. (16:9)

How can the *devas* vanquish the *asuras*? How can we individually deal with living in the *Kali yuga*, the age of violence and darkness? How can we contribute to wholesomeness? We must each ask ourselves these questions and come up with tiny, concrete follow-through answers that can be applied to our daily lives in simple ways—while keeping in mind the overall aim of liberation. *Kaivalya* refers to liberation as total independence, complete oneness. Our aim is to be fully free from the external environment without giving up on it or being drawn into its baser values. The wish to be free from the presence of evil and suffering ever encourages us to pursue our aim.

Transforming the Inner Asura

As we stand at the crossroads of a real new age, our survival depends upon our Knowledge. With Knowledge, comes mutual caring. Developing Knowledge, compassion and the capacity to help are the responsibility of *each* individual person. These qualities cannot emerge from group identity, organizations or educational systems alone. Individual initiative is required first and foremost.

Simply stated, the issue is: how capable and how motivated are we to look in the mirror and see what is reflected back? Can we experience our own lack of inner knowing, our lack of compassion, our greed? As we observe ourselves in action, in emotion, in intention, we will inevitably come to develop honesty. If we can see with a truthful eye, we cannot help but allow our human sensitivity to reawaken. But in order for this to occur, we must first be willing to stop and *look.*

Remember, our aim initially is not to remove the dirt—just to see. If we allow ourselves to see our intentions, see how critical the mind is of others, how blame, guilt, greed and pride provide a kind of shell that covers our sensitivity and prevents us from *suffering our seeing*, we will soon begin to experience remorse of conscience. The quality of the conscious suffering of conscience has a very different flavor than the self-pity, self-criticism and guilt of unconscious suffering. The first results from self-effort and *sadhana*, the second occurs automatically as part of the defense mechanism of the ego to maintain and balance the status quo. Through conscious suffering, help will appear. The partnership with great nature will be established.

If however, we are not yet ready to look, nature will force us by dragging us into "hell." Through the universal law of cause and effect, our self-centered actions inevitably lead to suffering.

> They torture their souls with insatiable desires and full of deceit, insolence and pride, they hold fast their dark ideas and carry on their impure work. Thus they are beset with innumerable cares which last long all their lives until death. (16:10-11)

And if we try to sidestep our seeing experience by fixing our faults, so that we look good to ourselves and others, we will only be strengthening our egoism and pride(17). To change before seeing-suffering is actually lived through, spoils the possibility for authentic transformation. What we do not want is surface *conformity* to an "ideal" image be it social or religious. For this leads to suppression and hypocrisy.

The *asuric* mind revels in appearances, in praise, in looking good. As he mistakes reality for the body, his religion is ostentation. "Look how good I am, how competent I am, how smart I am, how beautiful I am." Or the flip side of the coin, which is equally untrue, "see how bad I am, how stupid I am, how ugly I am." His point of reference always remains at the ego level. Fed by the cycle of desire, consumption and attachment fueled by conditioning and the media, his false sense of I remains the measure of all things.

Krishna is very clear that the more attached, angry and greedy we are, the harder we must fall, the more deeply we must suffer(19-21). By rejecting the partnership with the forces of nature, natural law in accordance with the three *gunas* decrees our destruction. Our false selves become shattered that the ego might surrender.

> In their chains of selfishness and arrogance of violence, anger and lust, these malignant men hate me. They hate me in themselves and in others. In the vast cycles of life and death I inexorably hurl them down to destruction, these lowest of men, cruel and evil whose soul is hate. (16:18-19)

Unlike the Judaeo-Christian ethic, the purpose of the fall in *Vedanta* is not punishment but the unfoldment of natural law. *All destruction carries within itself the seeds of construction—constructive destruction.* Total reliance on the body ego mind form as reality must be destroyed, so a connection with the Real center can begin to form. The process of making this connection is called the effort of evolution. We must be broken down again and again throughout many lifetimes, that we be allowed to re-form again, as what we already are—the living embodiment of the *Atma*. This is nature's built in mechanism for maintaining balance, in order to be able to sustain and support life on earth. It is said the entire *Mahabharata* war was fought as a bloodletting to remove poison from the earth. "The earth was to be cleansed of the poisons which were choking her."(Subramaniam, p.747)

It is important that the *asura* of highly developed intellect understand this basic natural law—for it applies to each and every one of us without exception. Without understanding, there is no motivation to change, or to place one's faith and trust in something other than matter, and develop one's inner wealth. However, *in the physical presence of the avatar, the doubting materialistic mentality can come to experience divine Reality.* But as the majority of western *asuras* will probably not meet an *avatar*, either in person or in astral body, it is still possible for us to approach Truth and become open to a teaching. Therefore, when Krishna advises that the science of spirituality, or scriptures, be the guiding force behind our behavior(24), he is speaking on the practical level of helping us to understand the workings of natural law, so that we will not become helpless, unconscious victims of the destruction and involution that is inevitable when lack of knowledge is combined with lack of ethics. And without beginning to process this knowledge, whose source is *not* the intellect, it is very difficult for the average, contemporary person to be motivated to develop virtue.

Krishna is also speaking on a deeper level. The scriptures of all religions offer more than authoritative knowledge. They are a living expression of the divine force on earth as experienced by realized souls. By understanding, experiencing and connecting with this force, we contact our Self through different levels of love, insight, intuition and consciousness. *In the light of this force, our asuric nature dissolves.*

We must fully comprehend how difficult it is to conquer the *asuric* nature. Now would be an apt time to recall the story of the battle between the gods and demons told in chapter ten, which reveals how to defeat our demonic nature and claim the nectar of immortality. As the *asura* lives under the backing of a powerful collective force, his individual mentality has connected with the total thought form of materialism, becomes entrenched in it and *is controlled by it*. The *asura* is utterly dominated by the archetype of materialism. Just as the minds of individuals are controlled by demonic forces, so are families, communities, societies and nations helplessly under their sway. To free oneself from this power requires more than good intentions and conscious decisions. *It requires an inner connection with the deepest level of the force of good.*

The connective link with the Self renders the *asura* powerless. But since it takes time and practice to learn how to make this connection directly, intermediaries are utilized. The "gods," the forces of good, are developed and incorporated into one's life. Gradually they take on battle with the *asuras*. As detachment develops, this helps greatly. But only to the extent the individual is able to connect with the Self is the *asuric* mentality transformed. Only at the deepest level can total transformation occur. Without this connection, all external teaching is only helpful conditioning, which accrues little by little, until inner readiness appears. When the teachings begin to serve as a link to practice, intuition and inner experience, they will not be misused for the props of ego enhancement or pride. Only through experiencing deep love, understanding and consciousness can the armor of the *asura* be pierced.

Psychotherapy and the Asuric Mind

The implications of all this for psychotherapy are enormous. When a person comes to a therapist for help, he is either in the midst of a phase of destruction or is very unhappy with the status quo—his life, work, failure in a relationship, feelings of alienation, lack of self confidence, and so forth. Amidst the plenty of material success he may dwell in an inner wasteland. When one can ask for help he is somewhat ripe for healing, more open to receiving knowledge, love and wisdom than ever before. If the therapist has little appreciation of human values in his own life—the values of universal love, compassion and sacrifice, how can any genuine healing take place? And without this broader knowledge of the universal law of cause and effect, there is no underlying basis for genuine evolution to proceed: personal growth of the ego, yes; inner evolution, no.

A certain degree of "ego development" is important, especially for young people. But it is essential to graduate to empathy and universal love. As love is our nature, young people can relate to this. Whereas ego development can lesson our conflicts and improve daily functioning, it does not necessarily lead to peaceful and contented living.

If one does not clear away the impediments to living his essence, his true nature of unobstructed clarity, then one's genuine inner contentment remains quite fragile, very subject to the flux of external events, even after many years of therapy. The goal of any psychotherapy worthy of the name should subtly aid the person from within in the purification of his emotions, so that he can proceed on his own to develop divine wealth. For this, the therapist must reflect inner purity, knowledge, compassion, and right motivation. Without fulfilling these criteria, future negative *karma* might keep the person chained to the bondage of attachment, suffering and self-defeating views.

Dissolution and destruction present us with a precious opportunity for openness, painful though it might be. Without maintaining direct contact with this opening and depth, all possibility for Self Knowledge and liberation can be lost. For it is the experience of our raw sensitivity that allows us to truly value love, and become capable of loving in a way that is both personal and universal.

Whereas these ideas and practices can be incorporated into any school of psychotherapy, in accordance with the openness of the individual therapist, they are not in themselves amenable to their own psychological theory. That would be like pinning a butterfly to the wall. For they transcend all method and theory. Compassion, mutual respect, *dharma*, open listening, relaxation, inner subtle energy, insight and nonconceptual experiential awareness fluidity is the root of healing, no matter what the school.

Likewise, these laws are not techniques that can be learned by the mind and incorporated into practice. They do not respond to lip service, greed or fad. They can only be lived, through the inner practice of contacting the being presence in one's Self and seeing the other as one's Self. This experience of love prepares a person to be able to face his *vasanas* so that his thoughts and emotions can be transformed and his negative *karma* purified. To the degree we can link our thoughts and actions to Truth, no new negative *karma* will form. Every experience in our lives is potentially an opportunity for working through *karma*, both "negative" and "positive."

To one highly trained in unconscious egoistic living, these ideas might appear idealistic, impractical or nonremunerative. But they are simple, factual requirements for healing wholeness to occur. Conflict resolution and improved functioning are not synonymous with total healing and ultimate freedom. *Truth and healing go together as two aspects of the same coin.*

The majority of persons who seek therapy are functioning primarily in a state of *tamas* and *rajas*. Without developing divine wealth, one remains fixated at these lower levels, unable to take the next step toward *sattva* and beyond, which leads to *satchitananda*—being, awareness, bliss. Without transforming some "negative" qualities into "positive" qualities, we cannot proceed to the practice of detachment and discrimination, distinguishing the Real from the unreal. And ongoing conscious contentment remains elusive. Rather than "teaching" positive qualities, it would be far more effective if authority figures could consciously serve as role models, based on our behavior.

When we are trapped in the vicious cycle of lust, rage and greed, our evolution is postponed. First we must see these qualities in ourselves, consciously suffer them, and then leave them behind.

> There are three gates to hell, the death of the soul: the gate of lust, the gate of wrath, and the gate of greed. Let a man shun the three. When a man is free from these three doors of darkness, he does what is good for his soul. And then he enters the Path Supreme. (16:21-2)

Unfortunately, what passes for psychotherapy tends to keep some people stuck in the vicious cycle of desire, anger and ambition. If there is no knowledge of any other way of being, one object of desire gets substituted for another, one position is replaced by a more powerful one, while the person's ego gets "strengthened" and he learns to adapt to a false ethic. But qualitatively, his values remain the same. He still clings to a foundation of straw.

Desire can be either a potential healer or a powerful imprisoner. It is a *sakti*, an expression of the divine energy of life, the force of the Goddess. To follow it rightly, with awareness, can lead us to our destiny. But when it is followed blindly under the tutelage of advertising agencies, the film industry, animal instincts and ignorant "authority" figures, we are destined for suffering. Only through suffering one's *karma* again and again, does the *asura* become fit to enter a path. With this rite of passage, the multiplicity of argumentation and relativity one day melts into unity. (For further discussion of psychotherapy and spirituality see Appendix Two.)

The Science of Spirituality

To view the scriptures or science of spirituality as one's true guide is to gradually apply the aspiration for Truth and Reality as a foundation for living. When we have no consciously chosen guide, it is very easy to fall prey to the predominating influence of the conditioning and values into which we have been born. *Without allowing oneself exposure to a higher influence, there is little lasting opportunity for evolution, for happiness, for liberation.*

Therefore, Krishna's advice to let the scriptures be our guide(24) is not spoken as dogmatism and should not be interpreted as such. He is not advising submitting to someone else's interpretation of Hinduism, Judaism, Christianity, Islam, fundamentalism, or what constitutes "salvation." Rather, he is lovingly leading us toward the science of spirituality in whatever form we can receive it and incorporate it into our lives, so as to uplift and guide us through the maze of joy and sorrow, birth and death. *The influence of the higher is our true mother and father.* When we allow this energy to permeate our thoughts and actions, our lives become worthwhile—a force for the highest good to enter into creation.

Whereas the sixteenth chapter does not expound the way of liberation, it does offer us the necessary prerequisites to liberation. It demonstrates in a clear and concise manner, the subtle forces that prevent the average contemporary person from living in ongoing joy and contentment. Sri Sathya Sai Baba has some excellent advice for the *asuras* of the world:

> Do not follow the body.
> Do not follow the mind.
> Follow your conscience.

This does not mean deny the body. This does not mean suppress the emotions. Rather, it points to a process of living whereby the desires of the body, the expression of the emotions and the idealism of the intellect are gradually being integrated under the rulership of our deepest, formless, essence Self. Only then can our inner conscience, Truth, become accessible—with ease like breathing, as an ongoing way of being.

Thus, the sixteenth discourse reveals not only the *yoga* of the knowledge of the divine and demonic powers, but helps us differentiate between the two. Through developing divine wealth and suffering our imperfections under the impartial gaze of the inner eye, compassion springs forth. And we prepare the groundwork for liberation.

Seventeen

YOGA OF THE THREE-FOLD FAITH

Sraddhatraya Vibhaga Yoga

	Gita verses
Three qualities of faith *(sraddha)*	1–3
Three kinds of worship	4–6
Three types of food	7–10
Three kinds of sacrifice *(yajna)*	11–13
Three qualities of austerity *(tapas)*	14–19
Three forms of charity *(dana)*	20–22
Significance of *Vedic mantra, Om Tat Sat*	23–27
The importance of *sraddha* in every action	28

whatever we do
do it with faith
whatever we say
say it with faith
whatever we give
give it with faith

a golden thread
sews all our actions
to the infinite

In the seventeenth discourse, Krishna further elucidates the universal law of the three *gunas* from the perspective of faith(*sraddha*). *Sraddha* is what motivates a person's thoughts and actions. It is formed from our interests and capacities as well as the past impressions imprinted on our unconscious, both personal and collective. As the driving force around which all feelings, desires, and behavior evolve, faith is the prime mover in determining our lives.

This prompting factor underlies the quality of our every action from eating and sleeping, to the career we chose, the recreation we pursue, our mode of speech and walk and generosity, the way we invest our money, and the kind of doctor we consult. Potential opportunities are lost and won based on the quality of our faith—faith in ourselves and in the lawful unfolding of events in the universe. Since all our choices are molded by our faith, this leads to the formation of our destiny.

The many faceted *sraddha* of which Krishna speaks is neither blind belief nor group conformity to authority or spiritual hierarchy. For blind belief can never pass for faith if the mind is questioning and alert. Steady faith stems directly from our *immediate experience*. Our emotions, for example, are greatly influenced by our faith. When we feel anxious or depressed, if we allow our discomfort to surface under the eye of the witness, we will notice that our inner state, which seems sometimes stuck and sometimes moving, is ever prodding us toward harmony with our self and with all of life. This kind of faith accrues with experience and leads to self confidence and trust—a real appreciation for life. Without a little bit of faith, man is destined to be fearful.

the pace of life rushes on
many events crowd into a
tiny time frame
pushing us into a
perpetual state of stress

tension, doubt, ambivalence
worry and joylessness
stem from fear and
lack of faith

Without faith in an inherently purposeful universal order *that includes oneself* based on knowledge and experience, it is very difficult to live with self confidence. Without some degree of faith in the presence of beneficence, it is almost impossible to feel centered and at home, peaceful in the face of difficulty, steady in the sea of censure, balanced in the quickness of change. The feeling that something higher than our own ego is supporting our efforts in spite of our "failures"—or even the hint that the higher might be offering us "failure" in order to help us in some as yet unknown way—can be a great help in navigating the waves of existence. And this faith will surely be granted if we can be open and patient, and truly seek.

to listen to the tiny seed
of still small voice within
and not be swept away by
conventional social opinion

to pursue the action of the moment
attentively in accordance with
our highest ideal

will lead us to faith
will guide us to the Real

Krishna is now offering us the raw material to discriminate between different gradations of *sraddha*, that through understanding and self-observation, this knowledge can be incorporated into our daily practice and serve as a beneficial force for our evolution. Another perspective is being presented to help remove the veils that cover our inherent perfection. The subtle implications of comprehending this knowledge lead with ease and naturalness to a finer quality of living.

The chapter opens with a question. At the close of the sixteenth discourse, Krishna emphatically states that the scriptures, or science of spirituality, is the prime source for determining the actions of a spiritual student. For the *asura*, instinctual and material desire is the unquestioned source of action. But for the aspirant, the knowledge and suggestions of the *sastras* are to go from the page into the heart and be incorporated into his life. This brings up a dilemna in the mind of Arjuna.

As a military man of action, he's not that well versed in scriptures. He's had some traditional education but never really pursued it at length. So he's asking about a person like himself who wants to be good, who has his own faith and follows some form of worship but doesn't know specifically about the laws of spirituality or about the kinds of actions enjoined by the scriptures. He may be a decent person, but has little interest in studying scriptures. Would this person be considered godly, neutral or demonic? The question is quite relevant for the contemporary person who rarely reads the sacred texts of any religion and therefore has no knowledge about applying their philosophy to his life. Would Krishna characterize such a person as *sattvic*, *rajasic* or *tamasic*?

Faith, Ego and Dharma

Before plunging into Krishna's response, let's ponder the relationship between the idea of faith and the concept of ego. Remember, it is the body ego mind form that is the vehicle through which we meet the world, experience our feelings and thoughts and perform our consequent actions. Therefore, if we have genuine faith in the existence of a force higher than our own ego, or perceived sense of self, our aim will be to live in accordance with this knowledge. Our thoughts, feelings and actions will revolve around contacting the essence ideal and living with the way of the ideal in the ongoing moment, no matter what the activity.

This manner of being offers spontaneity, movement, freedom and stillness. By not being tied to concepts, or goods that are canned and impressions that are stale, packaged living departs. For the ideal is not a concept but a dynamic way of being waiting to be discovered in the moment. We cannot really know what is right until we find ourselves face to face with the situation that tests our ideal. Until it is lived in the moment, the ideal remains theoretical; it stays mental. Where there is faith in that which is ungraspable, intangible to the senses and the mind, the need to control has been abandoned. There is the acceptance knowledge that whatever life brings is purposeful, provided we can meet it from the perspective of forging a connection with the highest.

In the *Mahabharata*, Yuddhisthira faces this very issue of the relationship between the ideal and the ego. He was such a totally honest person that, in his mind, to utter an untruth was akin to the most heinous crime. He was the very embodiment of *dharma*. In the midst of the war, his teacher Drona, who fought on the opposing side, began using divine weapons and killing everyone in sight. Drona had to be stopped. But he could not be defeated in battle. *He could only be defeated by a lie*.

Krishna explains through reason that the victory of good over evil depends on this lie. Arjuna could not tell Drona that his son Ashwattama was dead. But Yuddhisthira was able to sacrifice his ego, his individual right action, his personal *dharma* for the sake of a greater *dharma*. Universal eternal *dharma* is mightier than personal or ego-oriented *dharma*. And in order to experience liberation, all personal *dharmas* must be surrendered. But only to the highest Good, the one great all encompassing *dharma*. (In spite of this, the elephant Ashwattama was killed to mitigate the *adharmic* effect of the lie.)

Therefore, it is our faith in the highest, which helps us shed the false concept of ego. Without faith in a transcendent immanent energy through which events are ordered in partnership with our actions, there can be no motivation for surrendering the false sense of I. One's identity can be expanded with the idea of becoming more powerful, more competent, more good, more proud, but the falsehood of I cannot be surrendered without faith in the highest. When we can acknowledge that there is no me, that what I call me is a superimposition of the life energy onto inert matter, then we are utilizing the vehicle of life that has been lent to us for merging with the source of life. And our individual lives become universal.

This ongoing process is based on the quality of our faith. This is a faith that transcends and permeates matter, a faith that utilizes the higher Intelligence(*buddhi*) for freeing us from the domain of the lower thought and matter envelopments, by perceiving the ongoing interpenetration of *samsara* and *nirvana*. Through the deepest faith, the *gunas* can thus live *through* us without becoming the *substance* of us.

Three Forms of Faith

This leads us to Krishna's response to Arjuna's question about the quality of a person who has faith but no knowledge of spiritual science or scripture. There are levels of faith that can be considered analogous to ego development. Everyone has faith in something. Where one places his faith, stems from how strongly bound to matter he is and to what quality of matter he is bound. Are there any spaces in the ego which allow the light to enter and promote a give and take with the environment and the course of events? Or does one function as a fixed and rigid system, utterly predictable, with little slack in the rope of the *gunas*? For where a person places his faith determines the person. If one has no trust in his highest Self, his faith will be placed in his capacity to do, to get and to maneuver. Thus his choices will be more constricted, more concrete than the one who places his faith in the open expansive energy functioning *through* his innate intelligence. The former is small-minded, the latter is large-minded and open-minded, *connected* to the universal divine Intelligence.

> The faith of a man follows his nature. Man is made of faith. As his faith is so he is. (17:3)

In the area of worship, for example(4), the *tamasic* person places his faith in others to take care of him—the spiritual underworld of cult figures, mediums, and channeling of spirits, with a blind acceptance that stems from the inability to discriminate truth from untruth. In street life, the underworld figures of drug dealers, organized crime, politicians or nepotism of one sort or another are sought for protection. And in ordinary life, the god image of power gets projected onto parents, spouses, children and authority figures to give a sense of security and a feeling of being taken care of.

Because of the acknowledgement of one's inability to go it alone, *tamasic* faith has the potential for great receptivity and surrender. However, because the inner chaos is so strong and the discriminating intellect so weak, god and goblin become confused. One is mistaken for the other. If this person could surrender to the *source* of the underworld, as opposed to the underworld itself, his faith would slowly become more grounded, more balanced and more truthful. But first, the one with *tamasic* faith must be shown the difference between darkness and light, ghost and god, shadow and savior.

There are stories of powerful magicians who can change their forms at will. Without the proper protection, it is possible even for the most virtuous and intelligent person to be fooled by sound, imagery and the mind. The *Ramayana* offers an example. The evil demon Ravana manages to kidnap Sita when a magician assumes Rama's voice and cries for help. Her mind worries that Rama is in danger, so she insists on sending away Lakshmana, the brother-in-law who is protecting her. He doesn't want to go but she is adamant. Then she is coaxed out of her protective circle by what she thinks is a holy man. But he's really the magician-demon in disguise. Without the protection of her sacred space, Sita becomes easy prey for the kidnapper.

Black magic can rule the psyche as well as cast spells with far-ranging consequences—in a wholly unconscious manner. When a person learns to differentiate between the shades of spirit world and Truth, then he can be helped to say no to the entity or negative thought form that threatens to take over his life. This can occur on a literal level, or as a projection of unconscious contents, which thereby influence life events. Only when he is convinced that his goblin god is not conducive to his well being can he begin to look to a more genuine source for help.

Rajasic faith, on the other hand, is totally materialistic and tangible(5). One worships people with money, fame, and power. All the heroes of the media from Hollywood and rock star to athlete and politician become the focus of conversation and attention. Public opinion or what other people think also becomes a kind of god.

Rajasic faith is the accepted norm in our society. The person with total faith in egoistic action has sold his soul for the sake of position, praise or bank account—*too great a price to pay for the illusion of security*. This illusion is created by a mind that has placed all its faith in matter which, by definition, is bound to change and perish, thereby bringing disappointment and pain.

The *sattvic* person has faith in God as a form: a concrete body form to be worshipped, such as Jesus, Buddha, Mohammed or Krishna, or the phenomenal forces that rule the universe and the psyche, or the formless God. If one's chosen deity can serve as the force which links one to the universal transcendent God energy in all, then worship can be considered pure *sattva*. Where partisan divisions exist between this God or that, this scriptural logic or that, this religion or that, then worship is motivated by a *rajasic* need for egoistic power as opposed to *sattvic* surrender. The logic of dogma has little relationship to holistic faith.

Three Forms of Austerity

The austerity or self-discipline indigenous to the three types of faith can also be distinguished(5,6). The main purpose of *tapas* (austerity) in spiritual work is to train the body, emotions and intellect to develop will, to purify the mind and to unify the psyche behind its one grand aim—realization. But not only the spiritually minded perform *tapas*. The *Puranas* speak of many *asura*s who engage in austerity for the sake of being granted boons by the gods. The gods are helpless in the face of natural law. For every effort produces its effect. The boon must be granted even to the worst of demon, provided he has put in his proper time and effort.

There's a story about an *asura* named Bhasmasura who performs *tapas* and asks Siva, the Lord of *tapas*, for a boon. The boon is that whoever the *asura* touches on the head will be burned to ashes. After granting the boon, Siva realizes the demon plans to use his destructive power against Him, the Lord of destruction Himself. So he begins to run. He runs and runs with the demon trailing on his heels close behind. Siva is getting very tired. Just then, Vishnu intervenes and sends the irresistible Mohini to sidetrack Bhasmasura. He is spellbound and asks her to marry him. She consents, on one condition—that he first purify himself in the river by performing the ablution rites. One part of this rite consists of placing water in your hand and dropping it onto the top of your head. Needless to say, in the heat of passion, his years of *tapas* are totally forgotten. And he is burned to ashes.

The Lord of preservation comes to the rescue of the Lord of destruction that the balance of creation be maintained. The story teaches that self-control must never be given free reign to be used in an egoistic manner. It must always be practiced in service of the Self to maintain harmony, all inclusiveness and unity(14). The effects of egoistic *tapas* can be lost in a flash. *Unless the energy we gain from self-discipline is given back to the universe in the form of creative service for the well being of all, the energy will return to the jurisdiction of maya and vanish.*

In our society, where most people remain unconscious of the possibility of spiritual power derived from *tapas*, the principle still holds sway over the psyche. When we put in concentrated effort we get results. But effort that is severe and unharmonious exacts its toll on the body mind of the person.

Although the contemporary western *asura* may not stand on one leg for three months or stare at the sun for days like his harsh eastern counterpart, his mode of *tapas* is equally foolish. For example, the *rajasic asura* who takes total refuge in the god of work may be unaware of the level of stress he is inflicting on himself and others through anxiety, intense busy-ness and rushing. When one has little awareness or appreciation for his own body, he might care for it in superficial ways, which beef up external appearance; through tanning or gaining muscles, or in quick fix ways, such as fad diets, gulping handfuls of vitamin pills or taking unnecessary antibiotics. But genuine caring for the body as a valued temple reflects emotional appreciation and requires sensitivity to what is healthful and wholesome as a total way of living. Then one's very *lifestyle* serves to prevent illness and promote calmness and joyousness. Quick fix remedies based on consumerism become an anachronism.

Poisoning one's body with smoking, debilitating one's circulation by not getting natural exercise in the fresh air, consuming rich foods and alcohol as social obligation can all become habitual abuse to the body. Allowing oneself to live in a way that one's natural needs for food or sex are disregarded or suppressed can also be viewed as unconscious negative *tapas*. Likewise, when one's emotional need for nurturing and affection is ignored, this is foolish *tapas* that hardens the heart. Through not living the loving disposition inherent in each of us, the powers of life within can turn against oneself and others(6). The human heart not functioning in accordance with its expansive human capacity constricts. This can lead to unhappiness and heart attacks. Unwholesome *tapas* poisons the soul. To value the powers of life, they must be lovingly and humanly given the opportunity to be experienced. The enlivening powers are an expression of God residing within us.

> Every human being has to accomplish certain aims in life which are in tune with humanness. You have to realize that the Lord is the Indweller in all beings and experience unity in diversity. The entire creation is present within the human body. This is the mystery of creation. The human body is a marvelous creation. Every organ in the body discharges its special function and nothing else. Only the divine can create such a wonderful organism. The *Atma* is the master within the body. Never betray the master. Be grateful to God for endowing you with such a marvelous body.
> (Sri Sathya Sai Baba, SS5-95, p.127)

The same energy that goes into maintaining *rajasic* values can become constructive rather than destructive, as one's aspirations become attuned to the inner universal partnership. Krishna, like the Buddha after him is advocating the middle way. When this is applied to both secular and spiritual endeavor, the world and the spirit unite.

In *slokas* 8-22, Krishna proceeds to describe three kinds of food, three qualities of discipline, three forms of sacrifice and three ways of giving, which are all based on our *sraddha*. These four categories loosely comprise the substance of our actions—eating, self-discipline, sacrifice and giving. Through observing these four types of actions dancing through our lives, we differentiate between the *gunas*. This awareness brings detachment, sensitivity and deeper feeling experience.

Three Qualities of Food

The ancient wisdom suggests an innate connection between the food we eat and the disposition of the mind and body. In an untrained person with little control, the mind and body remain inseparable from each other; one invariably influences the other. When the body hurts, we succumb to pain. When the emotions are out of sync, the body becomes ill. But for the advanced *yogi, the mind controls the body.* When the mind is blissful, pain is of minimal significance.

Food is like medicine for the body and raw material for the mind. What we eat is an important determinant of the propensity of our mind and behavior. Through a process of observation, the *rishis* have classified certain foods and ways of eating, as serving to promote the *sattvic* mood, the *rajasic* mood and the *tamasic* mood. Likewise, it has been found that people with different temperaments are attracted to corresponding kinds of food.

Persons who are *sattvic* will gravitate toward a vegetarian diet that is very fresh, inherently tasteful and simply prepared. There is no need to cover the essence of the flavor by spices, rich gravies or overcooking. In order for food to be *sattvic*, it must be cooked with spotless utensils in a clean kitchen and be prepared by a person whose mind is calm, with money obtained by honest means. The food should not be canned, frozen, processed or reheated from the prior day but should be freshly prepared and eaten not more than three hours after cooking. No chemical additives, preservatives, MSG or goods with a long shelf life can be considered pure. *Sattvic* food promotes health, strength, cheerfulness and longevity. Whereas diet alone cannot guarantee a spiritual outlook, it can create the fertile soil for this way of being to sprout. Purity in food makes our spiritual work much easier by disposing the mind toward peacefulness.

Rajasic food, on the other hand, leads the mind toward passion and agitation. The *rajasic* person will be attracted to food that is spicy, sour, salty, bitter, fiery and served very hot. One under the spell of *rajas* loves garlic, hot peppers and thick red meat. The more of this he eats, the more stressed out he becomes. Reveling in animal flesh feeds the animal disposition. This leads to a temperament that is impatient, agitated, aggressive and impulsive. *Insensitivity to all forms of life, as well as to the human feelings of compassion and caring is promoted by eating other animals.* Whereas the *sattvic* person would find it difficult to tolerate the sweet chemical flavor of sodas and bottled drinks, the *rajasic* person enjoys them. *Sraddha* in expediency not only supports the instant food industry, but undermines a wholesome and nutritious caring for oneself.

Just as fast foods chains have spread throughout the earth, so the food of inane and violent impressions is taking root in underdeveloped nations via satellite TV and cyberspace. For example, in the villages of India some simple and "illiterate" people still maintain a moral and joyful family lifestyle based on their culture, communal life and customs. In the west, we wistfully wish for a return to "family values" and peaceful, crime-free living. The effect of exposing naive, uneducated people to western materialistic values via the media will systematically rob them of their own culture by inducing a low level of hypnotic, unthinking uniformity and admiration for violence and materialism. Western consumer advertising is now working hard to target the minds of Indian children, in the same way they have already taken over the wholesomeness of western children. Emerging nations such as India, which have hooked into satellite TV, must make a sincere effort to offset the inevitable barrage of mind pollution. One approach would be to show quality cultural programs that educate people regarding the intrinsic value of their own cultural heritage, by helping simple people appreciate their roots and way of life. Spell out to them the greed behind the mentality of materialistic consumerism and the tactics of the entertainment industry, with its reliance on sensationalism, sex and aggression. Demonstrate through examples what ongoing exposure to this mentality can do to the human soul. Education and warning are needed to prevent mechanical brainwashing from suppressing humanness.

We see how difficult it is to redress environmental pollution after the fact. It would be very good if we could learn from past mistakes and adopt *preventive medicine* by not fostering world wide mind pollution. The *quality* of technology must take precedence over the *unthinking materialism* of technology. The *rajasic asura* must be educated through facing responsibility for the long-term consequences of his actions, recognizing his greed and developing conscience. This process can be aided by intelligent exposure and inner readiness.

The *tamasic* person likes tasteless food, packaged food, frozen food. He keeps returning to the same container in the refrigerator days after it has been bought. As he has little appreciation for freshness, he sleeps a lot during the day, since his body does not receive the nutrition it needs. Then he compensates with caffeine. Content consuming almost rancid fruit and vegetables, the *tamasic* person is not aware that stale food also makes the mind sluggish and tired, depressed and reactive. But this food seems conducive to his temperament. Change the diet and the possibility improves for changing the character. The *Chandogya Upanishad* says:

> When the food is pure, the mind becomes pure; when the mind is pure, remembrance becomes firmly fixed; and when remembrance is acquired, there is release from all knots of the heart. (7.26.2)

Three Qualities of Sacrifice (*Yajna*)

In *slokas* 11-19, Krishna expounds on sacrifice, worship and self-discipline. As discussed in chapter four, sacrifice is the basis for all action, be it on the individual or cosmic divine level.[38] All action or inaction is some form of sacrifice. Our sacrifice can be conscious or unconscious depending on our inner attitude and feelings toward our actions. An action becomes a conscious sacrifice when this is not action for oneself alone and the heart is linked to something higher than the ego. The heart, the mind and the hand are then brought to work together in harmony.

Although the sacrifice explained in *slokas* 11-13 refers primarily to ritual forms of worship (*yajna*), it can also apply to any action. The attempt to establish a universal standard for beneficent action can be helpful. When we do something with love, for its own sake because it deeply feels right and does not contradict our knowledge, then our action is *sattvic*. When action is performed for reward, show, position or praise, it is *rajasic*. When done in a mechanical way, without any care or understanding, just because everyone else is doing it, the sacrifice is *tamasic*.

The ongoing *sadhana* of the spiritual student consists of the triple discipline of body, speech and mind, the integration of thought, word and deed(14-17). Ritual forms of daily worship (*puja*) present a framework for giving thanks to the forces that promote our evolution and also serve to offer the gift of finer energy to great nature. Whether performed as formal ritual or incorporated into our lives as appreciative, loving remembrance, "to attune with a higher ideal whereby the meditator develops in himself the qualities of the meditated is called worship"(Swami Chinmayananda). To experience gratitude to the teachers, who are firmly dedicated to evoking the spiritual life in all who can receive it, can serve as an ongoing example of what we ourselves are also capable. To base all our actions on the qualities of purity, *dharma*, *brahmacharya* and *ahimsa* leads to a life of harmony and contentment, thereby nourishing the world, as well as our self.

Traditionally, *brahmacharya* refers to sexual celibacy, especially as practiced during the student stage of life(14). Here however, Krishna is speaking to a householder with wives and children. Within its broader context, *brahmacharya* refers to *keeping the mind fixed in Brahman throughout all our activities*. Remembrance sanctifies our every action, does not allow the mind to become fixated on or obsessed by any thing that would keep it away from the concentrated all-expansive awareness of the life principle in its totality. The sages say, through performing every act as worship, the urges of the body naturally align themselves with divine will. In this way, mind control becomes organic.

Through awareness of words(15), through inner listening, the *sattvic* person speaks softly and kindly with a directness that is easy to understand, yet hurts no one through too brash an honesty. His words are always well-economized, never superfluous, violent nor impulsive. He does not waste energy through excessive speech or thought. As his speech reflects his inner ideas and feelings, his words wield power. Speech is a reflection of our inner being. Through our words, *karmas* are perpetuated, created or destroyed. Practicing mindfulness of speech serves to integrate the personality.

When we think one thing and say another, we are unable to trust ourself. And we become two-faced, hypocritical and slippery—untrustworthy. *When we say what we think others want to hear and do not live by our ideals, we develop a secret self-hate.*

> Words which give peace, words which are good and beautiful and true and also the reading of sacred books; this is the harmony of words. (17:15)

Harmony of mind comes from practicing calmness, inner silence, self-restraint, loving kindness and purity(16).This is the root of the triple purity of body, speech and mind. The purpose of all *tapas* is to harmonize our thought, word and deed(17). In this nonconflicted state of balance, our words become an expression of Truth. Again and again, we are taken through many different levels of the realm of *karma*, through many different rungs of purification till ultimately, we are granted leave from the cycle.

Three Qualities of Charity

The same basic principles of the *gunas* apply to giving. Krishna says charity must be given intelligently and stem from abundance, from the desire to give *without any expectation of receiving*. Whether we are giving money, love, time or knowledge, giving is to be for its own sake, not for recognition or expected result. When we expect something in return or give in ambivalence without wholehearted generosity, the gift is *rajasic*. And where there is no appreciation of the recipient and his needs, where there is insult or disrespect, the charity is *tamasic*. Maharaj says, "Clarity and charity go together. Each needs and strengthens the other."

These four categories of food, sacrifice, self-discipline and giving are the raw materials of life that the spiritual aspirant has to work with. *They are the means through which the body, emotions and intellect become attuned to the ideal.* Through awareness of our functioning in each of these four areas, we come to see where we are at a given moment. Are we attached to a particular *guna*? Can we allow a realignment with the awareness ideal to take place? What is it about our present mode of thought and action that is interfering with this alignment?

Witnessing the Four Categories

This manner of working allows us to apply directly to the circumstances of everyday living, techniques which until this point have been understood theoretically. *Slowly and steadily, the energy and concentration derived from meditation enters our daily lives and utterly transforms.* The process of integrating method with life can take place first in a semi-sheltered environment such as an *ashram* or spiritual community, where the ideas are practiced under the power and influence of the teacher. Later, when one is away from the physical presence of the teacher or the external vibrations of the spiritual community, the real challenge begins. Can one live the ideas and practices in such a steady manner so as to be able to maintain contact with this awareness energy purity without clinging or guarding, while at the same time, not unknowingly giving it away due to ignorance of the ongoing need for spontaneous vigilance?

The work is ongoing until total realization. Even one who has become accustomed to the experience of peacefulness, contentment and spiritual energy over the years can at any moment be unexpectedly challenged by some blatant form of *maya* without fully realizing it. Vigilance is essential. Unless the *sattvic* mood is maintained *throughout all four areas of living*, the spiritual energy can easily slip away. Until realization is complete, we can seemingly lose what has been seemingly won. For many a *sattvic* seeker, the most challenging task is the integration of spirituality and sexuality. The entire projecting power of *maya* is maintained by our confusion of sexual impulse with love, conjoined with our identification with the body, which is an expression of attachment. In a discourse about Krishna, Sri Sathya Sai Baba says:

> This was the first message given to the world by Sri Krishna: "Those who experience the truth that the *Atma* which dwells in all beings is the same as Mine, whether they are full of desires or free from desires, whether they are householders or renunciants, whether

> they perform the prescribed duties(*karma*) or not, they will abide in Me." This message was given to all mankind five thousand years ago.

Therefore, a space is being offered for varied ways of living as a human being. Married or single, ritualist or thinker, action or inaction, as long as we *live in remembrance*, all our actions, duties, instincts and desires will lead us to God.

> Wherever you may be, in whatever condition, consider your hearts as an ocean of milk, abode of God. God is omnipresent. When you lead your life with this faith, there is nothing greater than this. (Sri Sathya Sai Baba, SS,8-95, p.203)

Once we have reached the seventeenth chapter internally, there is an awareness of a responsibility for living the ideas that Krishna has been expounding. With urgency, a feeling that cuts through intellectual complacency forces us to face the fact that the problematic aspects of ourselves will not automatically vanish. That which seems to keep us from perfection still pops up from time to time, seeming to prevent our progress and our peacefulness, our lovingness and our presence. Whatever lurks in the mud will remain so until it is *karmically* worked through or burned to ashes in the fire of meditation and remembrance. There is no escape. Until the mind is wholly pure, the Self cannot be fully reflected in it.

Hence, the seeming repetition of the ideas of the seventeenth chapter is not repetitive at all—provided a connection can be forged between idea, practice and our daily functioning. Once spirit and world have been separated out from each other, they must be *reunited* again; to consciously *be* as they always *are*, in accordance with Truth. Without practice, the chapter can appear mundane. With practice, the discourse can lead each of us back to the Achilles heel of our mind, that healing might occur. Our *karma* must be continuously worked through at progressively higher and higher levels as well as lower and lower levels until it is extinguished. This is a prerequisite to liberation.

So the four categories of actions are being expounded that our witnessing consciousness might serve as the link, which filters through the ideal to our ongoing behavior in a flash. Through this presence, our desires, thoughts, and actions become uplifted to help us embody our God nature. Without this presence, our desires, thoughts and actions proceed automatically like those of the animal.

Abiding in Remembrance

There are several possible ways we can practice the ideas in the seventeenth chapter. The first can be described as the way of global awareness, a general awareness experience of the senses, perceptions, emotions, images, thoughts, and actions without trying to change anything: watching the quality of faith while forging a connection with the depth of one's consciousness. The second approach can be called a conscious attempt to maintain the vigilance of the *sattvic* mood in all our actions. This entails the aspiration to uplift the quality of our *tamasic* and *rajasic* faith to *sattva*, that our functioning can become more peaceful, more loving and attuned to the common good. It is wholly natural, spontaneous and unforced. The first is the way of being; the second is the way of effort-making. This effort however is not from an ego space, but rather is linked to the witnessing consciousness, feeling, or divine will. When both ways of living are incorporated into our daily lives, purification *spontaneously* proceeds.

A third form of practice advised by Krishna(23-28) is repetition of the ancient holy *Vedic mantra, Om Tat Sat*. This *mantra* offers a way of devotion to the formless *Brahman*. It serves to link the mind and action to the highest Reality—to uplift the body ego mind form from its limited, relative plane of action—to the free and unlimited. In its usage in the traditional *yajna*, it is said to have the effect of nullifying all mistakes in ritual action or scriptural recitation, provided the meaning of the *mantra* is comprehended and the motivation is for the benefit of all. Even if one's actions are imperfect, their negative effects will be nullified if they are performed in remembrance with positive motivation.

The *mantra* embodies a triple designation of *Brahman*. *Om* stands for the Absolute transcendent consciousness as the unborn Self in all beings, present throughout the three states of consciousness. The sound reverberating within the body induces sacredness. When *Om* is uttered before beginning an action, the divine is called to be present in the action.

Tat means That. That is *Brahman* in the world. To see all as *Brahman* dispels all selfish motivation. Whether our action fits into the category of sacrifice, food, gift or self-discipline, when awareness of That is present, our *vasanas* become extinguished and no new *vasanas* are formed from our action. Even if the action is not *sattvic*, awareness of That will nullify its *karmic* effects.

Sat means being, existence, "isness," Truth, Reality. Any work performed with *awareness being* allows us to serve as vehicles that radiate ongoing existence into life. By recognizing this Truth in all actions and all beings, the unified ongoing goodness auspiciousness enters into life consciousness. When true faith in ongoing existence presence underlies all actions, the effect is Truth. Then the four categories of actions are Real. They do not fall under the projecting power of *maya*.

> *Brahman* alone is free from blemish. Everything else has some trace of evil in it. The sinful man ought not to be addressed as sinner. For by doing so, the sin in him is further cherished. But by calling him good at all times, the goodness in him is fostered. This goodness is an effective means to reform the world. This is a great lesson in life to be learned by all. The word *sat* is used for this purpose. (Swami Chidbhavananda, p.834,5)

When actions are undertaken without heartfelt faith, knowledge awareness existence, they are not Real. They are relative, changing in accordance with the properties of the mind. They lose their eternal universal dimension. They are false. They are *maya*. They are *samsara* without any connection to *nirvana*. They produce no essential effect, or an effect contrary to the intentions of the doer. *Only when the faith of the performer of action is linked to Reality does human action have any real clout.* Otherwise, it is just activity buzzing around meaningless, imbalanced, signifying nothing, producing nothing.

Part of the following poem entitled "Buddha's Pity" helps elucidate what is meant by meaningless *karma* and the compassion of the *avatar:*

My children,
The Enlightened One, because He saw mankind drowning
in the great sea of birth, death and sorrow
and longed to save them
For this He was moved to pity.
Because He saw that though they longed for happiness
they made for themselves no karma of happiness
and though they hated pain, yet willingly made for themselves
a karma of pain;
and though they coveted the joys of heaven
would not follow His commandments on earth,
For this He was moved to pity.
Because He saw them consumed by the fires of pain and sorrow
yet knowing not where to seek the still waters of samadhi
For this He was moved to pity.
Because He saw them living in an evil time,
subjected to tyrannous kings and suffering many ills,
yet heedlessly following after pleasure,
For this He was moved to pity.
Because He saw them living in a time of wars,
killing and wounding one another;
and knew that for the riotous hatred that had flourished in
their hearts they were doomed to pay an endless retribution,
For this He was moved to pity.
Because many born at the time of His incarnation had heard Him
preach the Holy Law, yet could not receive it,
For this He was moved to pity.
Because some had great riches that they could not bear
to give away,
For this He was moved to pity.
Because He saw the men of the world ploughing their fields,
sowing the seed, trafficking, huckstering, buying and selling;
and at the end winning nothing but bitterness,
For this He was moved to pity.
(E. A. Burtt, p.240-l)

Faith Dissolves Ego

With the close of the chapter, we reach a deeper level in understanding the importance of *karma*. Opportunities emerge again and again in different forms throughout the course of our lives to help us nullify all our negative thoughts and negative acts, all our meaningless thoughts and meaningless acts, all the harm we have perpetrated on ourselves and others, both knowingly and unknowingly. As our level of faith deepens, it leaps beyond the realm of ego, beyond the realm of *karma*. No longer are there any distinctions between being, goodness and faith. Each is part of the same whole brought into life through the vehicle of the human being ever aspiring to live his God-nature.

Faith thus heals the psyche and the body. And the process of ever deepening faith involves understanding how *trust in oneself and trust in the universe of beings, things and events serve as the actual vehicle for healing to occur*. When seemingly difficult things happen, an opportunity presents itself to deepen one's faith, which thereby unifies the conflicted aspects of the personality around this one great wish for wholeness, health, peacefulness, happiness. The healing power of the greatest masters can manifest at will without the aspirant's faith, but for purposes of learning, understanding and autonomy, the disciple is taught through experience that the level of faith, deeply harmonized within oneself can connect us with the highest energy. And it is this energy that heals. Faith is the means of connecting with the healing energy that lives inside each of us.

When Jesus says to the crippled or the leper, "it is your faith which makes you whole," this is a living example of the most powerful energy of illuminated feeling intelligence connecting with the source of universal energy. When this connection is forged through grace of the higher, all physical and psychological imperfections melt into one wholeness perfection.

Where doubt and conflict dominate the psyche, half-hearted wishes or requests for healing will tend to be automatic and superficial, as they lack the backing of the unifying force of deeply felt emotion. This leads one into the realm of superstition, where faith is superficial and healing a mirage. The person will tend to justify his skepticism with the thought, "I was right all along. I knew it wouldn't work." Until life compels one to surrender wholeheartedly, the power of faith remains dormant, fast asleep in the cocoon of "rationality." Gradually, as we learn to turn within to the positive influences that help us value our Self, the indomitable force of life, we begin to awaken and experience the love that heals.

Reflections on Faith

Here are some thoughts, which illustrate the accessibility of the multifaceted diamond of faith to many different moods, psychological types and circumstances of living:

> Faith is not belief. It is the grasp on the Ultimate—an illumination.
> He who has no faith in himself can never have faith in God.
> It is faith that makes a lion of a man.
> (Swami Vivekananda)

> Faith is the bird
> that feels the light
> and sings when the dawn
> is still dark
> (Rabindranath Tagore)

> When the finite man stretches out his tiny hands to reach the Infinite, when the imperfect strives to attain perfection, certainly there must be a limit up to which he can consciously and deliberately move through intelligent self-effort. But a time comes when he must take a leap of faith. He must sincerely cultivate strong faith. Faith illumines the path and dissipates all shadows and suspicions. In the face of all doubts and difficulties, it is only the faith in one's heart that can sustain one's efforts and give the joyous assurance of success. (Swami Chinmayananda)

> Faith is the ability to see divinity in the flowing waters of a river. Faith is the secret power in man by which he successfully explores the unknown and wins laurels of his final victory. Faith is a belief in what is not known to us now so that we may come to know at a future date what we now only believe in.

This faith can be a positive help only when it is built upon full understanding and upon an ability to think independently. Men of 'blind' faith live and strive in thoughtlessness without discriminating whether what they are doing is right(*sat*) or wrong(*asat*). If an independent, right discriminating power is absent from a bosom, 'faith' cannot deliver any appreciable results. (Swami Chinmayananda)

When you are affirming healing for yourself or others, visualize the tremendous force of God's healing power as a white light surrounding you or the person for whom you are praying. Feel that it is melting away all illness and imperfection. Every uplifting thought we think, every prayer we utter, every good action we perform is impregnated with God's power. We can manifest this power in greater and greater ways as our faith becomes stronger and our love for God becomes deeper.

Know for certain that if it is ultimately for the highest good, cosmic law and even the will of God can be influenced by the power of prayer and affirmation, when one's thought is strong and faith is perfect. When one has forcefully prayed and positively affirmed healing with faith and devotion but the end result is contrary, then comes the time to surrender in inner peace to the higher wisdom of God. But until He has made His final pronouncement, He expects man to use his God given power, will and strength to resist all imperfection in this world of change and relativity. (Sri Daya Mata)

Daughter, be of good comfort; thy faith has made thee whole. (Matthew 9:22)

According to your faith be it unto you. (Matthew 9:29)

God is the Doctor. Seek Him, rely on Him. You will be free from diseases. (Sri Sathya Sai Baba)

There is infinite power inherent in the human heart. But despite such power, man does not have faith in himself. What is the reason for this? The reason is that he feels separated and believes he is different from divinity, which in truth is always inside him as his very core. This same divinity pervades the entire universe. When you deepen a firm faith in God you will have no fear whatsoever. You will recognize that the God you worship is One who is present everywhere in everyone and everything and also in yourself. This

> belief will remove all vestige of fear from your heart. But if you don't have that faith, then you will be ridden with fear.
>
> Your faith in the omnipresent is the key to developing fearlessness. Only when you lose faith will you develop fear. Only when you forget your true Self will fear arise. You have forgotten your true nature, you have forgotten *Atma*. You are considering yourself to be this little five foot body. But *the truth is that you are infinite in form and that your power is unlimited.*
>
> When you make an effort to remove the delusion and get a vision of the *Atma* you become merged in *Nirvana*. Then you can call yourself a real human being. If you do not make any effort along this path you are not a man but a 'man' in name only.
> (Sri Sathya Sai Baba)

Thus, the seventeenth discourse reveals the power of the threefold *yoga* of faith. Through living the science of spirituality, we are helped to purify the various levels of *sraddha*, until it is experienced as fully transcending all matter, *karma* and *guna*—in the realm of pure love.

Eighteen

YOGA OF LIBERATION THROUGH RENUNCIATION

Moksha Sannyasa Yoga

	Gita verses
Gradations of renunciation (*tyaga and sannyasa*)	1–12
Five causes of action according to *Sankhya* philosophy	13–16
Escape bondage through freedom from "doership"	17–18
Three kinds of knowledge, action, intellect, will, and happiness	19–40
Duties of the four psychological types(castes)	41–48
Realize *Brahman* through purity, mind control and renunciation of attachment to results	49–55
Realize *Brahman* through devotion and surrender	56–58
The power of *maya*	59–61
Realize *Brahman*, take refuge in the highest	62–66
Reveal the science of liberation *(Gita sastra)* to those who can receive it, for this is a great *yajna*	67–71
Arjuna answers Krishna's question and declares he is free of doubt	72–73
Sanjaya's adoration of the *Gita*	74–78

surrender all selfishness
to Me
in wholesomeness

imperfect though your work may be
offer everything to Me
with remembrance love

and you will be stainless
and you will be in Me
always

Throughout each chapter, many different *yogas* have been presented. Each practice demonstrates a different slice in the process of cutting through the coverings on our journey inward, that we might come to experience our innermost Self which pervades everything. In the concluding chapter, Krishna summarizes the major ideas of the *Gita* and continues to differentiate the three-fold nature of action, giving, sacrifice and self-harmony as the prelude for realization. Here the three forms of spiritual practice—action, devotion and knowledge—truly lose their distinct boundaries as they become integrated, applicable to any situation, any time, any place.

The aspirant is now prepared to understand and participate in helping the ego merge with *Brahman* on the battlefield of life, as all the disparate parts of oneself become connected through one ever present remembrance. In this way, we are offered the challenge of living out our Knowledge, making every thought and action part of some higher purpose and participating in a new beginning that has far reaching consequences for oneself, the society and for all creation.

The circle is being completed as we return to the beginning when Arjuna says, "I surrender to you. I am your disciple. Teach me." From beginning to end, *surrender, surrender, surrender is the culmination of the philosophy of the Gita*. The meaning has been given many times voiced loud and clear in different ways. But now after long preparation, as closure of the formal teaching nears, the spiritual aspirant becomes the disciple, better able to receive the essence and leave the shell. That which is understood with the heart and intellect does by itself come to be practiced. Felt understanding quickens the inner motivation toward liberation, as now the quality of surrender is at a different level. No longer prompted by helplessness, self-pity and confusion, the surrender of the eighteenth chapter is fueled by competence, love and Self confidence.

Commentators offer several meanings for the title of the chapter. To some, it is interpreted as liberation through renunciation of desire. To others, it means liberation through surrendering the results of actions to God. And others believe it is liberation itself that is renounced for the privilege of working on in the world out of love for the creator and his creatures, as his assistant or messenger of love. None of these interpretations is mutually exclusive but complement each other during different phases of spiritual *sadhana.*

Surrender and Renunciation

The discourse opens with a question. Arjuna asks to understand the subtle meanings of *sannyasa*(renunciation), and *tyaga* (abandonment, surrender, relinquishment)(1). This differentiation is crucial to the way one pursues spiritual work in daily life. Does the serious aspirant strive to renounce all actions based on self-centered desire or personal gain(*sannyasa*)(2)? Is it possible? Is it desirable? Or do we strive to surrender attachment to the reward of work, the fruits of one's effort, and anxiety regarding the results of our actions(*tyaga*)? What is the relationship between relinquishment and renunciation?

Krishna begins by reiterating that all action must not be renounced, cannot be renounced(5). Works of sacrifice, giving and self-discipline serve the function of purification for the individual, the society and the cosmos. Even the wise man needs to perform such actions, as long as there is no attachment to the result. To abandon obligatory duty is laziness(*tamasic*)(7), to forsake activity for some self-centered reason such as inconvenience or discomfort is egotistical(*rajasic*)(8); to act without attachment because it needs to be done is dutiful(*sattvic*)(9). This quality of action follows one's inner feeling, which is a manifestation of divine will. When performed for its own sake, dedicated to the higher, without any desire for reward or result, without attachment or clinging, this steadiness-being, beyond the opposites, purifies vasanas—brings peace and contentment.

> The relinquisher sees and has no doubts; he surrenders, he is pure and has peace. Work, pleasant or painful is for him joy. (18:10)

Swami Chinmayananda says of this *sloka*:

> When impulses such as jealousy, anger, passion or greed come to a man of *sattvic tyaga*(righteous relinquishment), he does not get involved in them as we do in our attachment and identification. A man of relinquishment readily discovers in himself a secret faculty to abandon his identification with the false, lower instincts in himself. He does not become a victim of his own mental impressions. He stands ever free and surely apart from the tumults of his mind.
>
> Such a person is said to be an educated and cultured person. An uncultured person is like a dry leaf that is tossed hither and thither by every passing breeze. It is the privilege of the animal alone to get faithfully colored by its own instincts and act according to the dictates of its impulses. It is only man, the inheritor of an intellect who can inquire into the nature of the rising waves of impulses, judge them in the light of the ideal he holds onto in himself and, if need be, stand apart and allow them to die away. But ordinarily, a person finds it impossible to stand apart and live, to act independently of his impulses. (THG, p.1007)

The gradual process of surrendering our "negative emotions" brings peace of mind. A calm mind is a contented mind. A peaceful person is a steady, joyful person. Thus, the direct path to the end of sorrow is the abandonment of agitation, through whatever means of surrender is suitable for each individual personality. When this occurs, even painful experiences can become joyful, for this is a means of connecting with one's Self. Love exuding from the Self melts individual pain into expansiveness.

Krishna again reiterates that action is an essential part of living, movement is an intrinsic part of life(11). It is our attachment to the *results* of work, anxiety for the end product that must be relinquished. And through the practice of working on in the world with acceptance, without giving way to fear or the desire to control, not focusing on *what* we do but in what *spirit* it is done, we work through our layers of *karma* both negative and positive. Then when we become fit for the ongoing practice of meditation, desire will gradually be surrendered of its own accord. In that moment, *natural renunciation occurs (sannyasa) through just being*, without any trying. This quality of living without identification with the ego transcends time and duality(12). When an action is performed by an ego wanting a result, positive, negative or mixed effects accrue. When an action is performed *through* a person as a vehicle of duty or an expression of love, with no identification with the action or attachment to the outcome, no *vasanas* are formed. No bondage occurs. *The action itself serves as a means for purifying past vasanas and bringing liberation.*

In a life of seeming constraints, one can be free internally, thereby releasing oneself from all constraints of the past. The link with the eternal is established in life.

> When work is done for a reward, the work brings pleasure or pain or both in its time. But when a man does work in Eternity, then Eternity is his reward.(18:12)

Thus, the distinction between surrender and renunciation:

> "*Tyaga* is that capacity in us with which from moment to moment we withdraw ourselves from the impulses of our mind, while *sannyasa* is the total renunciation of the entire tendencies, both good and bad, from their crystallization as the ego."
> (Swami Chinmayananda, THG, p.1012)

Love, Surrender and Ego

How then does the idea of ego coincide with surrender and renunciation both in theory and in practice? As a mental construct, the ego is made up of *vasanas* formed from past desires, impressions, thoughts, emotions and actions. Desires that are not connected with one's highest inner ideal, keep a person imprisoned by supporting ways of living that lead to false notions, suffering, stress and more entrenched *vasanas*. Through the practice of surrender, our thoughts and actions become linked with the "higher." Gradually, these values and way of being envelop the "lower," annihilating degrees of bondage. As our desires decrease, the *vasanas* melt and the false foundation comprising the ego also disappears, making way for that which is more the essence of the person. It is the emotions and desires that maintain the ego. Anger, greed, attachment, envy, pride and delusion serve to fuel our false sense of self. *As our emotional reactivity and ignorance subside, the illusion of ego loosens its grip.*

With the melting of ego, innate simplicity, openness and natural childlikeness emerge. Concepts, false notions and superimposition of reality find no place when we live spontaneously, directly in the moment. In this manner, the inert and agitated *vasanas* become subsumed into peaceful *vasanas*, thereby offering a joyful, freeing calm, a breathing space for the ego. When through the long-term practice of surrender all the encumbrances have vanished, the ego itself experiences *sannyasa*, the natural annihilation of all its separate desires, subsumed into pure being. Now divine will and divine love shine through the person.

So surrender of ego does not result from self-will, personal decision, or ongoing effort alone. Through the grace of continuous practice in partnership with the higher, the nitty-gritty of life becomes an experiment in ascending the mountain of Truth, leaving behind more and more of the nonessential as we travel along the way. When only the essence remains, then the ego has been renounced. There is no motivation of I separate from the essence. As long as there is a body, there is an individual, but now there is a harmonious interchange between the individual and the totality. We live in ongoing communion realization, a conscious servant of great nature, an expression of the whole.

> The giving up of these lower impulses of the passionate(*rajasic*) and the dull(*tamasic*) in our moment to moment contacts with life is abandonment(*tyaga*), which will give us sufficient mastery over ourselves ultimately to give up the very ego center which causes all these deflections. Renouncing our indulgence with the inheritance of the past and leaving all our anxiety for the future to serve the world as service to the Lord is abandonment(*tyaga*). And this final giving up of the perception of the finite in the acquired wisdom of the Infinite is the fulfillment of life called renunciation (*sannyasa*). (ibid., p.996)

It is a misconception to believe that only those with a "healthy" ego can practice surrender. Surrender is for everyone who wishes to live in wholesomeness, whether his ego is presently healthy or not. *To seek to establish the link with one's higher Self is the most supportive thing we can do for ourselves.* To live in this manner, the personal self is not negated but is experienced in the true perspective of the totality. Siva and Sakti coexist.

This way of being need not pose a threat to the ego nor induce any fear. The various methods that lead to surrender are as gentle as the inner receptivity of the person. It is when the individual ego fights to rule, that nature and the course of life bring fear inducing events in order to restabilize Her rightful harmony. The horrific aspect of the goddess Kali appears in conjunction with the *vasanas* of the individual or nation, and brings in her wake either the destruction of negative tendencies in a more forced manner than is palatable, or the love of the cosmic mother. We are each being given the opportunity to choose, based on the quality of our receptivity and level of inner purity.

Only when we attribute a sense of doership to the ego, are we enforcing a false sense of isolation and alienation, which leads to unhappiness, anxiety and unwholesomeness. Even the most inert, *tamasic* person, whose task is to be uplifted into action can be greatly aided by trying to work in the full knowledge of being supported by the foundation of a universal order. This can be experienced through familiarity with the laws of *karma* and/or the love of God as divine protector, the mother and father of all happenings. The greatest gift for anyone with a healthy or an unhealthy ego is to act on in the world and allow oneself to receive this loving support by simply reaching out for it from a heartfelt space deep within.

The *gopis* once played a trick on Radha. They gave her a clay pot with holes in it, which she was to use to fetch water for Krishna. When she saw the holes in the pot she prayed fervently to Krishna to help her deliver the water to him. Only with her powerful yearning and His grace was the task accomplished. In the same way, all our imperfections, which are simply a manifestation of the conditioned ego, when offered *to* God *for* God help us serve as the link which brings the waters of eternal life to perpetual fruition. By calling on the higher for help, seemingly impossible tasks can be accomplished.

Carl Jung's idea that the ego must be built up before it can be surrendered was based on his own individual method of inducing surrender through active imagination and archetypal dream imagery. It is definitely advisable for a person exposed to the sea of the collective unconscious to have a relatively healthy ego. However, this particular approach is only one limited means for inducing surrender. *The Gita is offering us more gradual and supportive paths of surrender through daily living.* The transpersonal, image inducing form of relative surrender does not necessarily lead to the give and take required for the surrender of one's interpersonal rigidity, or to humility, or to compassion for one's fellow beings—which are essential prerequisites for living happily in the world—nor does it include giving up anxiety for results in everyday life, which is the primary cause of stress and sorrow. More is required. On the other hand, contemplation alone does not lead to surrender, without practicing selfless service and other spiritual disciplines.

Through direct surrender to the teachings or to the *avatar*, realized soul, embodied God or formless God, personal love and devotion combine with loving consciousness, thereby blending individual caring and insight with transcendent love—a love which gradually expands to include all beings. The teacher can serve as one's focus and support in surrender.

As the aspirant proceeds, his trust and level of surrender will be tested again and again until it proves deep enough and broad enough to strip the ego of its remaining vestiges of the desire for control. As long as we live under the slightest illusion that the concrete world of the senses and mind is real, we live in confusion. We try to control outcomes by falsely believing our actions determine all events. Although this mode might appear workable in the beginning, it always falls apart in the end.

The various tests of surrender given to every ego on the path might induce fear at first but will only appear where there is inner readiness. When one has first experienced the supportive partnership with natural events and the loving presence of the personal/universal God force, the foundation is set for deeper surrender. Like all experiences on the path, it will happen when the time is right. Individual and cosmos interplay as one whole.

The Causes of Karma

To comprehend why it is not possible to give up action, there must be clarity regarding the content and origins of action (13-18). How do specific actions occur? What does it all consist of? Understanding these issues helps in the ongoing process of discriminating matter from spirit, that we will not be identified with or attached to the vehicle of action, the process of action or the result of action; also called the knower, the knowing and the known or the doer, the doing and the thing done(18).

The five sources of action delineated by the *sankhyan* sages consist of matter and can be observed throughout the process of daily living. These are:

1. the body
2. the ego
3. the five organs of perception(eye, ear, nose tongue, skin)
4. the five organs of action (hands, feet, mouth, organs of elimination, sex organs)
5. the total *vasanas* of the person called the presiding deity, the elemental forces ruling one's life, or fate.

All action is performed through these five means. *There is no self that performs these actions.* The construct called self continuously changes as different thoughts, desires and actions get deposited in the total mind.

So even the fifth category of action called fate is interdependent with all the others, in order for an action to occur. The way we engage in the first four sources of action will determine our destiny. Likewise, the formless *Atma* is neither responsible for action nor performs action but rather just *is—is* the existing substratum that allows action to occur. When we "do" or feel or think anything, who is "doing," feeling or thinking? Is it the hand, the eye, the ego, one's fate? To live in this ongoing awareness must dispel our identification with the actor, as well as our emotional reactions, expectations, blame or disappointment.

The root of all emotional reaction is some form of attachment. With total separateness as part of one whole, there is no place for negativity. From this clear discrimination stems a knowing acceptance that is neither resignation nor cynicism. No longer justified in imposing our beliefs on ourselves or on others, we see the illusory nature of the root substance of all expectations and consequent emotions. The mind stops clinging. The bubble that we thought was solid vanishes. Nothing is left for us but *being*—no self-centeredness, no ill will, no impositions, simply acceptance—just *being*. The chains of entanglement formed through the age-old labyrinth network of these five sources of action lose their power to bind. With discriminative knowledge insight, they simply dissolve.

All action is to help us evolve into the state of actionlessness and still participate in *dharmic* action.

Action and the Gunas

To help our pure discrimination expand, Krishna differentiates the three-fold aspects of knowledge, action, reason, will and happiness(19-40). The *knowing* that links the eternal with the ephemeral and the part with the whole is *sattvic* knowledge. *The inner urge toward unity exemplifies purity.* The mind that naturally unifies is smooth and flowing—neither isolated nor agitated. Unlike the *rajasic* mind with its tendency to see diversity, criticize, and cause divisiveness, or the *tamasic* mind which, in its fragmentation and concreteness, sees only the effect and avoids the cause, the very process of perceiving in a *sattvic* manner serves to purify and unite one with Self Knowledge(21-2).

> When one sees Eternity in things that pass away and Infinity in finite things then one has pure knowledge. (18:20)

Educational systems that are dominated by *rajasic* thought, systematically alienate a child from his naturally unified mode of perception. Through this externally oriented conditioning toward divisive perception, criticism and argumentation, the conditions that lead to overemphasis of concrete thinking and competitiveness are being imposed upon students.

Ancient India recognized three basic approaches to debate: *jalpa, vitanda and vada.* In the first instance, "the attempt is to smother the opposition and its arguments by vehement criticism and bitter rejoinders, spoken with an overbearing arrogance in assertions." In the second method, the debater "mercilessly criticizes the arguments of the opposition, exposing by means fair or foul both the real and imaginary fallacies in their line of argument, the aim being to destroy the edifice." In the third, "the one arguing is trying to read the letter and the verse as directly as possible with the object of *coming directly to truth*, without indulging in any hair-splitting argument."[39] If a teacher places more value on *sattvic* truth seeking rather than on *rajasic* "winning," the student will learn something truly valuable.

Unless educational skills can be expressed within a more total context, they can lead to more harm than good—especially if the child adapts too well to their insensitive effect. *An all pervasive external orientation gives a person the message that his inner Self is not important.* This robs him of his intrinsic sense of self worth and self confidence, and causes him to base his identity on external factors and results—which can never be fully relied upon. The capacity to do, to think and to follow through can be more fruitfully accomplished within a framework that embodies humanness. There is an essential place for the universality of the higher in education. In this way, education can lead to true culture rather than merely to social structure.

When inner feeling, perceptual imagery, creativity, communication, camaraderie, humor, tolerance, good will, relaxation, giving and the welfare of the whole is *equally* valued alongside cognitive skills, goal orientation, and individual "success," the way is being prepared for a more unified person to emerge from the educational system. This will thereby lead to a more human and contented society. Both hemispheres of the brain as well as the globe need to be included. Without this balanced emphasis, we are training our children to become mechanistic and egocentric—*tamasic* and *rajasic*.

When one's individual actions are perceived as a sacred trust performed as service to creator and humanity, all personal desire for reward vanishes. With this *dharma,* no new *karma* is formed. *Work becomes worship.* This quality of *sattvic* action does not lead to the bondage of new conditioning (23-26).[40] But *rajasic* work performed for praise or result can induce feelings of false martyrdom or disappointment when the outcome is different from one's intention. And *tamasic* work performed in confusion, without regard for the consequences to oneself and others leads only to slavery.

Of the three types of doers(26-28), the pure *sattvic* doer, untouched by the poles of opposites, unidentified with victory or defeat is steady in his pursuit of Truth. Resting in inner peacefulness, he requires no selfish motivation to work—be it external paycheck or inner emotional expression. Whereas the *rajasic* person works for perceived personal gain, either material or emotional, the *tamasic* person tends to be confused and subsequently dishonest with himself and others, filled with ill-will and consequent discontent, which he spreads to others.

The three classifications of wisdom(29-32) correspond to one's level of discrimination. In order to be free, we must know what constitutes bondage. Without this higher intellect (*sattvic buddhi*), we cannot *differentiate* right action from impure action, what is to be feared from what is not to be feared, courage from cowardice. As long as the objects perceived by the senses, emotions and thoughts are viewed as having an intrinsic existence of their own, one's discrimination is clouded. The differentiation proceeding from *sattvic buddhi* combines feeling with thinking and receives intuitive knowledge of right action directly from the *Atman. To act from this inner knowing is wisdom.*

The classification of will or fortitude(33-35) corresponds to the degree of inner harmony of the mind, the *prana* and the senses. When one's thoughts and actions stem from the higher intellect(*buddhi*), the Self can be reflected clearly, and the will naturally falls under the jurisdiction of the Self. When one's steadiness is motivated by externals such as reward, praise or religious ritual, the will is *rajasic.* And when one is so caught in inertia, one does not strive to surrender his self-pity, laziness, attachment or depression, the will is *tamasic.*

By attempting to work through deep-seated emotional issues, we willingly descend into *tamas*. As long as some link with the golden thread of Atma is maintained, this willing descent is *surrender for purification*. It exudes a very different fragrance than perpetual automatic *tamas* and requires faith in the ongoing process, which leads to the ultimate unfoldment of the Self.

Without mobilizing steadiness toward our highest inner aim, we remain caught in the prevailing *guna* of our past conditioning. Pure *sattva* cannot be conditioned because it is our inner nature. Through imbibing the flavor of the *sattvic* environment, through selfless service and making efforts in meditation, we are engaging in the process of gradually connecting with our own inner essence.

In classifying the three qualities of happiness (36-39), Krishna teaches that *sattvic* happiness stems from the inner joy that results from spiritual work. When the mind becomes pure, one dwells in peaceful, loving joy, experiencing insights from the Self. Unlike the fleeting false power and sensuality of *rajasic* happiness, or the segmentation and emotional denial involved in *tamasic* happiness, the sattvic way might seem painful at first. But if we remain steadily attuned to the inner, we come to experience that the *layers of pain are changeable and temporary* (37). Our suffering will one day vanish. Through the combination of self-effort and grace, the conditioning from the *gunas* becomes transformed into *sattva* and pure *sattva*. To the degree this occurs, our pain vanishes.

The more sensitive we become, the more discriminating we become, the fewer projections we have both in an interpersonal sense and from the perspective of confusing the five-fold aspects of matter with Reality. When we see the *gunas* playing through every aspect of embodied life (40), from the addict to the sage, we begin to free our Self from the power of our personal conditioning, our collective conditioning and the total conditioning of *maya,* which is supported by the interplay of the three *gunas*.

Four Psychological Types and Dharma

In *slokas* 41-45, Krishna reviews four basic types of human beings, relevant to all cultures, all times and all places. The spiritual teacher, scholar, healer, contemplative thinker is called the *brahmin*; the warrior, ruler, statesman is called the *kshatriya*; the businessman, lawyer, farmer, banker, doctor is called the *vaisya*; and the servant, laborer, hired help is called the *sudra*. These types stem from an inner configuration of the *gunas*(see chapters 4 and 14). No one type is intrinsically better than another.[41] In an attitude of dedication and surrender, when one pursues the work and obligatory duty conducive to his type, this *in itself* prepares the way toward liberation. When each type follows his or her own *dharma*, happiness results, both for oneself and for the society. *When one type follows the dharma of another, confusion results*(47).

For example, if the President of the U.S. is more a businessman than a leader, he will end up spending the majority of his time wheeling and dealing for contributions and favors rather than leading with courage, heroism and honesty. If writers and artists seem forced to go commercial in order to eat, the entire society constricts its soul. These examples are a deadly result of the mixing of castes, feared by Arjuna in the first chapter. In every field, to confuse the quality of intellectual, creative and moral value with average norms or the technology of moneymaking demonstrates how our society is dominated by *tamasic* and *rajasic* values. This entrenches us in mediocrity.

The four types can be distinguished by their *dharmas*(41-44). Each person develops internally by following the inherent duty of his inner type. The *dharma* of the *brahmin* is to cultivate peacefulness, simplicity, self-control, forgiveness, knowledge, wisdom and faith, while bringing spirituality to the society. In order to embrace true humility and selflessness, he must let go of all pride of scholarship, comparisons and self-righteousness.

The task of the warrior statesman is to develop skill, fortitude, courage, generosity, protectiveness and leadership, while serving the society. This means he must let go of all pride of power, kingship and physical strength in order to evolve. He must also learn to distinguish between the duty of protectiveness and the emotional clannishness of attachment.

The duty of the businessmen is to bring wealth, prosperity and good will to the society. This means he must learn to let go of all the agitation, nervousness and anxiety of the marketplace, and perform his duties with competence and fairness. If the *vaisya* allows his dealings with money to intrude on his relationships with other people, he will end up treating others as objects to be manipulated and controlled. Through valuing relationship and living human values, the *vaisya* can truly evolve, while bringing good vibrations to the community and serving the society.

The duty of the hired worker is to perform his *dharma* with right effort in an honest and truthful manner that will best serve oneself, one's employer, family and society. To perform all action as selfless service is the gift of purification. We each need to imbibe the attitude of the perfect *sudra*.

It is not right to impose on the business person the expectation of philosophical introspection, or the intense urge to self-perfection found in the *brahmin*, or the bravery, leadership and generosity present in the warrior. Likewise, it would also be inappropriate to impose on the *brahmin* mentality an emphasis on the worries of material life. For simplicity alone is conducive to contemplation. Each of us has our own *dharma* with its various admixtures. Each can lead to liberation. The more *attuned* we are to these four types in our own nature, the less will we impose our own way on others, and the more we will respect the boundaries and limitations of ourselves and others. *This mutual respect leads to harmonious living.*

No one type is better than another. The only "sin" is to try to perform work that is not right for oneself(47). When we have a gift that makes us feel joyful, it would be wrong to ignore the talent because its not remunerative or we feel pushed into conformity by well meaning, materialistic parents or an anxious spouse. At least try and see if it is possible to follow your bliss. Never allow the "practical" mind and superego to take precedence over a deep inner calling. Following false duty leads to inner death!

When we work at what is right for us, our work becomes steadily joyous, a means of purification, not a temporary false high that later leads to suffering(45). "The type of a person's actions, the quality of his ego, the color of his knowledge, the texture of his understanding, the temper of his fortitude, and the brilliance of his happiness will determine his caste." (Swami Chinmayananda, THG, p.1054)

Work as Worship

Whatever we do in life can become our spiritual work if it is done in a spirit of dedication, performed in the consciousness of service—to oneself, to others and to the creator. With this in mind, all work becomes a means of self-perfection. All work becomes worship.

> A man attains perfection when his work is worship of God, from whom all things come and who is in all. (18:46)

But the work itself cannot embody perfection because as part of matter, it is performed by an imperfect being, within a partial and imperfect medium(48). Nonetheless, it still serves as the means toward perfection. Some native Americans consciously place mistakes in their works of art in acknowledgement that only the Great Spirit is perfect.

In order for our work to become worship, it must be in tune with our nature; it must be our *dharma*. One criteria used by the sages to help determine our true *svadharma* is based on the *vasanas* with which we are born(48). Whatever we bring into this world that is inherently part of our own temperament that has not been grafted on by others is our own *dharma*, which is to be followed. Whatever has been internalized through parents, relationships or society in this life, that is not our own *is to be rejected.* Thus, separating out our essential nature from external influences is a major part of spiritual work.

Separating Essence from Conditioning

Swami Chinmayandanda says:

> There are two forces that control, guide, define and determine our actions: 1) the impulses brought forth by the pressure of the mental temperaments within and 2) the pressure of the environment. One is to follow faithfully the subjective *vasanas*, even if they be defective. But at the same time, we must courageously renounce all the demands that the objective world makes upon us from without.
>
> The *vasanas* one is born with are to be lived through without ego and desire while the *vasana* creating atmosphere into which one

> is born should not be allowed to contain one's personality. Krishna is very carefully indicating that a spiritual seeker must constantly strive hard to stand apart from the shackling effects of the environment. According to the *Gita,* man is the master of circumstance. To the extent he comes to assert this mastery, to that extent he is evolved. (ibid., p.1067-8)

Because the child loves the parents, he unfortunately tends to pick up their qualities. From a psychological perspective, all internalizations from parents, caretakers, teachers and loved ones, which do not accord with our inner nature are excess baggage. All mores and standards of time and place into which we have been born are to be internally shed on the way to Truth. *But for the average person, these externals are mistaken for himself.* Concreteness, literalism and matter become confused with Reality. For the spiritual seeker on the other hand, there is *nothing external for him to cling to* except divine wisdom, which serves as the link to the Self.

Psychologists point toward the necessity of internalizing the good mother and the good father as an important part of ego development. If this enlivening factor called "God" could be connected with at a young age simply by *not being lost,* and if human beings could serve as true carriers of divine consciousness, would there be a need to "internalize" the "good" parental archetype? The parent would rightly serve as the link to the Self. The ever present fullness of one's Self would just *be*. One's Self would not be taken away. To allow a child to honor his Self is all that is required. It seems very simple. But in order to sidestep all extraneous expectations and superimpositions, the parents must *live* the Self, the environment must reflect the Self, by not imposing the unreal. This may well be one of the major differences between the formation of the eastern and western ego—the degree to which we collectively honor and aspire to live the Self.

When we *live* the Self, there is no need for the superimposition of internalization to occur. Or what gets internalized is closer to Reality. This is one definition of living in the Golden Age, *Sathya yuga*. The further away societal internalization is from *dharma*, the more degenerated is the inner *yuga* in which we dwell. Therefore, even in the *Kali yuga*, it is possible for us to live internally in the age of Rama(*Treta yuga*), provided our minds have been purified to that degree. And when our inner purity reaches the level of the Golden

Age, there is no difference between liberation and daily living. *Nirvana* and *samsara* are One.

Unity and Individuality

Each of us can be a genuinely *unique* part of the whole, if we do not allow our individuality to separate us from the whole. There is a world of difference between group consciousness and group conformity. The western ego tends to be a slave to the opposites of group conformity combined with alienated separateness, which passes for "individuality." The eastern ego on the other hand, tends to be much closer to the unconscious and the group and less aware of its separate emotions and aloneness. But no matter where the origin of our birth, in addition to societal conditioning, the configuration of our past lives will determine the hemispheric fluidity of the functioning ego, as well as our natural propensity for introversion and contemplation.

Each of us, whether born in the east or west, north or south is of one essence. Both easterner and westerner must come to shed his cultural conditioning and function out of this unity. This is the challenge of the Aquarian age—to shed the crust of ego while living the uniqueness of our individual dharma, through our connection with the Self, the individual, the group, the society and the totality.[42] To live out our individual uniqueness, without strengthening the supremacy of the ego or imposing our separate individuality, is to accept being a *loving instrument* of our individual dharma as His servant, student, friend, devotee, disciple or messenger on earth, in a very simple, humble and quiet way—by just being. This is the secret of true individuality without egoism.

If we are to participate internally and externally in the new age, the challenge is unity. Integration of feeling and thinking, male and female, dissolution and creation, right brain and left brain, individual and group, compassion and contemplation, service and self-containedness are the precursors. And for those spiritual students still living internally in the *Kali yuga*, the primary means to freedom is to act on in the world without a sense of doership in accordance with the character with which we are born.

> The more our mind is ventilated with consciousness divine, the less will the ego assert and therefore no defects can pollute our actions. If there be an influx of wrong *vasanas* within, the earlier we exhaust them through action, without any ego or egocentric desire of enjoying their fruits, the quicker shall the load of existing *vasanas* be lifted from our personality. (ibid., p.1068)

If what gets internalized from the environment is to be grafted off from the psyche how is adaptation possible? Can we live in the world without adopting its standards? Can one be *in* the world and not be *of* the world?

If we make use of the social environment as a *tool* to help us shed the rigidity of the egocentric sense of rights, doership, disappointment and the "way things should be done," then adaptation is helpful. On the other hand, if we adopt an external mode of functioning as our *own* way, this form of adaptation is harmful, as it adds the unnecessary weight of identification to the ego. For the westerner to internalize "western values" or feel he must follow a western spiritual path is not necessarily his *own* way but the *way of his external conditioning*. If we remain in the awareness that everything we do in life is but a role in which we happen to find ourselves, part of the giant play of the universe in which we are all participants, then our long time practice of participation through surrender will culminate in a life of renunciation (49).

Renunciation and Internalization

Krishna is careful to inform us again and again that it is not work that is to be renounced but egoistic desire; the mental and emotional glue that binds us to people and things, which causes us to believe we are dependent on something external, something other than the joy of the Self for our happiness(48).

Jesus understood very well the power of internalizing parental and societal influences, which prevent a person from living his inner nature, his true Self:

> I speak that which I have seen with my Father and ye do that which ye have seen with your father." (John, 8:38)
>
> "Ye are of your father, the devil and the lusts of your father ye will do. He was a murderer from the beginning and abode not in truth because there is no truth in him. When he speaketh a lie, he speaketh of his own; for he is liar and the father of it. (8:44)

Jesus is speaking these words not to judge but to teach. The murder committed by the father is not necessarily literal but symbolic. A symbolic murder is equally as potent as a physical murder from the viewpoint of Truth. When we disregard Truth, we live a lie. *When we confuse the five-fold aspect of the material world with Reality we live a lie.* When the ego, with its selfish and conditioned ways, abrogates Truth unto itself, the *death of the spirit* occurs. The perception of Truth dies to that person. And when a father imposes too much conditioned life on a child, he freezes the child's soul by preventing him from relating to Truth, from imbibing Truth, from being Truth.

In the lust of attachment, the father allows little space for the child to unfold. By attempting to control, he imposes his egocentric will and society's external values. Through alienating him from that which is of *true* value, he kills the inner life of the child. Out of denial, fear, greed, egoism or simply ignorance, the father trains the child to live on the surface of things and never experience his own depth. He passes on his fear of feeling, reflection and inner searching. This places a thick wall around one's own Self, the source of life and lasting happiness. Since the child loves the father, he identifies with his actions and beliefs. There are however, many children of *asuric* parents who become seekers of Truth, and one day discover their expansive divine inheritance.

In the *Mahabharata,* Krishna acknowledges that Duryodhana was not to blame for his greed and jealousy. It was his father, the blind king Dhritarashtra who instilled in his son his own unfulfilled ambition and greed. Even the holy power of his mother Gandhari could not offset the boy's natural masculine identification with the beliefs and faults of his father. Due to psychological blindness, Dhritarashtra functioned primarily through the defense mechanism of denial. As a result, he fell under the sway of his evil brother-in-law Shakuni, who used him as a pawn to destroy the dynasty. If Dhritarashtra could have admitted that he didn't know and *turned to a wiser person for help*, as opposed to someone who told him what he wanted to hear, then death and destruction could have been avoided. When we stop being open to discussion with those who are capable of understanding and helping, then we are living under the spell of denial and the illusion of control. Unintentionally, we perpetrate evil.

In this way, we each serve to murder the life of the child, both within our own self and within our children. The antidote in this *Kali yuga* is to acknowledge the rightful place for father learning and Father learning—through discriminating between societal values and eternal values; through aligning and integrating eternal human values with our daily living in society. In other ages, societal values were a reflection of human values. Today they are not. To the extent this is recognized, much personal danger and suffering can be averted. "Render unto Caesar that which is Caesar's and unto God that which is God's."

The practice of surrender helps us develop detachment and thereby respect the inner autonomy of the child. The person with loving detachment offers his inner and outer child the opportunity for life—to develop in accordance with his own individual nature. This leads to Truth. And the culmination of practicing surrender through daily living is renunciation (*sannyasa*)(49). Through working in this egoless state, without desire, without identification, we come to move and live and act without action, one with the eternal, one with Truth. Through fulfilling our calling in life, we purge the personality of the crust of its extraneous influences, that we might one day enter the actionless state and continuously live our inherent perfection.

Becoming One with Brahman

Krishna then reviews the prerequisites for Self realization and the process of meditation(50-58). When the majority of *vasanas* have been purged, the body, emotions and intellect are balanced and free from the pull of the opposites. For this state of steady dispassion to be ongoing, the senses, emotions and mind must come under the natural control of the higher intellect. Then when we no longer perceive ourselves primarily as separate entities, we cannot experience hatred, greed, attachment, pride or anger, as these emotions arise from the separate ego. *We become fit to be one with the totality;* we perceive the light within ourselves and others as one light(54-5).

The light of love that illumines all creation is experienced as the foundation of life, whether one is working, eating, sitting, walking or talking. Through living this love, wholly permeable, wholly equal, we discover our true home—an ongoing inner space of peace and contentment that permeates everything no matter what(58). The refuge that begins as emotional need or intellectual greed becomes a *way of being*. Krishna promises:

> By love he knows me in truth, who I am and what I am. And when he knows me in truth, he enters into my Being.
>
> In whatever work he does he can take refuge in me and he attains then by my grace the imperishable home of eternity.
>
> Offer in thy heart all thy works to me and see me as the end of thy love; take refuge in the *yoga* of reason and ever rest thy soul in me.
>
> If thy soul finds rest in me, thou shalt overcome all dangers by my grace, but if thy thoughts are on thyself and thou wilt not listen, thou shalt perish. (18:55-58)

In His love for us, Krishna is revealing how we can value our inner Self and *live.* Without this valuing, our real Self is inaccessible and *we die.*

It is impossible to sidestep one's *karma* in life(59). Even if we try to escape, years later, when the opportune conditions to work it through no longer exist, our inner psychological nature will still express its tendencies. Just as Arjuna cannot escape from fighting the battle of *Dharmakshetra*, we too cannot escape from our inner tendencies without engaging them in their rightful field of expression, that they might one day be worked through and left behind.

The love of God and Goddess, as total omnipresent consciousness energy, offers us this opportunity through the divine decree of *karma.* Our suffering one day forces us to the point where the ancient archetype lurks—be it in the form of the instinctual level of the animal realm, or the culmination of long-term generational issues called the "sins of the fathers," as in the *Mahabharata*, or in the lingering negative thought-forms of a group, society or nation—that our primordial conditioning might be confronted, battled with and finally purged. But Ramakrishna reminds us:

> To be ever engaged in *karma* is not the goal of life. It is only a means to attain Godhood. Do not mistake the means for the end. The road to a town is not itself the town.

The Victory of Love

One cannot reach this space of ongoing love without fully participating in one's role in the battle of life with detachment, thereby rewriting the script of one's life; righting past wrongs, purifying past emotions and nullifying past *karma*. To connect with the God force behind all people, places, actions and things pervading all times in each moment is to open one's heart to the action of His grace(61-2). *This is the only victory.* It matters little the location of the field or the nature of our specific tasks or even the seemingly concrete outcomes. What matters is that in accepting the challenge of our individual lives, our tasks be performed in the ongoing awareness connection with the light from which we are all created, which continues through us, behind us, above us and around us. Through this awareness we participate in eternity. *Eternity becomes our home.* And Krishna promises His grace of supreme peace.

> God dwells in the heart of all beings, Arjuna. Thy God dwells in thy heart and His power of wonder moves all things—puppets in a play of shadows—whirling them onwards in the stream of time. Go to Him for thy salvation with all thy soul, victorious man. By His grace thou shalt obtain the peace supreme, thy home of Eternity. (18:61-2)

Swami Chinmayananda says:

> To the extent we identify ourselves with Him, His light and power become ours. And they are called His grace. Ere long, as a result of this grace accumulated within, through integration of the personality and constant surrender of the ego, the individual shall obtain supreme peace, the eternal resting place.

> Without bringing all levels of our being and all facets of our personality into our love for Him, we cannot drown our finite ego sense into the lap of the infinite Lord. Thus, a true devotee must reorient his being and surrender himself as a willing vehicle of His expression. Then all delusions end; the mortal comes to live fully the state of Immortality, of Godhood. (THG, p.1094)

The essence of the *Gita* is the call to surrender; a surrender that ultimately melts all extraneousness, smoothes all roughness, polishes all dullness, be it in the aloneness of the forest or the tumult of the marketplace; a surrender that practices its craft by rubbing shoulders with others in loving contact and hating contact, in the agitation of movement or in the enclave of silence; a surrender that sees equality permeating every socioeconomic class, every level of mind, including the crudest action or the kindest gesture; that whatever we do, wherever we be will be known as His place, which is also our place; or His act that is also our act. And when the attention awareness becomes so focused that His presence ever continues to make itself known, the desire to serve will be experienced as love; love without intention, love without words, pure love—not because we know it is right action or *dharma*, not because we long for merit or liberation, not even because our conscience or inner voice leads us there. Rather, out of love alone we come to serve and out of love alone we come to *be* served. *Love itself becomes the embodiment of surrender.*

There is no forest. There is no city. His temple of the universe has many landscapes, many rooms, many people, many creatures, many actions. And that which unites them all, the subtlest all pervading part of His body, the only substratum is the micro-atom of creation called love.

Thus the realized soul serves humanity not as service but as breathing; not as worship but as being; not as knowing but as awareness bliss. He does not give up liberation; it is the *concept* of liberation held only by the unliberated that is to be renounced. For the realized soul serves humanity however and wherever His love takes him. And those of us deeply aspiring toward realization are compelled to follow.

> It is possible for the *jivatman*(individual self) to merge in the *Paramatman*. He can then state, "I and my Lord are one." ...It is in

this way that Ishvara claims the ardent devotee as His own. He first reveals His attributes and glories to the devotee and then absorbs him in union. (Ramakrishna)

The Choice of Surrender

In the true spirit of respect for the autonomy of the individual, Krishna asks Arjuna to reflect deeply upon what he has heard and do what he chooses(63). Freedom of thought, speech and action is the only way. Krishna is neither salesman nor missionary. Out of love for his friend and humanity, He relates this secret Truth to Arjuna. Only if it feels right to his body, heart and intellect is he to surrender wholeheartedly, to the best of his ability. Likewise, when each of us knows deep down what is right for us, only then does it behoove us to practice and to follow. The gradual unfoldment of the process combined with our deepening openness will lead us to a point of conscious decision that is His grace alone.

> Give thy mind to me; give me thy heart, thy sacrifice and thy adoration. This is my word of promise. Thy shalt in truth come to me for thou art dear to me."
>
> Abandoning all *dharmas* come to me for thy salvation. I will make thee free from the bondage of sins. Grieve no more. (18:65-6)

When the sole motivation for action is love, all external duty can be surrendered. Love becomes the prime motivator, the prime mover. The deepest internal *dharma* called loving consciousness, naturally serves as the prime basis for our actions. This loving consciousness is not mediated through body, emotion or intellect. *It just is*. Through love we come to know Truth and live it.[43]

Now when Arjuna speaks(73) he knows with total certainty that all his doubts have disappeared forever. After losing the memory of his finite self, he has regained remembrance of his eternal Self, his original pristine awareness (*Atmabodh*). Through the process of surrendering to the Lord, he has been lifted up step by step until he reaches a space where he becomes a total instrument for performing God's will on earth. This is the journey of the spiritual seeker.

> The tadpole can live both in water and on land after it sheds its tail. The tail of ignorance drops off from man when he gets enlightened in Brahma *jnana*(knowledge of the transcendent God). He then becomes a *jivanmukta*—liberated soul. He simultaneously lives in the world and rests in *Brahman*. (Ramakrishna)

Scripture as the Word of God

Sanjaya's final words verify that he receives the *yoga* of the *Gita* directly from Krishna Himself(75). In the same way, we too can receive the *Gita* as *ultimate yoga* directly from the scriptures to our innermost Self. Otherwise, it is experienced as beautiful literature, logical theory or a series of verbal teachings and exercises. For any scripture to serve as divine word, it cannot be limited by interpretation, but must be received individually from *Paramatman*. When this happens, the gifts of intuitive understanding and wisdom gradually accrue, thereby uplifting the finite individuality to merge in the totality. It is hoped that the present work will aid each reader to forge a direct, personal, intuitive connection with the divine energy of the *Gita*.

To help us win the ultimate victory of liberation, Sri Sathya Sai Baba says:

> Understand the *Gita* well and observing its injunctions, establish yourself in the attitude of action without desire(*nishkama karma*). Do all duties as acts of worship. That is the sole task. Leave the rest to Him: the fruit, the consequence, the result. Then you receive the grace of God and your life on earth is sanctified and becomes worthwhile. (*Gita Vahini,* p.228)

Thus, the eighteenth discourse reveals the *yoga* of surrender, which culminates in the victory of Love, the essence of liberation.

Eternal Dharma

streaming forth into the cosmos
from the mind-born children of the creator
love in the total universe freely flowing
fully accessible beyond time and place
forever and ever

transcending the void
the impenetrable suction of a thousand black holes
beyond limits beyond relativity beyond subjectivity
this dharma was molded with creation
in the causeless first cause ever continuous

it is not separate from creation
it withstands destruction
it upholds the universe

the cornerstone of creation
this sanathana dharma
without which the cosmos would collapse
until it is again re-formed
inherent in the divine plan forever and ever

what force can possibly withstand conditioning?
what energy can simply allow a space
for all too malleable man
to discover his nature
amidst the confusion of whirlwinds?

how can the tiny soul
forge a link with the whole?
(in time and space while
transcending time and space)

the secret rests in connecting with dharma
infusing its essence with our essence
its breath with our breath
its soul with our soul everlasting

only then can dharmas be transcended

the mind-born rishis and divine avatars
send unfathomable love to all beings
through the everliving form
of sanathana dharma

VERSES FROM THE BHAGAVAD GITA

One

Arjuna says: And I see forebodings of evil, O Krishna. I do not foresee any good in killing our own relatives in the sacrifice of battle. 1:31

♦

Two

In my confusion I feel desolation. In my self-pity, I see not the way of *dharma*. I am your disciple; I take refuge in you. Teach me what is right for me. 2:7

Krishna says: The unreal has no being; the Real has no non-being. This Truth has been seen by those who experience the essence. 2:16

You have the right to work only, but not for the results of work. Do not let your motivation for action be influenced by reward, and do not become attached to inaction. 2:47

Perform work in this world Arjuna, as a man established within himself—without selfish attachments, and alike in success and defeat. For *yoga* is perfect evenness of mind. 2:48 (EE)

When a person attains peace, all suffering caused by the unbalanced mind ceases. And the mind remains firmly fixed in the wisdom of the Self. 2:65

♦

Three

A person does not reach the actionless state by not working; nor does he attain perfection by mere renunciation. 3:4

All actions are performed by the qualities of nature, the three *gunas*. But one whose mind is deluded by egoism thinks, "I am the doer." 3:27

Offer all your work to me with your mind on the supreme Self. Free from vain hopes and selfish thoughts, without mental agitation, fight your battle. 3:30

And perform your duty, even if it be humble rather than another's, even if it be great. To die in one's duty is life: to live in another's is death. 3:35

♦

Four

Whenever there is a decay of *dharma* and unrighteousness increases, then I am born as a human being. 4:7

He who knows my birth as God and who knows my sacrifice, when he leaves his mortal body, goes no more from death to death, for he in truth comes to me. (JM)

Freed from attachment, fear and anger, absorbed in me, purified by the fire of Knowledge, many have attained my Being. 4:9-10 (SwC)

He who sees inaction in action and action in inaction is wise among men. He is a true *yogi* and in all his works finds peace. 4:18

He who has given up attachment to the fruits of work, who is ever content, who does not depend upon anything, though engaged in action, he does not do anything. 4:20

Content with whatever comes, free from the pairs of opposites, free from malice, balanced in success and failure, though acting, he is not bound. 4:22

O Arjuna. He who makes pure his works by *yoga*, whose doubts are cleared by direct Knowledge, and who is established in the Self, is free from the bondage of ego-centered work. 4:41

♦

Five

Just as a lotus leaf remains clean and dry in water, he who offers all his actions to the highest, without a trace of attachment, is not tainted by evil. 5:10

The person of unity, harmonized in *yoga*, surrenders the reward of his work and thus attains final peace. The person of disharmony, ruled by desire, is attached to his reward and remains in bondage. 5:12

One who sees the Absolute abides in *Brahman*. His intellect is steady; gone is his delusion. When pleasure comes he is not shaken; when pain comes he is not depressed. 5:20

With conflict healed and sins destroyed, with mind disciplined and joyfully participating in the welfare of all beings, one becomes a *rishi*, a sage, and attains Absolute freedom, *moksha*. 5:25

♦

Six

For the person aspiring to ascend to *yoga*, union with Self, dedicated action is said to be the means. When he has attained Self awareness, abiding in peaceful serenity is the means. 6:3

Let a man lift himself by his own Self alone; and let him not lower himself. For this Self alone is the friend of oneself, and this Self is the enemy of oneself. 6:5 (SwC)

The person who has won victory over the mind is filled with peace and experiences only the Self. In heat or cold, in pleasure or pain, in honor or disgrace, he is ever in Him. 6:7

In deep solitude, day after day, let the practitioner keep the mind fixed in steady concentration, hoping for nothing, desiring nothing. 6:10

And when he sees me in all and he sees all in me, then I never leave him and he never leaves me. 6:30 (JM)

♦

Seven

I shall pass on to you this Knowledge combined with direct experience. When this is known in full, there is nothing more to be known. 7:2

O Arjuna. In this vast universe there is no other higher than me. All this is strung on me as clusters of gems on a string. 7:7

Know me O Arjuna as the eternal seed in all beings. I am the intelligence of the intelligent, the radiance of the beautiful. 7:10

And know that the three qualities of the soul come from me—peaceful light, restless life and lifeless darkness. But I am not in them; they are in me. 7:12

O Arjuna. By the delusion of the pairs of opposites—attraction and aversion, like and dislike, desire and hatred—all beings are subject to illusion in the world. 7:27

Those who take refuge in me, striving for liberation from old age and death, come to know Brahman, the Self, and the nature of action. 7:29

♦

Eight

At the time of death, he who leaves his body remembering me only attains my Being. There is no doubt about this. 8:5

Therefore, remember me at all times. Remember me and fight. Surrendering your mind and intellect to me, you shall in truth come to me. 8:7

There is a reward that comes from studying the *Veda*, or from sacrifice, *yajna*, or from leading a life of austerity, *tapas*, or from giving, *dana*. But the *yogi* who knows the truth of the two paths of light and darkness attains a greater reward—the Supreme state, his everlasting home. 8:28

♦

Nine

All this world is pervaded by me in my unmanifest form. All beings exist in me but I do not dwell in them. (SwC)

And in truth, they do not exist in me. Behold my divine *yoga*: I am the source of all beings, I support them all. Yet I am not rooted in them. 9:4-5

To those who worship me alone thinking of no other, ever united with me, I provide what they need(*yoga*), and preserve what they already have(*kshema*). 9:22

Whatever you do or eat or give or sacrifice, let it be an offering to me. And whatever you suffer, suffer it for me. 9:27 (JM)

I am the same toward all beings; to me no one is hateful or dear. But those who worship me with devotion are in me and I am also in them. 9:29

♦

Ten

He who knows me as birthless, without a beginning, the Lord of all worlds, this mortal is free from delusion and sin. 10:3

He who knows in essence the manifold manifestations of my glory and power, becomes harmonized in steady *yoga* and unites with me. There is no doubt about this. 10:7

To those ever steadfast in worshipping me with their love, I give the *yoga* of discrimination, *buddhi yoga*; and with this they realize me. 10:10

I am the beginning, the middle and the end of all creation. Among sciences, I am knowledge of the Soul. Of the many paths of reason, I am the one that leads to Truth. 10:32

O Arjuna. I am the seed of all beings. No being—either animate or inanimate, that moves or moves not—can ever exist without me. 10:39

♦

Eleven

Arjuna says: If you deem it possible for me to see your cosmic form, O Lord of *yoga*, then please show me your imperishable Self. 11:4

I see thee without beginning, middle or end—thy boundless power, innumerable arms, and thine eyes as the sun and the moon. And I see thy face as a sacred fire that gives light and life to the entire universe, in the splendor of a vast offering. 11:19 (JM)

Krishna says: Arise and win your glory. Conquer the enemies and enjoy the kingdom. They have already been slain by me. Be merely my instrument, O Arjuna! 11:33

Arjuna says: Thou God from the beginning, God in man since man was. Thou treasure supreme of this vast universe. Thou the One to be known and the Knower, the final resting place. Thou infinite presence in whom all things are. 11:38 (JM)

♦

Twelve

Krishna says: Fix your mind on me alone; let your thoughts dwell in me. Then you will surely live in me. 12:8

Knowledge is better than mechanical practice; meditation is better than mere knowledge. But higher than meditation is surrender in love of the fruit of one's actions, for with surrender comes peace. 12:12

The person whose love is equal for his friends or his enemies, who is the same in honor or disgrace, who is not bothered by heat and cold or pleasure and pain, who is free from the chains of attachment, and who is devoted to me—he my devotee is dear to me. 12:18

♦

Thirteen

Know me as the Knower in all the fields of my creation. To know the field and the Knower of the field is true Knowledge. 13:3

A constant yearning to know the inner Spirit and experience the Self ends in true Knowledge. To seek anything else is ignorance. 13:12

That *Brahman* is undivided and yet exists in beings as if divided. That *Brahman* is to be known as the supporter of all, the creator and the destroyer. 13:17

When one sees the Self in himself dwelling equally in all beings, he destroys not the Self by the self, he hurts not himself by hurting others. Then he attains the highest. 13:29

♦

Fourteen

Whatever forms are born come from the womb of Brahma, the great creator of nature. And I am the seed-giving father.

Purity, activity, and inertia—*sattva, rajas*, and *tamas*—are the three qualities of nature that seemingly limit the imperishable Self to a limited experience in the body. 14:4-5

Work done in *sattva* brings purity, work done in *rajas* brings suffering, and work done in *tamas* bears the fruit of ignorance. 14:16

When one sees no doer other than the *gunas* and knows that which is higher than the *gunas*, he comes into my Being. 14:19

♦

Fifteen

The real form of the tree of *samsara* is not perceived in the world—neither its beginning and end, nor its existence. Cut down this firmly rooted tree with the strong axe of nonattachment. Then seek sole refuge in that primeval *Purusha*, where there is no return to the projections streaming forth from the world of change. 15:3-4

Striving with determination, true seekers come to see the Self within. But those whose minds remain impure and thoughtless never see. 15:11

As I transcend the perishable and am higher than the imperishable, therefore I am called the supreme Spirit, *Purushottamah*, in the world and in the *Veda*. 15:18

♦

Sixteen

Fearlessness, purity of heart, steadfastness in the *yoga* of Knowledge, giving, self-harmony, conscious sacrifice, study of scriptures and straightforwardness…16:1

The divine nature leads to liberation; the demonic qualities lead to bondage. Do not grieve, O Arjuna. You were born to embody the qualities of goodness. 16:5

Led astray by lack of knowledge, entangled in the net of delusion, deeply attached to the pleasures of their cravings, they fall into a foul hell. 16:16

There are three gates to hell that destroy the soul—attachment, rage and greed. Therefore, one must let go of these three.

A person who is liberated from these three doors of darkness practices what benefits his soul. Thus he attains the Supreme goal. 16:21-22

♦

Seventeen

The faith of each person accords with his nature, O Arjuna. Faith is the essence of a person. As his faith is, so he is. 17:3

This is the discipline of speech: words that cause no excitable reactions in others, words that are truthful, beneficial, with good will, and the study of sacred texts.

This is the discipline of mind: calmness of mind, good-heartedness, silence, self-control, purity of thought and feeling. 17:15-16

The threefold discipline of body, speech and mind is called pure, *sattvic*, when performed with the highest faith, with no desire for reward, and with single-minded devotion. 17:17

Work performed without faith is *asat*, is nothing. Acts of sacrifice, giving or self-discipline done without faith produce no positive effect, both in this world and in the world to come. 17:28

♦

Eighteen

The sages understand renunciation, *sannyasa*, as refraining from all egocentric action motivated by desire. The learned understand renunciation, *tyaga*, as abandoning focus on the results of an action. 18:2

He who is free from the egoistic idea, "I am the doer," whose mind is free from ill will, even if he kills all these beings, he kills them not and he is free. 18:17

When one sees eternity in things that pass away and infinity in finite things, then one has pure knowledge. 18:20 (JM)

A person should not abandon the work born of his nature—even if it is imperfect. For all undertakings are enveloped by imperfection, as fire by smoke. 18:48

Make every act an offering to me; regard me as your only protector. Make every thought an offering to me; meditate on me always. (EE)

Fixing your mind on me, you will overcome all obstacles by my grace. But if from egoism and self-will you do not hear me, nothing will help you. 18:57-58

Abandoning all *dharmas* (reliance on external structures for support), take refuge in me alone. I will liberate you from all sin. Do not grieve. 18:66

ॐ

These verses were compiled from translations by Swami Chinmayananda, Eknath Easwaran, Juan Mascaro and Swami Vidyaprakashananda.

ADDENDUM ONE
BACKGROUND STORY AND CHARACTERS

The *Bhagavad Gita* is part of the *Mahabharata*, an eighteen-volume epic about the history of mankind. It was compiled by a *rishi* named Vyasa, who is credited with writing many important ancient texts. Indian holy men say the war mentioned in the *Mahabharata* occurred over five thousand years ago at the place called Kurukshetra, several hours northwest of Delhi. Western scholars attribute the *Gita* to more recent origins, anywhere from 1200 to 300 BC. What really matters, however, is that the work is timeless—as relevant today as it was thousands of years ago.

It tells the story of a time in history somewhat similar to our own; when human values were disintegrating and greed, anger and egocentricity were increasing in the human heart. This was a time when the end of an era was near, and destruction was somehow needed, that something new could be built.

In India, it is believed that when mankind is at its lowest point, in need of guidance and upliftment, God incarnates in human form to help humanity out of its rut and rekindle genuinely human qualities, such as love and compassion in the hearts of men and women. This incarnation is called an *avatar*, a divine descent. In Buddhism, the one who descends to help humanity is called a *boddhisattva*. Rama, Krishna, Buddha and Christ are considered major *avatars*. There are many *avatars* in the history of India, both animal and human; saviors and teachers with wisdom, compassion, and consciousness. But there are very few full *avatars*; persons who possess the sixteen full powers of God.[44] Krishna is considered such a person.

Ever since his birth, Krishna exhibited divine powers, especially the power of love that mostly everyone experienced in his presence. He had the beautiful capacity of playfulness, of bringing bliss to the hearts and minds of all good people who came near him. As a mischievous child, he is forever engaged in loving pranks or feats of impossible valor. At any age, he is a true friend to those who seek his friendship and love. But to those who degrade him or his teachings, he could appear ruthless. Yet his punishments are never out of spite, but to help save the demonic ones from their negative tendencies.

Even the evil Kamsa, the uncle of Krishna who relentlessly plotted the boy's death ever since his birth, dies with a smile on his face at the hands of young Krishna. The boundless love of Krishna is equal for both his friends and his foes. And those who remember Krishna go to Krishna, whether their minds are connected to Him in love or in hatred.

The five Pandavas are devoted to Krishna, especially Arjuna, who is his best friend and brother-in-law. Despite the fact that Arjuna was close to Krishna for so many years, Krishna never offered him the teaching of the *Gita* until he was in such need that he could receive it. In order to receive the teachings, he had to *surrender to Krishna,* take refuge in Krishna. He had to view Krishna not in the context of personal relationship, such as friend to friend or brother to brother but as one who supersedes the relativity of all relationship and *includes* all relationship. He had to view Krishna as his sole refuge, mentor and savior. Only then could he receive the teachings.

Although the hero Arjuna was an ordinary person like you and me, he was also special like you and me. He grew up under difficult circumstances. His father, King Pandu, head of the Pandava clan died when he and his four brothers were children, so they were all brought up in the palace of his blind uncle Dhritarashtra, who had assumed kingship. Because Dhritarashtra was blind, his wife also decided to wear a blindfold, a situation not uncommon today, when one spouse sometimes stops seeing or thinking for himself and seems to take on the views of the other, right or wrong. Primarily, Dhritarashtra was blind to the envy and greed of his own son Duryodhana. The father was unable to notice these qualities in his son because he had never been able to acknowledge his own negative qualities. Unknowingly, he conditioned Duryodhana to live in anger and jealousy. He denied a lot and was unreflective. He wavered between wanting to be fair and following the advice of an evil relative, Shakuni, who was secretly plotting the downfall of the dynasty. Because he was too weak to notice his own jealousy and selfishness, he was ensnared by evil suggestions. This manipulative advice reinforced his attachment to his own son Duryodhana, as he was driven to live out his unfulfilled ambitions through his son.

From the time they were children growing up in same palace, Duryodhana hated his cousins. Although the Pandavas were the rightful heirs to the throne, Duryodhana, in his greed for kingship, tried unsuccessfully to kill them. When the plot failed, then Dhritarashtra allotted them a barren kingdom in the desert far away. Because of their just rulership, this desolate kingdom bloomed and prospered. Sages flocked there and the inhabitants were happy. Duryodhana became jealous. Through a crooked game of dice, the Pandavas lost everything and were sent into exile for thirteen years. Dhritarashtra could have intervened and changed the course of events but was encouraged by his son to do nothing. He always capitulated to the wishes of his son.

When their exile ended, diplomatic attempts were made by Krishna to settle the feud. But greedy Duryodhana was unyielding. He wanted everything for himself and nothing for the Pandavas. Under the circumstances, war was inevitable. The two cousins went to Krishna for his blessing. He offered them two possibilities: all his armies at their disposal, as Krishna was also a king of neighboring Mathura, or himself driving the chariot. Arjuna was granted first choice. He opted for Krishna as his charioteer. Duryodhana gladly chose Krishna's armies. Now Arjuna was outnumbered by many thousands of men, weapons and elephants, eleven phalanxes to seven, but having Krishna as his driver was more meaningful than all the combat troops and powerful weapons in the world.

The symbolic meaning of the characters can be derived through knowledge of their Sanskrit roots,[45] as well as their past actions. Sanjaya is the minister of the blind king Dhritarashtra. The author Vyasa offered to give Dhritarashtra his sight to enable him to view the battle. The king refused; probably because something inside knew it would be too painful to witness the slaughter of all his sons. He also must have known history would say all this carnage and devastation could have been avoided had he only acted with fairness. But Dhritarashtra did accept the offer to have Sanjaya granted the inner vision to report everything that occurs on the battlefield—all speech, thoughts, actions and outcomes. As the enlightened knower, it is Sanjaya who relates the story of the *Gita*. Thus, Sanjaya symbolizes the voice of conscience within each of us, that inner aspect which knows Truth unequivocally. He then relates this Truth to the ego, who is given the opportunity to act on it. But as the king, or ego is blinded by his attachment, he is unable to receive Truth. When our inherent

Intelligence is covered by ignorance of Reality(*maya*) we cannot hear or see what is right. Although Dhritarashtra witnesses the teachings of Krishna along with Arjuna and Sanjaya, he is unable to benefit from them or put them into practice.

The five Pandava Princes were fathered by gods and represent different aspects of the five elements. Their lives reveal how matter can be harnessed to serve the forces of good. They each share one wife Draupadi, who is the embodiment of *dharma*. And they even manage to share her without jealousy or conflict! Thus they are a living example of how the five senses, ruled by the five elements, can be mobilized to work together in harmony as one balanced whole.

The one-hundred Kauravas headed by Duryodhana were fathered by blindness and represent devotion to egoistic power and personal desire. As they have little regard for the laws of right action, and function primarily out of self-centered passion and acquisition, nature decrees their destruction.

Drona was the teacher of martial arts to both the Pandavas and the Kauravas. His favorite is Arjuna. Although he is noble, intelligent and powerful, he is unable to side with the Pandavas. In his heart he knows they are just, but he is unable to think of leaving the Kauravas, as they supported him for so many years. At one bitter stage in his life, Drona knew poverty. This forced him to forsake his true *brahmin* upbringing to make his living as a warrior. Thus, Drona stands for the power of habit and past tendencies, the old order within, which prevents us from relating to the present as it is, unclouded by mental conditioning and emotional baggage.

Bhishma is the granduncle of both the Kauravas and Pandavas. He is a very great warrior-*yogi* and is ultra knowledgeable and just. He has the power of death under his command. But blind attachment to his father clouds his discrimination.

His mother is goddess Ganga. She brought him up in heaven until his teenage years, when he returned to earth to live with his father. The reunion with his absent father, King Santanu was intense, joyful and loving. Bhishma was a devoted son and a courageous warrior. But his father was unhappy and lovesick. So Bhishma took a "terrible vow" to sacrifice marriage and throne, that King Santanu could marry Satyavati and her own son would be king. Because he promised his father he would always support the throne of Hastinapura, he feels compelled to side with Duryodhana, in spite of the heartwrenching conflict that ensues. Thus, Bhishma represents an aspect of oneself that knows, and has impeccable strength and integrity, but reinforces problems because of the inner power of familial love and loyalty. An unnecessary and misguided sense of duty often clouds discrimination and provokes attachment. But in the end, Bhishma's awesome greatness is fully redeemed.

Through viewing each character in this way, we are led to expose and reflect upon the army of inner enemies that hinder us, as well as the inner allies that support us throughout our own life's journey toward liberation.

ADDENDUM TWO
PSYCHOTHERAPY AND SPIRITUALITY

The *Bhagavad Gita* presents guidelines for spiritual practice that can lead to total healing and the end of suffering. To become what we truly are—complete, whole and blissful—is to live out our inner radiance, which is the selfless Self. Through practice, seeing, and insight, obstacles are removed. Remembrance of our true nature returns. While the process leads us to the goal, it also *is* the goal.

Developing an integrated spiritual life occurs in stages. The first can be called the literal, tangible level where we accept what the mind and senses tell us, as real. At this stage, the life force gets projected onto externals such as money, material things, recognition and social life as entertainment. This limited way of being can be called the "way of the world" and its focus is on the gross body. The body is of great value, like a dormant seed waiting to sprout.

The second stage can be called the way of questioning, or the psychological, philosophical orientation where we begin to go within toward feelings, inner reflection, motivation, creativity, dreams and imagination. Here the life force becomes experienced within at both the personal and archetypal plane. The inner subjectivity of life is most valued and genuine relationships become more important than social life. The focus is primarily on the subtle body, but through experiencing deeper layers of the psyche, the causal body can also be included. When we enter the gate of this level, the seed has begun to sprout. As we encounter deeper archetypal places, a bridge from the psychological to the spiritual is formed. The forces of energy called gods and goddesses support us along the way. And when we pass through the final gate of this inner space, beautiful wonder buds are everywhere.

The third stage can be called the spiritual. Through our struggles, meditation, service and seeing, deeper purification proceeds. Momentary sparks of joy and unification lead us toward inner steadiness and mental concentration, ever linking the mind to universal energy. Gradually, devotion to Truth comes to dominate every aspect of our lives. And mind melts away without losing its capacity. At the culmination of this level, there are no more projections, no more reflections—everything is as is. Then the sages say, all life, all matter, all happenings all feelings, all beings, one's Self are experienced as part of One whole, ever complete. Now the focus is now—totality, unity, love, consciousness, *Brahman*, both at the formless and/or form level. The thousand petalled lotus is open.

One need not go through the second step of the psychological philosophical stage in order to embrace one's own spiritual nature. We can be plucked out of the mud at any time in accordance with our inner tendencies. But there can be a definite place for psychotherapy in the purification process. It must be acknowledged however, that although there are areas of overlap, therapy and spiritual work are *not* synonymous. For spiritual work originates from a *higher* level. Therapies with a spiritual orientation can serve only as a prelude and a link.

Therefore, in this age of melange and questionable alliances, the therapist should not take on the role of spiritual teacher. Spirituality should not be connected with money; for then it ceases to be spiritual. If the therapist reflects compassion, human values and a genuine inner presence, this in itself can aid healing no matter what the theoretical orientation of the therapist.

Meditation helps us *let go* of agitation and detach from our conditioning, through forming a link with a more subtle part of ourselves; beyond thought, beyond matter. This occurs through ascent—concentration on the "higher"(for example, *mantra*, God's form, energy, breath, awareness). Depth therapy helps us *go into* our emotions and receive the images that emerge from the unconscious, both personal and collective. This occurs through descent—concentration on the "lower"—emotions, images, dreams, needs, problems. Both disciplines guide us to go more deeply within and work through our confusion, for there is in Reality no "lower" or "higher." Although the mind and emotions are considered unreal, they do prevent us from experiencing the Real. Therefore they are a force, which is to be taken seriously. Both the personal and transpersonal levels ever interact and influence one another.

When therapy is rightly experienced, it should serve as a container for the deeper healing energies to emerge and permeate the ego. This can bring emotions to the surface, induce conscious suffering and pave the way for a new quality of energy, as well as initiate more balance between emotion and thought. It can also begin the healing process of parental and societal wounding, and lead to more authentic self-expression in the realm of creativity and relationship. But therapy alone cannot fully heal as it does not address issues of desire, attachment and universal love from the vantage point of Knowledge. Nor does it induce deep adaptation to life as a whole. Some therapy can aid partial adaptation to one's inner and outer environment, but more is required for wholesome living. Contact with the Self as synchronistic happening or dream image can be a harbinger of wonder and numinosity that has a healing effect, as it is a link to the higher. This induces faith based on experience. Any connection with deeper layers of the psyche is fundamentally a spiritual process. But this is only a beginning—a magical, wonderful, new beginning. In my experience, only ongoing, steady spiritual work contains the seeds for completing the process.

People who remain in therapy interminably still feeling incomplete, wounded and dependent on the external are usually clinging to *prakriti* and becoming more entrenched in the bondage of attachment. Their inner yearning might be better served by seeking the direct influence of a genuine teacher or teaching.

On the other hand, there are people who have been in spiritual work for years, and use this as an unconscious way of suppressing emotions or avoiding relationships. There are others who identify with the *guru*, the spiritual collective, archetypal unconscious contents or the teaching in a way that reinforces grandiosity and prevents them from working through their personal suffering. In this instance, the ego mistakes itself for God rather than dissolving in God. Then in other cases, a genuinely humble, open person, who never learned to assert rightful individuality may be having problems finding his essence-space or unnecessarily taking on the suffering and/or projections of others. In each of these instances therapy could be helpful, as well as for those seekers who feel the need for personal emotional intimacy as part of the healing process.

Ultimately, this is an individual issue; general external guidelines are difficult to draw. Each person has his own path that will unfold as he continues to go more deeply within. Both the spiritual seeker and the therapeutic client need to develop discrimination in their choice of helper. For me it worked well to be in a Jungian analysis before beginning meditation and spiritual training. Because my analyst did not tend to "interpret" my unconscious material but simply brought her awareness presence in subtle participation, this allowed me to form a relationship with my inner Self without reliance on the imposition of extraneous mental concepts. When the therapist imposes unnecessary theory or interpretation on the client, this can interfere with the genuine discovery of his own essence. Deep therapy should not be an internalization process but rather a cleansing process, whereby one can be helped to form a direct connection with one's own inner life—the deeper the better! If a person can develop an inner orientation that is open and not selectively defensive, this can lead to faith and trust based on experience and provide a good foundation for genuine spiritual work.[46]

Personal growth turns into evolution with the advent of surrender. For surrender we need devotion. In surrender, our motivation is for the Totality called "cosmos" or "God." Everything we do, say or think becomes linked to the universal life force, that we might serve the ongoing evolution of matter into spirit and thereby participate in uplifting creation.

There are numerous people who follow conventional religious traditions in an intellectual way or token manner. Their doubt remains because they have not yet established a link with inner experience. It is important to engage in methods that will help us leave behind the strictly mental realm and enter the realm of experience. To these human beings who long for something more but are afraid it doesn't exist, I acknowledge that I too was once an agnostic, a skeptic, a doubter. And for many years I was a seeker, a seeker who wanted to have faith but could find nothing to believe in. Then as deeper levels and interconnections between "outer" and "inner" became more accessible, I came to see there are genuine teachers; there are genuine teachings. These exist for each of us at our own level. All are available to our experience when we allow ourselves to follow our yearning. There is nothing more important.

When we sincerely surrender to our deepest yearning, the universal life force always responds. May we each discover the individual path that is right for us as we wind our way up toward the summit of the mountain! Here there is no more need for descent, as the summit is ever grounded in *now*.

ENDNOTES

[1] *Vedic* sacrifice(*yajna*) is undertaken to fulfill specific personal or communal desires. Whereas a personal *yajna* might be for wealth or health, a communal ritual beneficial for all might be performed for rain or world peace. The *Vedas* are the divine emanation of knowledge received by the *rishis* in meditation to help humanity. Later, they were compiled and divided into four sections by one of the twenty-three Vyasas. The *Yajur Veda* expounds the fire ceremony (*yajna*).There is a fire pit. Many different kinds of wood for fuel are placed inside. *Ghee*(clarified butter) is poured onto the flames as sacred *mantras* are intoned. The resultant positive vibrations are believed to help balance and nourish the cosmos. It has been suggested that while witnessing this powerful ritual, we mentally offer our negative qualities and desires to the fire of God, who will surely burn them to ashes, if we can but willingly surrender.

[2] The life energy of *kundalini* is the instinctive urge for evolution and one way of merging with the depths of one's nature called "God." The way of *tantra* is a technique to elevate this energy towards liberation. But one need not follow a *tantric* path to awaken the sacred *kundalini*. There are gentler ways of approaching realization. By following any geuine path and teacher, this energy can become available spontaneously, as its emergence and flow is a lawful part of the science of evolution. The particular path one follows is a matter of individual rightness.

[3] *Maya* is the name given to the inscrutable force of the Goddess, which causes human beings to mistake the unreal for the Real, the changing for the permanent. She causes us to believe that the input we receive from the senses, instincts, emotions and mind is true. So we become Her slaves. The sages say that the great Goddess of *maya* creates conditions that will help us transcend *maya*, when our time of ripeness occurs.

[4] The four developmental stages of life are: 1)student(*brahmacharya*), which emphasizes educational training, obedience and celibacy; 2)householder(*grhasta*), which emphasizes *dharma* and charity; 3)forest dweller(*vanaprasta*), which emphasizes service and self-discipline; and 4) renunciate(*sannyasin*), which focuses on surrender.

[5] Psychotherapy is certainly not a necessary bridge for all spiritual aspirants, but only for those who feel an inner need.

[6] The most essential qualities of the full *avatar* are His/Her total love for humanity, omniscience, omnipresence, omnipotence and the indomitable capacity for personal and universal upliftment.

[7] At certain phases of life, it might seem impossible to avoid following a strong desire, though the mind knows it is not in accordance with *dharma.* Performing such action can quickly perpetuate the fall needed to bring us wholeheartedly to spiritual work—provided the inner yearning for Truth is also present. Without the desire for perfection, performing *adharmic* action could inevitably cause our negative tendencies to become more deeply entrenched.

[8] Ramanuja is a very great devotee and exponent of qualified nondualism (*visisthadvaita*), who lived during the eleventh and twelfth century.

[9] This story was told by the renowned Sindi teacher, Dada Vaswami, during a talk at the Indian Consulate in NY. The *Gita* naturally evokes excellence in whatever we do.

[10] Any number multiplied by 8 decreases until 8 is multiplied by 9. Then it merges in 9, the God principle. For example, 8x9=72. 7+2=9.

[11] This story from the Puranas is retold by Swami Vivekananda and Eknath Easwaran.

[12] "He who among men is physically perfect, opulent, lord of others and most endowed with all human enjoyments represents the maximum joy of men. 100 measures of joy for man equals one measure of joy for the manes, who have won their world. 100 measures of joy for the manes who have won their world equals 1 measure of joy in the world of the celestial minstrels(*gandharvas*). 100 measures of joy in the world of celestial minstrels equals 1 measure of joy for the gods through action—those who attain godhead through their actions, as through ritual. 100 measures of joy for the gods through action equals 1 measure of joy for the gods by birth, as also for one who is erudite in the *Vedas*, taintless and unaffected by desire. 100 measures of joy in the world of Prajapati equals 1 measure of joy in the world of Hiranyagarbha(subtle total mind), as also for one who is erudite in the *Vedas*, taintless and

unaffected by desire. Hereafter, this indeed is the Supreme bliss, this is the world that is *Brahman*, O emperor, said Yajnavalka." (The degree of absence of desire determines a person's elevation to a particular sphere).

[13] This support vehicle operates both at the seen and unseen levels of matter. The subtle energy of directed concentration, contemplation, worship and yearning creates an ever-living force field, which helps all aspirants.

[14] Pandits have varying ideas about the specific time frame of *yugas*. Some believe the age of the present *Kali yuga* is about 2,400 years, and we are now on the brink of a new Golden Age. Yogananda posits a gap of 200 years between *yugas*. His *guru*, Sri Yukteswar gauged mathematical calculations of the revolution of planets around the sun and the sun around its distant star to form ascending and descending arcs of 12,000 years each. He correlated these with the day and night of Brahma. Others believe the day of Brahma is the lifespan of the solar system, while the day and night of Brahma is the lifespan of the universe.

The classical Hindu belief is that the start of the *Kali yuga* was 3102 BC. Sri Sathya Sai Baba says he has descended to earth to help usher in the Golden age, which will commence around the year 2025.

[15] This idea is similar to the Greek concept, whereby the Golden Age is found in the distant past and Silver, Bonze and Iron Ages reflect a systematic degeneration in the quality of life over time.

[16] "Therefore nothing is proved to be other than the *Atman*, which is distinct from the universe. The threefold appearance in the *Atman*(*Adhyatmika, Adhibhautika and Adhidaivika*) is proved to be without foundation. Know the threefold division consisting of the *gunas* to be but the effect of *maya*."(*Uddhava Gita,*23:7, p.341)

"This world of change which was originally non-existent is a *rajasika* projection of the *Brahman* and appears because of It. But the *Brahman* alone appears in multiple forms as the organs, the subtle elements, the mind(the gods) and the gross elements." (ibid. 23:22, p.347)

For a more systematic explanation of these three aspects of the aspectless Brahman, with applicable contemplation instructions for their dissolution, see *Panchikaranam of Sri Sankaracarya.* This includes an explanation by Sankara's student Sri Suresvara, which is very clear and suitable for the aspiring *jnani.*

[17] The great Bhishma lay bleeding with 1,000 arrows piercing his body, waiting for the auspicious moment when the sun would cross the equinox from the southern hemisphere to the northern (*uttarayana*). Before his heroic passing, Krishna assures Bhishma this is his last birth; that he will forever be remembered as an impeccable hero, and he will return to his rightful kingdom of the gods.

[18] The *Brhadaranyaka Upanishad* states that all pots and parts of pots are nothing but different conditions of the one mud alone—mere names, with no distinct substance of their own. Likewise, the world of names and forms is the one *Brahman* alone. There is no other essence.

[19] In a more detailed manner, Yogananda explains the transformation of the twenty-four *tattvas*(subtle elements) during the process of meditation. He says, "By ascent of the consciousness through the subtle centers of life and spiritual awakening in the spine, the *yogi* learns the inner science of changing the consciousness of gross matter into the consciousness of its primordial principles. He resolves the five vibratory elements along with their manifestation of the five senses, five organs of action and five life forces from grosser to finer principles; changing the consciousness of vibratory earth into the consciousness of vibratory water; the consciousness of water into that of vibratory fire; the consciousness of fire into that of vibratory air; the consciousness of air into that of vibratory ether; the consciousness of ether into that of mind (sense consciousness or *manas*); consciousness of mind into that of discrimination (*buddhi*); the consciousness of discrimination into that of ego(*ahamkara*); the consciousness of ego into that of feeling (*citta*). By thus dissolving the twenty-four principles successively into one another, the yogi then merges the consciousness of feeling into that of the primordial cosmic vibratory force (*Aum*) and the consciousness of *Aum* into Spirit. He thereby reaches the ultimate unity—the One from whom has sprung the many. By gradual steps the *yogi* in this way converts all consciousness of matter into the consciousness of Spirit." (p.268-9)

[20] The beautiful Indian Saint, Anandamayee Ma had a similar experience. While singing with devotees in Nainital, she perceived them all as myriad forms of Krishna (see painting in Battaracharya's *Anandamayee The Universal Mother,* p.46)

[21] This retelling of the story is taken primarily from Swami Sivananda.

[22] The 10th and 11th chapters can be viewed as expounding two aspects of the total mind, the immanent and the transcendent. Carl Jung calls the total mind the collective unconscious, which he viewed as consisting of archetypes or eternal ideas, the manifestations of life from primordial beginnings, accessible to the imaginal realm. To the advanced spiritual student however, the total mind is an ongoing living pulsation of sacred omnipresence.

[23] This arrangement of the "evolution" of matter is from Sri Krishna Prem, *The Yoga of the Bhagavat Gita*, page 205, with some modification.

[24] In the *Uddhava Gita,* Krishna describes the evolution and involution of the universe: "Before the origin of the *yugas*, the knower and the entire objective universe were verily one and homogeneous. The same was the case in the *Sathya yuga*, at the beginning of the cycle, when people were skilled in discrimination. That absolute and homogeneous Reality, the *Brahman*, which transcends mind and speech, became split into two—the objective world and the thinking subject. Of these two things one is *prakriti*, which has a dual nature, and the other Knowledge Absolute, which is called *Purusha*.

From the *prakriti* as I agitated it, there emanated the *gunas; sattva, rajas,* and *tamas,* with the approval of the *Purusha*. From them emanated the *Sutra*, with which the *Mahat* is united. From the transformation of that was produced egoism, which deludes all. Egoism is threefold—*sattvika, rajasa and tamasa*, which are respectively the cause of the mind, the organs and the fine particles of matter. It is both sentient and insentient. From the *tamasa* aspect of egoism there emanated the five elements; from the *rajasa* aspect the organs; and from the *sattvika* aspect the eleven gods and the mind. Directed by me, all these things acting together, made up an oval structure, which was an excellent abode for Me. In that oval structure, floating in water I dwelt.

From My navel grew a lotus epitomizing the world, and there the self-born Brahma manifested himself. With my grace he, the universal Soul endowed with activity, projected through hard reflection the three spheres, Bhur, Bhuvar, and Svar, together with their rulers. The Svar became the abode of the gods; the Bhuvar that of spirits; the earth that of men; and the spheres beyond the Svar, the abode of the *siddhas*. The Lord Brahma made the regions below the earth the abode of the *asuras* and *nagas*. Works characterized by the three *gunas* lead to the three spheres. *Yoga*, asceticism and renunciation lead to the pure spheres of Mahar, Jana, Tapas and Sathya, but *Bhakti yoga* leads to My abode(Vaikuntha).

Owing to Me who am Time and the Ordainer of everything, this world with diverse *karma* rises and sinks in this stream of the *gunas*. Whatever things come into being—minute or vast, thin or stout—all partake of the two principles, *Purusha* and *prakriti*. That from which a thing originates and into which it dissolves, abides also in the intermediate stage. That alone is Real. The modifications have a mere phenomenal existence, as in the case of metallic and earthenwares. That, using which as material, an antecedent state produces a consequent one, is alone the Reality. A state from which another state originates and into which it is dissolved, is also relatively called real. *Prakriti,* which is the material cause of this manifested universe, *Purusha* which is its substratum, and Time which is a factor in its manifestation—all these three verily am I, the *Brahman*.

Projection in its varied forms goes on for the experience of the soul, through an unbroken succession of causes and effects, until the term of continuance of the world is over, according to the will of the Lord. Then the universe which, pervaded by Me, is the scene of the births and deaths of multifarious creatures, is together with the spheres ready for the state called dissolution. Thus the bodies of animals are dissolved into food, food into seeds, seeds into earth, and earth into odor. Odor dissolves into water, water into its own essence sap, sap into fire, and fire into color. Color dissolves into air, air into touch, touch into ether, and ether into sound particles. The organs are dissolved into their efficient causes, the gods. The gods, My friend, are dissolved into the mind, which rules over all, and the mind into *sattvika* egoism. Sound is dissolved into *tamasa* egoism and the all-powerful egoism into the cosmic Intelligence. That cosmic Intelligence, endowed with the noblest qualities is dissolved into its own causes the *gunas*, the *gunas* into *prakriti* and that again into eternal time. Time is dissolved into the omisicent Being, the Being again into Me, the birthless *Atman*. The *Atman*, which is inferred from the projection and dissolution of the universe is Absolute and rests on Itself.

How can delusions caused by the seeing of difference rise in the mind or stay in the heart of a man who reasons in this way—like darkness in the sky at sunrise? Here in both a direct and an inverse order, I have described the Sankhya system, which breaks the knot of doubt. I am the Witness of the high and the low." (Swami Madhavananda, p.290-299)

[25] At the same time we are given freedom of choice, there is no total free choice separate from divine will, as the creative word or God in life principle is the omnipresent substratum for the ego and the six evolutes of the causeless first cause. We are however, being given the choice to educate our "lower nature" to connect with conscience, Truth, Love, Unity.

[26] By transforming our own inner poison, we each contribute to lessening the collective world poison. This can occur through personal inner psychological work with the emotions, through meditation, selfless service, self-observation, dedicated austerity and/or worship.

[27] The *Virat Purusha* or cosmic form body of God is extolled in the *Vedic* hymn, *Purusha Suktam*, which has been recited by devout Hindus for thousands of years.

[28] In the west, Jesus is an example of the personal God of Love who brings compassion to humanity. In India, He is revered as a great saint healer avatar, who is believed to have traveled widely in the east both before and after his crucifixion. There is a tomb of Jesus in Srinigar, India, which many worship as his burial place. Here he is known by the name of Isa, which means Lord of all living beings.

According to Peggy Mason, "Various early histories, such as the *Bhahavishya Mahapurana*, written in Sanskrit, state that Jesus, accompanied by Mary his mother and Thomas, after staying some time in Damascus took the long caravan route across northern Persia where he preached, converting many and earned the name of 'the healer of lepers.' This teaching pilgrimage took several years, traveling ever towards the east.

In the 'Acts of Thomas' and other sources, Jesus, Mary and Thomas stayed in Taxila (now Pakistan), whence they continued towards Kashmir. But Mary, not being able to bear further the hardships of the journey, died at what is now the small town of Murree, which was so named in her honor, some 30 miles from Rawalpindi. Her tomb at Pindi Point is an important shrine to this day."
(*Sai Baba*: *The Embodiment of Love*, p.34-5)

[29] To experience the cosmic form, love and grace is a prerequisite. For this realization to become permanent, ongoing devotion is required.

[30] The awakening power of love can be seen in psychoanalysis in the phenomenon of the transference. And all tendencies toward idealization can be viewed as the expression of the unconscious urge to discover the ideal within—one's spiritual center of love, perfection, consciousness, authority. When such a strong power reveals itself, the opportunity could be born for this love to become a cornerstone of initiation into embodied egolessness, genuine personal and universal relatedness, love of all fellow beings. But in order for this wholesome quality of evolution to proceed, the psychotherapist cannot be identified with the body and must possess right knowledge integrity. Otherwise, the powerful energy of love stays split-off, unconnected with its essence source. So it remains ego-centered or skin deep, in accordance with theory or the level of the conscious values of the body ego mind. Then a precious opportunity to approach the depth of the ideal is forfeited. The healing of personal, parental kinship wounds remains partial without direct contact with the source.

Sigmund Freud developed the concept of the transference based on his observations that the people he treated transferred to the therapist their emotions, sexual feelings and ways of relating derived from the libido, in relationship to their parents. Carl Jung included the archetypal dimension to the transference; that the power of these energies does not derive solely from a human connection but are an expression of transpersonal forces of life that become connected with ideas, aspects of living and instinctual feelings. The God image is viewed as an archetype, the inner reflection of a powerful force within the psyche. As long as something is a reflection, it is not experienced fully and consciously at its deepest level. But through experiencing the numinous power of the archetypal dimension of God, love, expansiveness, one comes closer to the Real. Since every gross, tangible thing and subtle intangible designation requires a way to be perceived by the body, mind and intellect, *Vedanta* would also consider the archetype a projection—a projection of the Self—but would not, I believe, consider the Self an archetype. For Jung only deals with the Self empirically, as he views it appearing in dreams and images.

Vedanta offers utter clarity regarding the different stages of love as an expression of God. Reality is the ongoing eternal source of love—not merely the *reflection* of an image. Love exists inside and outside all of us, always, everywhere, ever available.

[31] This point was expressed by Karunamayi(Sri Vijayeshwari Devi) during a talk in NY in July 1995.

[32] This story was told by Amritananda Mayi(Amachi) during a talk in NY in June 1995.

[33] To the degree the inner equipment is open to subtle, divine vibrations, our thinking stems from the higher Intelligence or direct intuition, rather than from ordinary reasoning or inference. These deeper experiences gradually pierce the shield of *maya.*

[34] In this context, mind is considered the sixth sense.

[35] Since by definition, *rakshasas* are too rigid to change in this life, it is up to the *asuras* to bring more human vibrations to the world and the universe, if we are to survive. *Vasista's Yoga* tells the story of Karkati, a vicious, insatiable *rakshasi,* who devoured people and caused them innumerable fatal diseases, including leukemia and cholera. After 8,000 years of strenuous *tapas* and subsequent insights,

even she became a realized soul. (see pages 93-107 in Swami Venkatesananda's translation)

[36] The *asuric* qualities of self-centeredness, arguing, and an orientation that focuses primarily on survival needs and materialism are indicative of an immature soul. The spiritually oriented person reflects a more mature level of soul development and inner evolution.

[37] Clearly, genuine "intelligence" relates to the quality of our sincere motivation and onepointed effort to embrace a teaching that will really help us cross the ocean of *samsara.*

[38] The five forms of *dharmic* sacrifice(*yajna*) performed in India are: 1) paying homage to the ancestors; to the accumulated effects of past wisdom and love (*pitri yajna*). 2) offering food to the needy on an individual and large group basis; respecting humanity(*nri yajna*). 3) feeding and caring for animals. Just as higher beings such as angels and *devas* help man, as part of the cosmic food chain, so man cares for those "beneath" him(*bhuta yajna*). 4) rites to the gods; offering the life force from the senses to the soul(*deva yajna*). 5) offering the soul to the all pervading *Brahman*(*Brahma yajna*). "This finality is attainable only after faithful performance of the preceding four ceremonies, which inwardly as well as outwardly acknowledge man's debt to the past, present, worlds of lower beings and worlds of higher beings. Thus proving his fidelity to creation, man is fit to touch the hem of the Creator's robe." (Yogananda, p.348)

[39] Swami Chinmayananda, THG, p.631.

[40] Sri Sathya Sai Baba helps clarify different kinds of *dharma.* He says, "Duty without love is deplorable. Duty with love is desirable. Love without duty is divine."

[41] Though the castes might be unequal in terms of innate intelligence and moral fiber, they are equal in terms of societal need and the possibility for evolution through following one's own *dharma.* For example, the Law of Manu places greatest responsibility on the *brahmins* for right conduct. This law states that for the same crime, punishment of a businessman should be twice as severe as for a laborer-servant, and that of a scholar-priest should be two to four times as severe as that of a warrior(see Coomaraswamy, p.12).

[42] Carl Jung's often quoted informal statement that westerners are better off following a western path as opposed to an eastern way seems quite outmoded today. I believe Jung based much of the philosophy of his psychology on the *Bhagavad Gita,* but he was unable to cross the bridge into eastern practice because of his personal *vasanas*. The east teaches us that the subtlest, all pervasive consciousness is self-luminous, self-experienced, fully independent. The "organ of perception" for transcendence has been called the "third eye" and not the mind, senses, or ego. However, if the intellect(*buddhi*) has been purified and conditioning dissolved, the higher can reflect through it. In this way, the higher Intelligence can serve as a mediating link to daily life. The higher Intelligence is part of the soul; independent, and not at all subject to the ego, except when it is veiled by the impurities of the ego, such as excessive attachment, fear and anger.

If one's essence is truly universal—and we are all children of the collective unconscious—then the "eastern" *yogic* path may be one's true *dharma.* But if a person's psyche is dominated by an inner Judaeo-Christian archetype, then the "western way" might be his *dharma.* As the 21st century proceeds and eastern spiritual teachers become generally accessible, more westerners will embrace the wisdom of the east as their true *dharma.* For the greatest gift of the East to all humanity is her universal Knowledge, which can be experienced.

[43] In the *Uddhava Gita*, Krishna summarizes the way of work and the criteria for relinquishing work:

"Placing one's *manas* and mind-stuff in Me with the body and mind delighting in Me, one should calmly do all work for My sake, remembering Me all the while. ...With a pure mind one should observe in all beings as well as in oneself only Me, the *Atman*, who am both inside and out and unobstructed like the sky. O great soul, he who, taking his stand on pure knowledge, thus regards and honors all beings as Myself—who has the same attitude towards a *chandala*(untouchable) and a *brahmana,* a thief as well as a patron of the *brahmanas*, a spark of fire as well as the sun, and a ruffian as well as a kind man—is considered a sage. Ideas of comparisons, jealousy, pity and egoism quickly depart from a man who always thinks of Me in all men.

Ignoring the derisive smiles of one's friends and leaving aside a merely physical view of things, as well as shame, one should prostrate oneself on the ground before every creature, from a *chandala,* a cow, an ass, or a dog. One should worship thus in thought, word and deed till one comes to look upon all beings as myself. To such a man everything is *Brahman,* owing to the knowledge that comes from seeing the Atman in all. *Seeing the Brahman all around, he is free from doubts and gives up all work.*

This looking upon all beings as Myself in thought, word and deed is to My mind, the best of all methods of worship. ...Any trifling activity whatsoever (such as fleeing as a result of fear or weeping from grief), *if it is unselfishly meant for Me,* becomes religion. Herein lies the wisdom of the wise and the cleverness of the intelligent; that in this very birth they attain Me, the Real and immortal, by means of something that is unreal and mortal." (Swami Madhavananda, p.359-362)

[44] The qualities of the full *avatar*(*purnavatar*) are different from *yogic* powers(*siddhis*), which can be developed from meditation and spiritual practice. For the full *avatar* is already born with these qualities, and requires no practice to develop them. Unlike the ordinary person who is born in accordance with his past *karma*, the *avatar*, when the need is great, *chooses* to descend to earth in human form solely to uplift humanity. Different *Vedantic* commentators have ascribed various numbers of qualities for the full *avatar* such as 12, 16, 22, and 64.

[45] For a more detailed explanation of the Sanskrit root derivations of all the names see Yogananda's commentary, p.65 – 90.

[46] In the beginning stages of psychotherapy a certain degree of internalization or identification with the therapist is a natural part of the healing process.

GLOSSARY

Abhaya – without fear

Abhyāsa yoga – yoga of repetition or practice

Adhibhūta – primordial elements, the fine substratum of material or gross objects.

Adhidaiva – world of the gods, the divine operating through the sense organs and objects, as the gods are considered the rulers of the sense organs.

Adhiyajña – the first sacrifice.

Adhyātma – the supreme Spirit, the Self.

Advaita – without two, nondualism, oneness. A primary exponent of *advaita* is Ādi Śaṅkara (788-820 A.D).

Āgāmī karma – results yet to come, future *karma*.

Ahaṅkāra – I, ego; means "I doing," an aspect of the inner instrument (*antaḥkaraṇa*). When one's sense of self is solely identified with the body mind form, this results in egoism, alienation, divisiveness and lack of unity.

Ahiṁsā – non-injury in thought, word and deed.

Airāvata – elephant of Indra that emerged when the ocean of milk was churned by the *devās* and *asurās*. He symbolizes wisdom and divine intuition.

Ākāśa – free or open space, ether, atmosphere, the subtle element that supports sound.

Akṣara – unmanifest, without form.

Amṛta – immortal, imperishable, nectar, the drink of the gods.

Ānanda – very great joy, bliss.

Ananta – endless, boundless, eternal, infinite.

Ananya bhakti – devotion without any otherness, singleminded devotion.

Antaḥkaraṇa – the subtle internal organ or inner instrument, the seat of mind, intellect, ego, outgoing thoughts, memory and soul conscience.

Aṇu – atom, the one atom present throughout the universe is consciousness.

Apara prakṛti –"lower" *prakṛti*, the visible world of matter.

Apsarā – divine dancer or courtesan.

Ardhanārīśvara – Śiva as part male part female. *Śiva* (consciousness, being existence) and *śakti* (dynamic, active energy) as One.

Ārtaḥ – a devotee whose suffering strengthens his closeness to God.

Arthārthī – a devotee who seeks wealth, meaning or something he treasures.

Āsana – bodily postures, the third limb of yoga in Patanjali's *Yoga Sūtras*.

Asat – not being, not existing, unreal.

Āśakti bhakti – very strong devotion to one's own god only, a narrow and incomplete form of devotion.

Aśvattha – an ancient tree in the pipal family, with a very large trunk, many branches and lush descending roots. *Yogis* meditate under this tree and devotees place holy objects such as stones, idols or *liṅgams* around it.

Asura – a self-centered materialistic person of demonic nature.

Ātmabodha – pristine Self awareness

Ātman – Self or God within.

A-U-M – the cosmic sound *Om* is a manifestation of the Absolute in the universe, throughout the three stages of consciousness. The letter *A* represents the waking state, *U* the dream state and *M* the deep sleep state (see *Māṇḍukya Upaniṣad*).

Āvaraṇa – the veiling power of *māyā.* Our impure emotions cover Reality and render it inaccessible to the psyche.

Avatāra – the embodiment of God in human form, who descends to earth to help humanity.

Avyakta – unmanifest, invisible, imperceptible, inapparent, indistinct.

Bhakti – devotion and love for God.

Bhakti yoga – devotion and loving remembrance is practiced and intensified as a means of linking the mind to God.

Bhāvasamanvitaḥ – equal loving consciousness, equality.

Bījākṣaram – seed syllable, a powerful root sound in *manṇtra*.

Bindu – dot, the seed potential of the energy of creation and destruction; before Om, between the Absolute and the manifest.

Bodhisattva – a compassionate being of the Mahayana Buddhist tradition, who sacrifices final liberation to help others awaken.

Brahmā – the aspect of the trinity that creates the universe; the active, dynamic force of imagination, which gives rise to forms and happenings.

Brahma Sūtra – a classical *advaita* text, by Bādarāyaṇa (Vyāsa), with commentary by Śaṅkarācārya.

Brahmacarya – celibacy; purity of thought, word and deed, the student stage of life.

Brahman – the Absolute, for which there are no words.

Brahmins – spiritual scholars and teachers, the first caste. These represent the head of the cosmic form of God and bring knowledge to the society.

Buddhi – the intellect, an aspect of the inner instrument (*antaḥkaraṇa*), which manifests as the reasoning process, discrimination (differentiating good from evil, the Real from the unreal), and the higher Intelligence or divine intuition.

Buddhi yoga – *yoga* of the higher Intelligence. Equal-minded steadiness in *yoga.*

Cakras – unseen centers of energy within the subtle body. Each center corresponds to a particular quality of energy related to physical, psychological and spiritual experience. The inner evolution of a human being is reflected by the progressive upliftment of divine energy through the *cakras*, initiated by meditation and spiritual practice.

Cit – higher consciousness, pure thought.

Citta – thoughts, feelings, memories that get deposited in the subconscious mind. One aspect of the inner instrument (*antaḥkaraṇa*).

Chitta gupta – the inner record keeper of all our thoughts and deeds.

Deva – god, a specific positive form of cosmic energy, as part of the whole.

Dhāraṇā – concentration, a technique of meditation, the sixth limb of *yoga* in Patanjali's *Yoga Sūtras*.

Dharma – law, righteous action, the inner essence of a thing.

Dhyāna – meditation, the seventh limb of *yoga.*

Divya cakṣu – divine eye, referred to as the subtle third eye between the eyebrows. As this gradually opens, our identification with matter dissolves and the eternal becomes more accessible.

Draṣtum – to see.

Dvaita – dualism. Here, God and man are considered two separate entities. A primary exponent of *dvaita* was Madhva (1238-1317).

Dvāpara yuga – the third cycle of time, which ended after the *Mahābhārata* War and traditionally is said to consist of 864,000 years.

Dyuti – the glow of beauty inherent in the realized soul.

Gandharva – divine musician.

Garuḍa – the eagle vehicle of Viṣṇu.

Gṛhastha – householder stage of life(second stage).

Guṇas – the three qualities of nature: *sattva, rajas,* and *tamas;* preservation, creation, and destruction. As the constituents of *prakṛti*, these are perpetually moving and changing.

Guṇātītaḥ – one who has transcended the *guṇas*.

Hiraṇyakaśipu – the seemingly invincible *asura* king who is the father of Prahlāda. He is finally killed by the lion Narasiṃha, who is one of the incarnations of Viṣṇu.

Hṛdaye guhāyam – the secret heart.

Īśvara – Lord of the universe. A manifestation of God as the total mind and controller of the universe.

Jalpa – in debating or arguing, an arrogant, bitter rejoinder meant to put down the opponent.

Jijñāsu – the intellectual seeker of truth.

Jīva – the person, the personal soul.

Jīvanmukta – one who is liberated while living in the human body. The *jīvanmukta* remains on earth to teach and serve as an example for others.

Jīvātman – the personal essence or individual soul.

Jñānam – Knowledge of Reality in *Vedānta*, or ordinary knowledge in daily usage.

Jñāna yoga – the path of Knowledge with an emphasis on linking the intellect to the divine through contemplation and self reflection.

Jñānī – a person of wisdom, one who experiences Reality.

Jñātum – to know.

Jñeyam – the act of knowing.

Kaivalya – liberation, total independence, complete oneness.

Kāla – time. Time accompanies thought, space and creation.

Kālī – the Divine Mother. In her fierce aspect, she's a fighter who drinks blood and devours time. In her beneficent aspect she gives *darśan,* helps the devotee overcome obstacles and grants liberation. The strength of her fierceness is truly benevolent.

Kali yuga – the age of strife, our present cycle. The most degenerate age, when qualities such as anger, hatred, egoism, envy and materialism predominate. This *yuga* is said to last for 432,000 years. According to Monier-Williams, it began on February 18, 3012 B.C.

Kāma – desire, lust, wish, longing, sensuality.

Kāmadhenu – the wish fulfilling cow that emerges from churning the ocean of milk. She demonstrates the power of our desires, which often materialize.

Karma – action, the fruit of one's thoughts, words and deeds.

Karma kāṇda – religious action or rite of worship.

Karma yoga – a way of linking the mind to God through dedicated action, action with remembrance, and/or desireless action.

Krama mukti – a steady, assured course to liberation, associated with the path of the sun.

Kṣara – perishable, melting away, as a cloud, water, or the body.

Kṣatriyas – the governing order or military, which later came to be known as the ruling caste. These represent the arms of the cosmic form, whose strength administers and protects the society.

Kṣetra – the field. The body, senses, mind, intellect and the environment are some of the components that comprise our field of experience.

Kṣetrajña – the knower of the field. *Ātmic* awareness is the true Knower.

Kuṇḍalinī – the *śakti*(energy) of the Goddess, which helps one awaken to enlightenment.

Kuṭastha – the unchanging universal consciousness, likened to the anvil that molds metal into its rightful shape.

Lakṣmī – the divine energy or Goddess, who is an expression of wealth, beauty, harmony, love and gracious living. She is worshipped as the Divine Mother in the *Śrī Lalitā Sahasranāma* (One Thousand Divine Names of the Goddess).

Layam – dissolution, destruction, melting, presided over by the energy called Śiva. Forms are broken down when something new is needed for personal and universal well-being.

Līlā – divine play, sport of the Lord, as manifested through the personal dramas of life.

Liṅgam – a phallus or oval shaped symbol of Śiva, as creator and container of life. Some are said to be self-created (*svayambhu*). Others are manifested by holy *yogis* to instill faith in the hearts of humanity. Śiva *linṅgams* have been worshipped in India from time immemorial.

Loka – place, world, or psychological space. Hindu mythology recognizes fourteen *lokas,* which comprise various levels of heavens and hells in the universe. These also exist within a person and evoke our subjective experience.

Mahābhārata – the great epic about the origins of life in Bhārata (India). The work consists of eighteen books and emphasizes ethics as well as history and mythology. It is the greatest teacher about life, human nature, universal righteousness, and spirituality. The *Bhagavad Gītā* is considered part of this text.

Mahat – large, huge, great; the total intellect principle in *Sāṅkhya* philosophy, called the great source of *ahaṅkāra* (self consciousness) and *manas* (mind); second evolute of *prakṛti* in the twenty-four tattvas.

Mahātmā – great soul, holy person.

Mahāsamādhi – the great union, when the soul merges with God when the body dies.

Mahāvākyas – great truths. Four pithy sayings that encapsulate the profound essence of *Vedānta.*

Mahāyuga – great *yuga*, consists of 4,320,000 years, which is the total of the four *yugas*.

Manas– mind, one aspect of the inner instrument(*antaḥkaraṇa*) through which thoughts enter the psyche and become deposited as *vāsanās*; often based on input from the senses and the sense objects.

Mantra – holy verbal sounds or syllables that bring the support of divine energy to the mind of the person who concentrates on them.

Māyā – the illusory world of change, *prakṛti*, the visible universe. When one mistakes Reality for what the mind and senses exerience, he is said to be ensnared in *māyā*.

Māyā śakti – the energy of the goddess, which helps a person evolve into his divine nature.

Mohinī – a beautiful temptress sent by Viṣṇu to sidetrack the *asuras* from claiming the nectar of immortality *(amṛta).* The word means confusion, one who deludes.

Mokṣa – liberation, release from worldly existence, eternal emancipation from the cycles of transmigration.

Mūla prakṛti – the subtlest root of matter. According to *Sāṅkhya* philosophy, the primary cause from which matter evolves.

Naṭarāja –Śiva as the cosmic dancer, who dances his dance of cosmic dissolution and creation surrounded by a circle of fire, dancing on the chubby infant of desire—indicative of Śiva's detachment.

Nīlakaṇṭha – blue-necked, a name of Śiva. When Śiva drinks the poison that emerges from churning the ocean of milk, it remains in his throat. His neck turns blue, as he does not swallow it. In this way, God takes on the sins of the world and remains untainted.

Nirguṇa – formless, the transcendent Absolute.

Nirvāṇa – liberation.

Niṣkāma karma – desireless action, performing one's duty without any desire for results. This principle is fundamental to *karma yoga*.

Nivṛtti – inner concentration; conscious attention remains within, spiritual awareness.

Niyama – inner purity, self study, contentment and surrender. Can also refer to observances and pilgrimage. Second in Patañjali's eight limbs of yoga.

Ojas – the power of strength, virility.

Om – the silent universal sound; the first manifestation of the Absolute in the world, from which the cosmos is said to manifest.

Om Tat Sat – a *mantra* of remembrance. If recited before beginning an action, this becomes a *yajña.* The meaning is *Brahman*, That, existence-being.

Parāprakṛti – higher *prakṛti*, the subtlest, unmanifest form of matter.

Parābhakti – the highest devotion, supreme devotion.

Paramātman – the supreme Self. The same universal Self in everyone and everything.

Parameśvara – the supreme Lord.

Prahlāda – the boy who was fully devoted to Viṣṇu since his birth. His demonic father, Hiraṇyakaśipu, tried to have him killed for his faith in God but all the plots failed. Prahlāda's faith, in spite of his family background and conditioning serves as an example for all pure souls everywhere.

Prajñā – conscious integrated awareness, wisdom, discrimination.

Prakṛti – matter both subtle and gross, which consists of the three *gunas* and is always changing.

Prāṇa – the subtle universal substance of life energy that manifests in the body as the five vital airs: breath, circulation, digestion, elimination, and the power of thought.

Praṇava – the subtle universal sound *Om.*

Prāṇāyāma – technique of gaining mastery over the five *prāṇa*s, through breathing techniques. Fourth in Patanjali's eight limbs of yoga.

Prārabdha karma – actions performed in past lives that are responsible for the present birth. Even the realized soul must witness the drama of this past *karma*, as it lives itself out.

Pratyāhāra – withdrawing the senses from the sense organs and disidentifying from thoughts. The fifth limb of yoga, in Patanjali's *Yoga Sutras*.

Praveṣtum – to enter into.

Prāvṛtti – dynamic movement of energy outward, an external focus on doing and accomplishing.

Prema – love for God.

Prema bhakti – loving devotion for God and seeing God in all.

Preyas – desired, agreeable, what is dear on the personal ego level.

Pūrṇāvatāra – full *avatāra*, one who fully embodies all the qualities of the divine incarnation.

Puruṣa – Self, God, the highest in a person.

Puruṣa – person, a reflection of the highest.

Puruṣārtha – self-effort, performing spiritual practices to clear away the obstacles to liberation. The four *puruṣārthas* or aims of life for a human being are desire, wealth, *dharma* and liberation. Desire, wealth and *dharma* are to be utilized for liberation.

Rakṣaṇa – protection.

Rākṣasas – demonic beings who are always trying to destroy goodness through killing, plotting, insatiable hunger and greed. Rāvaṇa was one of the most infamous *rākṣasas.*

Ṛṣis – experiential knowers of Truth, sages, seers of the *Vedas*. The seven *ṛṣis* are considered the progenitors of the human race. Some names are; Gautama, Bhāradvāja, Viśvāmitra, Jamadagni, Vaśiṣtha, Kaśyapa, Atri, Nārada, Bhṛgu, Dakṣa, Marīci, Āgirasa, Kratu Pulastya and Pulaha. Their influence is said to be ever present, helping humanity connect with the divine.

Sādhaka – a spiritual aspirant.

Sādhanā – spiritual effort.

Sādhu – a holy person.

Saguṇa – with form.

Samādhi – an inner state of merging the mind in God, the eighth limb in Patanjali's *Yoga Sūtras*. This occurs when the mind abides in absolute calmness and equality.

Saṁskāras – impressions that become deposited in the mind and influence our thought, motivation, and action. These crystallize into *vāsanās* or thought channels.

Śanaiḥ – slowly, gradually.

Sañcita karma – one's total *karma* from past *vāsanās*, which is often unconscious.

Saṅkalpa – egocentric will, desire or wish.

Sāṅkhya – philosophy expounded by the ancient *ṛṣi* Kapila about *prakṛti* and *Puruṣa*. Matter is that which changes and is related to duality, multiplicity, cause and effect. Spirit is the ongoing indestructible, changeless unity underlying all existence. The word means "numbering" and reveals the different subtle levels of *prakṛti* during the process of evolution and involution; from the divine ascent, creation or projection of matter and "world" to the divine descent of dissolution and destruction of projection and "world." Though matter and Spirit are considered distinct and separate, as part of one whole they form the universe.

Sannyāsin – renunciate. The true *sannyāsin*, be he householder or monk is not influenced by desire or egocentric will.

Śaraṇāgati – full refuge and total surrender, based wholly on loving devotion.

Sarasvatī – the goddess of knowledge, both secular and spiritual, as well as music, poetry, law, science and the arts. The aspect of the Divine Mother that brings *Ātma vidyā* or Self Knowledge.

Sarva loka maheśvara – the whole world is the great *Īśvara*. Everything is an expression of the divine. Śaṅkara's description of the tenth *Gītā* chapter.

Sat – being, existence, presence, happening.

Saccidānanda – existence, consciousness, bliss. An inner state of being-Reality experienced by the *yogi*.

Satya svarupa – the form of Truth.

Satya(Kṛta) yuga – the Golden Age, the first cycle of time, when people are considered good and contented. It is said to last for 1,728,000 years.

Śeṣa – the remainder or that which is left; the serpent who formed a couch for Viṣṇu to sleep on during the *pralaya* or dissolution.

Sevā – selfless service. Work is performed with the attitude of serving God and seeing Him in the other, as well as in oneself.

Śāstra – the science of scripture and spirituality.

Śiva – auspiciousness; that aspect of the trinity connected with dissolution and destruction. Śiva is also considered the One, the transcendent consciousness.

Śiva/Śakti – the complete God that includes male and female: still, silent consciousness (Śiva) and dynamic, active energy (Śakti).

Śraddhā – faith, the underlying motivation behind one's actions.

Sṛṣṭi – creation, unfolding.

Śreyas – most excellent, overall welfare, the bliss of final emancipation.

Śloka – verse, stanza.

Sthita prajña – person of steady wisdom. He or she is fully equal-minded.

Śūdras – people who serve. They are the fourth caste, consisting of laborers and hired help. These represent the feet of the cosmic form.

Svabhāva – one's own condition or natural state of being, innate or inherent disposition.

Svadharma – one's own duty or task in life. Each person must perform action in accordance with his intelligence, talents, abilities and level of righteousness.

Svādhyāya – study of one's own self, which includes scriptural study.

Svarupa – one's own form, or its own form.

Tapas – austerity, penance. This spiritual practice is rightly undertaken to help connect the mind with the highest. Only the *rākṣasas* and *asuras* perform *tapas* primarily for personal ego gain.

Tattvas – twenty-four constituents of *Sāṅkhya* philosophy: five elements, five senses, five types of corresponding sense objects, five organs of action, ego, mind, intellect and *Mūla prakṛti*.

Tejas – shining effulgence, an inner spiritual glow.

Tretā yuga – the second cycle of time, the age of Rāma. Here, man is still basically wholesome and happy but a little evil is present. This age is said to last for 1,296,000 years.

Turīya – the fourth state of consciousness, beyond the waking, the dreaming and the deep sleep states; a place of all-inclusive wholeness. (see *Māṇḍukya Upaniṣad*)

Tyāga – the aspect of renunciation translated as relinquishment. Attachment to desire for the results of action is abandoned, and not action itself.

Uccaḥśravās – the white-winged horse of Indra that emerges from churning the ocean of milk. He symbolizes the grace that comes from control of sexual energy.

Uttarāyaṇa – the northern path of the sun commencing on the winter solstice. *Uttarāyaṇa* is symbolic of the way of light and is therefore considered an auspicious time for the soul to leave the body.

Vāda – in debating, logical discussion with the underlying objective of discovering truth.

Vaiśyas – people whose vocation is commerce, farming or the professions, the third caste, which brings wealth to the society. These represent the thighs of the cosmic form.

Vāsanās – thought channels, conditioning from the past that has become crystallized, thereby influencing one's desires, motivations and thoughts.

Viśiṣṭādvaita – qualified nondualism. In this philosophy, Oneness remains supreme while the various subtle energies called gods and goddesses are recognized as part of one whole. A primary exponent of *viśiṣṭādvaita* was Rāmānuja (11th and 12th century).

Vedānta – knowledge of the *Vedas*, or the end of knowledge. For when one truly Knows, there is no need for knowledge, ritual, or teachings. As a philosophy, *Vedānta* emphasizes *advaita*, the essence of the Upaniṣads, but the word is sometimes used to include all Indian philosophy.

Vedas – A body of hymns divinely inspired through the *ṛṣis* to uplift the world. These are recited by pandits in ritual forms of *yajña* to enable the hearer to attune to the divine power inherent in their vibrations. The *Vedas* were later systematized into four categories of knowledge by Vyāsa.

Vibhūti – glory and sovereign power of the Lord. Holy ash, often placed on the invisible third eye between the eyebrows for blessing and spiritual healing. Some holy people, such as Sathya Sai Baba, materialize *vibhuti* to awaken faith or for healing. *Vibhuti* is associated with Śiva and symbolizes the eternal presence of the Soul.

Vicāra – pondering, deliberation, reflection, self-inquiry. Ādi Śaṇkara in *Ātma Bodha* suggests self-inquiry. Ramana Maharṣi, Nisargadatta Mahārāja and others also advise their disciples to pose the question, "Who am I"?

Vijñāna – discerning knowledge of the intellect, comprehending, recognizing.

Vikṣepa – the projecting power of *māyā.* When our ignorance causes us to mistake the concrete for reality, by believing what the senses and the mind experience is real. Reality is projected onto the changing forms of nature.

Viṣṇu – the aspect of the trinity that preserves and protects the universe. All the *avatāras*, such as Kṛṣṇa and Rāma are considered incarnations of Lord Viṣṇu, who pervades all.

Viśuddha sattva – total purity, which transcends the *guṇas.*

Vītaṇḍā – in debating, the use of destructive criticism to invent fallacies that will tear down the reasoning of the opponent.

Vṛkṣa – tree, that which can be cut down.

Vyāsa – a great *ṛṣi*, who continuously incarnates to help humanity. He is the compiler of the *Mahābhārata*, the *Vedas*, the *Purāṇas*, and other sacred texts. There are said to be 23 Vyasas.

Yajña – sacrifice, through group ritual with sacred fire and *Vedic* hymns; also conscious individual action, dedicated to the higher. Sacrifice maintains creation.

Yama – the god of death, who is said to escort souls away from the earth plane to their appropriate *loka*.

Yama – strengthening human values and will power through cultivating virtue: truth, noninjury, nonpossession, nonstealing, celibacy, faith, silence, patience, forgiveness and fearlessness. Patanjali classifies *yama* as the first limb of *yoga*, the root of the other seven limbs.

Yoga – a means of linking the mind to God in His personal or cosmic form. A physical approach, such as *haṭha yoga* serves to prepare the body to establish this connection.

Yoga yukta – one whose mind is steadily linked with God.

Yogi – a practitioner of *yoga,* one whose mind is linked to God. The word is used to designate one who is on the path, as well as one who is already realized.

Yuga – a cycle of time, an aeon that consists of four different continuous cycles, which have been called *Satya yuga, Tretā yuga, Dvāpara yuga and Kali yuga.* We are now living in the age of violence, the *Kali yuga.*

BIBLIOGRAPHY

Adidevananda, Swami(translator). *Sri Ramanuja Gita Bhasya.* Madras: Sri Ramakrishna Math, 1993.

Amritanandamayi Devi Sri. *May Your Hearts Blossom: An Address by Sri Sri Mata Amritanandamayi Devi at the Parliament of World's Religions, Chicago, 3rd September 1993.* Swami Amritaswarupananda, translator. Amritapuri, Kollam India: Mata Amritanandamayi Mission Trust, 1996.

Amritasivarupananda, Swami. *Amachi: A Biography of Mata Amritanandaji.* San Ramon CA, 1994.

Aurobindo, Sri. *Essays on the Gita.* Pondicherry: Sri Aurobindo Ashram Trust, 1993.

_____ *Letters on Yoga.* 1970.

_____ (compiled by Sri M. P. Pandit). *Vedic Symbolism.* Wilmot, WI: Lotus Light Publications, 1988.

Baba, Sri Sathya Sai. *Bhagavatha Vahini.* Prasanthi Nilayam, India: Sri Sathya Sai Books and Publications Trust, 1970.

_____ *Digest 2(Collection of Sathya Sai Baba's Sayings).* Switzerland, 1994.

_____ *Discourses on the Bhagavad Gita.* A. Drucker, ed. PN: SSSBPT, 1988.

_____ *Dhyana Vahini.* PN: SSSBPT, 1985.

_____ *Githa Vahini.* Tustin, CA: Sathya Sai Book Center of America, 1988.

_____ *Indian Culture and Spirituality.* PN: SSSBPT, 1990.

_____ *Jnana Vahini.* PN: SSSBPT, 1984.

_____ *Sadhana the Inward Path.* PN: SSSBPT, 1976.

_____ *Sathya Sai Vahini.* PN: SSSBPT

_____ *Summer Showers in Brindavan 1993.* PN: SSSBPT, 1993.

Bhattacharya, Dr. Buddhadev, Translator, Shri Asim Chatterjee. *Anandamayee, The Universal Mother.* Hardwar, India: Shree Shree Ananda Mayee Sanga Kankhal, 1995.

Brahma Sutra Bhasya of Shankaracharya. Sw. Gambhirananda, translator. Calcutta: Advaita Ashram, 1993.

Brhadaranyaka Upanishad. Madras: Sri Ramakrishna Math, 1992.

Burtt, E. A. *Teachings of the Compassionate Buddha.* New York: Mentor Books, 1955.

Calasso, Roberto, Translator, Tim Parks. *Ka:Stories of the Mind and Gods of India.* New York: Alfred A. Knopf, 1998.

Chandogya Upanishad, in *The Upanishads, An Anthology.* D. S. Sharma, ed. Bombay: Bharatiya Vidya Bhavan, 1989.

Chidbhavananda, Swami, *The Bhagavad Gita.* Tirupparaitturai India: Sri Ramakrishna Tapovanam, 1994.

Chinmayananda, Swami. *Discourses on the Mandukya Upanishad.* Bombay: Central Chinmaya Mission Trust, 1984.

_____ *The Holy Geeta.* Bombay: CCMT.

_____ *The Holy Bhagavad Gita*(videotapes)

_____ *I Love You (Letters to Children)* Bombay: CCMT, 1991.

_____ *A Manual for Self Unfoldment.* Bombay: CCMT, 1985.

_____ *Meditation(Hasten Slowly).* The Family Press, Napa, Ca, 1972.

_____ *Talks on Taittiriya Upanisad.* Bombay: CCMT, 1992.

_____ *Talks on Sankara's Vivekachudamani.* Bombay: CCMT, 1989.

_____ *Thousand Ways to the Transcendental, Vishnu Sahasranaama.* Bombay: CCMT 1989.

Coomaraswamy, Ananda K. *The Dance of Siva:Essays on Indian Art and Culture.* New York: Dover, 1985.

Dayton, Brandt, ed. *The Practical Vedanta of Swami Rama Tirtha.* Honesdale, PA: Himalayan International Institute, 1978.

Easwaran, Eknath. *The Bhagavad Gita for Daily Living* (3 vols.). Petaluma, CA: Nilgiri Press, 1985.

Gurdjieff, G. I. *All and Everything:First Series.* Aurora, OR: Two Rivers Press, 1993.

Hislop, Dr. J. *My Baba and I.* San Diego, CA: Birth Day Publishing, 1985.

_____ *Conversations with Bhagavan Sathya Sai Baba.* PN, India: SSSBPT.

Huxley, A. *The Perennial Philosophy.* New York: Harper&Row, 1970.

Iyengar, B. K. S. *Light on the Yoga Sutras of Patanjali.* London: Thorsons, An Imprint of HarperCollins Publishers, 1993.

Jung, Carl. *Psychology and Alchemy.* Princeton: Princeton University Press, 1976.

_____ *Psychology and the East.* 1978.

_____ *Two Essays on Analytical Psychology*. 1972.

Kramrisch, Stella. *Manifestations of Siva.* Philadelphia: Philadelphia Museum of Art, 1981.

Kasturi, N. *Loving God.* Tustin, CA: Sathya Sai Book Center of America, 1982.

Krishnananda, Swami. *The Philosophy of the Bhagavadgita.* Shivanandanagar, India: The Divine Life Society, 1980.

Leuverink, M., ed. *Mananam Publication Series: The Sages Speak About Immortality.*Piercy, CA: Chinmaya Publications, 1995.

_____ *The Sages Speak About Life and Death.* 1995.

_____ *The Power of Faith.* 1991.

Maharaj, Sri Nisargadatta. *I Am That.* Durham, NC: The Acorn Press, 1973, 1999.

Mascaro, Juan, Translator. *The Bhagavad Gita,* London: Penguin Books, 1962, 2003.

Mason, Peggy. *Sai Baba: The Embodiment of Love.* Tasburgh, Norwich: Pilgrim Books.

Mishra, R. S., M.D. *The Textbook of Yoga Psychology.* New York: Crown, 1987.

Monier-Williams, Sir. *A Sanskrit-English Dictionary.* Delhi: Motilal Banarsidas, 1899, 1990.

Moody, Raymond, M.D. *Life After Life.* New York: Bantam Books, 1975.

Osbon, Diane K., ed. *A Joseph Campbell Companion: Reflections on the Art of Living* New York: Harper Perennial, 1991.

Ouspensky, P. D. *In Search of the Miraculous.* Orlando, FL: Harcourt, Brace Janovich, 1949.

Pancikaranam of Sri Sankaracarya. Calcutta: Advaita Ashrama, 1997.

Prabhavananda Swami and Christopher Isherwood, translators. *Bhagavad Gita.* New York: Barnes and Noble Inc., 1995.

Prem, Sri Krishna. *The Yoga of the Bhagavat Gita.* London: Watkins, 1958, Element, 1993.

Radhakrishnan, S. *Bhagavad Gita.* London: George Allen & Unwin Ltd., 1948.

Reymond, Lizelle. *To Live Within.* Baltimore: Penguin Books, 1973, Rudra Press, 1995.

Sanathana Sarathi. Prasanthi Nilayam, India: SSSBPT, 8-88, 3-95, 8-95.

Sivananda, Swami. *Stories from Yoga Vashishta.* Shivanandagar, India: Divine Life Society, 1983.

Sogyal Rinpoche, Lama. *The Tibetan Book of Living and Dying*, San Francisco: HarperCollins, 1994.

Srimad Bhagavatam. N. Ragunathan, translator. Bangalore, India: Vighneswara Publishing, 1976.

Srinivasachari, P.N. *The Ethical Philosophy of the Gita.* Madras: Sri Ramakrishna Math, 1943, 1966.

Stevenson, Ian, M.D. *Children Who Remember Previous Lives.* Charlottesville, VA: University of Virginia, 1987.

Subramaniam, Kamala. *Mahabharata.* Bombay: Bharatiya Vidha Bhavan, 1980.

Tilak, Bal Gangadhar. Bhalchandra Sitaram Sukthankar, translator. *Srimad Bhagavadgita Rahasya,* Ninth Edition. Poona, India: Tilak Brothers, 1918, 1996.

Uddhava Gita: The Last Message of Shri Krishna. Swami Madhavananda, translator. Calcutta: Advaita Ashrama, 1997.

Venkatesananda, Swami. *Vasistha's Yoga.* Albany: State University of New York Press, 1993.

Vidyaprakashananda, Swami. *Gita Makaranda.* Kalahasti, India: Sri Suka Brahma Ashram, 1980.

Vivekananda, Swami. *Inspired Talks, My Master and Other Writings.* New York: Ramakrishna-Vivekananda Center of New York, 1958, U.S. Paperback Edition 1987.

_____ *Karma-Yoga and Bhakti-Yoga.* New York: Ramakrishna-Vivekananda Center of New York, 1955, U.S. Paperback Edition 1982.

_____ *Pearls of Wisdom.* Calcutta: Ramakrishna Mission Institute of Culture, 1988.

_____ *Raja Yoga.* New York: Ramakrishna-Vivekananda Center of New York, 1956, U.S. Paperback Edition1982.

Yukteswar, Sri. *The Holy Science.* Los Angeles: Self-Realization Fellowship, 1990.

Yogananda, Paramahansa. *God Talks With Arjuna: The Bhagavad Gita.* Los Angeles: Self-Realization Fellowship, 1995.

ACKNOWLEDGEMENTS

With gratitude to everyone who makes this knowledge accessible and to those whose quotes appear in this book:

Swami Adidevananda, Adi Shankara, Mata Amritanandamayi, Sri Aurobindo, Sri Sathya Sai Baba, Swami Chidbhavananda, Swami Chinmayananda, Eknath Easwaran, Sri Karunamayi, Swami Madhavananda, Sri Nisargadatta Maharaj, Juan Mascaro, Peggy Mason, Sri Krishna Prem, Ramanuja, Lama Sogyal Rinpoche, Swami Rama Tirtha, Lizelle Reymond, Swami Sivananda, Swami Vivekananda, Swami Vidyaprakashananda, Paramahansa Yogananda.

Advaita Ashrama Calcutta, Central Chinmaya Mission Trust, Divine Life Society, Mata Amritanandamayi Mission Trust, Sri Ramakrishna Math Madras, Sri Ramakrishna Tapovanam Tirupparaitturai, Sri Sathya Sai Books and Publications Trust.

For material quoted from:

The Bhagavad Gita for Daily Living, Volume I, by Eknath Easwaran, founder of the Blue Mountain Center of Meditation, copyright 1975; reprinted by permission of Nilgiri Press, Tomales, CA, www.nilgiri.org.

The Bhagavad Gita for Daily Living, Volume II, by Eknath Easwaran, founder of the Blue Mountain Center of Meditation, copyright 1979; reprinted by permission of Nilgiri Press, Tomales, CA, www.nilgiri.org.

God Talks With Arjuna: The Bhagavad Gita, by Paramahansa Yogananda, copyright 1995; reprinted by permission of Self Realization Fellowship.

Inspired Talks, My Master and Other Writings by Swami Vivekananda, published by the Ramakrishna-Vivekananda Center

INDEX